The Modern Olympics

The Modern Olympics
A Struggle for Revival

David C. Young

The Johns Hopkins University Press

Baltimore and London

© 1996 The Johns Hopkins University Press
All rights reserved. Published 1996
Printed in the United States of America on acid-free paper
05 04 03 02 01 00 99 98 97 96 5 4 3 2 1

The Johns Hopkins University Press
2715 North Charles Street
Baltimore, Maryland 21218-4319
The Johns Hopkins Press Ltd., London

Library of Congress Cataloging-in-Publication Data will be found at the end of this book.
A catalog record for this book is available from the British Library.

ISBN 0-8018-5374-5

*To Judy
and to all the athletes,
past and present,
who have graced
the Olympic Games*

Sow a single seed of a rare plant in the most secluded spot and if the soil and other conditions are favourable to its germination, it will grow up and bear another seed, and in time, produce plants sufficient to cover the length and breadth of the land.

—*Dr. W. P. Brookes, Much Wenlock,*
England, 1867

At certain epochs, certain ideas course through the world and they propagate themselves like veritable epidemics; and it is very difficult to monopolize them for the benefit of any one single man. One generally finds that without hearing from one another, even without making an agreement, several men have worked at the same time at the same project in different places.

—*Pierre de Coubertin, "Les Jeux Olympiques à Much Wenlock,"*
Paris, 1890

Your tree is in a flourishing condition.

—*Dr. W. P. Brookes, letter to Pierre de Coubertin, 1893*

Contents

Preface

I did not choose to write this book. Sometimes, in a rare fit of Platonism, I almost think it chose me. As a boy, I watched Harrison Dillard hurdle. I had never seen anything so wonderful in my life, nor have I since. Newspapers said Dillard practiced by dragging dimes off the tops of the hurdles with his shorts. I believed it. I read how the world's greatest hurdler had tripped in the trials for the 1948 Olympics but, qualifying in the 100-meter dash, had won a gold medal there. The hurdles took on a symbolic meaning for me. In 1952 I followed the Helsinki Olympiad to see if Dillard could get Olympic gold in the event where he was the best in the world. He did. In 1956 and 1960 Lee Calhoun's Olympic hurdling stirred my Olympic interest all the more.

In college, I majored in ancient Greek; I liked it best. I specialized in the poetry of Pindar, partly because of Pindar's genre, poems written for athletes who won in the Olympics and other ancient meets. I was an avid fan of track and field and a professor at the University of California at Santa Barbara, known for my Pindar scholarship, when Bill Toomey, 1968 Olympic decathlon victor, came to my office in 1971. He asked me to collaborate with him on a book about ancient and modern Olympics. That book never materialized, but I began a close study of ancient athletics, leading to my *Olympic Myth of Greek Amateur Athletics* (1984), in which I argued there were no "amateur athletes" in the ancient Olympics. Those studies drew me into the early history of amateurism and of the modern Olympic Games. Since the Tokyo Olympics, I had become fascinated with such questions as: How did this marvelous institution begin? How did the first organizers decide the first program?

Richard Mandell's book in 1976—which I devoured—and John Mac-Aloon's in 1981 answered most of my questions. But I noticed a reference to I. E. Chrysafis's 1930 book, in Greek, which told of some insignificant earlier modern Greek Olympics sponsored by a man named Zappas. I frequently visited Athens and knew the strange building, the Zappeion. On my next visit, I wandered into the Greek Olympic Committee office and asked about Chrysafis's book. A kind man, who knew no English, returned with the book and told me it was mine. The next week, pitching side to side in a rough ferry ride from Pierre de Coubertin's France to John Mahaffy's Ireland, I read Chrysafis's fascinating chapters. Thanks to my classical training, I could read the archaic, scholarly dialect it was written in. As my *Olympic Myth* went to press, I added a chapter on the Zappas Olympic Games.

Stephen Miller, then director of the American School of Classical Studies in Athens, read my book and told me that the Gennadius Library (administered by the American School) had just inherited Stephanos Dragoumis's papers. Dragoumis, long the head of the Zappas Olympic committee, is better known in Olympic history for telling Coubertin to "forget it" when the baron came to Athens in 1894 to arrange for the International Olympic Committee's Olympiad 1. I examined these papers and found a gold mine—previously unknown letters of Coubertin, some marked "Confidential," unknown letters of Demetrios Vikelas, first president of the IOC, and a letter from Dr. William P. Brookes, of Much Wenlock, England. I knew something of Brookes's Olympic contacts with Greece from reading Coubertin, Mandell, and MacAloon. But this letter said, "My friend Baron de Coubertin and [others including] myself are exerting ourselves to promote international Olympian festivals." I published parts of that letter, along with more on the Zappas Games and some materials I found in Lausanne (excerpts from the 1894 Paris congress minutes) in my 1987 article, "The Origins of the Modern Olympics." I was getting involved.

Soon Joachim Rühl wrote me from Cologne, saying that the new Brookes letter was important to his work on Brookes and the Much Wenlock Olympics. Rühl and I then corresponded and cooperated, helped by Wolfgang Decker, from Cologne, whom I had met in Athens. These two gentleman-scholars—unselfish giants of Olympic scholarship—sent me, unsolicited, the important *Diplomarbeiten* of their students: Anastase Kivroglou's on the Zappas documents, Benno Neumüller's on Brookes's Olympics, and Anette Keuser's on those in Liverpool. I then knew a book was almost written in the air somewhere, and it had fallen on me to finish it.

This book explains the history of the modern Olympic movement from its inception in 1833 until its culmination in the first successful international Olympiad of 1896. The survival of the modern Olympics after 1896 and their progress up to Atlanta in 1996 is another story, already well told by others. But these earlier Olympiads were the blood ancestors of Atlanta

1996. The early story has not been told. It is a single, continuous story: much pre-1896 Olympic activity, usually written off as a set of sporadic, unrelated "pseudo-Olympic" revivals, was in fact interconnected, even interdependent. Men and events directly influenced one another, and the documents tell the story. History, not I, chose the out-of-fashion chronological format for this book.

First, I needed to go to Wenlock. There in 1991, I was given access to the trunk that held the documents, and more, by Norman Wood of the Wenlock Olympian Society. I returned home and got to work, mostly with handwritten notes, some photocopies (difficult to get in Greek libraries and impossible at Wenlock; microfilm came later)—and Mandell's and MacAloon's books, Coubertin's writings, and others.

Anyone who has read this far knows that the book is not wholly mine but a common effort of the international scholarly community. I give formal thanks, first, to Mandell, MacAloon, and Coubertin. Though my account often differs sharply from theirs, without their important foundation work I probably never would have begun. I thank Dr. Judy Ann Turner, a historian and my wife, who endured everything, even when I had severe health problems, to stay my constant helpmate—and my best professional and scholarly consultant. The two gentlemen from Cologne, Rühl and Decker, contributed far more than their own excellent research. Without their students' work—without Neumüller—I would have been lost or three years later. Sam Mullins and Don Anthony, as well as Rühl, were instrumental in my getting a microfilm of the Brookes archives. And I thank the citizens of Wenlock for their hospitality.

Special thanks go to the anonymous employee of the Greek Olympic Committee, who gave an old hardbound copy of Chrysafis to an unknown American who could barely speak Greek. Christina Varda of the Gennadius Library was my helper for years, and I thank her almost wildly. Another Greek archivist, Fani Kakridis-Enz of the IOC Library in Lausanne, gave an unannounced American intruder, who could barely speak French, the "Congrès 1894" IOC file with the minutes of the 1894 Paris congress— without asking if I could read it. Anonymous (and 'onymous') librarians in Greece and America have met my sudden inquiries with surprising cooperation. And many colleagues have helped by their encouragement or exchange of research, even more surprising since much of my work goes against the grain in suggesting that Coubertin was not the only *renovateur.*

I especially wish to thank John Lucas, whose scholarly stature is matched by his open-mindedness and his belief in the good of the Olympic movement and the importance of the truth. Allen Guttmann, Tony Mangan, George Dales, Robert Barney, Nikos Filaretos, Kostas Georgiadis, Fernand Landry, Gareth Schmeling, Arnd Krüger, Paula Welch, Tom Adolph, Lucinda Adams, Bill Mallon, Ian Jobling, Donald Anthony, Antonis Tzikas, Dionysis Gangas, Robert Potter, and Ed Barton have given me encouragement or help when I needed it most. There are too many others to name—but I know their names. I thank Eric Halpern and the Johns Hopkins University Press for their speedy and professional action at all phases of publication.

To all the foreigners named above, my heartfelt thanks for their ability and willingness to speak English to us Americans who are fluent only in our native tongue. Would that we could reciprocate! At no point were my poor oral and aural foreign language skills a significant problem.

Many of the materials I use are in Greek or French. Knowing that many Americans do not read French well, that few outside of Greece read Greek, and that almost everyone who might start this book reads English, I have translated all quotations into English. I, more than most, realize the scholarly drawbacks there; *traduttore, traditore*, true in poetry, has some validity even in the everyday prose documents I use here. But to print both the original text and English translation would have made the book intolerably long and choppy and required much unwanted Greek type. I use and cite the French version of Coubertin's *Mémoires Olympiques*. All of the original correspondence between Brookes and Coubertin is in English, of which Coubertin had total mastery. All correspondence between Coubertin and Vikelas (and other Greeks) is in French. I use the modern spelling, "Vikelas," although "Bikelas" appears occasionally in citations. I read French and Greek (ancient and modern) and, though I am far from claiming perfect accuracy in the translations, I am confident I do not misrepresent the facts or the spirit of anything because of poor translation. Naturally, some will require to see the original for some items. If they are enterprising enough, they will; for I cite my sources.

Lay persons who read this book may wish to ignore the scholarly apparatus and extended notes, which might seem to encumber a good story. My account here was so often new, the documents published here for the first time—and at variance with standard Olympic history—that I needed to cite my sources constantly in order to maintain credibility, often to explain how so strong a variance could even take place. And in writing this book I was confronted, with amazing frequency, by that prominent human characteristic, error; wrong dates, names, and facts, even from the most reliable sources. I have no delusions about my own ability to be free of errors.

Abbreviations

AAA	Amateur Athletic Association, 1880, England
AAC	Amateur Athletic Club, 1866, England
AAU	Amateur Athletic Union, 1888, United States
IOA	International Olympic Academy, 1961, Greece
IOC	International Olympic Committee, 1894
NOA	National Olympian Association, 1865, England
NOG	National Olympian Games, 1866, England
USFSA	Union des sociétés françaises de sports athlétiques, 1890, France
WARS	Wenlock Agricultural Reading Society, 1840, England
WOC	Wenlock Olympian Class, 1850, England
WOG	Wenlock Olympian Games, 1850, England
WOS	Wenlock Olympian Society, 1860, England

The Modern Olympics

ONE

The Birth of the Olympic Idea, 1833–1858
The Poet and the Doctor

> Where are your Olympic Games?
> —*Panagiotis Soutsos, 1833*

It began as sheer poetry. Our modern Olympic movement—even the Olympic idea—seems to have begun as the glancing thought of a poet. He was a Greek, Panagiotis Soutsos, born in 1806 in Constantinople (Istanbul) and educated first in Chios, Greece, then in Paris, Padua, and Vienna, between 1820 and 1823. In Paris, as a teenager, he published his first book, *Odes of a Young Greek* (in French). He lived for a while in Transylvania, Romania, where he wrote what may be his best-known poem, aptly titled "The Traveler" (in Greek).[1] The dates of Soutsos's formative years are important, for these were years of turmoil and excitement for any Greek, and they help us understand why Soutsos conceived his Olympic idea.

The phrase "Olympic idea" is usually associated closely, personally, and strongly with Baron Pierre de Coubertin. For many people, it bears great emotional value in that respect, for standard Olympic history credits the baron with being the first to conceive the Olympic revival idea and with achieving it almost single-handedly. Yet others, such as Soutsos, had anticipated the idea and had already contributed to its eventual success. Coubertin's Olympic idea did not differ wholly from Soutsos's, and it is difficult to distinguish from the Olympic idea of Dr. W. P. Brookes, from whom Coubertin derived most of his own. Coubertin's version, indeed, differed in some of its international features, which became possible only as the earlier Olympic movement progressed toward fulfillment in Athens, in 1896. While many now complain that our Olympic Games have lost all sight of their underlying philosophy and origins, we have never determined exactly what those origins were. Furthermore, if we do not fully understand Soutsos's original motives—if we do not understand the entire history of the Olympic idea, including the roles of Soutsos, Brookes, and

Coubertin—we will never perceive how legitimate it is to call our modern Games "Olympic Games." Only with such knowledge can we grasp that our Olympiad xxvi, held in Atlanta in 1996, is indeed an authentic revival of the Games of ancient Greece.

As Soutsos approached manhood, Greeks had been under Turkish rule for about four centuries. In the early nineteenth century, by widespread military uprisings, they established their independence over the central and southern portions of the country. The traditional dates of this Greek War of Independence are 1821–28 (though much happened before and after). Beset by internal dissension and external meddling, the Greeks had trouble creating a stable government. In 1832 their allies, Britain, France, and Russia, imposed on them as their sovereign a teenage German prince from Bavaria, who became Otto ii, king of the Hellenes. Otto was only seventeen, but the Greeks had high hopes for his reign and their nation's future. On February 1, 1833, the new monarch arrived in the eastern Peloponnesus at Nafplion, the first capital of the new nation.

The young poet Soutsos, too, immediately moved to the new capital of Greece. He soon began to publish a newspaper there, naming it *Helios* (the Sun). He was only twenty-seven when he began to form his Olympic idea. In 1833, *Helios* published two original Soutsos poems, lyric poems with dramatic dialogue: "Dialogue of the Dead" and "The Ruins of Ancient Sparta; or the Arrival of King Otto in Greece."[2] These are strongly patriotic poems that celebrate the rebirth of the Greek nation after centuries of Ottoman rule. But they are not merely poems of freedom. To understand the authenticity of our Olympic revival we must enter Soutsos's poetic mind and know something of Greek emotions after Greece became free.

Soutsos felt the burden of ancient Greek history on his new nation, the heavy burden of ancient Greek glory. Many Greeks have felt it since. In his 1833 poems Soutsos pointedly asks how modern Greece can live up to its ancient reputation—how it might reestablish the culture and institutions that made ancient Greece great in the eyes of the modern world. Many Greeks saw that Ottoman rule had left them behind in modern European history and hoped soon to imitate successful modern nations such as France and England; but Soutsos focused more on restoring ancient Greek glory than on joining the new order of nineteenth-century Europe. The characters in his dramatic poems are a mix of recent Greek military heroes and figures from the distant past. The ancient characters themselves pepper their speech with the great names of antiquity, Marathon and Thermopylae, Homer and Aristotle. In "Dialogue of the Dead," a poem of fourteen pages, the ghost of the ancient philosopher Plato looks up from the underworld dismayed; if this is Greece, he wants to ask the modern Greek nation, "Where are your Olympic Games? . . . Your great festivals, your great theaters, the marble statues, where are they?"

Soutsos's Plato has the broad cultural scope of the ancient Olympics in mind. He goes on to say that they indeed featured glorious athletic events, such as the wrestling contest; but also that Herodotus came to Olympia to read his histories and inspired Thucydides to emulate him "in poetic prose." Soutsos's historical point of view is at once ancient and futuristic but not contemporary. The ghost of Modern Soldier responds to Plato:

> Rome, the ruler of the world, Rome fell; but it was not resurrected.
> Greece, O Glory! Greece alone died and was reborn.
> For its future growth, it enjoys a hidden momentum, a secret impetus
> . . . It will regain, wise people, its ancient rank,
> once again the leader in every form of greatness and beauty.
> The centuries to come will see those that have passed,
> and our ancestors will be reborn anew in living men.[3]

Here, in "Dialogue of the Dead," the notion of modern Olympic Games is just a rhetorical question, a kind of censure joined to the other cultural gaps Plato sees in modern Greece, including a lack of theater and a lack of art. But Plato's Olympic question seemed to stick in Soutsos's poetic mind; in the next poem, it turned from a rhetorical question to a proposal. Soutsos liked ghosts; true to his classical background, he called them "shades" *(skiai)*. In the "Ruins of Ancient Sparta," the shade of Leonidas, the greatest ancient Greek military hero, returns to his homeland, sits in the ruins, and addresses the newly arrived king and the new Greece:

> You have matched us ancients in bravery of battle.
> Now match the old times in education and culture *[paideia]*, too.
> Bring back to your land the days of Miltiades and Themistocles.
> Bring back the glorious days of Pericles for this rebirth. How long will there
>   be enmities and disputes!
> From this time on
> let the only contention among you be a rivalry for the national glory.
> And let the only contests that you have be those national games, the
>   Olympics, to which the olive branch once summoned the sons of Greece
> in ancient times.
> Greece your future is brilliant! In the old days,

even when torn asunder by dissent,[4] and divided into many kingdoms,
you were the focal point.
What will you now achieve united, marching forward under one king, with
wise steps, giant steps, to your original glory?[5]

We are yet far from Olympic Games. This proposal to restore the Olympics is still merely a poetic idea, a kind of symbol for restoring all ancient culture, expressed by a mere poetic ghost. But several features are of interest. Leonidas imagines an Olympic rebirth not just to restore athletic games but to head a broader movement, where the Olympics exemplify "education and culture." He further suggests that Olympics could foster among participants a feeling of brotherhood, a lessening of hostilities. Olympics could be a force for peace. The Olympic idea in its very germination with Soutsos was closely akin to the form it took in the minds of Coubertin and the later International Olympic Committee (IOC) charter. The crucial difference is that Soutsos had mainly patriotic motives, bordering on the nationalistic. The broader Olympic idea, with its emphasis on moral development and international competition, would come later. We may, however, perceive most of the basic elements of the Olympic idea here in Soutsos's first proposal.

Soutsos seems to have stumbled on the notion of an Olympic revival while writing a stanza of poetry. But that notion soon grew within him, taking on a more concrete form. The young author himself took a giant step. He removed this ghostly proposal from the poetic realm and presented it in real life.[6] In 1835 Soutsos wrote a memo to the Greek government,[7] whose capital Otto had now moved to Athens. The memo, sent to the minister of interior, John Kolletis,[8] proposed that March 25, the traditional starting date of the War of Independence, be made a national holiday of celebration. Furthermore—and it is crucial—Soutsos also formally proposed that the celebration include a revival of the Olympic Games. It is not wholly a coincidence that our own modern Olympic series began—the opening day of Olympiad 1, 1896—on March 25 in Athens.[9] Soutsos proposed that the revived Games rotate among four Greek cities in a four-year cycle, the first year in Athens, the second in Tripolis, the third in Mesolongion, and the fourth year on the island of Hydra. Again, Soutsos's vision passed beyond sports. "I had in mind," he writes, "besides these athletic games, the exhibition of agricultural goods and tools, along with industrial products; and to award prizes for poetry and the writing of history."[10]

Kolletis approved the proposals in Soutsos's memo and formally recommended them to the king. By a stroke of luck, the original of this important document has been found and published.[11] It is long and detailed. The four modern sites, it notes, would reflect the four major sites of the ancient Greek athletic circuit, the Olympic, Pythian, Isthmian, and Nemean Games. In fact, the document often invokes the names and glory of ancient Greece as justification and model for the revival. It is typical Soutsos. It gives specifications for each of the four stadiums (600 feet, the ancient length) and four hippodromes (1,200 feet). At each modern site there would be a throne for the king, whose presence would add the proper solemnity and command the respect of other countries for the Games. (Here, too, Soutsos anticipated Coubertin's emphasis on the participation of kings and heads of state). There would be special seating for the judges and ministers of state and marble pillars bearing the names of the heroes of the War of Independence. Each site would have a portico to display the works of art entered in the competitions and a theater for the drama contests.

Each commune would send, besides the athletes and competitors, two choirs of young people, twenty-four young women and twenty-four young men. Cash prizes would go to the victors in various categories—philosophy, literature, painting, and sculpture and chariot racing, horse racing, and footracing for the athletes.[12] The choirs and the intellectual and artistic contests are, of course, foreign to the ancient games. In a strange prelude to Coubertin (and Avery Brundage), the memo requires that "no runner in the stadium" should have led "an irregular life" and provides for prospective athletes to be challenged in this respect; that, too, is a modern feature, with no precedent in antiquity.[13] The festival that Soutsos and Kolletis proposed would last more than a week.

Soutsos was the first to have the rather strange notion, rarely questioned, that contests called Olympic Games could be held at sites other than Olympia. Today we accept that idea without thinking much about it. But it is a concept to give a classical scholar pause.[14] What does the word "Olympics" mean? Soutsos perceived that the word might mean the ancient Olympics held at Olympia—but something beyond that, as well: the king of contests, as the Olympics were king of the many athletic games in ancient Greece.[15]

When Kolletis approved all of Soutsos's proposal, it appeared that the Olympic Games would soon be revived, not in Olympia but in these other cities. But Kolletis was soon replaced, and in 1836 the new interior minister, Rhodartos, approved only that portion of Soutsos's proposal that made March 25 a national holiday (as it still is). The Olympic Games he dropped.[16] But in 1837, King Otto himself published a law establishing a

Committee for the Encouragement of National Industry. This committee was charged with promoting industrial growth throughout the year, identifying individuals who had achieved distinction by their agricultural or industrial products, and holding a great national festival every May. During the three-day festival the committee would award prizes to the outstanding individuals, display their products, and hold contests in the athletic games of ancient Greece.

Otto specified the athletic events to be contested: "discus, javelin, long jump, footraces, wrestling, and chariot racing." Winning athletes were to receive prizes, like those awarded in the agro-industrial contests, and to be "crowned with a laurel wreath."[17] Otto did not use the words "Olympics" or "revival." But the events themselves came from the ancient Olympic program, not current Greek or German practice, and the laurel crown harks back to ancient times (the prize at the Pythian, not the Olympic, Games). The entire law and the institutions it sought to establish seem only modified versions of Soutsos's original Olympic proposal, without the name—or all the antiquarian connotations—of "the Olympics."[18]

The following year, on the day of the new national holiday, March 25, some other Greeks proposed another revival. The people of Letrini, a small town near ancient Olympia in the district of Elis, formally voted to emulate their ancient ancestors by reviving the Olympics, "those noble games which were held every four years in ancient Elis," as "the Letrinian Games," as a part of each March 25 national holiday celebration. "Wishing to recall those noble times and wanting to make glorious the current celebration of the Rebirth of Greece," the Letrinians appointed a five-member organizing committee "to award the victors their prizes, as the ancient Eleans did."[19] As far as we know, this revival amounted to nothing. No record of actual games, if they took place at all, has been found.[20] But the Letrinians' revival activity is not wholly meaningless to our story. One member of this Letrini committee, Pavlos Giannopoulos, rejoined the Olympic movement as vice president of the 1875 Athens Olympic organizing committee and recognized Brookes's Olympic Games in England.[21] Furthermore, the Letrinians' motive, to ennoble the reborn nation by reviving its ancient glory, smacks of Soutsos's aims, indicating a tenor in Greece that would eventually lead to the actual revival. Soutsos was not alone in wanting Olympics revived.

Several years passed, and no Olympics took place. Otto's Committee for the Encouragement of National Industry did not even hold the nameless games announced in the 1837 law. But Soutsos did not give up. Rather, he redoubled his campaign to reestablish the Olympic Games. In 1842 he published another "lyric drama," this time focusing on a modern Greek hero, Georgios Karaïskakis, a prominent figure in the Greek Revolution. Before the text of the play itself begins, Soutsos addresses a long dedication to King Otto. He writes as if March 25 were still the date of the great games and hopes they will be the Olympics:

> And so I appropriately dedicate this poem to you, my king! A poem that celebrates the Greek struggle, since you have revealed by royal decree that every year on the 25th of March there will take place a universal festival to memorialize the resurrection of the Greek nation. And may it be that at this annual assembly . . . there may be held the ancient games of Olympia! And in this gathering of an inspired race may there be crowned the new Pindars, the new Herodotuses of Greece![22]

But this eloquent plea seemed to have no effect. Three years later, in a speech delivered at Karaïskakis's tomb in Athens before a crowd of fifteen thousand, Soutsos renewed his plea for an Olympic revival.[23] But the government seemed oblivious to his Olympic campaign, and Otto seemed to have forgotten his 1837 law. In 1851 Soutsos reiterated once more—at length—his call to revive the Olympic Games. As always, he speaks of true revival, of recreating antiquity:

> England has made its influence known on two hemispheres through its industrial expositions. Greece happens to have no power for that competition. But if Greece would re-establish the Olympic Games, and the Panathenaic Games on every [25 March], and for this festival every city of the first category would send a chariot of ancient Greek construction, and every town of the second category would send two mounted horsemen in ancient Greek style, and every town of the third category would send two wrestlers in ancient Greek dress, if in this festival there were exhibitions of ancient inscriptions that have been found, and of our antiquities, and exhibits of our own industrial products—if in such a festival, You, King!, the scepter of the Greek nation in your hands, should crown the epic, tragic, and lyric poets of merit, the historians of Greece; if wearing the ancient garb of Alexander of Macedon you would appear on your throne in the middle of the Greek amphitheater . . . [then the peoples of the world would respect Greece].[24]

The wording here in 1851, even down to such phrases as "every city of the first category," harks straight back to Soutsos's original 1835 proposal.[25] Here is a man obsessed with the Olympic idea, having already worked for it for some eighteen years, ever since Plato's ghost planted the seed in his poetic mind. He would need, however, to campaign a little longer, all in all a campaign of twenty-six years, before he would see Olympics revived in Greece. For still, despite his pleas and eloquence, nothing Olympic happened in Greece. Soutsos's dedication to his Olympic dream drove him to pursue it for decades as a lonely obsession.

Yet something had just happened in England. At this point—1851—we must leave Greece for a while and meet a major figure in the Olympic movement, Dr. William Penny Brookes (1809–95).[26] Brookes was born just three years after Soutsos, in the village of Much Wenlock, Shropshire, in northwest England. He, too, grew up far from the bustle of his nation's capital. He was first educated in his native land; but then, like Soutsos, he sought further training in Paris and Padua. Soutsos and Brookes studied in these two distant centers of European learning in precisely the same decade. Yet they seem to have formed their Olympic ideas independently; there is no indication that their paths ever crossed. Neither ever mentioned the other. But although they may never have met on the streets of Padua, their Olympic destinies were fatefully intertwined.

When he had completed his medical training, Brookes returned to his native village. There, for the rest of his long life, he practiced medicine and philanthropy. He was Much Wenlock's leading citizen. Early on, he began a program to improve the lot of the English working class in his area. His dedication to the working class is an important element in the history of modern Olympics, as we will see. It determined much of the history of amateurism, especially as it touched on Coubertin and the early IOC.

In 1840 Brookes formed the Much Wenlock Agricultural Reading Society (WARS) to encourage local farmers and working men to read and to improve their minds. He assembled books for them and obtained a public reading room "with a view of extending to the working classes those facilities and advantages which wealthier individuals can command at home."[27] In 1850 he decided to encourage their physical improvement, too, forming a subgroup of the society called the Wenlock Olympian Class (WOC). The name came from Brookes's admiration for the ancient Greek Olympics and a desire to emulate their ideals. The minutes of the 1850 founding meeting explain the original goals of Brookes's Olympian organization. They are so much at one with the goals later expressed by Coubertin and the subsequent IOC that they deserve to be quoted. The society members present at that meeting, held on February 25, 1850, decided

> that it was desirable that a class should be established . . . for the moral, physical and intellectual improvement of the Inhabitants of the Town & Neigh-

bourhood of Wenlock and especially of the Working Classes, by the encouragement of out-door recreation, and by the award of prizes annually at public Meetings for skill in Athletic exercises and proficiency in intellectual and industrial attainments. That this section of the Wenlock Agricultural Reading Society be called *The Olympian Class*.[28]

There is much here to note. First, the goal of "moral, physical and intellectual improvement" recalls Soutsos's notion; but it more clearly anticipates the "Olympic idea" of Coubertin. Noticeably absent from that idea here, in 1850, is the international element and the goal of fostering feelings of brotherhood and peace. But those notions Brookes himself would later be the first to add. Second is Brookes's explicit accommodation of the working class. That emphasis would later lead his Olympic movement into an open clash with England's southern elitist athletic clubs' amateur movement and eventually to the Olympic movement's defeat in England. It would hobble his international Olympic movement, as well. Third is the notion of recurrent Olympic athletic meetings. Soutsos had a four-year rotation around his nation. Brookes at this point still thought in local, annual terms. That would change, progressively and monumentally.

The first Annual Olympian Meeting was held on October 22–23, 1850. The Annual Wenlock Olympian Games were then held, like clockwork, every year thereafter. They continue till this day, a direct line from 1850, with a few gaps in this century, especially during the two world wars.[29]

The first Wenlock Olympian Games (WOG) in 1850 had nine events and offered cash prizes for each victor. Three of the events were typically English, hardly Greek: the cricket match, football, and quoits. The English—even Brookes himself—associated the game of quoits with the ancient discus, though it is more like our game of horseshoes.[30] Thus, Brookes may have viewed that much, at least, as a revival from antiquity. Another event, hopping 50 yards on one leg, is well known, but we would not think it Olympic. Yet the bulk of the program, five events, was track and field, the ancient Olympic staple and a sport still embryonic even in England. The Games included a high jump, a long jump, and three footraces in three age divisions—adult, boys under fourteen, and boys under seven. J. Bright won the long jump at 18 ft. 10 in., the only mark recorded; the high jump went to E. Poyner. The men's footrace winner was J. Hickman, who won a pound sterling (a significant amount in those days). In the "boys under 7" race, George Thomas won a little money, a book, and a laurel crown.[31] The laurel crown clearly proves that Brookes, from the start, had some notion of replicating features of the ancient games, which also had age divisions separating men and boys.

These games were immediately judged a complete success by a local newspaper, which gave an animated account of the football match.[32] Brookes's two sons, the newspaper reports, competed in the footrace for boys under seven but lost to Thomas. We can also detect Brookes's imprint in the pageantry, which would later grow and so impress Coubertin that it is surely the source for much of the pageantry in our own Olympic Games. Before the games there was a parade of the athletes and the committee to the field, led "by the Wenlock band with six flags." Bells rang throughout the town. After the games the band—closely followed by the "two young victors in the foot race, borne on the shoulders of two tall men, and their brows encircled with their laurel crowns"—led everyone, spectators included, in a procession back to the town.

Thus the Wenlock Olympian Games began. Over the next several years they continued with few, but significant, changes. The 1851 games increased the track-and-field program, having races of 200 yards and a half mile, and the hurdles "once around the course over 7 hurdles." The last was won by E. Poyner, who bounded "over the hurdles with the agility of a stag."[33] Poyner, from a nearby village, lost the long-jump contest to Mr. Mainwaring, a 'big city' athlete from Birmingham. Yet Poyner managed to triple anyway, this time winning the high jump and the half mile, as well. Archery and shot-put events ("throwing a stone of 15 pounds") were added.[34]

Program changes were made often between 1852 and 1856. Most significantly, some races were restricted to local residents, others open to "all England." The 1853 200-yard sprint, for example, had those two divisions. Both races were won by athletes from Wenlock. But the "local" and "open" divisions may somewhat parallel the later "amateur" and "professional" divisions.[35] In 1853 the amateur-professional controversy had not raised its ugly head, because amateurism as a concept had not yet been born. The 1852–56 Wenlock Olympian Games programs introduced nonathletic events, as well, especially for children. There were contests in arithmetic for boys, knitting for girls, and recitation for children of both sexes. The 1857 program expanded to twenty-five events. The focus, as always, was still on track and field, which comprised nine events. But a gymnastic event, pole climbing, was added; other events included a knitting contest for women; reading, spelling, and history competitions open to both boys and girls; and two separate art contests, one for boys and one for girls.

At the 1858 Wenlock Games, Brookes introduced an event with a medieval theme, "tilting at the ring." This event recreated an actual practice of medieval knights at their jousting tournaments. A mounted horseman charged under a frame from which was hung a small metal ring. His object was to dislodge the ring with his lance and keep it there as he passed under the frame.[36] This event became the featured attraction of all later Wenlock Olympian Games, and Brookes regarded it as their trademark. More importantly, the tilting bears a special importance in our own Olympic history. For when Coubertin witnessed the tilting at Wenlock in 1890, he was so impressed that ever after he conflated medieval chivalry with Greek athletics as he defined the Olympic spirit.[37] Furthermore, as we later see, the tilting event played a strange role in the 1859 Athens Olympics, though it did not appear on that program.

The tilting was full of ceremony and pageantry—the pageantry that would dazzle Coubertin decades later and enter our own Games. The Wenlock pageantry grew and grew. In 1890 Coubertin was especially taken with Brookes's inclusion of elegantly dressed women in the pageant and the fact that a young woman crowned the winning tilter with his laurels.[38] Thus, a reporter's comment on the much earlier 1855 Games—"the long lines of well-dressed females, who were seated on the rising banks commanding good views of the games"—has historical relevance.[39]

For the 1859 Wenlock Olympian Games, however, the program and pageantry changed even more; for by then Brookes had already become involved with the Greek Olympic movement initiated by Soutsos; and this new Greek influence on his 1859 Games was profound. Before looking further at Brookes's Games, we must return to Greece to catch up with the events that happened there during these early years of Brookes's activity in England. We shall return to Brookes, his involvement with the Greek Olympics, and the 1859 Wenlock Olympian Games in due course. Brookes's meetings of the Olympian Class from 1850 to 1858 had been minor affairs. I would not term them the first modern Olympics. Brookes tended to call them "Olympian Games" more often than "Olympics," but both he and the newspapers used both terms indiscriminately. That difference in name is irrelevant.[40] What matters is that Brookes did not claim to be reviving the ancient Olympics. Rather, I think, he was hoping to emulate something of the ancient Olympic ideals as he saw them. And, while Brookes's games were starting to attract athletes from nearby regions, they were still a local event.

Brookes's importance at this point is not in reviving Olympic games but in his forming an organization, named after the Olympics, with what he perceived as ancient Olympic philosophy and in implementing athletic games with that name and those notions. Because he took those little steps—when no one else had—he became so inextricably entwined in the web of Olympic history in Greece, England, and France that he eventually became its kingpin. For modern Olympic historians, he is the missing link in all phases of the Olympic movement. His importance grew gradually until he, if it must be any one man, might be seen as the founder of our Olympics. But, of course, the story is not that simple.

TWO

The First Zappas Olympiad, 1856–1859

I hope that History will take . . . a preponderant place in the
intellectual manifestations organized around the Games and on their
occasion. That is natural, for Olympism belongs to History.
To celebrate the Olympic Games is to vaunt History.
—*Coubertin, radio address, Geneva, 1935*

Brookes's vision, although at first limited and local, was immediately implemented. Soutsos's vision, in contrast, had been grand from the start, an attempt to revivify time. It was national, encompassing the whole Greek-speaking nation. Yet even after many years of his pleading, it remained a mere idea, of interest to no one but the visionary himself. In 1856, however, Soutsos's long Olympic efforts finally bore fruit, and the man named Evangelis Zappas enlisted in Soutsos's campaign to revive the Olympic Games. The practical side of the Greek Olympic movement starts here.

Evangelis Zappas, though a crucial figure in Olympic history, remains a kind of enigma.[1] He started out not as a businessman but as a soldier of fortune. Zappas was born in 1800 in Lambove, an Albanian-speaking village in northwestern Greece. Like many young men of his district, he began his career as a mercenary soldier for the fabled, notorious Ali Pasha, once the Turkish governor and later principal warlord of the region. But after serving under Ali Pasha, Zappas joined the Greek resistance forces. He became the aide-de-camp and constant companion of the noted hero of the Greek revolution Markos Botsaris, leader of a renowned band of Souliots.[2]

The war generally over but his native district still in Turkish hands, Zappas moved in 1831 to Romania, where he soon began to amass a great fortune in Romanian landholdings and agriculture and bought large shares in the Greek shipping industry. By the 1850s, he had become one of the richest men in eastern Europe, directing a vast financial empire from his large estate, Brostheni, near Bucharest, where he lived for the rest of his life.

It is not certain precisely how and when Zappas first heard of Soutsos's Olympic idea. Soutsos's family had a long-standing association with several districts of Romania, and it seems likely that some family member introduced Zappas to Soutsos or to Soutsos's printed Olympic proposals.[3] Alexandros Rangavis claimed Zappas "had read in one of Soutsos's newspapers . . . poetic bombast . . . an article on the ancient Olympic Games, with the—hardly practical—proposal for their modern revival in Greece."[4] However Zappas first heard of Soutsos's Olympic idea, he liked it. He attributed the impetus of his Olympic proposal directly to Soutsos, and Zappas's proposal sometimes follows Soutsos's in minute detail.[5] Without Soutsos, Zappas himself clearly would never have conceived the idea. Passionately devoted to Greece, like Soutsos, he too sought ways to incorporate former Greek heritage and glory into the new nation, to give it an identity worthy of Greece's past.

In early 1856,[6] Zappas wrote to King Otto as head of the Greek government, via regular diplomatic channels. The Greek ambassador to Romania, S. Skoufos, forwarded Zappas's letter from Bucharest to Athens. In this letter, Zappas proposed a permanent revival of the ancient Olympic Games, with cash prizes for the victors. He would pay for it all. Since it came from Romania, Otto gave Zappas's letter to Alexandros Rangavis, his foreign minister. Rangavis, who happened to oppose athletics, did not know what to do. For months no answer came from Athens. In April, Skoufos sent a telegram about the matter, and in May he wrote the government in Athens, seeking a reaction to Zappas's offer.[7] Still no reply.

Zappas was by then bombarding Skoufos with letters, asking about the Greek response to his offer. He even came to Bucharest in person to inquire. On June 6, 1856, Skoufos again wrote to King Otto and to the foreign minister, complaining of their failure to respond to these inquiries from Bucharest. Zappas's first letter is now lost. But Skoufos's June 1856 letter is preserved, as is most of the correspondence between Zappas and the Greek government respecting his Olympic revival in Greece. In this June 1856 letter Skoufos repeats Zappas's desire to revive the Olympic Games, the first edition to begin in Athens, "March 25, 1857." Zappas will pay for all, including a new Olympic building, where Greek art and industry may be exhibited. At the same time, the building can be a museum for antiquities, "visited by Greeks and foreigners alike." Zappas, Skoufos insists, "wishes to spare no expense."[8]

Finally, in early July, it seems that an answer of sorts finally came from Athens, under Rangavis's letterhead. Apparently recalling Zappas's war deeds, Rangavis bestowed on him several military honors. But his response to Zappas's Olympic proposal was obscure.[9] Rangavis later paraphrased that response: "I thanked Zappas for his . . . splendid idea; but told him also that times have changed since antiquity. Today, nations do not become distinguished, as then, by having the best athletes and runners, but the champions in industry, handiwork, and agriculture. I suggested that he found . . . Industrial Olympic Games."[10]

Skoufos quickly consulted with Zappas, and on July 15, Zappas wrote a personal letter to Rangavis, expressing mainly his feeling of brotherhood with the Greek minister. On the same day, he made a letter of credit—made out personally to Rangavis—for a large amount of money (two thousand Austrian florins) to pay for the first of the "Olympiads of Zappas," as he himself calls them.[11] Skoufos elaborated details of the apparent agreement in his own covering letter, then sent all three items down to Rangavis.[12] He thanked Rangavis on Zappas's behalf for the military honors. He notes that Zappas had now already sent a good deal of money for the first of the "Olympiads of Zappas." As for the "changes in the program" that Rangavis suggested (this must mean the industrial contests), Zappas agreed to leave that up to the organizing committee. But Skoufos also stressed—and it is important—that Zappas explicitly requested that Panagiotis Soutsos, along with his brother, Alexandros, be made a member of the Olympic organizing committee. This request confirms that Soutsos's Olympic initiative indeed lay behind Zappas's own Olympic efforts, that Zappas consciously sought to fulfill Soutsos's Olympic idea. For this reason, he wanted Soutsos himself to have a hand in directing the affair.

That Zappas and Soutsos shared personal friendship and communication is unmistakable; only the details are unclear. Thus on July 13, 1856—two days before Zappas's official response to Rangavis—a strange article appeared in Soutsos's newspaper, *Helios*. The author was the poet and editor, proposer of the Olympic revival, Soutsos himself; the headline read "Evangelis Zappas," and the subject was Olympic Games. Soutsos apparently knew, even before Rangavis, the exact nature of Zappas's generous offer. With obvious pride, Soutsos here reviews his own 1835 memo to Kolletis proposing an annual "revival of the Olympic Games"; he recalls, even reprints, some of his other speeches and writings advocating the same idea.[13]

Soutsos's July 13 article goes on to praise Zappas at length and to detail his wealth and generosity. It claims that once the Olympics are reestablished, Zappas's name should be ranked among the heroes of old, "beside the names of the Herakleses and the Theseuses, the founders of the [ancient] Olympics and Panathenaics."

Zappas and Soutsos had almost certainly been in contact; and perhaps Soutsos had friends in the government to tell him the moment Rangavis sent a response. For the timing is too close for coincidence: in Bucharest, Skoufos seems not to have informed Zappas of Rangavis's letter before July 10. On July 13, Soutsos's long *Helios* article appeared in Athens. Zappas wrote his official acceptance to Rangavis and sent the money on July 15.

A methodical correspondence between Zappas and the Greek government took place over the next two years, as they dickered over details of his gift and the Olympic Games. The term "Olympic Games" (*Olympiakoi Agones*) indeed occurs in these documents.[14] But all did not go smoothly. Rangavis, a poet and classics professor when not busy with the government, was the first of many Greek intellectuals who for decades formed an antiathletic clique that eventually ran the Greek Olympic movement aground. Rangavis simply did not believe that athletics were a worthwhile activity in modern times; they were a throwback to the primitive times of antiquity.[15] He tried to get Zappas to abandon the athletic feature of the new Olympics in favor of a wholly industrial festival. To industrial exhibits Zappas had agreed. That was, after all, part of Soutsos's own original plan. Zappas gave money to fund a building for the industrial exhibits. But Zappas would not forgo athletics. He still wanted to revive the true ancient Olympic Games, as well. He specified that the ancient Panathenaic stadium in Athens be restored as the athletic site, rebuilt with marble seats. He gave money and said he would give more. He told Rangavis to get the best architect available and to send him plans and estimates. Rangavis obtained and sent estimates so high that he thought them impossible: "The estimate . . . with marble seats in the stadium, went to 1,200,000 drachmas, which I viewed with much disquiet; with hesitation I sent it on to Mr. Zappas. But by return mail he replied that he accepted this expense if it were necessary."[16]

It was impossible to hold the Olympics as early as March 25, 1857, the date Zappas first proposed (this day obviously dictated by Soutsos's 1835 plan). He accepted a postponement to 1858. Soutsos, despite Zappas's request, was not appointed a member of any organizing committee. Rangavis seemed to dally. The Olympics were again postponed, despite Zappas's insistence that they be held as soon as possible. But by the summer of 1858, the newspapers seemed to know that the government was about to act further on Zappas's Olympic gift.[17] On July 18, 1858, Soutsos wrote to Zappas, sounding the old warrior out as to whether he, Zappas, would be willing to become a politician, to hold important public office in Athens. On August 8, 1858, Zappas wrote back to Soutsos, expressing joy at receiving Soutsos's letter, and the "brotherly love I have long had for you." But, Zappas explains, "I am not a political man; I decided that through a private life I could best help my country."[18]

Then it happened. On August 19, 1858, a royal decree came from Otto's palace, in his name; it was signed, apparently in his absence from the country, by his wife, Queen Amalia (once a student of Rangavis). This decree announced: "1) There are hereby established National Contests to be held every four years and called 'Olympics,' which have as their purpose to exhibit the products of the activities of Greece, especially, industry, agriculture, and animal husbandry. 2) The Olympic Organizing Committee will be the Committee for the Encouragement of National Industry."[19]

The decree specified that prizes would be awarded. For some competitions, there would be money prizes, cash in drachmas. For most, there would be medals of gold, silver, and bronze. The medals would bear Otto's bust on the obverse, with the legend Founder of the Olympics. The reverse would read First [or Second, or Third] Place Olympic Crown, Evangelis Zappas, Sponsor[20] of the Games. The decree sets the dates of the first modern Olympiad as the four Sundays of October, 1859. On the first Sunday there would be an opening religious service and academic competitions in lectures and books. The second Sunday would focus on animal husbandry contests and finish with a horse race, with a money prize.

The program for the third Sunday interests us most. On that day there would be the judging of the agricultural contests and "in the afternoon, solemn, public athletic games in the stadium, which will be fittingly prepared for the event. There will be money prizes ranging from 50–100 drachmas, and olive crowns." The stadium referred to is the ancient Panathenaic stadium in Athens, the same site where the first modern International Olympic Games were actually held in 1896. In 1858 it still lay buried, scarcely discernible under many layers and centuries of accumulated dirt, on the southeastern outskirts of Athens. On the fourth and final Sunday, prizes would be awarded in the industrial competitions; the day would culminate in the premier performance of a new Greek drama, the winner to be chosen by the Philological Department of the University. N. Theocharis was named chairman of the Olympic committee.

Construction of the building to display the agricultural and industrial goods was to begin soon.[21] Details of the various categories for the agricultural and industrial contests were specified in the August 1858 decree. It is an impressive list of more than a score of categories, including forestry; fishing; machines for making bread, wine, and sugar and for lifting and carrying; watches; soap; pasta; fire engines; architecture; wool; furniture; and photography. In addition, plans were begun—much money eventually spent—for those portions of the first Olympiad. Immediately after the royal decree was published, Soutsos's newspaper carried another article on Zappas, with the text of the decree, and noted, "All the newspapers of Greece have praised Zappas with one voice . . . because of his lavish philanthropy."[22]

For the athletic games in the stadium, however, the committee did not have elaborate plans—nor spend much money. From the start, it seemed clear that the athletic program of the Olympics was to be relegated to secondary, even minor, status. Even as the Olympic decree was published, a significant voice prominently protested this state of affairs. A leading Greek intellectual living in Paris, Mynas Minoides, published there the first edition of a newly discovered ancient Greek manuscript on athletics. He appended an article, dated August 13, 1858, commenting on the royal Olympic decree, several days before it actually happened. In both Greek and French he complained of the purposes for which the government intended to use Zappas's Olympic gift. "Did Mr. Zappas want to establish industrial contests? I don't think that this patriot, motivated by a zeal for the glory of ancient Greece, wanted to establish a palace for the exhibition of modern Greek technology—which is still embryonic." Minoides goes on to explain that Zappas never expected contemporary Greece to impress the world with its industry. "But for an authentic revival of the Olympic Games, where athletes, sprinters, wrestlers, and so on receive crowns, that's what will glorify Greece—that's the kind of thing which the Pindars and Simonideses of ancient Greece commemorated to make the athletes immortal." Minoides urges that the athletic Olympics be given more emphasis if there was to be an authentic revival of the ancient Olympic Games and that "the site of the stadium is there; all that is needed is for it to be excavated and seating made on the hill on each side"—not a great expense, he said, but of great importance.[23]

The Olympic web of events then began to weave itself in strange and wonderful ways. It is not surprising that news of the Greek revival immediately reached Minoides in metropolitan Paris, with its many Greek expatriates. But the same news also soon reached Dr. Brookes in rural Much Wenlock—thanks to some nameless Olympic hero who changed the course of history by writing from Athens to a Shropshire newspaper on September 4. On October 6, 1858, *Eddowes's Shrewsbury Journal* carried this small news item, scarcely three column-inches long:

A correspondent writing from Athens under the date September 4 says, "The Queen Regent has just signed a royal decree for the re-establishment of the Olympic Games, after being discontinued for nearly 1,550 years. They are to be held in Athens, in the ancient Stadium, which is still in a very perfect state of preservation . . . and are to take place in October, every fourth year, commencing in 1859. The Games are to include horseraces, wrestling, throwing quoits and other athletic sports."[24]

The correspondent goes on to give a few more details, such as the inclusion of the agro-industrial exhibitions; the name of the wealthy Greek, Evangelis Zappas (here wrongly called a Peloponnesian), who "formed the idea" and is paying for it all; and the prize medals, with Otto's bust on one side and Zappas's name on the other.

Brookes read this article in his local newspaper, clipped it out, and excitedly pasted it into his scrapbook, where it remains to this day. He then took pen in hand and, as was the custom in those days, wrote to the British ambassador in Athens, Sir Thomas Wyse. Thus began some quick, continuing correspondence between Brookes and Wyse.[25] Wyse replied, apparently asking Brookes what events he would recommend that the Greek Olympiad include. On December 23, 1858, Brookes wrote back to Wyse, sending a suggested program, apparently based on the 1858 Wenlock Olympian Games. That would have meant such things as high jump, long jump, hurdles, footraces at various distances, putting the stone—and tilting at the ring. He probably just sent Athens his 1858 program.

None of these 1858 letters is actually preserved. But they may be confidently reconstructed, especially from Wyse's next letter dated February 10, 1859, which does survive.[26] Wyse thanks the doctor for his advice; but, he explains, although the new Olympics will include athletic games, they feature agro-industrial contests. Dr. Brookes's proposed program for the athletic Olympics, Wyse suggests, is too ambitious, offering too many events to be implemented. Brookes was not easily daunted, nor was he content merely to send advice. Excited by the prospect of modern Greek Olympic Games, he wanted to participate more himself. Still assuming that the forthcoming Athens Olympic Games would follow his suggested program, on February 24, 1859, Brookes sent Wyse, in Athens, another letter and a gift of ten pounds sterling, designated as a prize for the victor in tilting at the ring. Wyse did not reply until July 14, but he then wrote Brookes that he had given the money to the Athens committee. Characteristically, Brookes sent still more letters.[27]

The clipping of that October *Eddowes's* newspaper article, because of the ensuing exchange between Brookes and Wyse, was a momentous event in our Olympic history. It not only spurred Brookes to a new flurry of Olympic revival activity, it also planted the germ of internationalism in Brookes's mind—and thus in our own Olympic movement, destined to be international.

Theocharis's Greek committee, however, did not follow Brookes's suggested program and scheduled no "tilting at the ring."[28] Belatedly, on September 30, 1859, it published a program that included footraces at three distances, three jumping events, two types of discus throws, two javelin throws, and a pole climb. Cash prizes were specified for each event, generally fifty or one hundred drachmas. Second in some events paid fifty drachmas.[29] An addendum to the official announcement, dated October 24, 1859, announces an additional prize, a bonus prize, which would go to the winner of the distance race. The announcement is amusing; but the prize itself and its winner, as we will see, play important roles in Olympic history:

> The Olympic Committee of Mudenlok,[30] England, has donated an additional prize of ten pounds sterling (= 281 drachmas) for a victor in the footraces in the forthcoming Olympic Games; so the winner of the race will receive, besides the 100 drachmas specified by the law, the stated prize thanks to the kind generosity of the Mudenlok Olympic Committee.[31]

The Olympiad as a whole proceeded much as planned. The opening had to be postponed somewhat, but on October 18 the opening ceremonies took place. King Otto and Queen Amalia went to the exhibition building, where they were warmly greeted by the organizing committee. In a religious ceremony, the metropolitan gave his blessing to the whole enterprise. Theocharis addressed the king in a formal speech (which Soutsos judged overly obsequious). Before leaving, the royal couple toured the industrial exhibits, which were still arriving and being arranged.[32] Soutsos's account begins: "Glory and honor to Evangelis Zappas, designer of grand plans. He waited and waited, and finally he brought to reality my idea, which was called 'poetic.' . . . Here is a man who brought to fruition what the whole nation ought to have done." Here as elsewhere, Soutsos's subsequent sentences are peppered with the great names of antiquity, Herodotus, Pindar, and others.[33] But his "poetic" idea[34] had indeed become reality. One cannot blame him much for a bit of gloating.

The next week the chariot races were held, divided into two classes, professional carriage drivers and "laymen."[35] The layman victor, Manuel Argyropoulos, won a pair of fancy English pistols, apparently the gift of

Prince Alfred of England, who looked on as four of six chariots crashed—an authentic feature: in one ancient chariot race, only one of forty-one chariots finished. The winner of the professional race, his name variously reported, won three hundred drachmas.[36]

Minoides' early perception of the Olympic committee's bias against athletics proved to be true. The royal decree had specified athletic games in the stadium. But the antiathletic Rangavis, with immense Zappas funds earmarked to restore the stadium in marble, had refused even to buy the property on which the stadium lay.[37] Therefore on November 15, 1859, the first Greek Olympic revival of athletic games took place not at the ancient stadium, as Zappas wished and the royal decree had stated, but at a flat city square that lay on what was then the northwest edge of the city. Then named Plateia Loudovikou, or "Ludwig Square," it is now known in Athens as "Koumoundourou."[38] King Otto and Queen Amalia attended.

These games were not much of a success and generally received a negative judgment in the contemporary Athens press. But they were not nearly so bad as the accounts of modern Olympic historians such as Mandell and MacAloon represent them. Their accounts, in fact, are so full of serious errors as to be wholly unusable.[39]

As in antiquity, athletes from all over the Greek-speaking world, north to south, east to west—from as far away as Turkey, Crete, Cyprus, and Albania[40]—came to compete in these Olympics. The weather was cold and windy. A large crowd encircled the flat square, but only a few could see the events well. The first event was the classic ancient Olympic footrace, the *stadion*, a sprint 600 feet long, one length of the course, or about 200 meters. That first modern Olympic winner was Demetrios Athanasiou, from a village not far from Athens. Next came the *diaulos*, a two-lap race of about 400 meters, as in ancient Olympia, won by Georgios Arsenis from Tripolis in the Peloponnesus. The other events followed. Kostas Chrestos of Argos tripled, winning the discus and both javelin throws. In the pole climb, a number of contestants climbed a soaped pole to claim the valuable prizes that lay at the top, such as a watch and silver candlestick holders.[41] In the featured distance race, the *dolichos*, seven laps or something under a mile, the leading runner collapsed (and apparently later died[42]). Petros Velissariou passed him, winning the race, Zappas's drachmas, and Brookes's British pounds. Velissariou had come all the way from Smyrna, now known as Izmir, Turkey, but then still populated by Greeks. We will hear much more of Velissariou soon; for he shared an important page of our Olympic history with Baron Pierre de Coubertin (literally a page—the Wenlock page of honorary members).

Here are the summary results of the 1859 Athens Olympics. Unfortunately, times and marks were not recorded. I recast the distances to their closest modern equivalents.[43] Second place was recorded in some events but not in others.

200 meters: first, Demetrios Athanasiou, Aspropotamos
400 meters: first, Georgios Arsenis, Tripolis
1,500 meters: first, Petros Velissariou, Smyrna
Discus (distance): first, Constantinos Vassilikis, Athens
Discus ("in height" [at target]): first, Kosta Chrestou, Argos;[44]
Javelin (distance): first, Kosta Chrestou, Argos; second, Nikolaos
 Markopoulos, Serrai
Javelin (at target): first, Kosta Chrestou; second, Elias Kyprios
Long jump: first, Demetrios Karathanasis
Jump "beyond the ditch"[45] (triple jump?): first, Benoukas, Soulion;
 second, Chestos Krekoukis, Eleusis
Pole climb: [the winners' names are not recorded]

The newspaper reports suggest these Games were generally poor, marked by disorder and impromptu entries. Most blamed this result mainly on the committee's failure to prepare for the Games and to prepare a site in the stadium where more spectators could have seen the events. When many people tried to crowd to the front row, they pushed on into the athletic field, and one policeman "who was supposed to keep order showed so much incompetence that his horses ran every which way and hit men and women." The same reporter, obviously displeased with what he saw, especially deplores the death of the distance runner.[46]

Another highly critical reporter was especially upset that Rangavis and the committee would not buy and prepare the stadium, even suggesting that he would rather have seen "Rangavis compete in the greased pole climb" and other committee members do the jumping and even fight one another "in the boxing match." His article clearly tends toward the absurd and exaggerates. He even states that the committee accepted "a sightless beggar" *(eis aommatos epaitis)* for the distance race (with no comment on his success). "In short," the writer concludes, "there was never a more ridiculous affair than the comedy with took place in the Plateia Loudovikou; and one would truly err if he were to term it Olympic Games."[47] If we grant this reporter's peevish tone toward the committee and his rather absurd exaggerations, the "sightless beggar" was probably no more than a nearsighted man, poorly dressed. The Greek words would allow the metaphor.[48]

Although not all who attended these games judged them so severely, it seems beyond question that the athletic games themselves were a general failure. Yet the importance of this 1859 Olympiad does not lie in its own significance as an Olympic revival; and it passes beyond the Games' value as an implementation of Soutsos's vision—even beyond their being the first of the important Zappas series and their lineal relation to our own. Their greatest importance lies in their influence on W. P. Brookes. The 1859 Athens Olympics, as Joachim Rühl was the first to note,[49] profoundly changed Brookes's own Olympic activity, impelling him into an Olympic vision that would affect the world. Without these games and the 1870 and 1875 Athens Olympics that followed, Brookes never would have been spurred on to found the movement for international Olympics, into which he would—decades later—draw Baron de Coubertin.

THREE

The Olympic Movement in England, 1859–1868

> The Olympian Games, discontinued for centuries, have recently been revived! Here is strange news indeed. . . . [T]he classical games of antiquity were revived near Athens.
>
> —London Review, *September 15, 1860*

In Wenlock, Brookes anticipated the 1859 Athens Olympics by holding his local Olympics on July 27, 1859, several months before the Greek Games of November. The Greek revival had inspired Brookes to organize a far more ambitious, splendid, and Olympic festival than any of the previous Wenlock meetings. He expanded the program to include, on the athletic side, archery, cricket, football, two tilting matches, and ten track-and-field events. He imitated the Greek Games by adding a javelin throw event (at a target, like one 1859 Greek event) to his own.[1] Recalling Pindar, poet of the ancient Olympics, he set a prize for the best poem on the Wenlock Olympian Games; a prize was also given for the best essay on physical education, Brookes's other passion. All in all, with the contests in knitting, history, and arithmetic and new contests in art and music, the program totaled twenty-nine events.

The *Shrewsbury Chronicle* of July 29, 1859, under the headline "The Wenlock Olympic Games," gave special attention to the expanded pomp and pageantry they contained. "Gay banners, beautiful flowers, festoons, colours, and every imaginable token of festivity was there to greet us." Among the many different mottoes on the sundry banners were, "Welcome to Wenlock," "Success to the Olympic Games," and (on a very long banner) "Long life and prosperity to our worthy townsman, W. P. Brookes, Esq., the promoter of the Olympian Games."

As for the Games themselves, the *Chronicle* reporter gives a vivid description of the one-mile hurdle event, open "to all England." The winner won a close race with a kick.

In this race three started . . . W. Roberts, S. Oare, and E. Thomas. . . . The lot got off well together. The hurdles—four—were all cleared well throughout. The racers kept within a couple of yards of each other round the course. On clearing the last hurdle, Roberts, who had reserved himself, put out, and showed up in front, cleverly passing his competitors, and out-distancing the one (Oare) by a yard and a half; and the second (Thomas) by three yards and a half.

After relating the day's events, the reporter quotes the words with which Brookes formally closed the festival: "Such meetings as these bring out free minds, free opinions, free enterprises, free competition for every man in every grade of life. The Olympic Games bring together different classes, and make them sociable and neighbourly."[2]

Brookes's remarks here may call to mind the words spoken by Soutsos's ghost of Leonidas—but they sound even more like the words of Coubertin or Brundage, who often listed among the more distinctive features of the IOC Olympics their availability to athletes of all classes and from all nations, bringing those athletes together in a setting that fostered friendliness and peace. "Baron Pierre de Coubertin ... was certain that if the youth of the world could be brought together on an equal footing there would be no better way to promote mutual respect, better understanding between different classes and races, and international good will. How right he was."[3]

The years 1860–61 were crucial for Brookes's Olympic efforts and our own Olympic movement. They saw the Olympic movement clearly define itself as such and expand both regionally and internationally. On February 2, 1860, Wyse wrote Brookes to tell him how the Wenlock ten pound prize was awarded. He named Petros Velissariou, of Smyrna, the winner. He also enclosed details of the November 1859 Athens Olympics—a copy, in Greek, of all the regulations and actual summary results, including the victors' names. He accompanied these documents with an English translation. Brookes soon had the translation and Wyse's letter set in type and published. All printed and handwritten versions of the letter and all the documents are extant in the Wenlock archives; Coubertin saw them there in 1890.[4]

First, however, Brookes called a public "meeting of the inhabitants of the town and neighbourhood of Wenlock," at which he read aloud Wyse's letter from Athens, along with the translated summary results of the 1859 Zappas Olympiad. Noting especially Velissariou, winner of the Wenlock prize, he made a motion to the members of the WOC present that they vote to send Velissariou a Wenlock silver belt decoration and make him "an Honorary Member of the Wenlock Olympian Class." The motion was seconded and passed, along with the resolution that the translated results of the 1859 Zappas Olympiad be forwarded to the mayors of all Shropshire towns. "It was also resolved that a copy of the Greek Games be forwarded to a Manchester paper, with invitations to Greek residents to be present at the [Wenlock Olympic] Games in August."[5]

This fresh news of the Athens Games had obviously spurred Brookes on all the more. In March 1860, Brookes sent copies of the Wenlock Olympian program to "all the boroughs of England."[6] He also, it seems, included in this mailing the printed Wyse letter and 1859 Greek Olympics results; a London paper later published a detailed account of the Greek "Revival of Olympian Games."[7] And he contacted the mayors of the other five largest towns in Shropshire County, proposing to expand his Olympic movement to the regional level. On May 3, 1860, his Wenlock group formally approved Brookes's expanded Olympic plan. "Resolved that it was desirable that annual Meetings for Olympian Games for the whole county, to be called 'The Shropshire Olympian Games,' should be held in rotation in the following Boroughs and other large towns: Shrewsbury, Ludlow, Oswestry, Bridgenorth, Wenlock, Wellington."[8]

The idea of movable Olympics calls to mind Coubertin's later notion of what he called the ambulatory Olympics; and the idea of a yearly rotation among several select cities was part of Soutsos's original proposal for the Greek revival. Indeed, the three men often thought alike.

The First Shropshire Olympian Games were held at Wenlock in common with the Eleventh Annual Wenlock Olympian Games on August 22–23, 1860. These eleventh Wenlock games also prove how strongly the recent Greek revival had influenced Brookes. They became more Greek, with Greek mottoes displayed on banners carried in the parade. The 1860 Games probably also saw the introduction of a new Wenlock Olympic medal that featured Nike, the Greek goddess of victory, surrounded by a quotation from the ancient Greek poet of the Olympics, Pindar.[9] They also included poetry, essay, and literary contests—and a javelin throw for distance (not at a target), like the ancient Greek event and our own.

The guest of honor at these Olympics, Lt. Col. Herbert Edwards, liked the games but not their new Greek associations. Addressing the assemblage, he lectured it on its mistake in emulating the Olympic Games of pagan ancient Greece. He even suggests they scuttle the terms "Olympic" and "Olympian Class." "I . . . suggest . . . another name for this particular class. . . . ["Olympic"] is not merely a classic name, it is essentially a heathen name; it tells of festal rites held in honour of a false God by a nation that knew not the True. . . . Let me advise you to call this thoroughly English class . . . the Shropshire Class of British Work and Play."[10]

Fortunately for our Olympic movement, Brookes refused then, and ever after, to drop the names "Olympic" and "Olympian" from his activities. He did, indeed, seek to revive what he thought were the ideals of the ancient Greek Olympics. And his new associations with the Greek revival of the Olympic Games sealed the name and the aims of his movement: Coubertin, fortunately, saw the Wenlock Olympian Games, not the Wenlock Games of British Work and Play.

Also, again obviously recalling Pindar's Greece, Brookes set at the 1860 Games a prize "[f]or the best ode 'To the Victor of the Tilting Match.' " The winning ode, composed by J. Douglas of Shrewsbury, was, in fact, set to music and "in the following year performed by the students of the Royal Academy of Music with great success before a crowded audience at the Hanover Square rooms, London,"[11] as Coubertin states; but it could not have played the important role in our Olympic history that MacAloon has assigned it.[12]

In October 1860, Brookes developed the international potential of his Olympic activity begun by the gift of ten pounds. Somewhat belatedly, he proceeded to send Velissariou the gift and the honorary membership his group had approved some time earlier. He wrote two letters to Greece, one to N. Theocharis, president of the Greek Olympic committee, and the other to Queen Amalia, the wife of King Otto.[13] To Theocharis, Brookes writes:

> I shall feel much obliged if you will do me the honour of presenting the accompanying silver decoration to Petros Velissariou of Smyrna, the Winner of the Wenlock Prize at the Olympian Games at Athens last year and of informing him that he has been elected an Honorary Member of the Wenlock Olympian Class. I enclose a program of the Wenlock Olympian Games for the present year, and copies of the Prize Ode.

By the fate of history's march—not by chance—Velissariou was thus the first to be enrolled on the Wenlock page of honorary members; and Pierre de Coubertin, thirty years later, was the last enrolled, on that same page.[14] But Coubertin had not yet been born when Velissariou's name entered the Wenlock Olympic rolls.

Queen Amalia's letter was longer. It explained the nature of the Wenlock Olympian Games, the great respect Brookes had for Greece and the royal family, and other polite niceties a Victorian Englishman might address to a queen. With the queen's letter, too, he enclosed gifts, namely, one of the new Wenlock Olympian medals and a belt clasp "with a design worn by women at the Wenlock Games."

On November 8, 1860, Brookes wrapped all these things up in a single package and sent it, with a covering letter, to Spyridon Trikoupis, Greek ambassador in London, to be passed on to the intended recipients in Greece.[15] Trikoupis was the father of Charilaos Trikoupis, whose own name is far better known in Olympic history—where he is virtually infamous as the Greek prime minister who opposed Coubertin on the question of holding the first IOC Olympics in Athens in 1896. Trikoupis, not acknowledging receipt of Brookes's package until November 21, explained that he was still waiting for a response from the royal palace in Athens about the gift for Queen Amalia, because the royal family did not accept gifts without being first petitioned for their approval.[16] The package for Theocharis, he assured Brookes, had been forwarded to Athens.

Brookes was ever active. Before Velissariou received his medal and honorary membership—even before Trikoupis responded from London—Brookes took another crucial Olympic step. He severed the Wenlock Olympian Class from the parent Wenlock Agricultural Reading Society, making it separate and autonomous and renaming it the Wenlock Olympian Society (WOS). The WOS was officially founded just after November 16, 1860—though it later recorded that its first honorary member, Petros Velissariou, was "elected in October."[17] This separation from the Reading Society probably resulted mainly from Brookes's desire to focus on his broader Olympic quest, to give that primacy over his previous work for his townsmen's intellectual, even physical, improvement. But it was also spurred, in part, by some internal dissension within the Agricultural Reading Society, where a few members from the local clergy opposed the Olympian Class and its athletic meetings.[18] Yet Brookes may have welcomed their desire to sever the Olympian group from the society; for he now clearly wished to pursue his Olympic idea as a thing in itself, independent of all else.

The new WOS would sponsor the Twelfth Annual Wenlock Olympian Games in 1861; and the Second Shropshire Olympian Games would take place, this time, separately. But before those Games occurred, Velissariou, now in the Greek army, had finally received, through Theocharis, the medallion gift and Wenlock honorary membership. On April 5, 1861, in beautifully penned Greek (perhaps by a calligrapher), Velissariou wrote back to Brookes. Formally accepting his honorary membership in the "Wenlock Olympic Society," he warmly thanks Brookes for his new Wenlock medal and, indeed, the earlier ten-pound prize. All these things, Velissariou says, are "high honors," for which he has "profound gratitude." He hopes that Brookes will convey those sentiments "to every member" of the WOS. Brookes obviously prized this letter; for he had it translated into English and pasted both versions in his running scrapbook.[19]

Velissariou's letter came with an even more important covering letter from Theocharis, president of the Athens Olympic committee, writing to Brookes on May 2, 1861. This long letter is a major Olympic document, because it shows that, at this point, one could actually speak of an international Olympic movement. After a full page explaining the difficulties in getting the package to Velissariou and acknowledging Velissariou's response, Theocharis states that he must also express his thanks on behalf of his own committee:

> [The Greek Olympic committee] is happy to have found in the same nation which has so many claims to our profound gratitude, a sister institution of the same name, so nobly announced by the benevolent co-operation which it [the Wenlock committee] has lent its [the Greek committee's] work from the start, and the generous expressions for Greece which it [the Wenlock committee] has incorporated in its own program.
>
> The Olympic Committee of Athens, being very grateful for all its acts of good will, sends its most cordial greetings to its esteemed sister committee, and expresses its wishes for the progress of the Wenlock Olympics and the achievement of the civilizing aims which unite [our two committees] in the same course.[20]

Yet Theocharis had presided over his first and last Olympiad, and was not himself to continue united with Brookes on the same course. The Greek movement was now forced into a long hiatus. For a while, the Olympic movement advanced only in England, progressing there briefly and feverishly and soon developing into a national movement that actually held important national Olympics, which have been inexcusably forgotten in modern Olympic histories.

A few weeks after Theocharis wrote that letter, which I judge one of the most meaningful documents in all Olympic history, the Second Shropshire Olympian Games took place, on May 20–21, 1861. This time they were held independently of the Wenlock Games, in the larger city of Wellington. The program generally followed the previous Wenlock program but with emphasis on intellectual as well as athletic achievements. Rifle-shooting events at various distances were added. The now formally constituted Shropshire Olympian Society took as its motto *Palmam qui meruit ferat* (May he who earns it win the prize). Brookes had already used that motto in Wenlock. Ten thousand satisfied spectators looked on.[21] Later that year,

on October 23, the Wenlock Games were held as usual, the twelfth Wenlock Olympics, but they were the first organized by the new WOS. The
program shrank to fourteen events—all athletic.

The Olympic movement then spread outside of Shropshire and, significantly for us, to Liverpool. The Liverpool Olympic movement was
rather brief, but it contributed several items to our own: first, the ubiqui-
tous motto, *Mens sana in corpore sano* (a sound mind in a sound body), a
Latin phrase with no connection whatsoever to the ancient Olympics; second, the concept of amateurism—again, wholly unrelated to the ancient
Olympics but later the bane of the entire modern Olympic movement.[22]
The Liverpool committee also played a significant role in forming, with
Brookes in 1865, the British National Olympian Association (NOA).

In the 1850s a number of cricket clubs formed in Liverpool, and participation also grew in German-style gymnastics (*Turnen*) and in track and
field. Interest in the last was perhaps sparked by an edition of the Scottish
Highland Games in Liverpool in 1858. But these Liverpool activities were
restricted to clubs formed by men in the upper social classes, "Gentlemen," as they called themselves. The first ever Amateur Athletic Meeting
was apparently held toward the end of the decade. And in 1861 the first
rowing club in Liverpool restricted its participants to "Gentlemen Amateurs." Working-class athletes were excluded from membership and from
competition.[23]

Two men, Charles Melly and John Hulley, spearheaded the movement in
Liverpool. Both firmly believed in physical education and opened separate
gymnasiums in the city, especially for *Turner*-style exercises. Both men belonged to the Muscular Christianity movement, which broke with medieval Christianity's concept of a hatred of the flesh. Muscular Christians
believed that proper cultivation of the body could further, rather than hin-
der, proper mental and spiritual growth. Thus when the two men formed
the Liverpool Athletic Club in 1862, "for the encouragement of Physical
Education," they chose as its motto the words *Mens sana in corpore sano.*[24]

Surely influenced by Hulley's friend Brookes, Hulley and Melly decided
that as one of its first acts the Liverpool Athletic Club would hold Olympic
Games. A full track-and-field program was drawn up, to include footraces
and hurdles at various distances, triple jump, high jump, pole vault, and a
discus throw—an event never before practiced outside of Greece.[25] There
were gymnastic contests and combative events, such as fencing and wrestling. There was also a literary prize set for the best essay on physical education and the topic *Mens sana in corpore sano.*

Unlike Brookes's Olympics, however, the Liverpool games offered no cash prizes; only medals were awarded. And "professional and semi-pro athletes" were barred. Entry was open only to "Gentlemen Amateurs," which clearly excluded working-class entrants. On June 14, 1862, the first Liverpool Olympics were held at Mount Vernon Parade Grounds. A large number of contestants and up to ten thousand spectators, many of the latter women, arrived for the Games. "[T]hey were of a highly respectable class, including the elite of the neighbourhood," one newspaper remarks. The names of all the first- and second-place winners are preserved and a few of the winning marks, which were not high by later standards. R. T. Parkinson's winning triple jump was 42 ft. 11 in. and Mr. Musgrove won the pole vault at 9 ft. 6 in. But everyone seemed to agree "[t]he Olympic Festival, taken altogether, has proved a great success."[26] The most notable feature of these Games is surely their introduction—to the Olympic movement and perhaps to all of history—of elitist "amateurism" and their exclusion of the working class.

In the autumn of that year Dr. Brookes presided over the third Shropshire Olympics, held again at Wenlock in conjunction with the thirteenth Wenlock Olympian Games. There, surely with a critical eye north toward his friends in Liverpool, Brookes said in his annual speech, "As Christians we should, on moral grounds, endeavor to direct the amusement of the working class." Brookes's activity started with a view toward the working class, and he never forgot it. This attitude would bring him in constant, even furious, conflict with advocates of class-exclusive amateurism, which eventually killed the British Olympic movement before hobbling our own. But Brookes's speech continued in otherwise full agreement with Melly and Hulley; the importance of physical education for a strong national youth that could protect the nation in battle:

> [W]hy not direct our attention to the physical improvement of those who are to constitute the living defenders of our freedom? I feel sure that the introduction of a system of gymnastic training into our national schools . . . would be a national good, would be the means of raising up . . . a race of healthy, active, vigorous youths, a noble, manly race, whose reputation for pluck, bodily power, and endurance, would inspire far more terror on the battlefield than the arms they bore.[27]

Brookes's campaign for compulsory physical education in the national schools was the item that much later caught the attention of Pierre de Coubertin and brought Coubertin to Wenlock in 1890, where Brookes drew him into the Olympic revival movement.

Coubertin was born on New Year's Day the following year, 1863. Had he been old enough, he surely would have also approved of the new policy announced for the second annual Liverpool Olympic Games; for it sought to become international. This time, the call went out to "Gentleman Amateurs of all nations" to come to compete in Olympic Games in Liverpool on June 13, 1863. Yet this international feature failed, probably because there were, as yet, no "Gentleman Amateurs" outside of England; and the victor list contains only Englishmen. Still, the Olympics were a great success. Swimming events were added. There were bands and much pageantry. Between twelve thousand and fifteen thousand people watched. One newspaper concluded that it was "a magnificent and truly Olympic Festival." But another seemed more concerned about the prospect of "professionalism" entering in and registered the first objection to athletes who had trainers, a question that would later plague the amateur movement: "It is quite true that Mr. Hulley, by withrawing all money prizes, has done much to promote the best interest in such sports. . . . [Yet] we think he needs to purify the games still further by insisting upon these trainers being kept out of the arena."[28]

The 1864 Liverpool Olympics were held in June at a new site, the Biological Gardens. Thousands thronged the area and created a scene reminiscent of the 1859 Athens Olympics; although there was a grandstand, standing spectators ringed the infield, so only those in front could see. The result was a pushing and shoving match that ended with many spectators on the racetrack itself. A highly class-conscious reporter was displeased that the site was "so contaminated in public opinion by the associations normally connected with it" and that betting men were there, allowed "to carry on their nefarious craft."[29]

Other newspapers judged the overall festival a success. One sought to evaluate the whole idea of an Olympic revival.

We hope that these attempts to revive the games of the Olympiad will not alarm the fearful and timid. . . . Ancient Greece . . . owed nearly all her wondrous skill in the art of life to her grand combined physical and mental education. . . . How striking does this revival of the Olympic Games illustrate the proverb "There is nothing new under the sun." . . . [N]ow, after the lapse of [two thousand years], we find the men of Liverpool entering the lists and competing in the very same games, which, in her prosperity, attracted the chivalry and the beauty of Greece and made the stadium ring with shouts of exultant joy.

It was a gratifying reflection . . . to consider that these men had come together—many of them long distances—not in the sordid hope of winning so

much money, but, as in old Grecian times, simply for the honour which rewards success. . . . Indeed, the most ardent admirer of muscular development
could have wished for no more earnest and unanimous public testimony to
the worth of the cause. It was a scene to recall the romantic days of ancient
chivalry."

These words, in fact, make Coubertin sound like an echo decades after-
ward.[30]

A year later, on June 19, 1865, Evangelis Zappas died in Romania. He
left his immense fortune to the Greek government, to fund continuation
of the Greek Olympic revival.

There were no 1865 Liverpool Olympics, but Hulley was the main official
at a Grand Olympian Festival held on August 9, 1865, at Lancaster, north
of Liverpool. The concept seemed to spread around the northwestern part
of the isle. The previous year, Hulley and Melly had agreed to start building a new modern gym, to be called the Liverpool Gymnasium. When
completed it was one of the best sports facilities in all Europe. It opened
in November 1865, with a number of prominent guests attending the
opening ceremonies. Among those guests were Dr. W. P. Brookes and
E. G. Ravenstein, president of the German Gymnastic Society, a *Turner*
group in London. Brookes and Hulley were already good friends—and
Hulley an honorary member at Wenlock.[31] Then and there, in Liverpool,
they formed a bond, along with Ravenstein, and founded a new Olympic
organization. They intended this organization to unify the several Olympic societies that had sprung up in England (Wenlock and Liverpool were
no longer alone).[32] They wanted to bring a truly national Olympic movement, along with national Olympic Games, to England. The three men
formally founded the first phase of the present British National Olympic
Committee, the current British Olympic Association, naming it the National Olympian Association (NOA). I excerpt a few items from the Articles of Foundation—which read not unlike our own IOC Olympic
charter:[33]

> RESOLVED. That a National Olympian Association be established for the en-
> couragement and reward of skill and strength in manly exercises, by the
> award of Medals and other Prizes, money excepted, at General Meetings of
> the Association, to be held annually and in rotation in or near one of the
> principal cities or towns of Great Britain. That Professional Athletes shall be
> excluded from competition.
> That the NOA will also pay homage to Mental Excellence, by electing

from time to time as honorary members, persons who have distinguished themselves in Literature, Art, or Science, or who have proved themselves benefactors to mankind.

That this Association shall form a centre of union for the different Olympian, Athletic, Gymnastic, Boating, Swimming, Cricket, and other similar Societies, enabling them . . . to assist one another; and affording to the most expert of their Athletes an opportunity of contending and distinguishing themselves in a National arena.

That the competition of this Association shall be international, and open to all comers.

· ·

That the first Annual Meeting will be held next July, in London.

That the Badge of the Association be a wreathe of oak, and its Motto *Civium vires civitatis vis*.[34]

Several items here deserve special note. The motto (the strength of the nation lies in the strength of its citizens) indicates Hulley and Brookes's shared notion that England's military security lay in the physical condition of its youth. Noteworthy, too, are the pledge to recognize mental excellence, as well, and the call for international competition.[35] We ourselves might notice first that the charter excludes professional athletes from competing but fails to define "professional." But the embryonic clubs of elitist upper-class athletes in southern England first noted that the NOA sought to be an umbrella organization for various British sporting clubs and had scheduled its first meeting for their own backyard, London, in 1866. And, although the NOA excluded professional athletes, it did not formally exclude the working class. On that question, if Hulley's Liverpool tradition incited him to dispute it, Brookes had carried the day.[36]

When news of Brookes's NOA and its plans reached London, the upper-class gentlemen of London and Oxbridge were resolved not to let the NOA proceed. They immediately formed a counter-Olympic organization, the Amateur Athletic Club (AAC), which would later transform into the British Amateur Athletic Association (AAA). The official historian of the AAA, P. Lovesey, puts it this way: "[A] shock-wave ran through the running grounds of the capital. The prospect of athletics controlled from anywhere but London was unthinkable. Never mind that Liverpool had staged four Olympic Festivals on a scale grander than anything seen in the South. The London contingent mobilized as if the French had landed."[37]

Interest in track and field had just begun among the upper classes in southern England. A club had formed in London in 1863,[38] and the first intercollegiate meeting, sometimes known as the first amateur athletic meeting, took place as a dual meet between Oxford and Cambridge, at Christ Church Field, Oxford, on March 5, 1864.[39] A few other clubs became vaguely organized in London. These "gentleman amateurs" founded a class-elitist style of amateurism even stronger than that in Liverpool. They refused to allow members of the working class to participate in any of their meetings; they even refused to share dressing rooms with any man who worked for a living. More importantly, they stated that they did not want to share valuable prizes with their countrymen from a lower social level. I have elsewhere collected some detailed contemporary comments of English gentleman amateurs on how necessary it was to bar working-class men from participating in athletics.[40] But these gentleman amateurs also looked askance at outsiders from the north (especially such a place as Liverpool), whom they tended to view as provincials.[41] The Amateur Athletic Club, the first organization ever formed with the word "amateur" in its name, was created in late 1865 "chiefly to inaugurate and manage an annual amateur championship meeting"—plainly on class-exclusive principles. The panic and urgency of the AAC's organization—sure proof that it was spurred by news of the NOA's announced London Olympics—are obvious in the AAC's first announcement: "The Amateur Athletic Club will hold their first annual champion games on the day immediately preceding the University boat race, on some ground in London. The programme will probably consist of the following events. . . ."[42] And Lovesey candidly admits: "It has to be said that the AAC prospectus, published in February, 1866, bears signs of having been cobbled together to thwart the National Olympian Association."[43] Thus regional, as well as class, warfare would finally bring Brookes's British national Olympic movement to its knees and give rise to the strange controversies that surrounded "amateur athletics" for many decades.

Brookes's NOA had announced Olympic Games in London for July 1866. The AAC quickly held, on March 23 at Beaufort House, their "first annual championship games," with a program much like that in the universities' new intervarsity meets.[44] It then directed its own athletes to boycott the July Olympics in hopes of running them aground. All but three of London's top "gentleman athletes," and all but four members of the AAC altogether, did boycott.[45] Yet the 1866 Olympic Games in London were still a great success. Although a majority of the known marks in the AAC meet were somewhat superior to those compiled at the Olympics, contemporary newspapers and most later historians have judged the Olympics as the superior of the two 1866 meets.[46] They were clearly grander in the number and nationwide representation of athletes and the number of spectators. They are a truly significant step in our Olympic history. Brookes was president of the Olympic organizing committee, and his speech given at those Games was what first caused Coubertin to admire Brookes and later find out about his Olympic ideas. Amazingly, modern Olympic histories seem to know nothing at all of these important London Games.[47]

The 1866 London Olympics began on July 31 with swimming events in the Thames.[48] They continued on August 1, with gymnastic and track-and-field events held in the original Crystal Palace. This structure was the new architectural wonder of the day, prefabricated, movable, built of iron girders and glass panels. Anticipating our Forums and Superdomes, it was also the first great indoor sports arena.[49] Ten thousand spectators and contestants were there. I give the summary results, noting first place only, though three places were recorded.

General competition (high jump, long jump, half-mile race, putting the weight, and rope climb): H. W. Brooke[50] and H. Landsberger (tie), both of the German Gymnastic Society (GGS, Ravenstein's group), London

General competition for members of army and navy: C. Amos, Fiftieth Light Infantry

Volunteers competition (a military event run in battle gear, like the ancient Olympic "armed race"):[51] J. W. Worrall, Honourable Artillery Company

100-yard dash: C. G. Emery, AAC, London, 10½ sec.[52]

175 yards: C. G. Emery, AAC, London, 18½ sec.

440-yard hurdles: W. Grace, Bristol, 1 min. 10 sec.

Half mile: W. Rye, King's College RC, London, 2 min. 13 sec.[53]

Steeplechase, half mile: H. W. Brooke, GGS, London, 4 min. 50 sec.

One mile: W. Rye, King's College RC, London (C. Nurse, Brighton, finished first, 4 min. 50 sec., but was disqualified; see below)

Two mile: E. Humphrey, Southampton Athletic Club (Nurse finished first at 10 min. 59 sec. but was again disqualified; see below)

High jump: Guy Pym, AAC, London, 5 ft. 4 in.

Long jump: J. G. Elliott, GGS, London, 17 ft. 2 in.

Standing long jump: A. Seeley, GGS, London, 9 ft. 6 in.

Pole leaping: J. Plowman, GGS, London, 8 ft. 10 in.

Vaulting: G. Henderson, Liverpool, 6 ft. 6 in.

Javelin[54:] W. A. Worsop, GGS, London

Shot put (36 lbs.): Mr. Hartley
Rope climb: H. Landsberger, GGS, London
Wrestling, Cumberland style: G. Henderson, Liverpool
Wrestling, catch-as-catch-can: A. Thiemain, GGS, and G. Henderson, Liverpool (draw)
Boxing, lightweight: P. McDonald, GGS, London, C. G. Emery, AAC, London, and A. Seeley, GGS, London (tie[55])
Boxing, heavyweight: J. Williams, GGS, London
Fencing: H. Hartjen, GGS, London
Fencing with bayonet and sabre: G. Henderson, Liverpool

On the next day, August 2, the Olympic Games continued with the gymnastic events, held in the buildings of Ravenstein's German Gymnastic Society at King's Cross. Ravenstein's group was thriving, with more than a thousand members, of whom most were Britons, the rest Germans living in London. In addition to an "amateur band, singing club, library of 2,000 volumes, ladies' class for athletics,"[56] the GGS now enjoyed a new gymnasium building, which was ideal for the event.

Indeed, the 1866 program is surprisingly comprehensive—with swimming, track and field, gymnastics, wrestling, boxing, and fencing, it was remarkably like that of the early IOC Olympiads. That fact alone makes the 1866 Olympics worth mention in Olympic histories, despite marks that are often mediocre, even for those days. But there is more of interest here, several Olympic firsts and the athletic debut of one of the world's greatest athletes, the most heralded athletic hero in all of British sports history.

Few Englishmen know that their revered W. G. Grace of Bristol was an Olympic champion hurdler long before he became the most famous cricket player of all time. Grace's later and current position in British sporting legend is even greater than that of Babe Ruth in America.[57] But on August 1, 1866, Grace, then just eighteen years old, took time off from a cricket match, went over to the Crystal Palace, and lined up with fourteen other athletes entered in the hurdles. There were twenty flights. The eyewitness accounts are vivid: "Grace took the lead from the start, followed by Collins and Emery. . . ; and Grace, making the pace a cracker, led by 20 yards at half the distance, and eventually won with ease by 20 yards; Emery, who passed Collins at the last hurdle but one, second; Collins third."[58]

The track-and-field steeplechase—now of course a standard Olympic event—was first contested at these 1866 Olympic Games. "Steeple Chase, half a mile.—There were two cross bars about 6ft high, a gate about 10ft, and several hurdles to get over, and a ditch to jump in. There were eight starters, but only four finished the course, and these at very wide intervals. H. W. Brooke, G.G.S., first, F. Collins, second, J. G. Elliott, G.G.S., third. Time, 4 min. 40 sec." This steeplechase event, a race devised for humans to imitate a standard equestrian event, was modified as it became more popular in following decades until it took its modern form as our contemporary Olympic event.[59]

These London Olympics also anticipated the case of James Thorpe. For the first time, an Olympic victor was subsequently disqualified for being a professional and stripped of his honors. The mile run had nineteen entries.

> C. Nurse (Brighton) entered and came in first, but was disqualified for not being an amateur. Immediately after the start Nurse took the lead, James 2nd, Rye 3rd, Humphrey, 4th, the rest together. . . . [A]t the half mile (2 min. 21 sec.) Nurse was first, followed by Rye and Humphrey, then King (who soon afterwards retired), the others nowhere. Soon . . . Rye made a rush for the lead, but was outpaced, and he was satisfied with second place. No change occurred in the remainder of the race until within 200 yards of the finish, Nurse put on a spurt, left Rye in the rear and won very easily in 4 min. 50 sec.[60]

When Nurse was disqualified, Rye (King's College) was declared the winner. Nurse also won the two-mile run but was disqualified there, as well. I find no record of the nature of the charges against Nurse and who lodged them nor who decided to disqualify him on what criteria. Those details, of such interest to us with our long history of amateur problems and our fallen hero, James Thorpe, seem not to have interested 1866 newspapers in the case of C. Nurse. As noted above, the NOA failed to define the term "professional athlete" in their charter papers. Amateurism of some kind was being enforced; but under Brookes's presidency the elitist amateurism of the AAC was surely not operative. The AAC boycott did not yet destroy these Games; some AAC members, Pym and Emery, even competed and won. One newspaper reports, "The Festival at the Crystal Palace appears to have been a genuine success." Another, in Oxford, notes, "The presentation of the prizes was preceded by an address from Mr. W. P. Brookes . . . who may be termed 'the father of the Olympian movement.'"[61] Before the formal dinner at the Crystal Palace, Brookes gave a long address to the assembled Olympians at the Handel Orchestra, a speech that pleaded the case for physical education. Indeed it was a published version of this same Brookes speech that later attracted Coubertin to the same movement—and thus to the Olympic idea and movement, whose paternity has always been assigned to him. We look at this important speech in more detail when we examine its influence on Coubertin.[62]

Because their movement was now national, Hulley and Brookes reduced some of their activity in their regional Olympics. No Liverpool Olympics were held in 1865; and the last Liverpool Olympiad, a significant festival, was organized by a different group in 1867.[63] There were no Shropshire Olympics after 1864. But Brookes kept up his annual local Wenlock Olympics. For the Eighteenth Annual Wenlock Olympian Games, held on June 11, 1867, he added some events from the 1866 London Games, such as a pole vault, gymnastics, and the newly invented "foot steeple-chase with a water-leap." At the closing ceremony, in a special tribute to its founder, the WOS gave a specially inscribed first-class silver medal, with Pindar's words inscribed on it, to Brookes, the man "who, if not the absolute originator of these manly sports, is, at all events the reviver of them in modern days, and the leading pioneer of the athletic movement."

In response, Brookes said:

> [I]t can reasonably be asked, in what way can it be possible, that the inhabitants of a small town like Wenlock, can contribute to the national welfare? In this way—drop a stone in the middle of a lake, and the little ring first formed will go on gradually increasing in circumference till, at length, the distant shores are reached.
>
> Sow a single seed of a rare plant in the most secluded spot and if the soil and other conditions are favourable to its germination, it will grow up and bear another seed, and in time, produce plants sufficient to cover the length and breadth of the land.[64]

These intriguing metaphors, in retrospect, may be far better appreciated in our own day than they could have been in Brookes's. They seem amazingly prophetic from our vantage point almost a century and a half after they were uttered, when the seeds of the growing Olympic movement have been repeatedly planted in so many fertile minds that it now reaches virtually every corner of the globe.

The second annual National Olympian Games took place in Birmingham later that month, on June 26–28, 1867. The prospectus, reflecting Brookes's influence, notes "[t]he Association will support all efforts made to introduce bodily exercises into schools as a regular branch of education." It also sought to better define "amateur" perhaps because of the Nurse case but probably more in order to satisfy and attract athletes of the AAC: "The competitions are strictly confined to Amateurs. Persons who have competed for Public or Admission Money, or for a Prize with

Professionals, or ever made Gymnastics or Athletics a means of livelihood, are ineligible."

But the AAC, which itself technically included all those same restrictions, was really more interested in social class. It had the added provision known as the mechanics clause—it excluded from amateur status anyone "who is by trade or employment, a mechanic, artisan, or labourer."[65] Brookes, with his concern for the working class, refused to place this clause in his NOA rules, and the AAC again asked its athletes to boycott the Olympics. The difference between the two definitions was and remained crucial.

From London, Bristol, Leeds, and elsewhere around England athletes came to the National Olympian Games at Birmingham.[66] But very few were from the top athletic clubs of the south, most of which obeyed the boycott. The boycott put a damper on the Birmingham Olympics but could not destroy them. On opening day, June 25, 1867, there were many athletes and spectators; the train taking them to the contest site on Portland Road was three kilometers long. The program had forty-two events, including (besides all the standard athletic events) a poetry contest, a pentathlon, special events for a boys division, and the first team gymnastics in Olympic history. Brookes's handprint was, of course, everywhere: the first and featured event was tilting at the ring. There was much impressive pageantry, obviously derived from Wenlock. The Wenlock Fife and Drum Band and another band from Warwickshire led the procession of athletes and spectators to the contest grounds.

The opening tilting event was presented with much fanfare and a special award ceremony, then and there, for the victor. The track-and-field events came next. A few of the marks were very respectable for the time, better than in 1866 and superior to those attained at the 1867 AAC Amateur Championships in London (10.25[67] in the 100-yard dash, 9 ft. 5 in. in the pole vault). But for the most part the AAC marks were somewhat better, and the athletes who had set them had stayed home in the south. The AAC had achieved a rather tight grip on most amateur clubs in England, seeking to make sure that it controlled them, that the mechanics clause would generally prevail, and that the NOA would lose its bid to become the major umbrella organization for British amateur athletics.

Later that same year Brookes introduced an innovation to the Wenlock Olympics that surely affects our whole Olympic history. For in order to show Baron Pierre de Coubertin a festival of Olympic Games in 1890, he resorted to this 1867 innovation as a precedent. Soon after the 1867 national Olympics, Brookes decided to stage a special autumn edition of the

Wenlock Olympian Games. A few years before, beset by press criticism of the events he had held "open to all comers" and even some internal dissension over the amateur question within the WOS, he had formed the Amateur Class of the WOS, apparently to satisfy these critics.[68] But he never would define "amateur" by a social-class division. In order to participate in this 1867 special autumn meeting for the Amateur Class, contestants were required to swear an oath that: "I will never compete for money, nor with Professionals, nor ever make Athletic Exercises or Contests a means of livelihood."[69]

Once again, we see Brookes anticipating Coubertin and, in this case, anticipating even the most zealous Avery Brundage. As early as 1906, Coubertin was recommending an Olympic oath; he repeated that call in 1913, after the Thorpe case, and finally drafted an oath that was first administered to the athletes at the Antwerp Games, in 1920. But Brookes's 1867 oath—with its denial of even future professionalism—is the one that Brundage recommended.[70]

The 1868 national Olympics were first scheduled for Manchester. Brookes introduced an amateur oath to the national Olympics, wherein athletes swore they had never competed for money or made any monetary profit from athletics. But there was no reference to abstention from future profit nor to social class.[71] This time, the AAC boycott, led by the powerful men in London, succeeded in thwarting the Games. Few top athletes signed up for the Olympics, and the festival was moved to the rather small Shropshire city of Wellington, not far from Brookes's own village. The National Olympian Games (NOG) sought to replicate the previous year's Birmingham program as much as possible, but there were no facilities in Wellington for swimming, boxing, and wrestling. The Games were not a great success, and nothing like the successful 1866 London Olympics nor even the Birmingham edition of the previous year. A newspaper reporter writes of these Games, "Olympic! The name has slipped glibly from the tongue."[72] But for a while it did not slip from the tongues of those in the NOA. The AAC had thoroughly tightened its grip on English sport.[73] Brookes and the NOA did not even attempt to hold any more National Olympics at this point, as class-exclusive amateurism reigned throughout the land.

Thus in less than a decade after the first Greek Olympiad, from 1859 to 1868, the British Olympic movement seemed first to flourish, then to wither. But the Olympic spirit would not die. Its seed had been planted in more than one country's soil. As Brookes saw his Olympic movement founder in England, Soutsos's own movement finally flowered in Greece.

FOUR

The Olympic Movement in Greece, 1869–1875

> Everything past affects the future, and no future can be built
> without taking the past into account.
> —*Pierre de Coubertin, 1923*

As the Olympic movement seemed to wane in England, it suddenly revived in Greece. Evangelis Zappas died in 1865, leaving his immense fortune for the modern Olympics, to be held every four years, "in the manner
of our ancestors."[1] His will specified that the stadium be excavated and
restored for the athletic games, with an adequate but simple building
nearby for the agro-industrial exhibits. The will contained a strange section: His body was first to be buried at a church in Romania. After four
years, it was to be dug up and decapitated: the portion below the neck was
to be reburied at a school in his native village in Greek Albania. The head
was to be reburied in Athens at the new Olympic building, with a plaque
bearing the words, in ancient Greek, *Enthade keitai he kefale Evangele Zappa*
("Here lies the head of Evangelis Zappas").[2]

By October 22, 1862, the Greeks had already run King Otto off the
throne and out of Greece. He did not formally abdicate; he was simply
compelled to leave. The Greek people, in a formal plebiscite, almost unanimously voted to offer the throne to Queen Victoria's second son, Prince
Alfred, who had attended the 1859 Athens Olympics and there gave a prize
to the chariot victor. But Alfred, on his mother's orders, declined. By June
1863, the Greeks had obtained another prince—like Otto, an unemployed
teenager of good European royalty—who both met their allies' approval
and would take the job and crown. On October 18, the Danish teenager,
now named King George 1 of Greece, arrived in Greece. His first several
years were especially difficult, with sundry internal problems—a military
insurrection in Crete, a new marriage, and serious questions of foreign
policy and alliances. These things complicated the task of the young man
learning his job and the Greek language.[3] The turmoil seemed to make
Olympic Games impossible. But George had thought of Olympic Games

as early as 1865, and in 1869 the government announced that the Second Olympiad would be held in October 1870.[4] They were indeed held, only one month later, in November 1870. Unlike the 1859 Athens Olympics—but much more like the later 1896 IOC edition—the 1870 Athens Olympics were an astonishing success.

The Olympic committee spent almost two hundred thousand drachmas on the 1870 Olympics. Most went to the agro-industrial contests, for a temporary building and glass cases to display the entries.[5] These exhibits were, in fact, a success and eclipsed the athletic games, especially because of their budget and emphasis. Various other competitions in rowing, swimming, and equestrian events were originally planned but later canceled.

The athletic Olympics were held in the stadium, as Zappas had intended and as the people had hoped. Athletics received only 6 percent of the total budget. But in 1869 the ancient Panathenaic stadium was indeed excavated and suitably prepared.[6] The notion that the stadium lay unexcavated until 1895—when Coubertin moved the Greeks to uncover their own ancient treasures—is simply untrue. Yet the 1870 committee spent only eighty-five hundred drachmas to excavate the stadium, not even one-twentieth of what Zappas had given for that purpose back in 1859. Of course, although Zappas had paid for marble seats, the spectators got wooden bleachers. Yet all could see perfectly, because of the stadium's ancient design.

The athletic subcommittee did a superb job with the minimal budget at hand. It anticipated Coubertin in aiming to revive the ancient Olympics in conformity with the conditions of modern life. Yet in many ways it was truly a revival. The call for entries went out about three months before the event. Athletes were to report in person to the Olympic committee in Athens for six weeks' supervised training and prelims. Victors would receive free seats for life at future Olympiads. All athletes would swear an oath they would not cheat and so on, just as in antiquity. The oath, of course, was unrelated to the Olympic oaths in Wenlock and Wellington (1867–68) and had nothing to do with amateurism—which, by early 1870, was still unknown in Greece.[7]

Furthermore, no athlete need forgo his Olympic dream because of money. The committee offered to pay travel expenses for needy athletes and also their uniforms and room and board while in Athens. It offered cash prizes, as Zappas's will required.[8] Once again, athletes from all over the Greek-speaking world, east to west, north to south, Crete to Constantinople, made their way to the Olympic Games in Athens. On the big day, November 15, 1870, the athletes and the stadium were ready. Thirty thousand spectators flocked to the renovated stadium to see the revival of the Olympic Games, bigger than almost any crowd at Coubertin's IOC Olympics from 1900 to 1920.[9] Thus the 1870 Olympics took place in the modern world's first real stadium, with record Olympic attendance unmatched, outside of Athens, until Paris, in 1924.

The games opened with an Olympic hymn. The program, not so elaborate as Brookes's programs in England, was still sophisticated for the time. It included track-and-field events and the gymnastic contests that were common then. The athletes contended, as best they could, in disciplined fashion and sporting spirit for Olympic victory. The large, orderly crowd applauded the athletes' performances. King George crowned each victor with an olive wreath, the prize in ancient Olympia—just as he later did in the IOC Olympiad 1, 1896.

By a strange coincidence—there are many in Olympic history—the principal organizer and coach (*gymnasiarch*) for these 1870 athletic Olympics was the German schoolteacher Julius Ening. Ening came to Greece to work in King Otto's palace. But when Otto was expelled, Ening remained in Greece to teach. One of his pupils was a boy named Demetrios Vikelas, who later became the first president of our own IOC, handpicked by Coubertin. Vikelas played a major role in organizing the first International Olympic Games in 1896 and in fact saved our Olympic movement at that time. But in 1870 he was no longer in Greece, nor was he in touch with his old teacher, now the head Olympic coach.[10] Vikelas's Olympic destiny was still far off.

The first 1870 victor was Evangelos Skordaras, a butcher, who won the 400 meters just ahead of Georgios Xydeas.[11] Three athletes won double victories. Georgios Tsantelas of Eleusis won both the long jump and the triple jump; he placed second in the javelin. We wish we knew his marks; but here the 1870 revival, unlike its modern counterparts in England, was too authentic. As in ancient Greece, officials kept no record of distances or times. To beat one's competitors was all that mattered, in 1870 as in 470 B.C. But we have the summary results for first through third place in ten events. I list only first place.

400 meters: E. Skordaras, Athens
Running triple jump: G. Tsantelas, Eleusis
Running single long jump: G. Tsantelas, Eleusis
Wrestling: K. Kardamylakis, Crete
Discus throw: S. Ioannou, Kallipolis
Javelin throw (at target): S. Ioannou

Pole vault (for distance): K. Kardamylakis
Pole climb: Th. Troungas, Athens
Rope climb: G. Akestorides, Constantinople [i.e., Istanbul]
Individual tug-of-war: I. Psychas, Kyme[12]

The games formally closed, and the clapping crowd, before dispersing, waited patiently as the king and queen, hand in hand, basking in Olympic euphoria, walked out of the stadium to their chariot.

The newspapers praised the Olympic games as a grand success, beyond anyone's expectation.[13] The king warmly thanked the committee. As the English press now called Brookes the father of the Olympian movement, the Greeks now called Zappas the founder of the Olympics. They thought he would be pleased.[14] The 1859 Games may seem not to deserve the title of first modern Olympics, since they were not, in the final judgment, successful. Some may say that the 1866 London Olympics, too, fall short of earning the title. Although a success, they were technically an English production, not a revival of the Games of Greece. But it is hard to deny the term first modern Olympics to these 1870 Athens Olympic Games, held in the ancient stadium, the same stadium as our IOC Olympiad 1, the 1896 Athens edition. The 1896 Games were, indeed, the first truly international modern Olympics. In contrast, all the 1870 contestants were Greeks (some citizens of Turkey); but so, also, all Olympic athletes in antiquity were Greeks. Therefore, the 1870 Olympics cannot be deprived of the ancient name on that account without making nonsense of the ancient Olympic Games themselves.

At first all seemed to go well with these 1870 Games. But 1870 is a crucial date. Coubertin was six years old; the Greek crown prince Constantine was two. The class-elitist concept of amateurism, as defined by the AAC, not by Brookes, was only four years old. But it now spread to Greece. The main thrust of this early amateur movement, as we have seen, was not so much against athletic profit as against a social class, namely, the working class—a movement to keep it out of competition.

The first sour note in 1870 soon came from Philip Ioannou, a classical scholar and professor, a social elitist, one of the judges at the 1870 Games, and a member of the Greek antiathletic clique. Even before the Games, in a speech paid for by the Olympic committee, he spoke out against the athletic Olympic Games because "the useful arts should be valued ahead of demonstrations . . . of . . . physical dexterity." Besides, he said (in words diametrically opposed to those of Brookes and Coubertin), now that technology had replaced the warrior on the battlefield, "physical strength and athletic development . . . have lost . . . most of their former worth."[15] After the games, he attacked them on amateur grounds, clearly drawing his concept from the English AAC amateur definition, not from Brookes's Olympic movement, which tacitly welcomed the working class. In his official judge's report, Ioannou said that the 1870 Olympics were a travesty because "some working men had competed," men "scarcely pried away from their wage-earner jobs."[16] Besides Skordaras (the 400 meter winner and a butcher), Troungas, victor in the pole climb, was a stone cutter, and Kardamylakes, the Olympic champion wrestler, was an ordinary manual laborer. He had come all the way from Crete to contend, because the organizing committee provided for the poorer, working-class athletes.

Men from the working class had competed. Even worse, they had won. This fact was always at the heart of the problem.[17] Amateurism, as defined by the AAC, was designed to save first place for the upper class. Accordingly, Ioannou said that the 1870 edition "was a pointless parody of the ancient Games" (a comment later taken out of context and used by Coubertin's supporters to discredit the Zappas Greek Olympics).[18] Ioannou criticized the organizing committee for not enticing the "well-educated youth" and deplored their absence from these Olympics. He suggested that athletic training be introduced into the schools and university and that gymnasiums for that purpose be built in the major cities of Greece, with a central gym in Athens, headed by the current coach, Julius Ening.

In effect, Ioannou and his clique of judges proposed that only upper-class youths be allowed to compete in the next Olympiad, that the general public be banned. That proposal did arouse more "interest among the cultured portion of society, especially the men of the schools, for whom Ioannou's words were a veritable gospel." But most of these recommendations were quickly forgotten and never implemented.[19] Almost nothing happened to prepare for the Greek Olympiad III, now scheduled for 1875. But in a crucial respect Ioannou and his fellow Athenian aristocrats carried the day: this next Olympiad was, indeed, limited to young men from the more "cultured" class. Class-oriented amateurism, in the manner of the AAC, now ruled in Greece as in England.[20]

Appointed as coach and organizer for the athletic games of Greece's Olympiad III was Ioannis Phokianos, a well-educated man with immense influence on the history of Greek athletics and physical education. His belief in elitist, class-focused amateurism was unswerving. But elitist amateurism never actually opposed cash prizes, if given to the right people.[21] Phokianos therefore made no objection when the Olympic committee announced cash prizes for the athletes, as before. But entry rules were structured so that only students would compete, essentially young men from the university—obviously, the "higher social orders," as one newspaper described them. All contestants were required to train at Phokianos's gym in Athens, where he sought to bring "young men from the cultured class, university and high school students . . . instead of the working class men who had come to the first two Olympiads."[22] Allowance was made for Athenian public and private high school students and, one sentence read, "even others" could be accepted—if the committee decided to approve them. In the event, it seems, all the competitors were students. Entrants were required to get an entry application at the university and have their student status certified by their school authorities.

The 1875 agro-industrial contests took the lion's share of money and attention, as before. As in 1870, competitions in such categories as rowing, swimming, shooting, and equestrian events were announced, but apparently they were later canceled. Newspapers followed closely the final preparations for the athletic events in Phokianos's gym, one noting with pleasure that the "social class" *(taxis)* of the young men was "much more respectable" *(polytimotera)* than in previous Olympiads.[23]

The athletic events again took place in the Panathenaic stadium, but on May 18, not in the fall, like the previous two Olympiads, nor on March 25, as Soutsos wanted. These 1875 Olympics were a fiasco. The Olympic committee spent almost no money to prepare the stadium. The track, flat in 1870, had high and low spots after several years of unattended weathering. In the spectator areas thornbushes and rocks remained uncleared, making it difficult for people to move around and assemble. Except for a few dignitaries and wealthier people, spectators sat haphazardly on the ground. Crude wooden benches were set for paying spectators, but even some of these broke when used. There was none of the regal pomp that Soutsos had imagined. The royal family did not even attend; most of those who did regretted it.[24]

The young athletes of the "cultured class" did not, after all, improve the Olympic Games. Some made light of their own poor performances, and spectators laughed as much as they applauded. Only twenty-four athletes competed (one newspaper said fifteen), compared with forty at the 1870 games. The crowd too was smaller, twenty thousand at the highest estimate, while another guess was ten thousand to fifteen thousand. Disorder reigned, both on the field and on the sloping banks around it, where the people sat or stood. The Games lasted only two and a half hours. For much of that time the judges—Ioannou still among them—made long, boring speeches to explain their decisions. A band played between events, but not Greek music. It played polkas, Offenbach, and other "facetious compositions." The last two scheduled events, the horizontal bar and parallel bars gymnastic events, were canceled, partly because the crowd was restless and it was growing dark, partly because Phokianos associated those events with professional acrobats, whom he despised.[25] The whole affair turned out so disastrously that Phokianos, disgraced, left town.

The official 1875 committee report, full of data on the agro-industrial exhibits, avoids all mention of the athletic competitions held that day. The victors' names are known from newspaper reports and other sources; I list them as I listed the winners in 1859 and 1870. Again, second and third places are known, but I give only first place.

> Footrace (200 meters): V. Tringas, Amphissa
> Pole vault (distance): A. Petsalis, Parga
> Javelin (at target): M. Tzavaras
> Pole climb: K. Soutsos, Nafplion
> Discus (distance): Z. Saropoulos, Macedonia
> Mounting the inclined pole: A. Ioannidis, Athens
> Wrestling: M. Tzavaras
> Rope climb: K. Molakidis, Smyrna

The newspapers the next day denounced the newest Olympics as a dismal failure and betrayal of Zappas's intent, pointing especially to the disorder both in the stadium and in the stands.[26] "[E]verything assumed the color of comedy. . . . The crowd seized every opportunity for merriment. . . . Neither the judges nor the competitors took any interest in the form of the proceedings. Products of another society, another kind of civic life, the athletic Games of the Ancients, when revived today, become nothing but a direct mocking of Antiquity." This report in *Aion*, May 19, 1875, has especial significance because it was written by Timoleon Philemon, who later obviously changed his mind about Olympic revivals. He was the able secretary-general of the organizing committee for our IOC Olympiad 1, in Athens, 1896, once coming to Coubertin's aid.[27] Yet in 1875, Philemon joined the chorus of reporters who criticized those games as wholly unsuccessful.

Another noteworthy report is that of the *Ephemeris*, May 20, which begins by cataloguing the mistakes made prior to the games, especially the committee's failure adequately to prepare the stadium, which it could easily have done had it cared much about athletics. The report then explains that while some people approved of the plan to revive the athletic Olympics, others viewed them as "pointless and out of step with the spirit of the times." This is an obvious reference to the persistence of the antiathletic clique among the educators and aristocrats. This clique was founded at the outset by Rangavis, who regarded athletics as a throwback to primitive times. And Ioannou was clearly a prominent member, since he believed modern warfare techniques had rendered physical strength and athletic development rather worthless. This antiathletic clique later played a major role in Greece's failure to hold further national athletic Olympics, squandering Zappas's money given for that purpose on other things. This clique was also responsible for Greece's refusal to answer Brookes's many calls in the 1880s for international Olympic Games there and an international Olympic movement. And it was generally the same clique that opposed Coubertin and the idea of hosting the 1896 IOC Games in Athens.[28]

The *Ephemeris* further notes that whereas the upper classes had not competed in previous Olympiads, this time no working men competed. Instead, there was "the idea that only the educated youths would enter the stadium. This exclusivist idea seemed somehow to violate the explicit stipulation about these contests, namely, that they are Panhellenic." The article stresses the ancient idea of "equality for all in the stadium of the contests." The reporter writes, with obvious sarcasm, "We trust that, after the splendid example which was provided by this year's honorable youth from the high schools and University, in the next Olympiad the Stadium will be full of contestants from every class pursuing the prize with equality of rights." Dr. Brookes—Coubertin and Brundage, too—would have cheered.[29] But the reporter's hope went unfulfilled; for there were never again Greek national Olympics in that stadium, only the IOC Olympiads of 1896 and 1906. And there have been no more Olympics of any kind since 1906 anywhere in Greece, despite Greek hopes for 1996.

The most scathing account of the 1875 Olympics was neither written nor published by Greeks. It was published in England and was the work of an Anglo-Irishman, John Mahaffy, whose attendance at the 1875 Athens Olympics is one of the momentous events in our whole Olympic history. Certainly, he and his writings had a profound impact on the lives of such men as Coubertin, Brundage, Jim Thorpe, and Bill Toomey. After the 1875 Games, Mahaffy got interested in the ancient Olympics, too. He was the first to assert (quite wrongly) that the ancient Olympic Games were for "amateur" athletes only, inventing the myth of ancient Greek amateurism that became our own and plagued our Olympic movement for almost a century.[30]

Before misleading the world about the ancient Greek Olympics, Mahaffy misled Olympic history about the modern Greek Olympic series, publishing an article on that topic soon after he returned from Greece that same year. "Were we to propose the resuscitation of the Olympic Games in the Panathenaic stadium at Athens, we should be in anxious dread of comparisons with the victors of Pindar's day. . . . Nay we should fear an accusation of absurdity in transferring Olympia to Athens."[31]

Our own IOC Olympiad I took place in that very stadium in Athens. What would Mahaffy have thought of "transferring Olympia to" Seoul or Atlanta! He ridicules the Greeks for the very idea of reviving the Olympics and for the shape of the stadium, "like a huge oblong stewpot." Though all our modern stadiums are shaped the same way, Mahaffy had never seen one before. It was, in fact, the first stadium of the modern world, based on the ancient stadium design because the Greeks had discovered long ago how to allow many spectators to view events on the field.

Mahaffy heaps especial ridicule on the revival of the discus throw.[32] He calls it one of the "features in which the new Olympic games seemed strictly a parody on ancient manners"; another was the javelin. "In our sports we never throw the discus," he smugly said, never foreseeing that—mainly because of the modern Greek Olympic tradition—the javelin and discus would later be revived in modern sports and remain, as in antiquity, essential Olympic events.

Concerning the athletes themselves, the actual competitions, the organization, award ceremonies, order, general atmosphere, and failure of the Games, Mahaffy was even harsher and more full of satire and ridicule than the caustic Greek newspaper reports.[33] Yet Mahaffy's modern Greek was so bad that he mistook the words for "parallel bars" and "horizontal bar" in the program for types of horse races. He seems to fuse Zappas Olympiads I and II together, giving a date between the two. He did not know who Zappas was and could not even spell his name. Nor did he know who Phokianos was or that Phokianos restricted competition to the upper-class youth of Greece.

Had he known of the elitism of the 1875 Olympics, he would have been delighted as he watched. Mahaffy himself was so strongly class elitist that it drew the attention of even his sympathetic friends and biographers. "He was an out-and-out social snob: that is, he would rather have sat down to a bad meal with a stupid aristocrat than to a good meal with an intelligent tradesman."[34] Thus, he thought the disorder he saw in the crowd "was inevitable, when ten or eleven thousand people of all classes are gathered together." When speaking of the Athenian upper class, Mahaffy sarcastically comments on the "richer classes (they can hardly be called upper, as all Greeks profess to be equal)." But his class elitism had a more telling effect in his 1879 article on the Olympics, because there he states that the ancient Olympics were, at least before later "corruption," open exclusively to the "Gentleman Amateurs" of the Greek aristocracy—no mechanics, artisans, or labourers allowed.[35]

Mahaffy's 1875 article has little value as a source for reconstructing the 1875 Olympics, but it had a powerful and pernicious influence on modern Olympic research. The foremost Olympic scholars have seized on it as the only eyewitness account of the Zappas Olympics available to those who cannot read Greek. MacAloon well recognized some of Mahaffy's patent sarcasm, satire, and exaggerations; but even he knew nothing of Mahaffy's own immense shortcomings—notorious among his contemporary peer classicists—in accuracy. Modern historians incorporated Mahaffy's erroneous version into our own Olympic histories, badly misjudging and misrepresenting the entire Greek Olympic movement—minimizing the Greek contribution to our own Olympic revival.[36]

Decades later, Georges Bourdon further damaged Olympic history by another error-riddled article (1926) that had the same effect as Mahaffy's, misleading Olympic historians into ignoring or discounting the Zappas Games. At one point, Bourdon candidly reveals the purpose of his article: "to discredit the [modern Greek] Olympic Games" *(pour discréditer les jeux olympiques [de la Grèce])*. Bourdon had been connected with Coubertin's Olympic efforts from the day of their inception in 1892.[37] In an apparent effort to rid Coubertin once and for all of the specter of the earlier modern Greek revival, he wrote an article discrediting the Zappas Olympics, published in the official 1924 Paris Olympic Book.

Bourdon mentions only the 1859 and 1870 Athens Olympiads, omitting the 1875 edition and mistakenly asserting that the Greeks held no Olympiads after 1870. This is a minor error compared with the other gross inaccuracies of his report. Bourdon wrongly claims that the 1870 Games were an abject failure and that the modern Greek Olympic movement amounted to nothing:

> To tell the truth, these two days called olympics, were more country fair amusements *[amusements forains]* than serious sporting competitions. Everything remained to be created. . . . This institution [the Greek national Olympics] was not viable, and two tries were enough to make that test. The day after, as the day before that day in Athens in 1870, the field was open. It was

to a French initiative *[initiative française]* that would redound the lofty merit for re-establishing the great Games. . . . It was a French appeal *[appel français]* that was going to move the world.[38]

One cannot miss Bourdon's motives for wanting to discredit the Greek games; he feared they might detract from the Frenchman Coubertin's frequent claim to be the sole author of the whole Olympic revival idea and project. Bourdon succeeded, but he dealt historical truth a nearly fatal blow. Coubertin's claim as sole founder of our Olympics went unchallenged for most of a century, and the Greeks themselves scarcely know the role their own forefathers played. Modern Olympic historians accepted Bourdon's and Mahaffy's damning judgment of the Zappas Olympiads;[39] it became a commonplace in Olympic history.

Greece's vital role in reviving the Olympics was far from over in 1875, as an examination of Coubertin's IOC Olympiad 1 reveals. But the Greek Olympic movement existed in suspension for a while thereafter. One more item about the 1875 Athens Olympics, however, merits mention. It shows how complexly intertwined our Olympic roots are, from Olympia, Greece, in 1838, to Atlanta, in 1996. And it suggests that there may be many unknown contributors to our Olympic movement, however minor their roles. Pavlos Giannopoulos was a member of that earlier, 1838 Olympic committee appointed by the town of Letrini, near Olympia, to organize an Olympic revival. In 1875 he was vice-president of the Zappas Olympic organizing committee. In Giannopoulos's official report on the 1875 Olympiad, one reads these unexpected words: "Dr. Brookes in Wenlock, England, has founded Olympic Games, and he warmly greeted our first Olympiad in 1859."[40] Brookes was still remembered in Greece. That the Greeks and Brookes continued to take an interest in each other's activities becomes apparent as history compels a return to Giannopoulos's "Dr. Brookes" in England.

FIVE

National Failures, International Dreams, 1869–1888

I often think of a remark of O'Connell's that "There are but two classes in the world; one to hammer, and the other to be hammered at." So I shall hammer on.

—*W. P. Brookes, 1883*

In 1868 the British National Olympian Games had faltered so badly—a victim of class-exclusive amateurism—that Brookes temporarily gave them up. But he abandoned neither his Olympic dream nor his local Wenlock Olympian Games. They continued to evolve in regular annual celebrations, taking on more connections with the ancient Olympics. To the 1868 Wenlock Olympics, which took place somewhat before the national Olympiad, Brookes had added a pentathlon event, called general competition. He had introduced this pentathlon at the 1866 London Olympics. At the Wenlock version he set as the prize (valued at fourteen pounds) one of the special silver Wenlock medals with the ancient Greek theme, featuring the Greek goddess Nike (Victory) and the quotation from Pindar.[1]

In 1869 this Wenlock pentathlon was won by the 1866 London Olympic champion, H. W. Brooke, an athlete from the German Gymnastic Society in London, which was still headed by E. Ravenstein. Ravenstein's contingent had indeed come up from London; but the Games did not attract the better athletes from Birmingham and other larger cities, as they had several years before. For the first time the footraces took place on a handicap basis, whereby the best runners were required to give their inferiors a head start. Handicap races, common in the latter part of the nineteenth century, were designed to make the race more exciting for the spectators and to encourage local runners to enter; but they also discouraged the best athletes from competing.

The 1870 Wenlock Olympian Games took place as usual, but for the first and last time with value prizes wholly absent except for tilting at the ring (which paid a silver goblet) and the general competition (the prize for which was a silver medal—again won by Brooke). There was nothing else remarkable. That same year saw two other events momentous to our Olympic history: first, the 1870 Athens Olympics and second, France's resounding defeat in the Franco-Prussian war, which beckoned Coubertin to his life's mission. It is unclear whether Brookes knew of the 1870 Athens Olympics. But he took full cognizance of France's defeat and saw it as a warning.[2]

The local Wenlock Games continued in 1871–72.[3] The 1872 Wenlock Olympics took place on their new permanent grounds, a beautiful area northwest of the village named Linden Field—the very spot where Coubertin himself later saw his first Olympics in 1890 and planted a tree, which now bears his name and continues to grow and thrive to this day. For the 1873 Wenlock Olympics, Linden Field was in perfect condition. Some athletes came from larger cities, such as Birmingham and Manchester.[4]

Brookes's local Olympics were not yet in obvious trouble. For this brief period he seemed to let his grander Olympic ambitions lie fallow so that he could focus more on his other great obsession, his concern for mandatory physical education in the state schools and the quality of national health and preparedness. He saw France's military defeat at Sedan as a clear warning to Britain. But since these are the very matters that later drew Coubertin to Brookes, I postpone many details to the following chapter on Coubertin. Here I include only those physical education items of direct relation to Brookes's Olympic activities, following his Olympism to its logical conclusion, his proposal for international Olympic Games.

Brookes soon tried to resume the British national Olympics. With Ravenstein and Brookes still listed as honorary secretaries (Hulley had left the group), the NOA announced National Olympian Games to be held in Much Wenlock on May 25–26, 1874. The venue, Linden Field in Wenlock, clearly indicates the close tie this fourth British national Olympiad had to Brookes. But these Games differed from earlier NOA Olympiads in several respects besides their village setting.

The organizers emphasized the Games' connection with physical education for the youth of England more than any connection with ancient Greece. The prospectus for the third Olympiad in 1868 makes reference to the NOA's goal of introducing bodily exercises into schools as a regular branch of education. But the 1874 prospectus was more specific and aimed at the government. It states as its goal "[t]o promote Physical Education generally, but especially, by gymnastic exercises, in our National Elementary Schools, under the authority of the Committee of the Council on Education." Furthermore, Brookes had once set a prize, obviously thinking of Pindar and the ancient Olympics, for the best poem celebrating a victory at his games. Now the NOA set a prize for the best essay "on Physical Education, with special reference to our National Elementary Schools." These national Olympics also listed a number of contests "for Wenlock National School Children."[5]

In another innovation Brookes assembled prominent politicians and other high-ranking dignitaries to be listed on the program as officials or organizers of the Games. Coubertin later employed the same practice (a well-known trait) and regularly sought prominent politicians to head his conferences and titled nobility, even royalty, for his letterheads.[6] The NOA somehow got the earl of Bradford to consent to serve as president of the 1874 national Olympics committee. Lord Bradford reportedly accepted "for political reasons 'rather than from any fondness for National Olympian Festivals.' "[7] He did little more than put in an appearance at Wenlock. The list of names on the NOG council included several other titled nobility and men who had been knighted.

Most notable on the Wenlock NOG council list is the name of Thomas Hughes, the author of *Tom Brown's School Days*. Hughes's *Tom Brown* is the most discussed book in all Olympic scholarship. Coubertin's reports of its profound impact on him lead Olympic scholars to view that book as the main inspiration for all of the baron's later work.[8] In 1874 Brookes clearly hoped that heading his program with Bradford, Hughes, and other notables, many of them already active in the physical education movement, might lend authority to his plea for compulsory physical education in the state schools.

Of course, the powerful Amateur Athletic Club in London spurned these Wenlock National Olympian Games. Brookes did manage to get the name of William Waddell on his NOA committee list. Waddell was one of the head men and honorary secretary of the London Athletic Club, the AAC's only remaining rival in London. Yet all Brookes's efforts could not produce a first-class athletic meeting. The program was interesting enough, with a full complement of standard track-and-field events and gymnastic events such as the horizontal bar, the parallel bars, and an event called the horse. Because the venue was Wenlock, there was also tilting at the ring. But the AAC boycott again persuaded the best athletes in England to stay away, and the athletic performances were noticeably inferior to those of the AAC-sponsored national Amateur Championships that same year. The pageantry, processions, and prize ceremonies were of the

Wenlock kind that entranced Coubertin sixteen years later. But as athletic Olympic Games, the Fourth National Olympian Games had little importance.[9] The AAC's opposition again took its toll.

Brookes's local Wenlock Olympics went on. The 1875 (twenty-fifth-anniversary) edition of the WOG program announces: "Professional Athletes are excluded from all contests; strangers, therefore, wishing to contend must produce such certificates or other evidence as will satisfy the Judges that they are not professional athletes." But Brookes still would not define "professional" along the class lines followed by the AAC. The local newspaper notes "the goal at which the society is aiming—the harmonious development of body and mind—as a national concern."[10] The 1876 WOG saw ten thousand spectators and the first bicycle race at any Olympic event; but the number of competitors was comparatively small.[11]

Despite the mediocrity of the 1874 National Olympian Games, Brookes and his NOA now scheduled its fifth Olympiad for August 15–16, 1877. Since the major cities, such as London and Birmingham, would no longer cooperate as they once had, the NOA chose a local site, again in Shropshire, namely, Shrewsbury, near but larger than Wenlock. Why, after so much failure, would Brookes persist in attempting National Olympian Games, especially when they were not feasible outside his local Shropshire? No clear answer appears. Had Brookes finally heard of the renewed Olympic revival in Greece, the Zappas Olympiads of 1870 and 1875, and gained courage from it? Whatever his motivation, Brookes now openly sought to associate these NOA Games with modern Greece. He thus began his historically crucial correspondence with John Gennadius, then chargé d'affaires at the Greek embassy in London. Gennadius was no sportsman but a diplomat and book collector, later founder of the famous Gennadius Library in Athens. From 1876 to 1893, Gennadius was in frequent contact with Brookes on the topic of Olympics. For more than a decade, from 1880 to 1893, Brookes hounded Gennadius to help him found international Olympic Games.

It is another quirk of fate that much of our Olympic history depends on three Greeks who all lived in London for varying periods of time in the latter half of the last century and knew one another in the 1860s. Their personal relationships strongly affected the Olympic movement. Those three Greeks are Demetrios Vikelas, first president of the IOC; Charilaos Trikoupis, son of the former ambassador with whom Brookes corresponded in 1860 and the prime minister of Greece in 1894, notorious for opposing Coubertin and the 1896 Athens Olympiad; and John Gennadius. Vikelas and Trikoupis become major figures later, actually determining the course—the life or death—of the modern international Olympic movement in its phase initiated by Coubertin.[12] Gennadius plays a significant role here, during the earlier Brookes phase.[13]

Whether spurred by the renewal of the Zappas Olympiads or just hoping that the luster of ancient Greece might make these 1877 NOA Games more attractive to prospective athletes, in July, Brookes wrote to Gennadius in London. Gennadius was then serving his first term there as Greek chargé d'affaires. Brookes persuaded Gennadius to ask King George of Greece to honor the 1877 British Olympics by giving a special prize for the victor of the pentathlon, just as he, Brookes, had donated the prize of ten pounds for the 1859 Greek Olympics, won by Velissariou. He wanted the king to donate, in his name, a silver cup, with a suitable inscription in Greek. George readily agreed to match Brookes in Olympic prize gifts. On August 8, 1877, Gennadius replied to Brookes that the king had donated the cup and that he was authorized to "present to your Association from the part of His Majesty and as a prize for the Pentathlon, a cup with a suitable inscription of the value of Ten Pounds Sterling."[14] The Greek inscription on the cup reads:

> George I, King of the Hellenes,
> for the man who won the Pentathlon
> at the Modern Olympics of the British
> at Shrewsbury in August, 1877.

The Modern Olympics of the British at Shrewsbury in 1877 were hardly worthy of the high-sounding name. They were held in conjunction with the Shrewsbury Flower Show, hosted by the local horticultural society. The AAC, of course, induced the better athletes of England to boycott the Games, producing competitions and performances that were unremarkable. Besides tilting at the ring, the highlight of the Games seems to have been the unveiling and presentation of King George's pentathlon cup, won by a local Shrewsbury law student.[15] Brookes's speech was thankful: "To the monarch who now reigns over the Hellenic Kingdom, and who takes a lively interest in our modern Olympian games, we feel deeply grateful for the honour he has conferred on the National Olympian Association and the town of Shrewsbury by the gift of a prize for the Pentathlon."[16]

George indeed displayed a lively interest in later modern Olympic Games—Coubertin and Vikelas's 1896 IOC Games—but in 1877 it seemed that no one but Brookes cared about the Olympics. Only a handful of Englishmen sided with Brookes and the NOA in their conflict with the aristocratic southern athletic clubs the AAC controlled. Among that handful was a writer for the *Athletic World* who, in 1878, praised Brookes and the founders of the NOA and deplored the division in English sports, suggesting all clubs unite under the NOA:

> What a blessing it would be to all concerned, or connected with amateur athletic sport, to be in a state of union one with another. . . . The National Olympian Association was established for this special purpose. . . . There is no institution in England more entitled than the N.O.A. to hold an Annual Championship Athletic Meeting. It is thoroughly representative, which the Amateur Athletic Club is not.[17]

But such egalitarianism did not prevail in England, and the exclusivist AAC, which still explicitly barred working-class men, had already become England's athletic umbrella.

Brookes's local Wenlock Olympics ran into difficulty, though they hobbled on. In 1877 Brookes again held a special autumn meeting of the WOG, open only to Wenlock inhabitants, "to give local athletes a spurt."[18] But even the regular annual Wenlock Games soon became an almost wholly local affair, attracting even less interest and fewer first-rate athletes from outside and encountering financial trouble. Neumüller illustrates the decline with a case in point. The athlete H. W. Oliver won several events in 1877 and 1878, including such races as the mile hurdles and the mile run. But in 1879 he did not come to Wenlock, which was no great distance from his home. Instead, he competed at the AAC Amateur Championships held in London, where he won the two-mile hurdles. Neumüller attributes the Wenlock Games' decline to their increasing emphasis, renewed in 1878, on handicap races, wherein the better athletes had little incentive to compete. He also cites the proliferation of athletic meetings all over England. In the early years of the Wenlock Olympics, they were among the athletes' few noteworthy opportunities to compete.[19] By the late 1870s there were many athletic meetings elsewhere, reducing the number of spectators who would travel to Wenlock to watch.

By 1880 the financial state of the WOS was so imperiled that its Olympic Games omitted the pentathlon, along with the rather expensive medal that regularly went to the victor. In his speech Brookes openly confessed the financial trouble, saying the WOS would need to petition "friends of the Society," asking for donations. The ladies of Wenlock held a bazaar, selling pottery and furniture. By such means the society ended the year with a balance and continued to host Wenlock Olympic Games the following years. But the athletes' marks and crowds were not what they had been a decade before.[20]

Brookes's efforts to establish physical education in the schools had occupied much of his time in the 1870s. With the national Olympic movement moribund and his local Olympics maimed, one might expect Brookes to have given up his Olympic idea, to concentrate wholly on this other avocation. But Brookes was not a quitter. Instead, he simply thought grander Olympic thoughts. In 1880 he boldly took perhaps the most crucial step in our entire Olympic history: he conceived the notion of founding recurrent international Olympic Games, formally proposed it, and sought to implement it.

Precisely when Brookes first conceived the idea of international Olympic Games is not clear, but it was no later than the autumn of 1880. Brookes wrote to Gennadius, still Greek chargé d'affaires in London, sometime before November, proposing that international Olympic Games be undertaken in Athens. Brookes kept no copy of his own letter.[21] Much of its content may be inferred from Gennadius's extant reply, dated November 8, 1880.

> I beg to apologize for so delaying my answer to your last most courteous letter. Yet not only have I been overweighed by pressing obligations, but your proposal itself required consideration and the expressions of opinions which I could not take upon myself without consulting with others.
>
> The result is, that while thanking you most cordially for the lively interest you have not ceased to take in Greek matters and while congratulating you upon all your Society's aims [illegible] and the most excellent proposal you now make to us, we regret deeply that in the present and troubled and critical circumstances of the kingdom it would not be possible to carry out in a befitting manner the theme of your proposal. If, as we must hope, later on a more settled and satisfactory state of affairs be established [illegible] I have every reason to believe that such a proposal would meet with a ready and cheerful response.
>
> I am very thankful to you for the interesting papers you were so good as to send me. [Gennadius then comments on the photo of himself enclosed, as per Brookes's request.[22]]
>
> I shall consider it an honor to be enrolled, as you kindly propose, amongst the honorary members of your Society, though I feel I am but little qualified for that honor; the more so as I am not sure I shall remain next year in England.[23]

Gennadius's name was immediately placed second on the select roll of honorary members of the WOS, right after Velissariou's, and just two names before Coubertin's. The notation says Gennadius was elected November 1880.

Gennadius's rather imprecise references to Brookes's proposal might lead some to doubt that Brookes had just suggested the revival of international Olympic Games in Greece. But Gennadius's later letters and published newspaper accounts remove all doubt. In his official report of the 1880 activities of the WOS, delivered January 18, 1881, Brookes makes clear the precise nature of his proposal, even paraphrasing from Gennadius's November letter.

> Your Committeee has suggested the holding of an International Olympian Festival at Athens, when the present critical state of affairs in Greece is ended, as her friends earnestly hope. . . . The proposal has been favourably received by Greeks resident in England, and will, no doubt, be cordially responded to by the Authorities in Athens, and by the principal Athletic Societies of Great Britian, many of whose members would gladly avail themselves of an opportunity of visiting the classic land . . . ; and of contending in a generous rivalry with the Athletes of other nations, in the time-consecrated stadium at Athens.[24]

There is no great difference between this plan and what finally took place at Athens in 1896; we can no longer attribute the very first conception of the idea to Coubertin.[25] Yet there was a meaningful difference between Brookes's 1880 proposal and the baron's full proposal of 1894: Coubertin recommended a world-wide selection of sites.[26]

Brookes was sadly wrong when he predicted that his plan would "be cordially responded to by the Authorities in Athens, and . . . Athletic Societies of Great Britain." Both would turn a cold shoulder to his idea of international Olympic Games. And who were those "Greeks resident in England" who had favorably received the proposal? Brookes probably counted Gennadius among them, on the strength of his remarks quoted above. Another may be one Socrates Parasyrakis, who is listed among the donors who contributed a small amount to the impoverished WOS account in 1880.[27] In the Greek language newspaper of Trieste, *Kleio*, on June 25, 1881, there appeared an account of Brookes's proposal in an article signed by "S. P.," which Brookes thought, perhaps rightly, was written by Parasyrakis.

> *Olympic Games in England.* Thirty-one years ago in the very old town of Much Wenlock, England, there was founded a Much Wenlock Olympic Society for the advancement of athletic exercises, and there are annual Games held there to which all who wish to participate come from every part of England. . . . The founder of this admirable Society is Dr. Brookes, who works tirelessly for the noble goals of the Society. . . . [O]ur representative in England, the

Honorable John Gennadius, is among the Honorary Members. For the Olympics held in Athens in 1859 the Wenlock Olympic Society voted to give ten English pounds as a prize for the victor in the footrace. . . . In 1877 H.M. George, King of the Hellenes, donated a cup worth ten pounds as prize for the victor in the Pentathlon. . . . Brookes, this ardent philhellene, is now at work so that an International Olympic Festival may be held soon in Athens. From that a great deal of good will result in a variety of respects. So we do not doubt but that the Greek government will provide every facility for the Festival's achievement.[28]

The international proposal was now in print outside of England, and it was soon published in England, as well. In 1882 Brookes sought a site for yet another attempt at British National Olympian Games and petitioned the Shropshire town of Ludlow to undertake holding them. His speech there was reported in the newspapers, which carefully noted that Dr. Brookes "had been trying to establish an International Olympian Association at Athens, and hoped in a few years to see his efforts become successful."[29] Thus, Brookes even foresaw establishing the IOC but would base it in Athens. Yet Ludlow voted down hosting national Olympics, on financial grounds. Brookes got the athletic club of the village of Hadley to hold a National Olympian Festival in conjunction with its own town Games in June 1883. These Sixth (and very last) Annual National Olympian Games were again a failure, however, not worthy of the name.[30] Only local athletes competed. The elitist amateur movement had already dealt the NOA the final lethal blow. It robbed the NOA, on paper, at least, of its one remaining claim to be the legitimate umbrella for all England, namely, its egalitarianism, in contrast with the AAC's class exclusiveness. The AAC had been reformed, reorganized, and renamed the Amateur Athletic Association (AAA) in 1880, when it was forced to abandon the notorious mechanics clause.[31] Working men were no longer explicitly barred. Yet the AAA remained de facto elitist and had even further tightened its control of English sport by stating that, effective January 1, 1883, athletes "competing at sports held under rules not approved by the AAA will render themselves ineligible to compete at Meetings held by associated Clubs."[32] Thus, any athlete who competed in the June 1883 NOG at Hadley would therby be rendered ineligible to compete in major English events.

Disappointed but not defeated, Brookes said in the course of these very last National Olympian Games: "I often think of a remark of O'Connell's that 'There are but two classes in the world; one to hammer, and the other to be hammered at.' So I shall hammer on in the belief that others will succeed me who will strike with more effect, and what is right in itself and good for the nation will ultimately prevail." These are words of hope and prophecy, almost a prescience of Coubertin, who had just turned twenty years old. Brookes could not actually have known of the young Parisian. But he seems to have somehow known that there would be a Coubertin, another to carry on the Olympic effort.[33]

Thus denying utter defeat, Brookes pursued his other two obsessions, physical education in the schools and his new international Olympic dream. He began a barrage of letters to Gennadius, trying to get Greek help in founding international Olympics. In 1881, just as he himself had feared, Gennadius was indeed removed from his post as Greek chargé d'affaires in England; for Charilaos Trikoupis was now prime minister of Greece. For more than a decade, when Trikoupis was in, his political opponent Gennadius was out, and vice versa. Gennadius soon returned to London but was again demoted in 1882, this time to the Greek legation in Vienna. Brookes was somehow able to follow him. From Vienna on October 16, 1883, Gennadius wrote Wenlock. He thanks Brookes for the doctor's recent letter and enclosures, agrees with his efforts to establish physical education in the schools, and writes: "[A]s a Greek I can but feel indebted to you that you combine with this idea the project of a revival of the Olympic Games. I heartily hope and wish for the realization of your double object and I believe that if circumstances are favorable you will find a very sympathetic response in Greece."[34]

This letter leaves no doubt about the specific nature of the project in which Brookes sought Greek cooperation, making it certain that Brookes conceived an international Olympic idea before Coubertin. But the international Olympic conceptions of the two men were significantly different. Brookes's idea was an international competition called the Olympic Games; his January 1881 phrase, "contending in a generous rivalry with the Athletes of other nations," can leave no real doubt on that question. But the rest of that 1881 sentence—"in the time-consecrated stadium at Athens"—reveals how his notion differed from Coubertin's. Later documents verify that Brookes sought repeated international Olympiads, not a one-time event. Yet Brookes never plainly explained his plan beyond proposing an international festival at Athens. Would subsequent Olympiads take place in Athens, too? in England? elsewhere? Perhaps Brookes did not clarify this point because he could get no one else interested in even one Athens Olympiad. Coubertin's conception was, clearly and from the start, to internationalize the site as well as the athletes and competitions—so that cities and citizens worldwide could host, watch, enjoy, and participate in the revived Olympic Games.

By 1885 Trikoupis was out in Athens and Gennadius back in London, soon elevated to the permanent rank of minister for Greece there. Brookes hammered at him with his international Olympic idea, writing sometimes more than once a year. Gennadius continued to reply with brief, polite, temporizing letters, essentially saying "thanks, but no thanks" on the question of Greece helping with international Olympic Games. Four such letters came from Gennadius in 1886 and 1887, one even referring, in apparent response to the doctor's inquiry, to the Zappas modern Greek "Olympian Games." All were designed to cool but not kill Brookes's Olympic ardor.[35]

In order to grasp why Gennadius did not respond more favorably to Brookes's idea, we must return to Athens and follow the course—or derailment—of the Greek Olympic movement. Greek political life had been chaotic. The Zappas Olympic committee had held no more national Olympics since the failed Olympiad III in 1875. But it was far from idle in the 1880s and not out of money. The Olympic committee was now wholly controlled by the antiathletic faction, headed by Stephanos Dragoumis, infamous in Olympic history, along with Trikoupis, for opposing Coubertin in 1894.[36] And this antiathletic committee was spending Zappas's money. It built the magnificent building called the Zappeion, which still rises in splendor from the National Gardens in downtown Athens. Its stated purpose was to make a site for the Olympic agro-industrial exhibits. Gross cost overruns and contractor delays ran the cost to over a million drachmas, an immense amount at that time.[37]

As the Zappeion neared completion, the Olympic committee announced that Olympiad IV would take place in October 1888. Trikoupis was again back in power (Gennadius again demoted to lesser assignments in The Hague and Washington, D.C.). The 1888 organizing committee announced that the athletic games, expressly "public games," would take place in the ancient stadium, the agro-industrial exhibits in the Zappeion.[38] Earlier Olympiads required athletes to report four to six weeks ahead, but 1888 athletes were told to come no earlier than ten days before the Games began. The committee never intended to hold them, took no step and spent no drachma to prepare the stadium or any portion of the athletic program.

When the time came for Olympiad IV, Zappas's head was duly sent to Athens, to be enshrined in the Zappeion at its formal opening on October 20, 1888. The head is still there today, behind the plaque that reads, "Here lies the head of Evangelis Zappas." And the agro-industrial Olympics indeed took place, but for the last time. A long official report lists all the winners in sundry categories. But no athletic games were held. Dragoumis and his committee silently scuttled the 1888 athletic Olympics; perhaps he had consulted with Trikoupis, as he did in 1894.[39] At any rate, the Zappas Olympic committee, which still exists today, held no athletic Olympic Games in 1888 and none thereafter.[40]

Several prominent Olympic historians, the few that know of the Zappas Olympics, assure us that there were Zappas Games in 1888—or 1887, 1877, or 1889. The confusion is the result of the following event.[41] Phokianos, who had left Athens in disgrace in 1875, taking another position in Salonike, had been recalled to run the Athens Central Gym. When he found out that the 1888 athletic Olympics would not be held, he undertook to produce them himself, at his own expense, in the following year. Instead of public games in the stadium in 1888, these games, called "Olympics" by some reporters in the press, took place in 1889 in Phokianos's small gym, near the large, weedy stadium. The general public was barred, and the privileged few, the upper-class Athenians whom Phokianos invited to his little display of socially elite athletes, were aghast as the athletes and their friends ran amuck. There were few seats in the gym, and athletes blocked the spectators' view, tried to display their prowess before their event was called, and pushed one another into the crowd until "ladies and young women were made uneasy."[42]

There was such disorder that the games were canceled in their midst. Dragoumis and cabinet ministers fled the scene. A few days later Phokianos restaged the games for an even smaller, more select audience, which was satisfied enough, as were some newspapers. But since these Games were produced by a private individual and not open to the Greek public, I do not reckon them as part of the Zappas Olympic Games series and forgo listing the victors of the restaged version.[43] Zappas left an immense bequest to the Greek people for the revival of the Olympic Games in the stadium. The great majority of Greeks loved athletics and wanted the Olympics to be held and to succeed. After the wholly successful 1870 Olympiad, they had been denied the right to compete; now they could not even watch. Yet the Greek Olympic revival movement was not dead; it was just ailing, and in the wrong hands.

Greek Crown Prince Constantine, George's oldest son, now rose to lead the Olympic movement in Greece. He has not entered the story before but will eventually play a critical role in our Olympiad 1. Constantine's Olympic activity formally began on June 22, 1890, when he signed a royal decree announcing the government itself would resume the Greek Olympic series in a four-year cycle, beginning with an Olympiad v in 1892.[44]

Political turmoil in Athens continued, however, Trikoupis and Deliyannis exchanging the prime minister's office sometimes twice in the same year. It is probable that the 1892 Games somehow fell victim to these politics. Trikoupis and Prince Constantine later became bitter political enemies, especially when Trikoupis opposed the IOC Olympics of 1896. Perhaps his antipathy toward both Constantine and the Olympic Games had begun earlier. Whatever the cause, the 1892 Greek Olympiad was never held.

Many Greeks, however, still wanted Olympics and athletic meets. Phokianos weathered the storm of criticism after the 1889 fiasco, retaining direction of the central gym. In 1891 he merged his group with the Omonoia Club, forming the Panhellenic Gymnastic Society. Besides seeking to hold athletic contests, the Panhellenic's charter—soon published by the government newspaper—had as one of its major goals the refounding "of the Ancient Olympic Games."[45]

In May 1891 the Panhellenic Gymnastic Society held its first athletic meet. The royal family, which had starred at the 1870 Olympics but avoided the next two, attended the Panhellenic Games, which went rather well. George announced he would patronize these games and next time would give valuable prizes. Briefly in power, Prime Minister Theodoros Deliyannis—known later, when once again in power, as the welcome friend of IOC Olympiad I—gave government support to the Panhellenic Games. Prince George, the king's second son, offered to chair the judges' committee for its next games. The government let the Panhellenic hold girls' gymnastics in the Zappeion.[46]

Obviously, the royal family and the Panhellenic Gymnastic Society were acting in lieu of Dragoumis's Olympic committee. When Constantine's plans for Olympiad V in 1892 aborted, the Panhellenic forged on. The second Panhellenic Games, held on May 14–15, 1893, were officially held under the patronage of Prince Constantine. Prince George was president of the organizing committee. These second Panhellenic Games started out auspiciously enough, with a special hymn for the occasion. The lyrics were written by a young Greek poet and Oxford student, Constantinos Manos, who played a significant role in the 1896 IOC Olympics.[47] The music was composed by Spyros Samaras—the same man who composed the hymn for the 1896 Olympics, to this day the official Olympic hymn and performed for every IOC Olympiad. Even Barcelona, in 1992, heard his music, as will Atlanta in 1996.

Several organizers of the IOC Olympiad I helped here in 1893. Many Greek athletes who competed in 1893 later competed in the first International Games, including Miltiades Gouskos and Soterios Versis, both best known for throwing close behind the American Robert Garrett in the 1896 Olympic shot put and discus. Some 1896 Olympians had competed in Phokianos's 1889 Olympics, as well.[48]

The 1893 Panhellenic Society games were not a total success. Phokianos's colleague from the Omonoia Club insisted on slow, boring group gymnastic displays punctuated by polka music and the like; there were other technical problems. The royal family, attending, was not pleased. Yet instead of withdrawing its support, it increased it, in hopes of improving the enterprise. King George offered some land to the society, and his sons joined it as active members and patrons. Crown Prince Constantine, especially, assumed a strong position in its organization.[49] The Panhellenic Gymnastic Society, now in the role vacated by the do-nothing Olympic committee, had the royal family as its general manager. Prince Constantine, who had sought to hold Olympic Games in 1892, already perhaps looked ahead to something bigger than these 1893 contests of the Panhellenic. His activity here in 1890–93 makes his able organization of our own international Olympiad I, in 1896, come as no surprise.

In England, meanwhile, Brookes continued to hammer away at Gennadius with copies of his writings, photographs, and invitations to attend the Wenlock Olympics in person and to hound him again and again about starting international Olympics in Greece. At least five times more in the years 1888–91 Gennadius had to fend Brookes off. In 1892, the year Greece failed to hold its announced Olympiad V, Brookes wrote Gennadius yet another time—he would not miss a year—urging that his recommended Olympic revival take place in Greece. On January 12, 1893, Gennadius sent Brookes a reply, apparently the last letter Gennadius ever wrote to Brookes.

Dear Sir,

I am extremely sensitive of the kind and friendly motives which have dictated your letter. . . . No one can regret my imminent departure from your hospitable country more than myself [illegible]. When in Athens I will not fail to repeat by word of mouth what I have more than once written regarding your Philhellenic [illegible] and the excellent work you have initiated and brought to such a flourishing condition in your part of the country. And being at one with you as regards the advantages of physical training, I shall do what I can in strengthening a feeling in that direction, which is already alive in Greece.

I shall thus inquire if there exists any [illegible] connected with such a movement which I think is not yet the case—and will certainly recommend . . . [illegible].[50]

It is unfortunate that some crucial parts of this letter seem illegible; for the word "movement" can only refer to Brookes's international Olympic movement. But what is most remarkable about Gennadius's 1893 letter is this: it proves that, although Coubertin himself had in Paris proposed an international Olympic revival on November 25, 1892, he still failed to inform Brookes (his "oldest friend") of his own interest in—and proposal for—international Olympic Games.[51] Had Brookes known of Coubertin's proposal, he would not have pinned all his hopes on the always reluctant Gennadius. Coubertin unquestionably knew that Brookes was proposing international Olympic Games—in Athens, at least. Why did the baron not tell his good friend in Wenlock that now he, too, was making that proposal, but developing it further—expanding it to encompass host cities around the world? I know no answer. When Brookes finally learned, two years later, of Coubertin's modification of the international Olympic idea to make it worldwide, he deemed it an improvement, telling the baron that his plan "embracing as it does all nations, is a really superb one, and deserving of the support of all nations."[52] Brookes would have given Coubertin's proposal his wholehearted support in 1892, had he known of it then. Perhaps he could have helped Coubertin in the difficult months that lay ahead.

Even stranger is Gennadius's later silence about Dr. Brookes. Gennadius had, almost countless times from 1880 to 1893, rebuffed Brookes's attempts to spread his notion of international Olympic Games to take place in Athens with Greek cooperation. Yet just three years after he wrote this last 1893 rejection letter to Brookes, Gennadius himself published an article heralding the 1896 Athens Games, attributing the whole origins of the modern Olympics to France and to Coubertin: "They are due to the sudden growth of athletic sports in France . . . [and] an International Congress . . . in Paris . . . 1894. . . . Baron Pierre de Coubertin, the secretary and moving spirit of the Congress."[53]

Knowing of Brookes's long efforts to achieve precisely what he now praised the baron for achieving, why did Gennadius not even mention Brookes? Again, I have no explanation. It all remains part of the mystery that has confused all previous Olympic history, somehow veiling Brookes's ideas, efforts, achievements, and influence with almost total silence.

SIX

Enter Pierre de Coubertin, 1883–1890

I quite agree with you that bodily training in National Schools is of very great importance. . . . I will be delighted to talk the subject over with you when we meet in October. . . . [I]f it is convenient to you I can proceed directly to Much Wenlock.

—*Coubertin, personal letter to Brookes, 1890*

It is a commonplace of modern Olympic history that Coubertin's interest in physical education, sports, and even Olympics was rooted in patriotism. He conceived the idea that France had lost the Franco-Prussian War because of the physical degeneracy of the young men in the French army; on the other side, he thought, the superior physical training the youth in the German army received in their German schools put them at a great military advantage. Naturally, Coubertin's surroundings strongly influenced his ideas. But an already existing Olympic movement also strongly influenced Coubertin's own successful Olympic revival. A number of scholars have explored Coubertin's intellectual development and the French sociopolitical climate of his day.[1] Allen Guttmann's *Olympics* contains an excellent, concise version of this commonplace, while displaying his gift for phrases that often capture the essence of what others want to say.[2]

Guttmann begins by noting that Coubertin (born in 1863) was a boy when the French army, under Emperor Napoleon III, experienced its "humiliating defeat" in 1870 at Sedan, thus ending the Franco-Prussian war. Coubertin grew up in the shadow of that national humiliation: "Like most Frenchmen, the young Coubertin burned with a desire to avenge the defeat and to recover the lost provinces" (Guttmann). After a brief period of military officer's training and a short stay in law school,[3] he decided his real calling was as a social reformer. In the early 1880s, "Coubertin was haunted by memories of the Franco-Prussian War. He attributed the defeat not to the arrogance of Napoleon III . . . but rather to the physical inferiority of the average French youth" (Guttmann). While some as-

68

sumed that modern warfare had rendered physical fitness of small value on the battlefield, Coubertin believed a soldier's physical abilities remained important and that the German soldiers' superiority came from their gymnastic training in the German schools. French schools, in contrast, still focused wholly on a traditional academic education—literature and philosophy—generally ignoring physical education. Coubertin, therefore, chose as the principal area for his social reform the French system of education.

> In his many books and articles, Coubertin appealed to his countrymen to mend their ways, to become as hardy as their perennial foes, to steel themselves for the task of revenge. He concluded, however, that there were better paths to physical prowess than . . . Germanic physical education. . . . Coubertin looked, therefore, across the channel to his nation's friendlier rival, England. (Guttmann)

Coubertin became an out-and-out Anglophile, convinced that England's elite private schools and universities provided an education so productive of physical, moral, and spiritual excellence that their system should serve as a model for French educational reorganization.[4] He visited various English schools and colleges in 1883, seeking the essence of English "sporting pedagogy" (Coubertin's phrase). He thought he observed it in practice. But seeking in print a definitive theoretical or philosophical statement of sporting pedagogy, he decided he could find nothing better than Thomas Hughes's *Tom Brown's School Days*.[5] Hughes's book was a novel about a young man's education at the Rugby School, during the headmastership of the well-known Thomas Arnold.[6] As a young teenager, Coubertin had been impressed by Hughes's book. As an adult, he reread *Tom Brown* and it profoundly affected him. The impact of *Tom Brown* is integral to the commonplace history: "Pierre re-read Thomas Hughes. This time, however, he read as Nietzsche read Schopenhauer, as one reads perhaps once in a lifetime: to further the formation of a philosophy. . . . Pierre ate up *Tom Brown*" (Mandell). He carried an English version with him throughout his 1883 tour of the English school system, saying it was his aid in revivifying Thomas Arnold and to understanding his work. Although Coubertin misjudged the extent of Arnold's emphasis on physical education and sports,[7] he came almost to idolize Arnold and idealized the sports of England.

Ever thereafter, Coubertin regularly cited the Rugby School and its former headmaster, Thomas Arnold, as embodying the essence of this superb English educational regimen. "It may be said without exaggeration that Coubertin's 'ethnography' of the public schools was devoted simply to verifying what he had read in Hughes's famous book. *Tom Brown* controlled not only the aim of his eye and the questions he asked, but also his judgment" (MacAloon). Coubertin's belief in something he called the Arnoldian system impelled him to urge France to value and practice English sports and to require them in French schools. Although such open Anglophilia made his proposals suspect and unwelcome among many French, Coubertin pursued his obsession with vigor. But the powers that directed the French educational system—whose Anglophobia nearly equaled their French patriotism—never really accepted Coubertin's ideas or implemented his reforms. Fortunately, as part of all this patriotic sports activity and promotion, he conceived the idea to propose a revival of the Olympic Games. His proposal succeeded magnificently, ultimately embracing the whole world: "At the end of his life, Coubertin would judge himself a failure with regard to France, but he never recanted or thought himself a fool. Along the way, he took up another dream, even more unlikely and outlandish: the resurrection on an international scale of the Olympic Games. This dream he succeeded in drawing into the world's waking life" (MacAloon, 52).

Thus, the institution of our Olympic Games originated in Coubertin's belief that France lost the war to Germany because of inferior physical training. So modern historians account for his proposal to revive the Olympic Games.

This commonplace of Olympic history and Coubertinian biography is substantially true—except for the premise, which contains a fundamental error. Coubertin did not get the idea to revive the Olympics on his own; he got it from Dr. W. P. Brookes. Even his notion that France lost the 1870 war to Germany because of physical degeneracy was not original with the baron, nor did it derive only from the French sources often suggested. He probably got that idea, too, mainly from Brookes.[8] In fact, with an uncanny prophetic ability, in 1866 Brookes had expressed a foreboding of France's humiliating defeat at German hands in 1870, the event that motivated Coubertin.

Brookes, as a young medical student in 1830, concluded that physical exercise would cure physical degeneration, and that led him to found the Olympian Class in 1850. He early anticipated Coubertin in arguing that degeneracy from exclusive mental training would lead to poor soldiers. By 1862 Brookes was making public pleas for the introduction of physical education in the schools, claiming that such training of the youth would greatly help the fighting ability of the nation's army.[9] In the speech he gave at the first National Olympian Games in London, 1866, he expresses those same ideas with a specific comparison of the French and German soldier, noting the role physical education played in their respective trainings. His exact words bear special importance because the young Coubertin read them carefully and devoured them eagerly, as the even younger Coubertin "ate up" *Tom Brown.*

Brookes's 1866 Olympic speech, titled "Address on Physical Education," indeed concerns physical education as much as Olympic Games; it recounts recent German history:

> Towards the close of the last century a German, named Gutsmuth[10] introduced into his own country a system of gymnastic exercises. . . . After him Frederick Jahn introduced gymnastic schools into Prussia, but these . . . were at last suppressed. . . . But when debility and disease, mental as well as bodily, began to increase, the ban against physical education was relaxed . . . and from that period until the present, physical exercises . . . have been encouraged and supported throughout the length and breadth of Prussia.

Brookes cites "some very able articles . . . in the *New York Herald* showing the physical degeneration of North Americans of both sexes for want of Physical exercises." Next comes the section that surely caught the baron's eye in 1889—on France:

> Again, if we turn to our neighbours the French for information on this subject, we find that out of 1,000 youths registered in 1863, as the contingent to be furnished by certain cantons for the conscription, 731 were rejected . . . as physically unfit to bear arms, a degeneracy which a writer in the *Siècle* attributed to two causes, viz., excessive labour in the manufacturing districts, and the want of physical training in the public schools.
>
> Ought not, then, even these two instances I have quoted [America and France] of declining physical stamina of certain races in the present day, as well as the lesson that history teaches of the decay and fall of some of the greatest nations of old . . . be a warning to us?[11]

Seeking, like Coubertin, to reform the school system, Brookes faults England itself for "a great and a culpable neglect of physical education." England had created its empire, he argues, because of the "manly sports of our forefathers" and the hardiness of its race. "There are some, I know, who think that, in the present day, bodily training is no longer necessary . . . that the era of physical force and with it the Olympian games has passed away—a pleasing but a dangerous delusion." Perhaps Brookes refers to Edwards's 1860 Wenlock anti-"Olympic" speech.[12] The doctor then recalls some recent military campaigns, especially the British defeat of the Russians at Inkerman: "What was it. . . ? Was it the skilful manoeuvres of our generals or the practised precision of our riflemen? No . . . it was the close quarters . . . the bayonet home thrusts . . . the invincible valour . . . and the powerful muscle of the British soldier. I say, then, that the era of physical force has not passed away."

He reiterates his point, that only by physical education in the schools can England maintain an army strong enough to preserve England's freedom, then closes his speech: "[T]he maintenance of the physical stamina of the people is an object not unworthy of the attention, the patronage, nay even the support of the state." Brookes continued to hammer on these themes, including French physical degeneracy versus German robustness—probably far more often than Coubertin did—for the rest of his life.[13]

The importance for us of Brookes's 1866 speech may lie most in its profound influence on Coubertin when he read it in 1889. For Brookes it was an opportunity to promote Olympian Games and insert his favorite metaphor, his trees: "[O]ur institutions . . . like our native oaks, are slow in their growth, like our oaks, too, they take the deeper root." It was also the first truly national forum from which Brookes could fight for physical education in the schools, the battle that would draw Coubertin to him and to his Olympic Games.

By 1869 Brookes and others had succeeded in getting the education authorities at least to contemplate these things, so he pressed on. Shortly before an important meeting of these education authorities in Manchester in late 1869, he wrote to one of them:

Happily for the aristocracy and the upper section of the middle classes in the country, the masters in our universities and large grammar schoools are so thoroughly imbued with the Greek and Roman ideas on this subject that they wisely endeavour in the training of youth to secure a just balance and a proper exercise of all the faculties of man. I shall be thankful to hear that the Educational Congress at Manchester decide to recommend bodily training as a branch of education in our national elementary schools for the sake of those who come after us, to prevent the degeneracy of a great nation.[14]

Here Brookes restates the themes of his 1866 London Olympics speech, directing his fears about "the degeneracy of a great nation" to individuals he regarded as influential. Brookes's attempts to persuade powerful and prominent individuals to support his cause persisted, as he sought men prominent in British physical education, such as Thomas Hughes, for the council of the 1874 National Olympian Games at Wenlock.

Even as the Wenlock Olympics dimmed in the late 1870s and while

Brookes tried to form an international Olympic movement with Greece in the 1880s, his speeches, correspondence, and all else show how fervently he still pursued the issue of physical education. His letters to John Gennadius closely linked Olympics to physical education. In his speech at the final 1882 NOG in Hadley, he kept up his theme, and in an 1884 address to the WOS he repeated his tree metaphor, with a special slap at the immovable Education Department:

> [O]f the seed which you have sown of that best preventive of national degeneracy, physical education, much, I regret to say, has fallen on stony ground and much, without effect, upon the half cultivated soil of the Education Department, a soil choked with the weeds of official prejudice. . . . [U]nder the powerful and fertilizing influence of public opinion, and through the . . . advocacy of several distinguished persons . . . some of the seed is beginning to germinate, and, if the harvest is slow in ripening . . . you may rest assured that it will . . . produce fruit abundantly.[15]

In 1888 Brookes wrote a letter to the National Physical Recreation Society, which was published in its March 1888 journal. This item, too, Coubertin himself certainly read and digested well, since it would have surely been included in the first package that Brookes sent to Coubertin in 1889. The published version, titled "National Disaster the Penalty for National Degeneracy," once more using the French as a warning, criticizes their "decline in physical stamina" and notes the "dangerous consequences to France of the continued neglect of physical education." Brookes refers specifically to France's recent defeat in the Franco-Prussian war, which he attributes to the superior physical training of the muscular German soldier.[16]

By this time Coubertin had begun to publish his own long string of books and articles advocating the introduction of physical education in the French schools, citing the British public schools as the model the French should imitate. In early 1888 Coubertin formed the Comité pour la Propagation des Exercises Physiques, better known to us as the Comité Jules Simon. Immediately, a rival organization sprang up, the Ligue Nationale de l'Education Physique, headed by Paschal Grousset. Grousset, strongly devoted to French manners, openly opposed the importation of English sports into French schools, wanting to maintain there a distinctly Gallic flavor. Grousset and his group were immediately active, wishing to establish their influence in all levels of French education, throughout the land, "everywhere" (*partout*), as Coubertin put it, even "in the colonies." Grousset even proposed an annual national athletic festival that would be a modern French parallel to the ancient Olympic Games. The baron immediately attacked his rival and the Ligue—and belittled the idea of modern Olympic Games:

> [Grousset's Ligue] makes a great fuss, it sets out at war, it has reminiscences of the Olympic Games and visions of ceremonies at the foot of Eiffel Tower, where the Head of State will crown the young athletes with laurel. And then, at the very time they talk about military defense, they declare they do not want to exert political action. . . . This is all a lot; it is even too much.[17]

Ironically here, probably the earliest reference to any notion of modern Olympic Games in all of his writing, Coubertin mentions the idea only to disparage it in a list of the excesses of his rival. Physical exercise as promotion of national military defense comes off rather poorly, as well.

As Coubertin battled with other early French physical education activists, his reading of authors such as Hippolyte Taine and Frédéric Le Play tended to confirm his idealistic notions of English education.[18] Coubertin had first visited England in 1883. In 1886 he returned, touring various English schools including Rugby, the locale of Hughes's book about Tom Brown. There he had his supposed vision at Rugby Chapel.[19] He soon began to publish articles on English schools and education, culminating in his first book, *L'éducation en Angleterre* (1888). The next year, he published another, *L'éducation anglaise en France* and toured America, visiting universities from north to south. The result was a third book, *Universités transatlantiques* (1890). But before he left for America,[20] Coubertin came in contact with Dr. W. P. Brookes, of Much Wenlock. That contact would affect his life far more than his professed idolatry of Tom Brown or Thomas Arnold.

There are hundreds of pages of Olympic history full of details about possible influences on Coubertin: Thomas Arnold, French thinkers and writers, Le Play, Taine, Coubertin's family, France and its politics. Almost incredibly, Olympic historians have failed to notice that by June 1889, Coubertin was already reading, digesting, and quoting Dr. Brookes's writings.[21] He knew Brookes's ideas before he went to America, before he founded the journal *Revue Athlétique*, and before he formed the Union des sociétés françaises de sports athlétiques (USFSA).

Coubertin himself dated his first knowledge of Brookes and his work to 1889. Early in that year the baron put notices in several English newspapers explaining his interest in British sports and physical education, requesting that Englishmen with similar interests communicate with him. That request was answered by Brookes, who sent Coubertin some of his writings. Coubertin acknowledges, at least twice, receipt of these documents from Brookes.[22] Later that year Paris held a grand Exposition Universelle. For that occasion Coubertin and other advocates of French sport arranged to hold, in June, an International Congress on Physical Exercise. Both before and after that congress, Coubertin placed much weight on it, tending to regard it as the first of a series of congresses important to his movement and to his life's work; and he seems to have organized it single-handedly.[23] For his speech delivered there on June 15, 1889, Coubertin came armed with a copy of Brookes's 1866 Crystal Palace address. Well into his speech, he approached the climax: "After that, how can one not agree with these words uttered by a perspicacious speaker at an athletic contest which took place some twenty years ago at the Crystal Palace." Coubertin then quoted verbatim from Brookes's speech delivered at the 1866 London Olympics. He obviously paid especial attention to Brookes's observations on the French soldier's weakness versus the German soldier's strength.[24] Here Coubertin publicly recognizes the theme of French degeneracy in a context of military readiness. He attributes it not to Taine, Didon, Le Play, or himself but to Brookes, from whom it seems highly likely he indeed got it.

In fact, in opinions written prior to this speech endorsing Brookes's ideas, Coubertin apparently turned his back on the notion of physical education and sport as a kind of military training, probably again in reaction to Grousset's notion of exercise as military defense. Coubertin wrote, rather surprisingly, "[I]t's citizens more than soldiers that [France] needs. . . . It's not militarism that our education needs, but freedom," and even repudiated the claims of military "muscles."[25] Yet he reversed his opinion after he read and quoted Brookes's speech on France's physical degeneracy. It is this later attitude that has informed modern Olympic history, not his earlier ideas, which seemed to be the contrary.

Another remarkable feature of Coubertin's 1889 congress speech is his extremely vague description of the occasion of Brookes's speech: "at an athletic contest . . . at the Crystal Palace." The occasion was, of course, more precisely, the first British National Olympian Games. The baron's inattention to the title of this "contest" seems ready proof that Coubertin, in June 1889, had not yet conceived the idea of reviving the Olympics. If he had any such plan, surely he would have pounced on the occasion of this speech he quotes so approvingly as ammunition for his own Olympic idea.[26]

Coubertin soon sent the news of his June 1889 speech to Brookes. A Shropshire newspaper proudly reported in November: "It is a pleasure to us to note, from the report from the proceedings of the above Congress, that the efforts of our Countryman, Dr. Brookes ... were alluded to by Monsieur Pierre de Coubertin at the close of his eloquent ... speech by a quotation from Dr. Brookes's address at the National Olympian Festival ... in August 1866." [27] And in the very first issue of his new *Revue Athlétique* (January 1890), Coubertin announced: "I have received some interesting documents from Mr. W. P. Brookes, who is following with lively sympathy, from his home in Much Wenlock (England) the movement for a physical renaissance in France." [28]

About this same time, early 1890, Coubertin played the principal role in founding the USFSA, the French athletic organization parallel to the British AAA and the American AAU (Amateur Athletic Union). This was the major institution for Coubertin's own activity. The initial stages of the USFSA, and details of the baron's travails, are well described in other Olympic histories, [29] allowing focus here on the main thread of our own Olympic history, which now ties an indissoluble knot between Coubertin and Brookes.

Brookes and Coubertin had obviously corresponded before June 1889, but how, how often, and when are unclear. After 1889 much more information appears. In late July 1890, Brookes finally succeeded in getting the National Physical Recreation Society to pass a resolution favorable to compulsory physical education in the national schools. He immediately took the initiative—as he had so often with Gennadius—and mailed Coubertin a copy of the resolution. He sent various other things along with that July letter, including his photograph, a request for one of the baron, and—as so often with Gennadius—an invitation to Coubertin to come visit him in Wenlock.

All these things are clear, because the original of Coubertin's replying letter, dated August 9, 1890, is extant. In it, Coubertin acknowledges receipt of Brookes's July package, and—in contrast with Gennadius—announces that he will indeed come visit Brookes in Wenlock. It was a fateful visit, indeed. The letter (in English) bears the letterhead of the USFSA. Since it is so far unpublished and obviously has great historical value, I quote some portions:

> Dear Dr. Brookes
> I was very much interested in reading the resolution adopted at the meeting held in London on the 27th of July and I wish you every success in your attempt to bring forth a general reform in your National Schools. The case is not quite the same with us. Physical training has already been made compulsory in the elementary schools of France.

The programme runs thus: [there follows a list of the several levels of French education, noting which exercises or sports are specified for each educational age level; Coubertin then notes that the program "is not yet carried out everywhere as it ought to be" because many teachers lack experience in physical education].

I quite agree with you that bodily training in National Schools is of very great importance to the whole nation; but it is of no less importance that boys above fifteen and young men should be fond of athletic games and sports and enjoy out of doors life and every manly form of recreation. Such was not the case with us and I shall do my best to make Athletics popular amongst my countrymen, for I firmly believe that the wonderful "Expansion of England" and the "Grandeur of the British people" are the consequences of athletic education and that you are indebted for it to cricket, football and rowing.

I will be delighted to talk the subject over with you when we meet in October. I must go to Birmingham and Rugby and intend starting toward the 20th of October; if it is convenient to you I can proceed directly to Much Wenlock. I leave it to your choice.

I sent some days ago my book on American Colleges "Universités Transatlantiques" and the last number of the Athletic Review containing the proceedings of our general meeting held in Paris on July 6th—You were kind enough to send me your photograph. I beg to return mine regretting that I have not a better one for it gives the idea of one much taller and stronger than I am.

With renewed thanks, believe me, Dear Dr. Brookes,

Ever yours most truly
Pierre de Coubertin[30]

Exchanging photographs was a favorite practice of Brookes, who seemed fascinated with photos and had asked Gennadius for his photo much earlier. The photo Coubertin sent Brookes is but a small portrait and looks much like any other photo of the young Coubertin.[31]

One significant feature of this letter, a feature of all Coubertin's references to Brookes and his work prior to October 1890, is worthy of note. Until 1890, the young baron seems to have no thought of an Olympic movement or interest in Olympic Games. He had seen references to them but simply did not notice. When Coubertin quoted so approvingly from Brookes's 1866 London National Olympian Games speech, he made only vague reference to its exact occasion ("at an athletic contest"). In this letter, the words "Olympic" and "Olympian" never occur. Brookes had sent programs of the Wenlock Olympics to Coubertin (even the article on Wenlock tilting). But Coubertin still focused only on Brookes's efforts in physical education. He expresses no interest in or recognition of Brookes's Olympic activities. He had ridiculed those of Grousset. It does not seem possible that Coubertin had any view to initiating an Olympic revival before he visited Wenlock.[32]

The train brought Coubertin to Wenlock in late October 1890.[33] He had very romantic first impressions of the village: "What characterizes it is the veil of poetry which envelopes it and the scent of antiquity which comes from it. Clearly Dr. Brookes . . . more keenly than any other has sensed this mysterious influence which Greek civilization, across the ages, still exerts on humanity."[34] Coubertin stayed only a couple of days; but they were crucial days in the history of our Olympic roots. Happily, there are three good articles about what happened: two by Coubertin himself and another in a local Shropshire newspaper.[35] Brookes had prepared well for the visit, obviously seeking to impress the young Frenchman with his enterprise. The annual Wenlock Olympics had already been held at their regular time in May 1890. But, invoking an old Wenlock tradition, Brookes decided to stage a special autumn edition of his Olympics in honor of his guest and "to enlighten Baron Pierre de Coubertin, a French gentleman, who desires to introduce athletics more largely among his own countrymen."[36] In fact, if Coubertin came expecting merely to discuss physical education, he must have been surprised at the Olympic emphasis that Brookes placed on his entire visit.

These autumn Olympics had little athletic significance, for even the regular meeting was, by then, mediocre. But in pageantry Brookes put on the full show for the baron, including the usual procession of competitors and villagers from the Gaskell Inn in town to Linden Field, led by a herald on horseback. Many in the procession were elaborately dressed. When everyone arrived at the field, there was a triumphal arch waiting, bearing the words "Welcome to Baron Pierre de Coubertin and Prosperity to France." Other banners displayed, in ancient Greek, quotations from the ancient authors. On their arrival at Linden Field, Brookes asked Coubertin to plant his tree: "The members of the Wenlock Olympian Society have a custom which they have great pleasure in carrying out, viz., that of paying honour to distinguished personages by dedicating beautiful trees as memorials to them. We are happy in having an opportunity of performing this ceremony in remembrance of your visit to Wenlock and to Linden Field."

Perhaps Brookes had some deep thoughts as the baron worked his spade; for he believed in nurturing the symbolic value of his trees, just as he cared for the botanical item itself.[37] Brief speeches and hymns followed, and champagne was poured onto the tree. When Coubertin ceremoniously planted his own tree, he observed those that had been planted in honor of others at other events: Queen Victoria, King George of Greece, the Prince of Wales, and various other dignitaries. "You see," he soon wrote of his tree, "that mine is not in bad company."[38] To this day, Coubertin's tree grows ever larger and thrives in Wenlock—as do the Olympic Games and movement around the world.

Next, the Games were held, including the regular track-and-field events and tilting at the ring. There were elaborate ceremonies to award the prizes, especially for the tilting event, where a woman crowned the winner in a ceremony reminiscent of medieval days. MacAloon well argues that our current Olympic award ceremonies probably derive partly from this moment. Later, Brookes held a formal dinner for about sixty people at the Raven Inn.[39] There were songs and speeches. Coubertin was by now already an honorary member of the Wenlock Olympian Society, his name appearing just inches below those of Velissariou and Gennadius on the official roll. To reciprocate, Coubertin announced that Brookes had been made an honorary fellow of his French athletic organization, the USFSA. He then posted a USFSA gold medal as a prize for the next Wenlock Olympics. Brookes spoke, praising Coubertin, France, and physical education, and added "I believe in the Latin motto: *mens sana in corpore sano.*" The evening was capped off by a ball held in the public library.[40]

On so busy a day, there was little time for discussion between the two men. But the day before or the day after, Brookes and Coubertin spent some time together. Aged and ailing, Brookes seized the opportunity to pass the Olympic torch to the young Frenchman. It seems obvious that Brookes viewed Coubertin as the man he had hoped Gennadius would be.[41] He probably talked more of Olympics than of physical education. Brookes filled Coubertin's ears with the history of the modern Olympic movement. He told him of his local Olympian Society, its founding many decades before, and its yearly games and of the Greek national Olympics of Zappas. In his archive room, Brookes showed Coubertin the summary results of the 1859 Athens Olympiad—the events, the athletes' names, Velissariou and the rest, all in English translation. Brookes told Coubertin about the British national Olympics, the London 1866 Olympiad, and other Olympic Games held in Birmingham and Shrewsbury. He informed the baron how he and the Greeks had exchanged gifts on the occasion of certain Olympiads. Brookes's Olympic correspondence, Coubertin noted, was "voluminous." Most importantly, Brookes told Coubertin about his ultimate Olympic dream, to begin an international revival, with the first international Olympic Games to be held at Athens.[42]

Yet even as his train left Wenlock, Coubertin himself almost certainly remained without interest in Olympic Games. Soon after he returned to Paris, he wrote an article praising Brookes's work in physical education. But the baron, perhaps recalling his earlier contentions with Grousset, still seemed to scoff a bit at the very name and idea of reviving the Olympics, asserting that, in modern times, there was "no longer any need to invoke memories of Greece and to seek encouragement in the past."[43]

SEVEN

The Baron at Work, 1890–1894

> To study History it is necessary to abandon certain prejudices
> which are firmly in place.
> —*Coubertin*, Histoire universelle, *1926*

Soon after returning to France, Coubertin wrote up his Wenlock experiences and published them on Christmas Day 1890 in his new journal, as "Les Jeux Olympiques à Much Wenlock—Une page de l'histoire de l'athlètisme." The article's title is interesting in itself. Apparently still having no notion of proposing an Olympic revival himself, Coubertin has no qualms about calling Brookes's games Olympic Games. He even gives Brookes credit for reviving the ancient Olympics: "[I]f the Olympic Games which modern Greece could not bring back to life are revived today, the credit is due not to a Greek but to Dr. Brookes."[1]

After giving his general impressions of Wenlock and Brookes, Coubertin briefly reviews the development of Anglo-American sports in the previous few decades. He quotes Brookes's Wenlock use of the motto *Mens sana in corpore sano* but also associates it here with Kingsley and Muscular Christianity. Focusing directly on Brookes's Wenlock Olympian Society, he mentions as its goal the "development of physical, moral, and intellectual qualities"—hardly different from that later stated by his own IOC, where they are better known as part of the Olympic idea. He then explains the actual Olympic Games that he witnessed, paying especial attention to the pageantry, tree planting, processions, and award ceremonies. The event that most impressed Coubertin was tilting at the ring, which he relates in detail. This tilting match probably inspired the medieval portion of Coubertin's subsequent Olympic idea.[2]

In this 1890 article Coubertin reveals surprising candor about Brookes's Olympic movement and previous Olympic revivals. He writes freely of the British National Olympian Games. "An attempt indeed occurred around 1866 to expand and generalize the Olympic Games. A festival took place that year at the Crystal Palace. It was repeated the next year at Birmingham, then at Shrewsbury, if I remember right."

Strangely, in view of his later claims and activity, here he again makes light of the very concept of Olympic Games in modern times. No scholar, as far as I know, has ever noticed this strange comment, Coubertin's second mention of the idea of reviving the Olympics. He here, as he had with Grousset in 1888, disparages the very idea he is famous for conceiving. After a brief account of the British national Olympic movement, he says: "This movement was not without use: it gave the partisans of athleticism an occasion to get together and be counted. But soon the eagerness for physical exercises manifested itself with an irresistable power. There was no longer any need to invoke memories of Greece and to seek encouragement in the past. They loved sport for its own sake."[3]

Those are not the words of a man already burning with the idea of founding modern games inspired by the "ancient Greek Olympics," even if Boulongne claims that "from 1888 on" Coubertin had "dreamed about making the Olympic Games live again."[4] By autumn, 1892, the baron had changed his mind on Olympics and presented Brookes's "unnecessary" idea as a brilliant idea, all his own.

Coubertin also notes explicitly that Greece had had a modern Olympic movement; that Brookes had corresponded with the Greek king and succeeded in getting the king to donate a cup to the "contest at Wenlock"; and that "he [Brookes] had favored the revival of the Olympic Games at Athens."[5] The last sentence cannot be misunderstood as a reference to Brookes's support of the Zappas Olympics in Athens—the baron was not that confused. In context, immediately following mention of the 1877 gift of a cup to Brookes's Games, it is surely a reference to Brookes's proposal for international Olympics to take place in Athens. But, probably because he himself has as yet no interest in an Olympic revival, Coubertin leaves vague precisely what kind of revival Brookes "favored" for Athens, and when. He continues: "But patronage was not all. The Greeks took part in a contest and then left off (se reposèrent). I have seen in the Wenlock archives the results of the contest and the names of the winners. Since then, nobody has heard any more talk of Olympic Games at Athens."

The last comment is, of course, quite wrong. Just months before Coubertin wrote that sentence, Prince Constantine had officially announced the Athens Olympiad v for 1892. And there had been, indeed, several more Olympiads at Athens after the one whose victor list the baron examined that day in Wenlock. But here Coubertin's error perhaps comes from forgivable ignorance. It is possible that Brookes himself did not know of the post-1859 Greek Olympiads.[6] If Brookes did not know of later Greek Olympiads, we have no reason to expect Coubertin to inquire further on his own. I do not think Coubertin is already, in 1890, consciously minimizing or ignoring these other national Olympic movements.

Even later, in 1897, in his second article about Brookes's Olympic Games ("A Typical Englishman"), Coubertin still notes Brookes's national "Olympian festivals" in Birmingham, Shrewsbury, and Wellington; but he says nothing about the London Olympiad, of which he knew very well. Perhaps by then that most obvious British Olympiad would have marred his next sentence, which summarily dismisses Brookes's activity in England: "But no regular movement was started." In 1897 he still reports Brookes's attempt to establish international Olympics at Athens—but again only to dismiss it.

> Dr. Brookes even endeavored to promote a festival in Athens; many young Englishmen, he thought, would gladly avail themselves of such an opportunity of visiting the classic land. But the proposal was declined by the Greek government. A festival of this kind could hardly be planned as long as the Paris Congress had not met to reorganize and revive the Olympian games on a permanent and broader scale.[7]

This time Coubertin makes no mention of any modern Olympiads in Greece—though by then he knew, through Vikelas, all about them in painful detail. As the years progressed Coubertin seemed to forget more and more about his predecessors in the Olympic movement in England and Greece. He increasingly minimized their role, eventually giving Brookes no credit for the Olympic idea, and consciously misrepresenting the Greeks' activity so that it appeared that Greece had had no Olympic revival whatsoever.[8] But I speak of these things later, returning now to Christmas Day, 1890, and to our immediate story.

The year 1890 ended as a highly eventful year for Olympic history, with relevant events happening quickly at several places. Brookes exchanged letters with both Coubertin and Gennadius; Constantine announced resumption of the Greek national Olympics; and Coubertin founded the USFSA, visited Brookes in Wenlock, and published his first article on the Wenlock Olympics—all in one year.

Over the next few years, as well, many more crucial events took place almost simultaneously in England, Greece, and France. Brookes invited the baron to attend the regular 1891 spring Wenlock Olympics. In April, Coubertin replied to decline the invitation, explaining his need to be in Paris for several athletic meetings to be held there that spring. But he kept his promise about the medal for those Games: "The Golden Medal I want to send you to be given as a prize at your next festival is ready." He includes instructions for obtaining the medal from his friend J. J. Jusserand, who will bring it to England.[9]

Brookes then wrote Coubertin often. On July 20, 1892 the baron finally wrote him back: "You must forgive me if I have not answered your last letters for I am now 'swallowed up' by the work I have to do."[10] He proudly writes of the growing numbers and activities of the USFSA. He talks of several specific sports and the question of professionalism. The letter continues:

> I am delighted to hear that my golden oak is growing all right and I only wish I could go and see it and accept your kind invitation. I remember very sweetly the days I spent with you at Wenlock.
>
> We shall have an eight day festival in Paris from Nov. 20 to Nov. 27 to commemorate the foundation of the Union five years ago. . . . Next spring I shall take over to America a French team to compete in New York, Boston, and Chicago. It may be that we shall play football in England before then.

Coubertin clearly reveals his own plans for many months in advance—especially November. Therefore, what is most surprising about this letter is that, while Coubertin tells Brookes of the jubilee of the USFSA to be held in November, just a few months away ("festival . . . to commemorate"), he makes no mention at all of Olympic Games. If Coubertin already had some intention or notion of proposing an international modern Olympic revival at this jubilee, he surely would have mentioned it in this letter. He knew it had long been Brookes's own plan and desire. His silence about any forthcoming proposal to revive the Olympic Games in this July 20 letter suggests that Coubertin still—in late July 1892—had no thought of making that proposal, no notion of pursuing Brookes's idea himself.[11]

In an ironic bit of timing, on September 10—sandwiched chronologically between Coubertin's July letter to Brookes and Coubertin's own first Olympic proposal in November—a Shropshire newspaper printed a summary history of Brookes's efforts in the modern Olympic revival movement to that date. It also paraphrased parts of a speech that Brookes delivered to a crowd of six thousand people. The article states that Wyse and Brookes corresponded prior to the 1859 Greek Olympics in Athens and gives other details. It then summarizes what was obviously the end of Brookes's speech: "If he lived long enough, Dr. Brookes hoped to go and witness an international festival at Athens, or upon the old spot where the Olympic Games were started."[12]

So in September 1892, six thousand people heard Brookes's international Olympic proposal, and many more read about it in the newspapers.

Coubertin himself and previous Olympic historians have dated the origin of the modern Olympic movement to November 25, 1892, that precise

·

day, two months later, when Coubertin first proposed an Olympic revival at that USFSA jubilee. In fact, the first sentence in Coubertin's own Olympic history, *Mémoires olympiques*, is a tantalizing nonsentence, consisting of nothing but that date: "One evening in November 1892 ... Friday the 25th, to be precise" (ellipsis in original).[13] The jubilee itself was premature. The USFSA was not yet five years old. But Coubertin counted not from the inception of the USFSA itself but from the start of one of its founding clubs.[14] Coubertin always planned his conferences with great care: he sought an impressive setting and orchestrated the events carefully. On that eventful evening there were three speakers, in a room in the Sorbonne. First, Coubertin's friend Georges Bourdon spoke on ancient sport; then his friend Jusserand spoke on sport in medieval times. Finally, Coubertin himself spoke on modern sport.[15]

He argued the case for international sport competitions. Near the end of his speech, he noted that if such international games were instituted, "the cause of peace will have received a new and powerful ally." That strong emphasis on the Olympics' potential as part of a peace movement is another significant feature of Coubertin's Olympic idea that distinguishes it from its predecessors. The baron closed this speech with an impassioned plea that his audience also help him "to pursue and realize ... this grandiose and beneficent project; namely, the re-establishment of the Olympic Games."

It was the first time Coubertin himself had uttered the words of this proposal. It is certain that he first heard the notion of an international Olympic revival from Brookes. Yet he never credited Brookes with any priority or influence in forming his own idea. In his 1908 book Coubertin carefully claims that he conceived the idea all by himself. He explains that he first saw there was a need to internationalize sport. Then he writes:

When and how this need associated itself in my mind with the idea of re-establishing the Olympic Games I couldn't say. . . . I was familiar with the term. Nothing in ancient history had made me more of a dreamer[16] than Olympia. This city of dream ... raised its colonnades and porticos unceasingly before my adolescent mind. Long before I thought of drawing from its ruins a principle of revival, I would rebuild it in my mind, to make the shape of its silhouette live again. Germany had exhumed its remains. Why should France not succeed in renewing its splendors? From there it was not far to the less dazzling but more practical and more fruitful project of reviving the Games.[17]

If Coubertin's mind since adolescence had been entranced with thoughts of ancient Olympia, nothing he had so far done or written before

1892 shows it. He makes only a couple of rather insignificant references to ancient Olympia in his earlier writing—clearly derived from his reading other authors' chance references to Olympia, not from reading even one book, article, or excavation report on ancient Olympia itself. And his knowledge of ancient Greece was always superficial, at best.[18] Even when he speaks of Brookes's and the Greeks' modern Olympics, he reveals no special interest in ancient Olympia or its games. As we saw, he even somewhat belittled such ideas in 1888 and 1890: "There was no longer any need to invoke memories of Greece and to seek encouragement in the past."

In 1908 Coubertin reveled in recalling what happened that "evening in November 1892" after he made his first Olympic proposal in the Sorbonne. He reported the audience's reaction as if his proposal to renew the Olympic Games was so novel as to be beyond comprehension.

> They could not comprehend the meaning of such an anachronism. They thought I used the phrase symbolically. I had to realize that, since they had not spiritually walked around the exedra of Herod Atticus and the tomb of Pelops [in Olympia], as I had done for a long time, those in the audience located the Olympic Games in their mental museum at the same level as the mysteries of Eleusis or the oracle at Delphi; things long dead which could be revived only at the opera-house.[19]

Coubertin in later years still maintained that his proposal for an Olympic revival was so novel that it baffled those who heard it.[20]

Like Brookes before him, however, Coubertin found little or no interest in his countrymen for the Olympic revival idea. Yet he did not seek Brookes's support nor, it seems, did he even inform Brookes of his own Paris proposal. For in December, Brookes proceeded to bother Gennadius again about Brookes's own plan for international Olympics in Athens.[21] Clearly, had Brookes known of Coubertin's proposal, he would have focused on helping the baron, not on pursuing the indifferent Greeks once more.

Indeed on May 30, 1893, perhaps frustrated by another lukewarm reply from Gennadius, the aged, possibly failing Brookes wrote a long, even rambling, letter to Coubertin. It tells of many things: the recent Wenlock Olympics, Brookes's own misfortune (he had broken his leg),[22] his education in Paris long ago. He ends the letter thus:

> I should be delighted if you could visit Wenlock in the Summer time, for I look upon you as one of my most valued friends, and take a deep interest in the cause you are so ably advocating and carrying out, a cause which will be of immense benefit to your Country. I earnestly hope that henceforth the

only contests between England and France will be athletic contests. . . . I have been endeavouring . . . to induce the Education Department to introduce compulsory physical education into our National Elementary Schools. . . . France, under your guidance . . . is wisely endeavoring to extinguish that physical degeneracy which was the cause of her recent disasters. . . . I shall shortly enter upon my 85th year, and am beginning to think that my zealous but ineffectual labours for the good of my country are fast coming to a close. I shall be glad to hear from you when you have time to write, and I remain yours Sincerely W. P. Brookes.[23]

This letter has obvious historical value and touches on topics that we associate with Coubertin. It shows that Brookes himself viewed athletic contests between nations as a desirable alternative to contests in war.[24] It shows that Brookes expressed directly to Coubertin his opinion about how French "physical degeneracy" caused her military defeat by Germany. And it especially reveals a tender respect for the baron and their common efforts in physical education. But it does not reveal any knowledge whatsoever of the Olympic revival proposal Coubertin made in Paris in November 1892. Had Brookes any such knowledge he surely would have mentioned it in so long a letter, rather than speaking only of Coubertin's "cause" of physical education.

We may conclude then that Coubertin, when his Olympic proposal aroused no interest in France, did not seek any support or advice from Brookes—although Brookes had just sent him that sympathetic letter. He decided to pursue a different course. Virtually everyone interested in sports, in every country that now had sports, was interested in the question of "amateurism," a term that has always generally defied definition.[25] Its fuzzy meaning and application caused repeated difficulties throughout the sporting world. USFSA member Adolphe de Palissaux proposed that the organization sponsor an international congress in hopes of resolving amateurism's many thorny problems. Coubertin seized on the idea, and with de Palissaux, caused the USFSA, in August 1893, to approve a preliminary program for such a congress. It was scheduled for June 1894.[26]

Coubertin's real plan for the congress, it seems, had less to do with amateurism than with reviving the Olympic Games. In the fall of 1893 he again visited America, hoping to drum up interest in his Olympic revival.[27] He went to Chicago where, amid other activities, he visited with W. R. Harper, president of the University of Chicago, who seemed mildly interested in Olympics. On the West Coast he went to the University of California campus at Berkeley. In San Francisco he visited one of the major West Coast athletic clubs, the Olympic Club. He later said it had a "predestined name."[28] The Olympic Club had, in fact, earlier that same year held its own Olympic Games; but these were mainly a theater production, with members playing out roles as ancient Greeks and Romans. Coubertin later makes a vague, oblique reference to this "Olympic" Revival of the Ancient Greco-Roman Games but fails to connect it with the San Francisco Olympic Club and his visit there in 1893.[29] It is difficult to believe that members neglected to inform Coubertin of this recent, important club event. He returned to the East Coast via Texas and New Orleans, hoping to find support for his Olympic idea.

Finally, in Princeton, he found some interest in Olympics. William Sloane, whom he visited on his previous trip to America, welcomed the idea warmly and agreed to serve as a commissioner for the June 1894 Paris congress. These two men developed a lasting friendship, and Sloane would play a major role in carrying out Coubertin's ideas in America (and in later IOC meetings).[30] So also C. Herbert, secretary of the AAA in Britain, agreed to serve on the secretariat of the 1894 Congress of Amateurs; but he had no interest at all in Olympics. When dinners were held for Coubertin with prominent sports figures in New York and London, the baron found no support for the idea of reviving the Olympic Games.[31].

In January 1894 Coubertin mailed a circular advertising the congress to take place in June 1894. The document listed the three sponsoring members as the committee for the congress, Herbert, Sloane, and Coubertin himself. Herbert represented "England and the English Colonies"; Sloane, America; and Coubertin, "France and Continental Europe." This January version of the circular called it an International Congress of Amateurs and contained eight agenda items. The first seven concerned the frequent questions raised by the concept of amateurism, such as definition, gate money, value of medals, betting, methods of disqualification. But the eighth and last item read, "The possibility or re-establishing the Olympic Games. Under what conditions would it be feasible?"[32]

The front matter to the program itself (or a slightly later version) confirms that from the start Coubertin viewed the international Olympic Games as in part a peace movement: "[I]t is possible to believe that these peaceful and refined contests would constitute the best of internationalism."[33] Here Coubertin is repeating a theme prominent in his initial 1892 Olympic call ("the cause of peace," above). Although Soutsos, on the national level, and Brookes, speaking internationally, had already suggested that revived Olympic Games might promote peace, it was Coubertin who strongly stressed their special potential for peace. He referred to it often, sometimes even focused on it, and developed it in practice so that it could contribute, in fact, to thawing the Cold War in the period 1950–76. It seems one of the baron's most original and greatest contributions to Olympism.[34]

Coubertin certainly sent this January flyer to a number of people in rather distant places. Sloane and Herbert received multiple copies, to distribute in their own regions, as did Leonard Cuff in New Zealand. It is unclear how many were sent to European addresses at this time.[35] But responses were few and slow. Even Coubertin himself admits that he had attracted little interest in the congress by spring 1894. At the end of March he was still seeking a suitable dignitary to serve as president of the congress and influential names to list as its honorary members.[36] But in early April he seems to have succeeded in getting a president, Baron A. C. de Courcel, a senator and former French ambassador to Germany.[37] That acceptance apparently triggered much more activity from Coubertin.

He then asked the Racing Club of Paris to hold the grand congressional banquet—in Paris, a true fête—on the evening of June 21; on April 12, the club agreed. He eventually obtained more than fifty names for the list of honorary members, an impressive addition to the printed program. The membership included influential politicians, titled nobility, and sportsmen from around the world. Coubertin always sought the sanction of royalty and the nobility to add luster to his projects. Therefore, at the head of the list were four impressive royal names, "the King of Belgium, the Prince of Wales, the Crown Prince of Sweden and Norway, and the Crown Prince of Greece."[38] The last prince, of course, was Constantine, who only two years earlier was compelled to forgo his own Athens Olympic Games announced for 1892.

Coubertin placed especial importance on Constantine's support in Greece. He says, "I charged my friend Charles Waldstein . . . to lay the question before the Greek royal family."[39] Waldstein, at that time head of the American School of Classical Studies in Athens, was excavating ancient Argos in southern Greece. In early April, the royal family paid his Argos excavation a rare visit. Waldstein, fulfilling his charge, told Constantine of Coubertin's own plans for an Olympic revival, and the two apparently had a long talk about Olympic Games. On April 15, Waldstein wrote Coubertin, informing him of his conversation with the crown prince and of Constantine's consent to be an honorary member. Waldstein and Constantine's conversation may have concerned something far more important than his honorary membership.[40]

Once assured on those things—de Courcel's presidency, the site for the fête, and support from the Greek royal family—in early May Coubertin sent out a flurry of invitations for his congress in June and requested that delegates send ahead their opinions on amateurism and the revival of the Olympic Games. These new invitations, sent to various people in Europe, differed from the first flyer. Coubertin now called his Paris meeting the International Athletic Congress, dropping the words "of Amateurs" from its previous title. Amateurism remained first on the program, and the first seven points concerning amateurism remained the same. But Coubertin now made much more of the Olympic feature of the congress, expanding the former point VIII to three points and making a separate heading:

Olympic Games

VIII—The possibility of re-establishing them.—Advantages from the athletic, moral and international points of view.

IX—Conditions to be imposed on competitors.—Sports represented.—Material organization and frequency of the revived Olympic Games.

X—Nomination of an International Committee responsible for preparing their re-establishment.

The last two items conflict with the closing paragraph of the January, eight-point program (which incongruously is kept in the ten-point program, as well). That paragraph gave assurances that the congress had as its object "to express opinions on the different questions submitted to it, to consider measures for international legislation, but not to inaugurate it."[41]

In Wenlock, sometime in May, Dr. Brookes finally received a program and circular invitation to the congress. There is no certain indication he was sent a personalized version; it may have been just the regular form letter.[42] On May 22, 1894, Brookes (who never procrastinated) wrote Coubertin as follows:

Dear Baron Coubertin,

I have called a Meeting of the Members of the Wenlock Olympian Society to be held on Thursday next, May 26, to consider the various propositions contained in the circulars you sent me, many of which they will be satisfied to leave to the decision of the Congress. In one, however, you will, I feel assured, have their cordial concurrence, viz., the establishment of an international Olympian Association and the arrangement that such gatherings be held in rotation in or near the Capitals of all nations joining in the Movement. This has long been a cherished idea of mine so far as making Greece the centre, but the plan of your Congress, embracing as it does all nations, is a really superb one, and deserving of the liberal support of all nations.[43]

Coubertin must have sent, with Brookes's circular, a copy (or text) of his "Le rétablissement" article, published in the middle of that same month.

The May circular mentions nothing about when or where the proposed new Olympics would be held; Brookes's words, "in rotation in or near the Capitals of all nations," probably reflect the baron's plan as stated in his "Le rétablissement."[44]

If Brookes thought Coubertin's intention to "embrac[e] . . . all nations" was "superb," why did he not include that worldwide feature in his own international Olympic proposal? "Rotation around the principal cities" was integral both to Brookes's Shropshire Olympics and to his National Olympian Games. Why did he abandon that course for the international Games? I here speculate on an answer, hoping to shed more light on Coubertin's "superb" improvement in the proposal, that significant difference between Coubertin's 1894 idea and Brookes's of 1880. Although the difference is only fourteen years, they were different times, and the two men were of different ages. Brookes's roots were early-nineteenth century, and, born in 1809, he was wholly a nineteenth-century man, "from another age," as Coubertin put it.[45] When he made his proposal in 1880, there was no international community of athletes, none even in Paris. Britain and its colonies, past and present, had athletics; Greece had an Olympic tradition. The rest of the world must have looked like an athletic desert in 1880 (German-style *Turner* are not relevant here). The idea of Olympic Games in the various "great capitals of the world" (Coubertin) was unthinkable in 1880. Both Brookes and Coubertin were practical men.

The young Coubertin, in contrast, nearly breathed in the future and expected to start his Olympics in 1900; he prophetically predicted that "the athletic renaissance" would "later be regarded as one of the characteristics of the 19th century," even if "today the word makes people laugh."[46] The athletic renaissance, partly due to Coubertin's own efforts, made international hosting of athletic contests perhaps feasible in 1894. Yet even then, attempts to hold international Olympics outside of Athens failed until 1908; they did not fully succeed until 1912. Brookes would have been foolish to propose rotating sites in 1880.[47]

After praising Coubertin for his "superb" notion of worldwide sites, Brookes's May 22 letter advises Coubertin to act quickly. Brookes offers his personal support ("[you] may rely upon my warm advocacy of your movement in all quarters where I have influence"). He pleads that his own bad health and advanced age will prevent him from attending the congress in person ("I wish I were younger"): he promises to send his society's opinions on the agenda topics soon.

By that time, late May, just weeks before the announced June 16 date of the congress, Coubertin had received many responses and a significant number of acceptances from Europe, from such places as Scotland and Switzerland, as well as France. Those respondents who refer to Coubertin's own letter of invitation as dated in "May" all answer to his invitation to an International Athletic Congress. That name had now wholly replaced the title on the January program, International Congress of Amateurs. But the baron soon made the transition from a congress on amateurism to a congress on Olympic Games complete. At the last minute, in early June, with the congress scheduled to open on June 16, Coubertin changed its name once more, giving it and the official program its third and final title: Paris International Congress for the Re-establishment of the Olympic Games.[48]

The baron later chuckled as he recalled this last-minute typographical legerdemain. "Suddenly the name changed. The words 'Congress for the Re-establishment of the Olympic Games' appeared on the invitation letters."[49] That title headed the actual program handed to delegates. The slow substitution of the words "Olympic Games" for "of Amateurs" illustrates the trick Coubertin played on the sporting world. He rightly perceived there would be very little interest in a congress to revive the Olympic Games.

Others, whose support he wanted, always cared much more about amateurism than Coubertin did himself. So he used it as a ploy to get the Games revived. In 1931 he could write:

> Amateurism. That! Always that. It had been sixteen years since we had naively feigned to be done with it. . . . Today I can risk the confession; I was never much concerned about the question of amateurism. It had served me as a screen [*paravent*] to convene the Congress to Re-establish the Olympic Games. Seeing the importance which others lent it in the sporting world, I would show the expected zeal in that direction, but it was zeal without real conviction.[50]

And as early as 1896 he wrote: "The programme of the Congress was so drawn up as to place to the fore questions of a purely sporting nature and to dissimulate the principal question, that of the revival of the Olympic Games. I was afraid that it would elicit sarcasm or would even discourage those with good will by the very magnitude of the project."[51]

There was one man who, Coubertin certainly knew, would not be discouraged by the project of reviving the Olympic Games, namely, W. P. Brookes. On June 13, almost the eve of the congress's opening, Brookes, for the second time that month, wrote Coubertin across the channel: "I cannot express how much interested I feel in your forthcoming international congress." In a four-page letter he again expresses a wish that he were younger and could attend in person and praises the baron for his efforts. Then he explains some of his own society's policies with respect to a number of specific questions on amateurism listed on the program. On the last page he suggests, "I hope the Congress will not omit the crowning of the victor in a Pentathlon, or in the greater number of contests with the olive wreath."[52]

Just two days before, Brookes had written what he thought was an even more important letter to Greece. On June 11 he wrote to the prime minister of Greece, Charilaos Trikoupis. Apparently, the aged Brookes confused the then prime minister with his father, Spiridon Trikoupis. Brookes had corresponded with the elder Trikoupis many years before in London, when Trikoupis was ambassador to England. It was the elder Trikoupis who helped Brookes deliver letters and gifts to Velissariou, Theocharis, and Queen Amalia in 1860.[53] Brookes thought he might have some personal influence with the Greek prime minister. Brookes's letter is valuable for its timing, just before the congress, and for the way it links the earlier Zappas Olympics and Brookes himself to Coubertin's proposal for an Olympic revival. It proves that Brookes himself saw Coubertin's present Olympic activity as the culmination of all previous activity in the Olympic movement.

Dr. Brookes's letter to Trikoupis begins with reference to his own Olympic Games in Wenlock and praise for the idea of crowning modern victors with the olive crown, following "the noble and highly appreciated example of the ancient Greeks."[54] He then continues with the point—but he is addressing the wrong Trikoupis:

> My friend Baron Pierre de Coubertin of Paris, and the other advocates of physical education, myself among the numbers, are exerting ourselves to promote international Olympian festivals, and I earnestly hope they will be successful, and be honoured by the patronage by his Majesty, the King of the Hellenes. The remembrance of my correspondence with Sir Thomas Wyse ... and yourself relative to the Olympian Games at Athens in Nov. 1859 ... is a great pleasure to me.

The letter closes with a status report on the tree Brookes had planted for King George ("a flourishing condition") and stress on Brookes's "profound respect" for George, "your august sovereign." But it is unlucky that Brookes has the wrong Trikoupis. Praise for George was perhaps not so welcome to this Trikoupis as Brookes assumed. Trikoupis immediately gave Brookes's letter to Stephanos Dragoumis, head of the do-nothing

Olympic committee. Dragoumis, it seems, just filed it away and was done with it—an act that wholly accords with the way Dragoumis and Trikoupis later rebuffed Coubertin, trying to derail the international Olympic project and to prevent the 1896 Athens Olympics from taking place. We may be certain that Trikoupis did not hurry to the royal palace to seek the king's patronage for the games, as Brookes had obviously hoped.

Before we turn to the famous June 1894 Paris congress and the topic of those 1896 Athens Olympics, it is appropriate to summarize the events from January 1890 to June 1894 in list form. For so many things happened almost simultaneously in several places that a synoptic view helps to place each one in perspective.

January 1890: Coubertin, in *Revue Athlétique,* acknowledges receipt of papers from Brookes (early 1889, before his speech in June).

Early 1890: Coubertin is instrumental in founding the USFSA by merger.

April 30, 1890: Gennadius writes Brookes acknowledging recent letter and papers from Brookes.

June 22, 1890: Constantine proclaims resumption of Greek Olympics in a four-year cycle, Olympiad V, scheduled for Athens in 1892.

August 9, 1890: Coubertin writes Brookes, intending to visit him.

Mid-October 1890: Coubertin visits Wenlock.

December 25, 1890: Coubertin publishes his first account of that visit, "Les Jeux Olympiques à Much Wenlock."

April 21, 1891: Coubertin writes Brookes, declining invitation to attend the 1891 Wenlock Olympics but promising to send a medal.

May 1, 1891: Panhellenic Gymnastic Society holds first athletic games in Athens; it announces its intention to host Olympics.

1892: in Athens, the Olympic Games that Constantine announced for this year are not held.

July 20, 1892: Coubertin writes Brookes, explaining his plans for the November jubilee of the USFSA but making no mention of any intent to propose Olympic Games.

September 10, 1892: a Wellington newspaper publishes full history of Brookes and the Olympic movement, from Brookes's contact with Wyse and the Zappas Olympics of 1859 to his current efforts for international Olympic Games in Athens.

November 25, 1892: at jubilee of USFSA, Coubertin makes his first mention of his desire to revive the Olympic Games.

December 1892: Brookes writes Gennadius once again urging
Greece to help form international Olympic Games.

January 12, 1893: Gennadius writes Brookes, acknowledging his December letter and saying he will do what he can to spread
Brookes's cause and "movement" in Greece but fears Greece is
not ready.

May 14–15, 1893: second Panhellenic Games are held in Athens,
"under patronage of Prince Constantine," with Samaras's hymn
(and the 1896 IOC Games' athletes, Gouskos and Versis).

May 30, 1893: Brookes writes to Coubertin about sundry things,
still not knowing of Coubertin's 1892 proposal for an Olympic revival.

August 1, 1893: USFSA decides to hold a conference on amateurism.

Autumn 1893: Coubertin, in America, discusses a possible Olympic
revival with several Americans, including Sloane.

January 1894: Coubertin sends the flyer for 1894 congress (with the
eight-point program) to sports organizations in distant countries.

Early April (?) 1894: Coubertin asks Waldstein to communicate with
the Greek royal family concerning his Olympic revival plan.

Early April 1894: de Courcel agrees to preside over congress.

April 12, 1894: the Racing Club of Paris agrees to host the major
fête.

April 15, 1894: Waldstein, after long conversation with Greek
Crown Prince Constantine, writes Coubertin that Constantine
will be an honorary member of the congress.

Late April and May 1894: Coubertin sends ten-point version of invitation to many people in Europe.

May 23, 1894: Brookes writes Coubertin; he now has an invitation
to the congress, and encourages Coubertin in his rotation principle.

June 11, 1894: Brookes writes Trikoupis in Athens: "my friend . . .
Coubertin . . . [and I] are [promoting] international Olympian festivals."

June 13, 1894: Brookes writes Coubertin with advice on amateur
rules.

June 16, 1894: scheduled opening day for the congress.

EIGHT

The 1894 Paris Congress and D. Vikelas

Life is like a trip on a train, when we sit with our backs to the engine.
We preserve, more or less, our somewhat jumbled impressions of it all,
and we know in general what trip we have taken. But we never see
exactly where we are going, and do not know what obstacles the train
may meet, nor even how or if we will reach our destination. And all the
time we are riding toward the future, with our backs turned, turned
toward that invisible destination.

—*Demetrios Vikelas*, I zoi mou, *1908*

A few days before Brookes wrote the two letters with which the last chapter closed—in the last days of May 1894—a man in Paris received in his mail a package that transformed Olympic history. That man was Demetrios Vikelas, destined within three weeks to become the first president of the IOC. From Vikelas the line leads directly, through Coubertin, Brundage, and all the rest, to the present president, Juan Antonio Samaranch. Vikelas and his presidency are crucial to the history of the IOC and the modern Olympics. Without him, there might not have been any modern Olympics, at least not as we know them.[1] Yet until that fateful day in late May 1894, Vikelas had never had anything at all to do with athletics and had never heard of Coubertin nor his congress. How did such a man become the first IOC president? Who was this man, Vikelas? A full understanding of Coubertin's 1894 congress, the 1896 Olympic Games, and the early years of the IOC requires some background on its first president.

Demetrios Vikelas was a Greek, born in 1835 on the Greek island of Syros to a family with its roots in Constantinople.[2] Educated first in Greece, he migrated to London at the age of seventeen, to work in his uncles' business and to continue his education. Already fluent in English, French, and Greek, he learned German and Italian. He continued in the family's London business and married a woman from London's Greek community. There he also met the younger Trikoupis, Charilaos, son of the ambassador and later the chief opponent of Coubertin's Olympic plans in Greece. Trikoupis and Vikelas became good friends in London but eventually parted over politics; their relationship may have affected Olympic history. For a quarter of a century, from age seventeen to age forty-two, Vikelas lived in London managing his commercial affairs, which mainly concerned the marketing of grain. Although he never enjoyed the life of a businessman, he did become wealthy.

Vikelas's real love was literature. Throughout his life he produced many books and articles of various kinds in several languages. At sixteen he published a Greek translation of French playwright Racine and, in England, some Greek translations of Shakespeare, Milton, and Robert Burns. He then wrote a volume of his own original Greek poetry and an ambitious history of medieval Greece. The last received high praise from European reviewers, quickly earning Vikelas a place among belletrists. He wrote continuously on sundry topics for various journals, including articles about England (in Greek) and about Greece (in English). He published on political questions, on questions of language, on almost everything.

In 1876 Vikelas and his uncles closed their London business and moved it to Athens. But Vikelas lived in Athens only one year before expatriating again, this time to Paris where his chronically ill wife could get better medical care. He then abandoned business and turned wholly to literature. He translated more Shakespearean plays into Greek and wrote an original book of short stories in French and travel books on countries such as Sweden and Scotland. His own novel about the Greek War of Independence, *Loukis Laras*, was so well received that it was translated into virtually all European languages. That book's English translator was, in yet another coincidence, John Gennadius. There is much more to Vikelas's literary career, but the varied activity recounted above demonstrates Vikelas's obvious qualifications to serve in an international organization. But international athletics? The question now seems all the more puzzling: How did such a literary man become the first president of any athletic body, particularly of the IOC?

Vikelas himself tells the tale in a long-ignored article he wrote in Greek, "The International Olympic Games," from which I translate a portion.[3]

> One evening last June, the mailman brought me a package, from which I withdrew a certificate that made me a member of the Panhellenic Gymnastic Society. I knew absolutely nothing about this Society—and had not asked for membership, nor did I have any qualifications. The next morning the mailman, coming again, resolved my perplexity. He brought me a huge envelope,

containing a letter from the Society, asking me to represent it at the International Athletic Congress. It was an official document, accompanied by letters from friends of mine, members of the Society, requesting that I say "Yes"— and specifically *by telegram*, since the Congress was to begin in a few days. My first impulse was to say no. I did not even know that an International Athletic Congress was soon to meet in Paris. What did I have to do with athletics!

He did not say no. "How could I say 'no' to dear friends?" he asks. Vikelas does not name these friends; strangely, he sent his telegram response to—of all people—Alexandros Rangavis, who had thought athletics wholly out of date when Zappas first proposed an Olympic revival. Rangavis, whose role here is otherwise a mystery, had apparently recommended Vikelas's name as the Panhellenic representative in Paris. But Vikelas had other friends in the Panhellenic Gymnastic Society who perhaps could not act so publicly. The foremost members of the Panhellenic were the three princes of the Greek royal family, led by Crown Prince Constantine. At that time, as Coubertin said, the Panhellenic was "under the patronage of the Crown Prince. Prince George is the honorary President, and Prince Nicolas is an honorary member." Were Vikelas's friends headed by Constantine himself? The evidence seems to suggest it. The Greek prince was one of the few, along with Brookes, not likely to discourage Coubertin's Olympic designs. Constantine had hoped to hold Olympics in Athens in 1892. In April 1894 he had met with Waldstein and, at the least, agreed to honorary membership in Coubertin's congress; he was instrumental in the first IOC Games, in Athens in 1896. It was Waldstein, too, who told Coubertin to obtain a Greek representative for the congress.[4] Vikelas, a royalist who worked closely with Constantine on the 1896 Games, attended Coubertin's Paris congress.

The congress opened grandly, as the baron had planned, with an inaugural session chaired by de Courcel. For the occasion Coubertin had the noted composer Gabriel-Urbain Fauré adapt for a modern choir an ancient Greek hymn discovered only a few years before. Fauré apparently directed the presentation himself. Coubertin described the result: "The 2,000 people present listened with religious silence to the divine melody which lived again to salute the Olympic revival across the dimness of the ages."[5] The next day the delegates viewed bicycle races and tennis. Over the next several days, Coubertin kept them busy with athletic presentations, dinners, receptions, and visits to Parisian dignitaries. The high point was the night of entertainment *(fête de nuit)* on the evening of June 21 at the Racing Club grounds. There were numerous lanterns and even electric lights; many titled dignitaries, princes, counts, and marquesses, besides the delegates; footraces and displays of drill teams. The evening was capped off by a grand fireworks show, which climaxed with a display that "represented the two rings of the Union interlaced with the monogram of the racing club." (Thus fireworks at recent Olympiads, which show the five interlaced rings, are precisely in keeping with Coubertin's tradition.[6] After the elaborate closing fireworks display at the Los Angeles Olympic Games in 1984, some television reporters speculated that Coubertin would have been repulsed by its extravagance. On the contrary, he would have cheered. For he first had the idea.)

There were also conference meetings in the Sorbonne. After two plenary sessions, the delegates divided, according to their preference, into two committees. One was scheduled to forge a set of amateur rules; the other, to consider a revival of the ancient Olympic Games. Coubertin's friend Michel Gondinet was elected president for the amateurism committee, and his American friend William Sloane became its vice-president. For the Olympic committee, Vikelas's 1895 account, more detailed than Coubertin's, explains:

> Most of the delegates enlisted in the committee on "amateurism." But I enlisted in the other.... So we divided then into two different rooms of the Sorbonne, so that each committee could organize, choosing its president and secretary. Imagine my surprise, gentlemen, when, as if by previous agreement, many of those present proposed my name as president. Me! President of an athletic committee!

Vikelas's narrative so far is probably accurate enough. It is surprising indeed that Vikelas, who had never had anything to do with sports, should be chosen for so important a position as president of the committee on the revival of the Olympic Games. All other offices for the congress were filled with Coubertin's friends and sporting associates. Since Coubertin had arranged everything ahead of time, it seems likely that Vikelas's election was, in fact, "by previous agreement." But why, one wonders, of all available delegates, would Coubertin want Vikelas to head that committee? It is not certain that they had even met. Right after agreeing to represent the Panhellenic, Vikelas had called at Coubertin's house in hopes of finding out more details about the congress; but "unfortunately," he wrote to Rangavis, the baron "was not home."[7]

In his 1895 article, after relating the committee's deliberations on specific points, Vikelas turns to the main question. But it seems Vikelas does not tell all details exactly as they happened: "As to where the first games would be held, there had been a few imprecise ideas exchanged, but it was decided to postpone the question for a decision in the plenary meeting of the Congress."

The important question—how Athens was chosen as the site of the first international Olympics—remains a mystery to this day. There are several accounts, at least three from Coubertin and another from Vikelas. The difficulty is that each of these accounts differs from the others, and in general they are mutually exclusive. Even worse, all of them are contradicted by an even stronger witness, the minutes of the Olympic committee of that June 1894 congress. The minutes clearly suggest that the delegates, in fact, first voted for Olympic Games in London for 1896. Coubertin writes, "it had to be Athens"; the phrase "Athens, 1896" now rings as if predestined in our ears. The actual 1894 minutes make astonishing reading—difficult reading, as well. They exist in two different handwritten drafts in French, both dated June 19 and clearly written in great haste. Some portions are illegible to me, and at other places there are words or whole sections crossed out and overwritten.[8] But one can determine this much: many—probably most—of the delegates expressed a preference for London as the initial 1896 site; Coubertin, opposing London, proposed Athens, instead; when some delegates objected to Athens, the baron had the matter of choosing an initial site tabled to be considered later, at the final plenary session on June 23.

One version of the minutes once read: "[At] the first meeting, the opinion of the majority of delegates was in favor of London, but the question of the absence of Mr. Herbert, delegate from the British Amateur Athletic Union [illegible] the question was reserved to be [resolved?] at the general assembly of the Congress." This passage was later crossed out (perhaps days later) and replaced with these simple, decisive words in the margin: "at Athens in 1896 and at Paris in 1900." The other version clarifies several of these obscurities but adds a few more problems. For example, it reads "the opinion of some" where the first version says "of the majority":

> The opinion of some is that the first games could take place at London in 1896, the second at Paris in 1900. . . . As to the site of the first games, de Coubertin sees some difficulties in . . . choosing London. . . . He proposes to take . . . Athens. M. Duval objects that Athens is a bit outside the center of Europe, especially for the first meeting of the games. He proposes—and Viscount de La Rochefoucauld seconds his motion—to choose London. M. de Coubertin moves that the question be tabled until the arrival of Mr. Herbert, delegate of the British AAA; [motion to table] adopted.[9]

There can be no doubt but that there was a strong sentiment to schedule the first Olympics for London. A German journal article of 1894 proves the minutes accurate, that their mention of "London in 1896" is not an inexplicable aberration.[10] Yet no Olympic history—no version by Coubertin, Vikelas, or any source except the 1894 minutes themselves and the 1894 German article—makes any mention of the London motion. Knowledge of it was successfully suppressed for nearly a century. One wonders why.

The suppressed London motion proves wrong or misleading all published versions of the procedure by which Athens was chosen. Vikelas wrote that no precise discussion of a site had taken place at the June 19 meeting; that the idea of proposing Athens was all his own, original with him; and that he himself did not think of it until the evening (June 22) before the final congress meeting (June 23), when he proposed it in great fear that all the others present would ridicule it.[11] Vikelas's version is, in light of the June 19 minutes and his own June 19 note to Coubertin, patently false. It is, I fear, even a conscious misrepresentation of the facts.[12]

Coubertin gives confusing reports of the Athens choice, misleading Mandell and MacAloon into basic errors on this question.[13] Yet Coubertin's reports, in the main, tell the truth, with only slight inaccuracies. They confuse only because they seem to contradict one another. In his 1894 account Coubertin writes: "The choice of Athens was proposed by the delegate from Greece. Warmly supported by messieurs de Coubertin, Sloane, Gondinet, and de Villers, this proposition was adopted unanimously."[14] But in 1908 he suggested that Athens was first his own idea:

> After consulting with M. Bikelas about the resources which the Greek capital might present, we resolved he and I to propose it as the first site. I still keep this little note from the Greek delegate dated June 19: "Dear Baron de Coubertin: I did not see you after our session to tell you how touched I was by your proposal to start with Athens. I'm sorry that I could not support you more warmly."[15]

These two apparently conflicting and confusing reports make good sense when one determines that there were, in fact, two separate proposals of Athens. Several details of the historical truth remain obscure, but what is without doubt true is the following: Coubertin first made the Athens proposal in the smaller Olympic committee meeting on June 19, whereas Vikelas made the formal proposal at the final plenary session on June 23.

Vikelas's "little note," from which Coubertin quotes here, is dated June 19; it confirms what the June 19 minutes say; namely, that Coubertin proposed Athens at the June 19 Olympic committee meeting. That meeting is the very session which Vikelas's note mentions. But this little note bears importance far beyond merely confirming the minutes on Coubertin's June 19 Athens motion. Coubertin quotes only its first few lines, omitting all the rest. But the full note survives, and its ending is remarkable: "Mr. Criésis told me that your telegram was immediately sent to Athens."[16] This otherwise unknown telegram, sent from Coubertin to Athens on June 19, serves as the key to unlock much of the mystery of how Athens was chosen. Besides matters already mentioned, the choice of Vikelas as committee president and the suppressed London motion, there is still more to the mystery. The strangest thing of all is the case of King George's premature telegram. On June 21, Coubertin received a telegram from King George of Greece. It read: "With deep feeling toward Baron de Coubertin's courteous petition, I send him and the members of the Congress, with my sincere thanks, my best wishes for the revival of the Olympic Games. George."[17]

It was a very nice telegram, and Coubertin read it later to the assembled congress. The difficulty? The mystery? This telegram arrived a few days too early. It came on June 21, when the subcommittee on Olympics was still deliberating. The congress did not even vote to revive the Olympics until June 23.

In addition, for what did King George give Coubertin his "sincere thanks" on June 21? One would naturally assume it must be Coubertin's choice of Athens for 1896. Yet according to received Olympic history the delegates themselves had not even heard of—no one in Paris had even thought of—a proposal for a Greek site by that June 21 date; Vikelas first voiced it on June 23. And what was Coubertin's "courteous petition" King George refers to? Ordinary Olympic history knows of no such thing and simply cannot accommodate the king's telegram; it is too anomalous to fit anywhere.

Yet now, in light of Vikelas's "little note," much becomes clear: Coubertin's petition, to which King George refers in his own telegram of June 21, is certainly this other telegram, dated June 19, which Coubertin sent to Athens. Both were transmitted through the office of Mr. Criésis, Greek chargé d'affaires in Paris.[18]

We can reconstruct the events as follows. At the June 19 subcommittee meeting Coubertin's motion to begin with Athens ran into trouble. Vikelas, apparently surprised by the motion, balked. Others, pushing for London, objected to Athens. Coubertin moved to table and then went or sent to the office of Mr. Criésis. Criésis then transmitted that same day, June 19, a telegram from Coubertin to King George.

The contents of Coubertin's telegram are not known. But since he was otherwise occupied with holding the congress, he must have felt some urgency in sending it. And he sent it on the same day that he proposed Athens as the initial site. George called it a "petition" or "question" (*demande*). One would surely expect, then, that the telegram queried the king about Greece's willingness to host the first international Olympiad in 1896. Perhaps it went something like this: "Will you hold the Olympics in Athens, 1896?" But there is another possibility. Perhaps the gist of Coubertin's telegram was even, "Your Majesty—is our deal on or off?" Was it, even less probable, "What should I do?"

We must consider these possibilities; namely, that before Vikelas made his June 23 Athens proposal, even before the congress began to meet, Coubertin and the Greek royal family had some tentative agreement that Athens would host the first international Olympiad. That would clearly resolve a number of items that make up the mystery of the choice of Athens, which otherwise must remain an enigma. First, it would explain why the unlikely Vikelas was picked for the Olympic committee's president "as if by previous agreement." Second, it would explain why Coubertin, the Anglophile, forthwith rejected London, insisting on Athens and why the very existence of the London motion was covered up. Third, it would account for the wording of King George's telegram, including his premature "sincere thanks." If the King was thanking the congress for choosing Athens, perhaps Coubertin's telegram had not made it clear that this expected result, "Athens, 1896," had not yet taken place.

I am not the first to suspect something lurking behind the official IOC version of how Athens was chosen. Mandell writes, "It seems to me likely that there must have been some preliminary discussions before the motion at the last banquet. Coubertin . . . was unlikely to decide impulsively on the site and date of the first modern Olympic Games. The fact that the Greek king accepted the invitation at once suggests that Bikelas . . . had a mandate when he left for Paris and that Coubertin was aware of it and was prepared to act on it."[19] Yet the king was no more likely—all communication had been by telegram—"to decide impulsively" than Coubertin, even on June 21. And Vikelas never left for Paris. He was already there, and he himself insisted that he had no mandate. He claimed he acted all on his own, with no authorization from the Panhellenic or the Greek government to propose Athens.[20] He perhaps had no official mandate, certainly nothing that could be made public; had he such an official charge, he would have supported Coubertin's motion at the June 19 meeting. But on June 22, the day after the king's telegram and the day before he proposed Athens at the plenary session, Vikelas wrote Phokianos, "I expect opposition to the Athens proposal because of its remoteness; but I will try to uphold it, trusting that I rightly interpret the desire of the Society and all of Greece."[21] He still seems a little uncertain, at least for a nonconfidential message. If anyone in Paris was aware of a mandate when the congress began and "prepared to act on it" openly, it was Coubertin, not Vikelas.

There are, however, difficulties in assuming a prearranged choice of Athens. If some previous agreement dictated Vikelas's selection as committee president, one wonders why the directors of the drama cast him in a major role without giving him more of the script. Vikelas's note of June 19 suggests that Coubertin's own suggestion that day was the first Vikelas had heard of any Athens proposal. That is why he hesitated to support Coubertin. Perhaps some piece of communication went astray somewhere.

Another difficulty comes from Coubertin's reported original plan to begin the Olympics at Paris in 1900; he says the decision for 1896 arose only as the congress proceeded and six years seemed too long a wait.[22] But even if Coubertin did not at first intend to start in 1896, perhaps he changed his mind as early as April 1894, shortly before or after Waldstein's conversation with Constantine.

If there was a previous agreement, one can readily guess exactly when and where it was made: Waldstein's long meeting with Crown Prince Constantine and the Greek royal family in April 1894.[23] Coubertin placed high value on this conference. At no other time does he seem to have asked a friend to intercede on his behalf in this way. And, to adapt Vikelas's metaphor, history is one of the few travels we take where we can sit with our backs to the engine and still see the destination. Was it mere destiny that made Constantine later become president of our 1896 IOC Olympiad 1 Athens organizing committee? Or was it that the prince himself had been in that Olympic mood all along, ever since his announced Athens Olympiad of 1892 collapsed?

The greatest difficulty in any theory of a prearranged agreement is the lack of concrete proof. If the agreement did exist, one would expect to find some wholly compelling telltale mark, like the German article that confirms the London motion. I see no such conclusive item in the evidence so far available. But any prior agreement between Coubertin and the Greek royal family would have necessarily been confidential, not to be made public at the time.[24] I do not claim that any prearrangement is certain, though it remains highly probable.

NINE

The IOC
First Faltering Steps, 1894

Indeed as Victor Hugo put it, the whole civilized world has a common grandmother in ancient Greece, but we [Greeks] have her as our mother. So we are in a way the uncles of the rest of the peoples.

—*D. Vikelas, Paris congress, 1894*

Coubertin's Paris congress climaxed with a final plenary session at a sumptuous banquet, presided over by Baron de Courcel. An orchestra played during dinner. After dinner, Coubertin gave the first speech.[1] I quote some parts, which well reveal the baron's character, beliefs, and aims:

> If I look around me for the people to whom I should show my gratitude, on the evening of this congress which fulfills the hope of the first ten years of my adult life . . . [there are too many to name]. In this year 1894 and in this city of Paris, whose joys and anxieties the world shares so closely that it has been likened to the world's nerve center, we were able to bring together the representatives of international athletics. . . . And in the evening electricity transmitted everywhere the news that hellenic Olympism had re-entered the world after an eclipse of centuries.
>
> The Greek heritage is so vast, Gentlemen, that all who in the modern world have conceived physical exercise under one of its multiple aspects could legitimately refer to Greece, which contained them all. [But] . . . since the middle ages a sort of discredit has hovered over bodily qualities and they have been isolated from the qualities of the mind. . . . This was an immense error. . . . The adherents of the old school groaned when they saw us holding our meetings in the heart of the Sorbonne: they realized that we were rebels and that we would finish by casting down the edifice of their worm-eaten philosophy. It is true, Gentlemen, we are rebels and that is why the press . . . has understood and helped. . . . [I]f I were to go on, this gay champagne would evaporate with boredom; I therefore hasten to . . . lift my glass to the Olympic idea, which has traversed the mists of the ages like an all-powerful ray of sunlight and returned to illumine the threshold of the twentieth century with a gleam of joyous hope.[2]

Earlier that same day, Vikelas had proposed Athens as the first Olympic site.[3] As we saw, he had chaosed ged his mind since chairing the June 19 meeting at which he had not supported Coubertin's Athens motion. He had changed his mind that same day, within hours of that meeting. In the previous chapter, I cited the beginning of Vikelas's June 19 note, about Coubertin's Athens proposal, and its end, about sending the telegram to Criésis. The middle reads: "It did not occur to me until later that the celebration of the Olympic Games at Athens in 1896 could coincide with another Franco-Hellenic occasion. The French School is to celebrate its fiftieth anniversary and on that occasion one can expect to see many of the literary and scholarly celebrities of Europe. What do you think of this coincidence?"[4]

So by the evening of June 19, Vikelas, too, had chosen Athens as the initial site. His king's cautious but clear telegram response to Coubertin on June 21 had been the go-ahead signal Vikelas had waited for. At this final plenary session on June 23, Vikelas rose to make a stirring, patriotic plea on Greece's behalf.

> The next day [June 23] the Congress convened and first of all deliberated and voted on, one by one, the decisions of the other committee, the one on amateurism.—Later it became my own committee's turn—When we reached the undecided question: where would the first games take place, 1896, I asked for the floor. I claimed Greece's rights with regard to the re-establishment of a Greek Institution. Indeed, as Victor Hugo put it, the whole civilized world has a common grandmother in ancient Greece, but we [Greeks] have her as our mother. So we are in a way the uncles of the rest of the peoples. Here is our only advantage, if it is an advantage. Here is the source of my request that the restored Olympic Games be inaugurated on our Greek soil. . . . I said something along those lines.[5]

Coubertin completes the story: "The choice of Athens was proposed by the delegate from Greece. Warmly supported by messieurs de Coubertin, Sloane, Gondinet, and de Villers, this proposition was adopted unanimously."[6]

Contrary to common belief, Michel Bréal did not make his proposal for an Olympic marathon race on this final day of the congress, nor on any other, but Coubertin indeed persuaded the congress to approve Paris as the site of the 1900 Games and to endorse his nominations for the new international committee.[7] Its precise name was not yet the International Olympic Committee; it was the International Committee of the Olympic Games. Vikelas, by acclamation again, was chosen the first president;

Coubertin had decided that the presidency should always fall to someone from the next host country. After the 1896 Games, it would thus devolve upon Coubertin himself. For now, Coubertin took the post of general secretary, where he could exercise much power over the whole enterprise. The treasurer was M. Callot, Coubertin's friend from Paris.

The other IOC members were mainly names to put on the letterhead to give it an impressive and international flavor; some had attended the congress, others had not. They were General Boutowsky, of Russia; Jiri Guth, of Bohemia; Commandant Balck, of Sweden; Leonard Cuff, of New Zealand; and William Sloane, of the United States. Cuff's letters had strongly supported the baron's congress; Sloane was his close friend in America, who had given him personal help there. Also appointed were Dr. Zubiaur, of Argentina; C. Herbert and Lord Ampthill, of England; Franz Kemeny, of Hungary; and Count Lucchessi-Palli, of Italy. The last was soon replaced by Duke d'Andria Carafa, and Count Maxime de Bousies, of Belgium, was soon added.[8] Most of the work, it was understood, would be done by Coubertin and Vikelas.

Crown Prince Constantine of Greece lost no time. Coubertin writes: "Apart from the telegram [from King George] . . . the first commitment, semi-official if not official, for our project was brought us by a note from Lieut.-Col. Sapountzakis, aide de camp of the Crown Prince, addressed to Vikelas, July 3, 1894. 'The Crown Prince,' it said, 'learned with great pleasure that the Games will be inaugurated in Athens.'" The note went on to assure the IOC that "the King and the Crown Prince will confer their patronage on the holding of these Games."[9] Constantine later conferred more than that. He eagerly assumed presidency of the 1896 Athens organizing committee and organized the Games of our IOC Olympiad 1.

Coubertin, too, was quick to act, creating a new publication, the *Bulletin of the International Committee of the Olympic Games*. The first issue, dated July 1894, appeared—with some apology—only in French. It is obviously all Coubertin's own work and calls for all correspondence to be sent directly to him. The top of the first page of this first issue already bore the Latin motto, *Citius, Fortius, Altius* (Faster, Stronger, Higher). Coubertin then announced the journal's purpose: "[The *Bulletin*] will contain the official communications of the International Committee and will keep its readers up-to-date on everything that concerns the Work of the Re-establishment of the Olympic Games." After a list of the new committee's members came the headline "Athens, 1896," with a lengthy justification for the decision to begin in Athens and predictions of the Athens Games' success. Most of this first issue consists of an elaborate account of the June congress in Paris: the events leading to it, its program, a list of honorary members and official delegates (including those who did not attend in person), the various outings and receptions. The last page gives the results of the congress's decisions on the several questions of amateurism and the decision to revive the Olympic Games. There is a list of probable sports for the first celebration in Athens and notice of the 1900 Games for Paris and "thereafter every four years, in other cities of the world." We do not know how many copies of this first issue were printed. But Brookes received one in Wenlock.[10]

The plan was for Vikelas to go to Athens first, to begin negotiations with politicians there, and with Dragoumis's Zappas Olympic committee; for Vikelas assumed that it would form the basis of the Athens organizing committee. Coubertin was to follow soon.[11] On August 8, just before leaving Paris, Vikelas wrote Coubertin explaining the disposition of fifty copies of the *Bulletin:* fifteen to the Panhellenic, a number to Athens newspapers and Greek language papers in Trieste and New York, and others to various important Greeks, including Trikoupis and Dragoumis.[12] He also left the manuscript of an article for the next issue of the IOC *Bulletin*, to be published in October.

This second issue contains Coubertin's only post-1890 recognition of the Zappas Olympic Games. By 1908, the baron would even assert that no Zappas Games had ever taken place in Athens. Here, as editor, he publishes Vikelas's article, which presents the Zappas Olympics as a kind of harbinger of the 1896 IOC Games.

THE OLYMPIC GAMES
in the Past and in the Future

... This glorious name has already been revived in Athens. It was applied to contests in art, industry, and athletics funded by the generosity of two Greeks, Evangelis and Constantine Zappas, which were intended to take place every four years. The actual project is more vast. The Olympic Games, as now proposed, would extend their influence well beyond the ethnographic limits of Greece. All civilized peoples who are influenced by ancient Greece would take part.[13]

Soon after writing these words, Vikelas, as president of the IOC, left for Athens. But he stopped in Vichy. It was late September when he sailed from Brindisi, Italy, to Patras, Greece, and went on to Athens. On October 4 he wrote the baron a somewhat optimistic letter, saying that Greeks he met along his trip welcomed the Olympic Games. But the letter was not wholly optimistic. Vikelas noted some financial concerns in Athens. He had not yet met with Prime Minister Trikoupis. The king was in Denmark; the prince, not in Athens but in Tatoi, Greece, where the royal family had another home. Vikelas still hoped for good results from Dragoumis's committee. But the next day he wrote Coubertin another letter. He had met with Trikoupis, and Trikoupis "would have much preferred" that the question of Olympic Games had never arisen. Since it had, he "would do what was possible." But Trikoupis was very concerned about the financial question. Vikelas insisted that Coubertin's presence was absolutely necessary and pleaded with him to come soon. This letter ends, "It goes without saying that everything I write you is for you only, 'Private and Confidential.'" Coubertin easily perceived that this letter meant all was not going well.[14]

Perhaps Vikelas was not, after all, the best messenger to approach Trikoupis for help in hosting the Olympic Games. Long ago in London, the two men had been friends; and after Trikoupis left England in 1865, they corresponded. But their once cordial friendship had, over the years, noticeably gone cold. The source of their disagreement was Greek politics. Trikoupis had immersed himself in an active political life and was often an outspoken critic of the king and the monarchy in general. Vikelas, generally a royalist, disapproved of this side of Trikoupis's politics and several times openly criticized Trikoupis's political policies and stands. By 1894 there was an outright rift between the two old friends.[15]

Vikelas sought to convene Dragoumis's Olympic committee at the Zappeion, still hoping it would function as the basis for organizing the 1896 Games. He also hoped for Coubertin's immediate arrival. But on October 14, before Coubertin came, even before his meeting with the Olympic committee took place, Vikelas received a telegram with bad news from Paris. His wife's health had taken a turn for the worse, and she was probably dying.[16] Vikelas hurried back to Paris, penning a brief letter to Dragoumis as he left.[17] Arriving in Paris on October 20, he had little time to confer with Coubertin. For Vikelas wished to be at his wife's bedside, and Coubertin was soon to leave for Athens. Yet they met briefly, at least once.[18]

Vikelas gave Coubertin a letter of introduction, addressed to Dragoumis and dated October 20, asking that Dragoumis welcome his French friend. And on October 22 he himself wrote Dragoumis, asking him to share the letter with Trikoupis. In this letter Vikelas explains that, although his wife is very ill, he feels compelled to write Athens on behalf of Coubertin and the Olympics. He says that he met with Coubertin and reported their (Trikoupis's and Dragoumis's) reluctance to hold the games. "I tried to convince [Coubertin] to postpone his journey to Athens, but it was impossible. He believes the reasons for cancelling the first Olympic games are insufficient. He will try to convince you and I agree with him."[19]

Vikelas predicts (as was the case) that wealthy Greeks abroad would solve the financial problems. But Vikelas's letter did not move Dragoumis, and Dragoumis would not wait for Coubertin. Before the baron arrived in Athens, Dragoumis convened the Zappas Olympic Committee, which then decided to have no part in Olympic Games.

On November 1, Dragoumis wrote a long, official letter to Coubertin, telling him not to bother coming, that Greece could not hold Olympic Games. He gave reasons: Greece was in the midst of a financial crisis and had no money to host the Games. Despite Greece's ancient Olympic tradition, he said, "the exact notion of what you call 'Athletic Sports' " did not yet exist in modern Greece. Dragoumis told the baron to wait for Paris in 1900 to hold the first international Olympic Games—to forget about Greece. That is Dragoumis's clear message. I need quote no more here; Coubertin himself published this letter, and its full text is now well known.[20]

Coubertin was already on his way to Athens. He and the letter crossed en route between Athens and Paris. The baron arrived in Athens on November 8.[21] When immediately handed a copy of Dragoumis's November 1 letter of rejection, he wrote a reply. He spent the next day handing out his business card and seeking to meet with the Zappas Olympic committee. But the following day, November 10, he was visited at his hotel by Trikoupis, who hoped to dissuade him at the outset.[22] He spoke firmly against the idea of 1896 Olympics in Athens and told the baron that he himself would see that Greece could not host the Games. But Coubertin was not dissuaded. In fact, he was encouraged by an Athens more modern than he expected and by the widespread support for the Olympic Games expressed by the Greek public and in the press.

Over the next several days he met twice with Prince Constantine. Those meetings gave Coubertin much encouragement, for Constantine seemed "definitely on our side." He talked with several other Greeks favorably disposed to the Games and probably with Dragoumis. He also watched with interest the press reports on the controversy of holding the Games. He took especial delight in a political cartoon wherein Trikoupis boxed with his political opponent, Deliyannis, over the question of Olympic Games.[23] On November 16, at the invitation of some new Greek friends, N. Politis and S. Lambros, Coubertin gave a stirring speech promoting the Games at a meeting of the Parnassus Literary Society. There, in order to allay the financial objections voiced by Trikoupis, the baron gave a very low estimate of the cost of holding the Games, suggesting a total budget of about one hundred fifty thousand francs, or two hundred fifty thousand drachmas.

He also made a ringing appeal to Greek patriotism. Apparently Dragoumis's claim that Greece had no notion of "Athletic Sports" allowed Coubertin at least to feign a belief that some Greeks were turning down the Games for fear their athletes would lose. To diffuse that supposed objection to his plan, he first said he "would not bet two drachmas" that Greek athletes would not win some Olympic crowns. Coubertin's Jesuit education had given him excellent training in rhetoric, and he knew very well to play the patriotism card in the fiercely proud new Greek nation. Here he saw his opening. He probably looked several members of his intent Greek audience in the eye as he shot out a reminder and a challenge:

> Finally, Gentlemen, did your fathers carefully weigh their chances of victory before rising up against the Turks? If they had, you here would not be free men this very moment. Those are considerations one simply does not examine; they are unworthy of you!
>
> When we had begun to play football matches against the English, we expected to lose. But the seventh time we played them, we beat them. . . . Dishonor here would not consist of being beaten; it would consist of not contending.[24]

This rhetoric impressed the baron himself so much that he later returned to that last sentence, transforming it only slightly, until it became something of a creed for his Olympic movement: "The important thing in the Olympic Games is not winning but taking part." Every four years we hear—more than any other phrase associated with the modern Olympics—variations on that theme from this 1894 Parnassus Society speech.[25]

Coubertin correctly saw that it was a successful speech, rallying more Greeks to his side. Sometime within the next two days Coubertin again met with Trikoupis, who still refused to cooperate. The baron did, however, ask for and receive a pledge of neutrality from the prime minister, who agreed not to oppose Coubertin actively if the baron proceeded on his own. "He promised it—not without mental reservations, I am sure."[26] At the same time Coubertin obtained permission to hold an organizing meeting at the Zappeion. He wrote a letter to the editor of the newspaper *Asty*, which had also published his Parnassus Society speech. In the letter he announced Trikoupis's pledge not to interfere and his permission to use the Zappeion. "A committee will soon be formed which will make a call to your compatriots to cover the expense." Coubertin closed by resorting to his rhetorical training again and throwing out another challenge to the Greeks: "In our country we have a proverb that says the word *impossible* is not French; someone told me this morning that it was Greek. I do not believe anything of the kind."[27]

On November 19, Coubertin again wrote Dragoumis, telling the president of the Zappas Olympic committee that Trikoupis had agreed not to interfere and had given him permission to hold a meeting in the Zappeion. Coubertin again sought Dragoumis's help. That very day Dragoumis sent the baron's letter to Trikoupis, asking what he should do; Trikoupis answered that Dragoumis should come to his office.[28] Unfortunately, there is no record of their conversation in that office. Two days later Coubertin met with Dragoumis—and again with Prince Constantine.[29] Constantine agreed to cooperate in every way and to serve as honorary president of the new committee. But Dragoumis refused to be a member of the committee, even refused to be present as the baron sought to organize a committee. Apparently he did, however, give Coubertin some names of prospective committee members.

All this is made clear in yet another letter that Coubertin addressed to Dragoumis on November 22. This previously unknown letter has such remarkable historical importance that I quote portions. It is prominently marked "Confidential" across the top.[30] The letter begins, "I have called together, for Saturday at 2 o'clock at the Zappeion, the people whose names you gave me." The letter goes on to broach sensitive political questions and other matters:

> A scruple occurs to me, and I tell you about it confidentially. The Crown Prince, who received me again yesterday, has accepted the honorary presidency of the committee. But what are the relations of Mr. Deliginge—about whom you and I spoke yesterday for the presidency—with the royal family? Are they not very bad since the incident of minister Deliyannis's recall? I'm relying on you for this, asking you to guide me. I will also ask you to come to the Zappeion Saturday, even though you do not want to take part in the committee, that you may help me a bit to [illegible; introduce?] myself in front of those who attend.

The letter closes by expressing Coubertin's hope to visit Mrs. Dragoumis very soon ("today or tomorrow") and other personal but formal niceties.

Vikelas had perhaps misjudged the political situation and especially his own relationship with Trikoupis. But Coubertin, fully aware of political tensions in Athens, misjudged Dragoumis's own personal politics even more. Dragoumis was no doubt the next to last person in Athens (Trikoupis being the last) to whom the baron should have confided sensitive political questions concerning Deliyannis, the royal family, and especially any mention of Prince Constantine. As we shall soon see, Dragoumis was Trikoupis's strongest political ally, and Constantine was Trikoupis's worst political enemy. And Dragoumis, like Trikoupis, was a firm enemy of the Games. The same letter even suggests that Dragoumis had recommended to Coubertin names of Trikoupis's people who would oppose the prince and the Games; others, Coubertin observes, were out of town. Dragoumis, I think, clearly intended to sabotage the baron's plans.

On the next day the *Nea Ephemeris* printed an article reporting the forthcoming meeting of the Olympic committee at the Zappeion to deal with the question of international Olympic Games; Coubertin had predicted the cost would only be about 125 thousand drachmas.[31]

One day later, on November 24, at the Zappeion, a meeting indeed took place.[32] Dragoumis came but stayed only long enough to introduce Coubertin to the others present, who numbered about thirty-two. He then quickly left, to disassociate himself from anything that took place at the meeting.[33] The baron presented the assembly a program for the Games, which he had drawn up before leaving Paris. He soon announced to this group of Trikoupians—and a few new friends whom he had invited on his own, including A. Mercatis (Constantine's friend since childhood) and G. Melas—that the crown prince would be their president. The title of Honorary president mentioned in Coubertin's letter to Dragoumis was gone. Coubertin and other reports about the meeting clearly state that Constantine's presidency was now real, not an honorary title or figurehead.[34] That fact alone probably alienated many of Trikoupis's supporters from the start. The baron then declared the men present in the room the Athens Olympics 1896 organizing committee. Four vice presidents were chosen, led by S. Skouloudis. Mercatis and Melas were named joint secretaries of the committee. Coubertin took the results of the meeting to Constantine, who approved it all.[35] Thinking his work now done, the baron prepared to leave Athens.

First, however, on November 27—as reports of the meeting and Prince Constantine's presidency appeared in the papers—Coubertin was the guest of honor at a dinner hosted by the Panhellenic Gymnastic Society.[36] The next morning he left Athens for Patras in the northwestern Peloponnesus, the port city for ferries to Italy. In Patras he was welcomed by another Greek athletic club, the Panachaean Athletic Society, which supplied him with a personal guide to visit ancient Olympia the next day. Thus on the morning of November 29, Coubertin, for the very first time, entered the site of the ancient games, "this city of dream," as he had called it—the ancient city that had so entranced his "adolescent mind," he claimed, that it led him, independently of Brookes, to the idea of reviving the Olympic Games.[37]

Much later he wrote of that first visit to Olympia: "We arrived there in late evening. I had to wait for dawn to see the outlines of the sacred place, of which I had so often dreamed. All morning long I wandered among the ruins." One morning seems a rather brief first visit for a man who claimed his life's work had been inspired by this sacred spot. The site is hard to examine so quickly. Coubertin did not feel compelled to return to Olympia again until 1927, when he attended a special ceremony, held in his honor, celebrating the revived Olympic Games.[38] Yet Coubertin somehow felt so attached to the site that he left instructions that his heart be cut from his body after his death and entombed separately at ancient Olympia.[39] The symbolism is obvious; but it is still surprising that he spent so few of his living hours at the scene of such inspiration.

From Patras, Coubertin crossed to Italy, then traveled on to Naples to visit his friend, the Duke d'Andria Carafa. There, on December 7, he gave a speech on the Olympic revival to the Naples Philological Circle. He felt the speech did not go over well: "Far from the harmonies of the Hymn to Apollo and from the silhouette of the Parthenon, to evoke the Olympic Games apparently lacked any power." His summary metaphor seems especially apt; after the speech, he said, he was left "with a feeling of having thrust a sword into water."[40] Yet back in Athens things were going even worse. By then, December 7, all Coubertin's efforts in Athens had already evaporated.

TEN

Politics, Trade Unions, and Wedding Bells, 1894–1895

The History of the World is but the Biography of great men.
—*Thomas Carlyle*, Heroes and Hero Worship, *1841*

At the very moment that Coubertin wandered the ruins of Olympia, his Athens organizing committee was disintegrating. By the time he reached Naples, the committee had dissolved itself, due to politics. In Greece, politics are pursued so earnestly that the language has a special verb, *politevomai*, meaning to engage in politics. Many members of the committee, including Skouloudis, the foremost vice president, belonged to Trikoupis's political clique.[1] As soon as Coubertin left town, they met, decided Athens should not host the Games, and resigned en masse.[2] Drafting a report stating that they judged it impossible to hold the Games, they attached their formal resignations and submitted the package to Prince Constantine on December 6. But Constantine tossed it in a drawer, saying he would consider it at his leisure.[3] Eager for Athens Olympics ever since 1890, Constantine had firmly decided Athens would host the first international Olympic Games in 1896.

On the same day, the Greek Parliament held a long, often acrimonious, debate over the question.[4] Full details would be of great interest to students of Greek politics, of international law, and of the 1896 Olympics themselves. Here I recount only what bears on our specific subject, the revival of the Olympic Games.

Speakers' opinions divided, pro and con, along political lines. Trikoupis's supporters spoke against the Games and generally tried to thwart those who favored holding them. Those who favored hosting the Games generally belonged to the opposition party of former Prime Minister Th. Deliyannis. When strongly pressed by Mr. Papamikhalopoulos as to what the Zappas Olympic committee was doing about the Games, Dragoumis finally snapped back, "the Olympic Committee has nothing to do with the international games." Trikoupis, when grilled even harder about what the government was doing, finally spoke: "[A]ccording to the newspapers, the Government has not undertaken the organization and expense of the games." These glib replies and that of Skouloudis—who explained that the organizing committee had decided to dissolve itself—exasperated some members of Parliament. After Trikoupis spoke, Mr. Zygomalas interjected:

> So, the matter is reduced to a joke, when it is an extremely serious question. ... While today the whole world thinks that the Games will take place in Greece, while the eyes of the entire civilized world, with inquisitiveness and interest, are turned on us—the descendants of those who first founded the Olympic Games—the government of the place works against it, the Olympic Committee loses all its courage, and the organizing committee is ready to commit suicide.

He cited Coubertin's much smaller estimate against Skouloudis's six hundred thousand drachmas and predicted that many Greeks, rich and poor, would contribute money. He then invoked the memory of Zappas: "The Olympic Committee and above all the government have every right to use some of the money left by the memorable Zappas, whose desire and main intention was that Games like this be celebrated in Greece." Dragoumis shot back a curt, one-sentence reply: "There is none."[5]

Zygomalas was not the only delegate to enlist Zappas's name on Coubertin's behalf. Mr. Evtaxias's speech, too, saw the baron and Zappas as coworkers on a single idea, to bring Olympic Games to Greece. Had it not been for Zappas, the Athens Games of 1896 surely would not have taken place. Zappas's actions, his will, and the previous tradition of Zappas Olympic Games had made Constantine an advocate of Olympic Games before the formation of the IOC in 1894. Many Greeks had the Olympic desire implanted in them long before Coubertin came to Athens. And men such as Zygomalas, who wanted the international games there now, could—and did—appeal to Zappas's aspirations and bequest as precedent for Coubertin and Vikelas's renewed attempt to revive the Olympics. They became open advocates of Coubertin's plan because they saw it as a major step fulfilling the previous Zappas Olympic tradition. It was not merely a strange new notion imported by a Frenchman.

When Dragoumis claimed there were no Zappas funds anymore, there ensued a long discussion of Zappas's money, his will, and the finances of his recently deceased cousin, Konstantinos. Dragoumis insisted there was no money available, while the Olympic supporters argued the contrary. It is true that, when Konstantinos died, the Romanian government seized the holdings and capital still in Romania, triggering a celebrated case in international law. But there was now also Zappas money and land in Greece, which Konstantinos's will left to the Greek government. Complex details have no relevance here. But it may be of interest that (according to William Sloane, his American friend) Coubertin (aided by his and Constantine's friend, A. Mercatis), induced the Greek government eventually to appropriate some Zappas money for the 1896 Games.[6]

In Naples the next day Coubertin gave his speech, feeling as if he had "thrust a sword into water." He did not then know of the deteriorating state of affairs in Athens; but he later received an accurate report of the December 6 Greek Parliament debate.[7] That debate did nothing to change the minds of Trikoupis, Dragoumis, and Skouloudis, but it did further inflame the Olympic desires of the Greek people. During the next few days, while the question itself was at an impasse—apparently in Prince Constantine's drawer—the Athenian press printed letters to the editor on the topic. One called the three main Olympic opponents' comments "extremely sad," a "renouncing of all the expectations." It emphasized how eagerly the crown prince wanted to host the Games and concluded "The world is observing all these things." Another said that some unnamed "patriots" intended to ask Constantine to form a new organizing committee. It stressed the international features of the proposed Games and the author's desire that Olympic Games now, as in classical Greece, be held in the stadium. In late December the status of the Olympic question remained unchanged. "Great sorrow," one letter said, had come to Greece and Athens, "the city of Pericles," because it now appeared that the Olympic Games would not be celebrated.[8]

Soon, however, on Christmas Day, Demetrios Vikelas returned to Athens, having buried his wife in Paris. He sought to pick up the pieces, to salvage the embattled Olympic proposal. The next day he held a news conference to promote the idea of holding the Games, and on December 28 he met with Trikoupis again, hoping their former friendship might persuade the prime minister to stop opposing the Games.[9] Perhaps encouraged by his presence, more private donors pledged money to the Olympics, and athletic clubs banded together to lobby for the Games.[10] Vikelas conferred with Constantine, too, and by January 7, 1895, was able to give a status report to the press. He announced that the crown prince had accepted the presidency of the organizing committee and believed it was possible to hold the international Games. The basic financial plan was to trust in the patriotism of the Greek people. Foreigners would indeed compete in Athens. Vikelas added that Athens must have the first IOC Games; otherwise, they might never again occur in Greece.[11]

In those last days of December and the first few days of January 1895, Vikelas was, with Constantine, feverishly working behind the scenes to form a new organizing committee. He also eagerly awaited news and instructions from Coubertin. On January 10 he wrote the baron in Paris, reporting the progress in Athens but also begging Coubertin to fulfill his promises to help: "Here now yet another mail delivery arrives without a word from you. It's becoming disturbing. I've been here 15 days and haven't got a message of four words from you. If the next mail brings nothing again, I don't know to what extremes I might go. . . . You understand, don't you, that everything is going very well here." He explained about the new committee: it would have an administrative council of ten to twelve people; Timoleon Philemon, former mayor of Athens, had agreed to serve as its secretary-general; the president, Prince Constantine, would soon convene a meeting of the new organizing committee, whose members were already chosen. "[T]he committee is already formed. I consider that part of my mission achieved. As for the money, it will be found. People are not going to let the Crown Prince expose himself to a checkmate. . . . I'm waiting for the velodrome plans from you. . . . But you must come to my aid. Write me." [12]

On January 14, he wrote, "Again the mailman and no letter. If I don't get anything by tomorrow morning, I'll begin moving." Vikelas explains that he has an appointment the next day to see Philemon and to arrange a meeting with the crown prince to submit the plans for the stadium. "I'm waiting impatiently for the plans and specifications that you would want for the velodrome, I'm waiting for answers to my various questions—what don't I wait for? And nothing comes! Not even any copies of the first number of the *Bulletin*. Nothing!" [13] Vikelas continued to shower the baron with letters, always asking him to take a more active role in the preparations.

Coubertin himself says, "During January and February 1895 the letters from Vikelas came three times a week. His zeal and his activity exerted themselves beyond calculation." The baron also acknowledges that Vikelas kept asking him for the velodrome plans, made suggestions for the formal invitations to athletic clubs, and spoke of other matters. [14] Finally, on January 17, Vikelas received a letter from Paris explaining the baron's inattention to matters Olympic: he was distracted by making plans for his coming marriage. [15]

Sentiment for holding the Games had been growing for weeks. The previous day, January 16, Vikelas had met—at their sudden invitation made on that date—with the heads of the Athenian trade unions to discuss

Olympic Games. In a powerful, impromptu patriotic speech, Vikelas seemed to convince one and all that the Games should be held. It was a kind of triumph for the translator of Shakespeare—who here quoted Homer to men from the working class. He closed with a rousing, challenging appeal that workingmen act in lieu of their reluctant leaders:

> Think how much an influx of tourists might benefit you. We now have an excellent, unexpected opportunity. Let's take advantage of it. If doubts from our side should become known, they could offend the tourists. You men— make the good beginning. Work together within your trade unions—only there—as much as you can and quickly, in order to be the first. Present it— for the success of the affair—and you will thus demonstrate the power and significance of the trade unions.

His strategy worked. Now virtually all the general populace of Athens was on his and Coubertin's side. "Thus thanks to Vikelas's presence in Athens the situation relative to the Games changed completely 'from one day to the next.' "[16] Much more changed soon, partly, in fact, due to the working public's pro-Olympic sentiment.

Trikoupis's economic policies were not working, and he had just announced a plan to raise taxes. On January 20, just four days after Vikelas's speech to the trade unions, Trikoupis's opponents assembled in a mass rally in Athens's Ares Park to protest against Trikoupis's actions. There, suddenly, a nearly unthinkable event took place: Crown Prince Constantine appeared, mounted on horseback and with a security guard; he commanded the chief of police not to break up the anti-Trikoupis rally.[17]

Trikoupis was, of course, incensed by the prince's independence and his daring, almost hostile, action. He immediately demanded that King George chastise his errant oldest son. George declined. All the more angry, on January 22 Trikoupis submitted his resignation to the king. George accepted it.[18] Two days later he appointed N. Deliyannis as his new prime minister. He was soon replaced, in the elections of April 1894, by T. Deliyannis, who was already accustomed to trading that post off and on with Trikoupis. But this time Trikoupis would not return.

Once Trikoupis's government was out, Constantine pursued his own Olympic plans. He lost no time. On January 24, as the new prime minister assumed office, the crown prince called a meeting of the new Olympic organizing committee for the next day at the Zappeion. Thus on January 25 a new committee was indeed formed. It was immediately a fait accompli. Vikelas's letters to Coubertin prove that he and the crown prince had been working out the details for weeks in advance. The committee was just as Vikelas had written Coubertin two weeks earlier. Constantine was president, and Philemon the secretary-general. The administrative council of twelve men was appointed. The prince also appointed a treasurer and four more secretaries. Two of these, Coubertin's friends Melas and Mercatis, were holdovers from the original November committee. Constantine had agreed to place on the new committee anyone from the original committee who chose to recant his resignation. In his speech at this same meeting he announced he would ask the trade unions to nominate a member, since they "so willingly expressed their desire to contribute to the success of the International Olympic Games."[19]

The next day the press reported on the meeting and the new committee. The *Nea Ephemeris* noted Prince Constantine's speech and said that things had begun well for the revival of the Olympic Games. Constantine's rather long speech was indeed a clarion call to that task. But its eloquence did not come from its seemingly impromptu delivery. The speech had been written well ahead of time, in anticipation of the happy occasion. In Paris, in fact, Coubertin had received a copy of that speech from Vikelas long before the prince delivered it in Athens.[20] The *Nea Ephemeris* article reported that the Paris congress had chosen Greece as the first place for the revival of the Games, that Greece had responded gratefully and heartily, and that there was little time left. From this point on, the new Athens organizing committee was functional, working hard, quickly, and effectively to organize the Games.

Coubertin seems not to have shared the Greeks' sense of Olympic urgency. On January 17, 1895, Vikelas had at last received a letter from Coubertin, in which the baron told him his plans to get married. But Vikelas was not the first Olympian to know. Coubertin first informed Dr. W. P. Brookes in Wenlock—why he wrote Brookes first is unclear. International Olympics in Athens were originally Brookes's own suggestion, but Coubertin did nothing else to recognize his priority. Inexplicably, the baron's letter to Brookes must have been written in Olympia or Naples, as the first organizing committee in Athens was disbanding. For on December 11, 1894, from Wenlock, Brookes wrote the baron, in Paris, a long, remarkable letter.

Dear Baron Coubertin,

The pleasure which I always derive from your letters was greatly enhanced by the information contained in your last that you were about to be married. . . . I must ask a favour from you, viz., that you will write a week before your marriage and tell me on what day it will take place, as I wish to invite a few friends to dine with me, and to drink to the health and happiness of yourself and your bride.[21]

Brookes eagerly invites the newlyweds to visit him in Wenlock and observe the 1895 Wenlock Olympics. He praises Coubertin's work on the Olympic Games. Brookes again stresses the Olympics' potential as an agent for world peace, fully agreeing with the baron's own emphasis: "I earnestly hope . . . that you will be successful in all your noble efforts for the promotion of the welfare of your Country and the benefit of other Nations, efforts which cannot fail to promote a friendly feeling and a desire for peace among the civilized nations of the earth." Brookes took a keen interest in the current Olympic developments, which he still viewed in much the same terms as he had himself first imagined them. Though he gave Coubertin the credit, he must have taken some pride in the progress of what he had conceived and again called the Olympic movement.

> I am looking forward . . . to the receipt of the next *Bulletin* respecting the International Olympian Association and the arrangements for the first festival at Athens. The Greek Government should, I think, gladly acquiesce in the honour France wishes to confer upon Greece by holding the first festival at Athens, which will be a mark of the respect and good feeling towards Greece of all the nations which have joined in the movement.

Brookes congratulates the baron on his ability "to organize a splendid international institution"—and expresses the wish that he "were 20 years younger, i.e. only 65 instead of 85; how pleased and proud I should have felt to have been one of your Lieutenants. I hope, however, that I shall live long enough to rejoice in the success of your patriotic and philanthropic undertaking."[22] The letter closes with some practical advice as to how Coubertin might get "the wealthy Greeks in England" to contribute money to the 1896 Games.

Coubertin surely gained some pleasure from such encouraging words of praise from Wenlock, but there is no indication that he answered Brookes's letter. His pen became rather dry. The next month Vikelas often begged Coubertin to write him and to take a more active role in the preparations in Athens. Vikelas, when he received his letter from Paris announcing the wedding—on January 17, in the midst of his own work in Athens—responded with mixed joy and fear. He was joyous to learn that Coubertin was soon to be married;[23] but he expressed fear that the marriage plans were distracting the baron from his role in the Olympics. He complains of Coubertin's inattention to that matter and of the difficulties he experienced in performing his own role. He tells the baron about his January 16 speech to the trade unions, then writes:

> What a business you make me carry out. And you leave me without help. Write me more fully; your fiancée won't [illegible; begrudge?] me that. She will have pity on the poor mortal that you have [illegible; made?] president. What a job! I understand why presidents submit their resignation. But I really don't understand this one of yours. That took me by surprise and I am full of worries. What will happen in France? I impatiently await further messages.

The letter closes, "I write you in haste. I am in a moment due for a meeting with the Crown Prince. . . . I will submit to him the plans for the stadium. Next week the Committee will begin to function. At least I hope so."[24]

As we saw above, the committee did begin to function then. But in the following weeks Vikelas did not get much help or further information from Coubertin. He repeatedly wrote to Paris asking the baron for information and begging him to take a more active role in organizing the 1896 Games. He also earnestly requested that Coubertin return to Athens to help in person during the winter of 1895–96.[25] But Coubertin did not come, and he did very little for the actual preparation of the Games. Rather reluctantly, it seems, he eventually did take care of some small matters, such as getting a design for the Olympic medals and drafting the format of the official invitations to potential participants that the Greeks should send. Coubertin's inertia at this time, obvious in Vikelas's letters, is in the main confirmed by the baron's own account.[26]

As secretary, Coubertin was expected to do much more, especially to get commitments of participation from various national teams. But in almost all cases, his efforts were wholly lacking, bungled, or too late. In the end, only Hungary and the United States sent national teams of any size, more the work of Kemeny and Sloane than of Coubertin. In France, Coubertin managed to form a national Olympic committee on paper but could not foster any significant desire or support for participation in the Athens Olympics.

Both Brookes and Coubertin thought England and its universities would be strong sources of many athletes for the initial international Olympiad. But the baron's attempts to recruit athletes in England were remarkably inadequate and much too late. On February 7, Vikelas wrote him about formation of national Olympic committees. Sloane, he said, could form a good committee in America, and Mr. Alexander, U.S. ambassador in Athens, was in contact with Sloane:

As for the English Committee, we must get Professor Jebb on it. They write me from Oxford that he would be a very important connection. [He then quotes, in English:] If there is any sort of committee which he can be asked to join, I should urge you to do it without delay. Whether he joins or not he will be more sympathetic for having been asked. . . . If he joins you have a most necessary helper in the University world [end of English passage] at Oxford as well as Cambridge. Please send him the enclosed letter, and send him numbers of the *Bulletin*.[27]

But apparently Coubertin did not write Jebb. The invitation the Cambridge Athletic Club later received was in German. And at Oxford, the Olympic announcements were so inconspicuous that one student stridently complained:

> [N]o edition of the rules was ever issued in English until shortly before the games, when a private firm produced one. . . . What was done to persuade Oxford and Cambridge men to compete in the Olympic Games? Practically nothing. . . . An obscure notice, indeed was posted up in Oxford and a paragraph inserted in an unimportant Oxford journal, but it was not till March . . . that any direct appeal was made to the . . . University Athletic Clubs. Even then the inducements and persuasion directed to them were of the mildest nature. . . . When an athletic meeting is scarcely advertised at all. . . .[28]

The day after writing his February 7 letter, Vikelas finally received another letter from Coubertin, dated February 2. But its focus was apparently not the recruitment of foreign athletes to compete in the Games. Its main concern must have been Coubertin's suspicion that his own name might not be prominent enough in the Athens preparations and newspapers. In responding, Vikelas feels compelled to begin his letter by reassuring the baron on that matter and writes that he encloses newspaper clippings of two items issued by the Olympic committee and "published in all the newspapers. . . . You will see that your name figures in both of them. Be totally assured on that subject. Your name is always spoken. People know that you are the founder."[29]

Thus, the baron's suspicions of the Greeks appeared at the outset. Yet Vikelas's letters are enough to disprove Coubertin's claims—accepted later by other Olympic historians—that the Greeks methodically excluded Coubertin and all mention of his name from their preparations. The question whether or not the Greeks ignored Coubertin has little relevance to the story here; but Coubertin's inactivity is relevant, because it explains why few nations sent athletes to Athens in 1896. Why did Coubertin seem to lose interest in the Olympics at this most crucial time, from December 1894 until well into 1896? And Vikelas's January 17 letter has raised another bothersome question: did Coubertin in fact seek to resign from the IOC just as preparations for IOC Olympiad 1 got underway?

MacAloon has asked the first question and perceived most of the answers. "Why through all of these potentially fatal difficulties did Coubertin remain in Paris?" At other times, he notes, the baron would go abroad and "flatter, cajole, inspire, and manipulate" to achieve his aims; that "the recruitment of teams and tourists" would probably have succeeded better had Coubertin carried on his normal public relations, calling meetings, making press releases, and such things. MacAloon wonders why he did not seek support in England, at least. The answer: "[B]ecause there were other strong claims upon his attention during these fifteen months."[30]

These other claims were two: first, Coubertin was married on March 12, 1895; second, he was busy writing a book on French history in 1895 and the first part of 1896. At first, one can scarcely believe that Coubertin would occupy himself writing a history book throughout the actual preparations for the first IOC Olympiad—especially when the Greeks had so clearly sought his advice and aid in carrying out his Olympic proposal, which, he said, fulfilled "the hope of the first ten years of my adult life." The timing is nearly incredible. Why would he be writing a history book precisely when the Olympics needed his attention most? There may be no satisfactory answer. But his engagement and marriage might have somehow related to his neglecting Olympic affairs to write history.

Coubertin's bride was Marie Rothan. Almost nothing certain is known about their courtship and the early years of their marriage. Some Olympic histories state that Marie supported and encouraged Coubertin's Olympic plans from the start, with deep faith and personal devotion. But this notion, I fear, comes not from historical evidence but rather from one fanciful piece of romantic historical fiction, Eyquem's obviously unreliable biography of Coubertin.[31] In view of Vikelas's comments in his letters and Coubertin's actions, it is much more likely that Marie Rothan Coubertin discouraged the baron from devoting himself to the Olympic project. Furthermore, she might well have encouraged him to write the history, since her own father had himself written extensively on French history.[32] I merely speculate; but perhaps the young bridegroom sought to please his bride by following in her father's footsteps.

On the question of whether Coubertin tried to resign from the IOC, Vikelas's January 17 letter merits careful scrutiny. It appears to say that the baron attempted to resign. But could it really say that? The idea prompts dismay. The IOC was Coubertin's personal creation, and he continued as an IOC member—that much is certain. Yet Vikelas's words, "this one of yours," seem clear enough and can, in the French, refer only to the previous word, "resignation," just shortly before.[33] One might assume that Vikelas exaggerates, referring sarcastically or metaphorically to Coubertin's inactivity rather than to any actual resignation the Baron had submitted. But Vikelas's next two sentences suggest that he did not use the word as an exaggeration, that he is genuinely taken aback and profoundly disturbed by a real notice of Coubertin's intent to resign: "That took me by surprise and I am full of worries. What will happen in France?"

Coubertin's other actions in 1895, wholly dissonant with his attitudes and aims both before and after this period, make it more credible that he indeed sent Vikelas his resignation. As MacAloon perceives, 1895 is the only year from 1886 to 1937 in which Coubertin published nothing. Ordinarily, he published many articles a year, often dozens. Furthermore, in 1895 Coubertin personally abandoned the journal *Revue Athlétique*, which he had himself founded in 1890. And, perhaps most surprising of all, he in fact resigned from the USFSA, the French athletic union he had founded and to which he had devoted immense energy for years.[34] Abruptly, as he married, the baron seems to have unilaterally divested himself of nearly all ties to his athletic pursuits. Therefore—though the magnitude of the act at this time seems so improbable that some uncertainty must remain—it is highly likely that Coubertin did seek to resign from the IOC.[35] If so Vikelas, as president, simply refused to accept his resignation; for he continued to harass him for information, advice, and aid. And Coubertin acceded to Vikelas's nonacceptance; he came to Athens in 1896 as secretary of the IOC. Whatever the cause of Coubertin's Olympic inactivity in 1895, the Greeks, indeed, needed to make almost all the preparations on their own, and with their own money.

ELEVEN

The Greeks at Work, 1895–1896

If in such a festival, you, King!, the scepter of the Greek nation in your
hands, should crown the [winners]; if . . . you would appear on your
throne in the middle of the Greek amphitheater . . .

—*Panagiotis Soutsos, 1851*

Immediately after Constantine recreated the organizing committee on
January 25, he formed special committees and appointed their members:
one subcommittee for each category of events, such as athletics (track and
field), fencing, cycling, and the rest.[1] On these committees he placed people knowledgeable in each of these athletic categories. He added three
more special committees: one to host the foreign athletes, another to over-
see restoration of the Panathenaic Stadium, and a third to organize the
Greek athletes for participation—in essence, a Greek national Olympic
committee. The crown prince convened all these new committees at the
Zappeion on February 13, announcing the charge of each committee and
introducing its members. Right then and there, each committee chose its
president and began its work. Now assured that all was progressing as
hoped, Vikelas left Athens for Paris on February 18, an "earnest patriot
and distinguished scholar, accompanied by the parting blessings of a grateful Greek populace," according to the newspapers.[2]

Clearly, the most difficult task fell to Constantine and the Board of
Twelve. They needed to find the money to finance the Games. The committee's most daunting task was the restoration of the stadium. Everyone
knew the expenses for the stadium would be immense: the plan was still
to restore it with all the rows and seats in marble splendor, as Zappas had
first envisioned it when he gave the money for that purpose many years
before. But, of course, the Zappas money was no longer available. What
had not been squandered or seized by Romania, Dragoumis would not
release. The cost would now be far greater than in 1859. As Vikelas had
suggested from the start, the principal source of revenue lay in private
donations from patriotic Greeks, those in Greece and those living abroad.
As early as December 1894, some private donations had come in. One of
the first noted was ten thousand drachmas from Constantinos Manos, a

Greek poet then studying at Oxford.[3] Manos later played a significant role in the actual Games.

Once the new committee had begun its work, many more donations from individuals and principalities—in villages the hat was passed—came in; some were large, most were rather small. All such donations eventually totaled over 332 thousand drachmas. But this amount, it turns out, would not even pay for constructing the velodrome and the rifle range. Coubertin's early estimates of a total budget of 200 thousand to 250 thousand drachmas was as ridiculously low as Skouloudis and Dragoumis had charged. The first realistic estimate for renovating the ancient stadium alone was calculated at 585 thousand drachmas, but even that proved to be far too low. Large donations were obviously needed; and wealthy Greeks living abroad had always been the best source of financing for special projects in Athens.

As the Board of Twelve pondered these difficulties, one of them, George Rhomas, proposed that George Averoff be approached for an immense gift. Averoff, a wealthy Greek originally from Zappas's home area of Epiros but at the time living in Alexandria, Egypt, had already privately funded a number of important buildings and institutions in Athens. Although some other members hesitated to solicit Averoff's help, Constantine and Philemon, the secretary-general, approved. The crown prince personally wrote to Averoff asking for the donation. Sometime before June 1895, Philemon left for Egypt with the prince's letter and the planned request. Averoff himself did not balk.[4] For the second time an expatriate Greek from the distant northwest immediately agreed to fund the rebuilding of the stadium in Athens. The plans by the architect, A. Metaxas, were forthwith approved by the stadium committee, Constantine, and Averoff. Averoff agreed to a budget of 585 thousand drachmas; he did not refuse when it was later raised to 920 thousand.

Averoff's philanthropy having solved the greatest problem, the stadium, the committee turned to other wealthy Greeks in hopes of financing the velodrome and the rifle range. No such generous donors stepped forward. At some point, however, apparently after T. Deliyannis was once more elected prime minister in April 1895, the new government assured the committee of two substantial sums. The first amounted to two hundred thousand drachmas, revenue expected from the sale of Olympic tickets; the second was four hundred thousand drachmas, predicted as income from the government's sale of commemorative Olympic stamps.

One may wonder that so high a figure was projected from ticket sales and especially from the stamps. But all sources agree that the sales of tickets and stamps reached their goals and the six hundred thousand drachmas the government had guaranteed eventually reached the organizing committee.[5] The rifle range was built in the district named Kallithea, and the velodrome in New Phaleron—near the tomb of the national hero, Karaïskakis. Soutsos, in his poem on Karaïskakis, had petitioned Otto to revive the Olympic Games, which he associated with Karaïskakis. Had he been alive to see the velodrome beside his hero's tomb, Soutsos would have been much gratified; he and Karaïskakis were remotely part cause of the structure.

The fencing committee had no worries about a new building; those contests were scheduled for the Zappeion itself. At last, some Olympic athletic events would be held in the Olympic house that Zappas built. Not far away, beside the imposing ruins of the ancient temple of Zeus, the tennis courts were planned, along with a field for the cricket matches, still on the program. In the Bay of Phaleron, south of Athens, jetties were made to accommodate the spectators for the rowing events planned there. The venue for the swimming events would be the picturesque little harbor of Piraeus, Marina Zea, from which hydrofoils now depart for the islands to the south. Thus, all the special committees arranged the details for the category of contest to which each was assigned.

This work progressed, the months began to slip away, and publicity about the Games trickled out. Athenian newspapers continued to solicit private donations and to print the names of donors, whether individuals or villages, of even small amounts. In Paris, on April 5, Vikelas gave a speech about the 1896 Olympic Games, their origin and prospects. Because this speech, noted previously, gives details of the Paris congress not found elsewhere, it remains an important document for the history of the IOC and the Olympic Games. Fascinating too, in retrospect and in view of current Greek tourism, is a section on how the Games could help Greece initiate a tourist industry—"such as exists in Egypt." But this speech was given to the Greek Students League there, not the Parisian public.[6]

The *Nea Ephemeris*, Nov. 20/Dec. 2, reported on Olympic progress in America. The New York newspapers, it said, were printing information on the Games in Athens. Most of this New York information eventually proved false, but that helps us to know why Athenians expected so much to happen that did not. President Cleveland, the Athens paper claimed, had an active Olympic committee working under him. The university athletic clubs would not be able to attend, since classes would still be in session at the time of the Olympics. But the New York Athletic Club had expressed its hope to defeat its transatlantic rival, the London Athletic Club, in Athens. Neither team, in the event, even came to Athens.

By the fall of 1895, however, several controversies began to mar the Olympic spirit in the Greek capital. A major dispute arose over control of the Greek national team and which athletes could compete. The Oxford student, Constantinos Manos, sought to torpedo the entire existing athletic structure of Greece and supplant it with his own. Full details are highy complex and relevant only to the history of modern Greek athletics. But the Manos affair itself bears on our own story. It compelled the IOC to make the first amateur ruling in its history; and it well reveals the continuing long arm of British elitist amateurism, which wrecked Brookes's Olympic movement in England, mildly marred the Games of 1896, and later caused great difficulties to countless modern Olympic athletes.

The most established club in Greece was the Panhellenic Gymnastic Society, of which Vikelas had so suddenly become a member, headed by Phokianos. The other main Athenian club was the National Gymnastic Society, directed by Ioannis Chrysafis, later the most important Greek Olympic historian. Chrysafis had studied under Phokianos, and the two clubs were generally on friendly, cooperative terms. But that cooperation was tenuous. The National Gymnastic Society announced it would sponsor athletic contests for all clubs in Greece, to be held in August on the island of Tinos, a kind of mecca of modern Greek religion. The Panhellenic at first refused to attend, but in the end it participated, along with the other athletic clubs of the Greek-speaking world. These games on Tinos, in August 1895, were intended to be a preparatory meeting, to some extent preliminary trials, for the Greek national Olympic team.[7]

The special committee for organizing the Greek Olympic team paid little or no attention to the Tinos Games nor indeed to the athletic clubs themselves. Constantine had fallen under Manos's spell and appointed this Oxford student-poet one of the four secretaries of the main organizing committee. Now staying in Athens, Manos intruded his own personality on the organizing committee and—something he obviously learned at Oxford—the English elitist amateurism that Brookes had fought against for so long. On October 9, Manos published in the *Asty* an article in which he declared that all members of the existing Greek athletic clubs, such as the Panhellenic and National Gymnastic Societies, were ineligible for Olympic competition. Since these clubs, he said, had salaried directors (Phokianos and Chrysafis), they were not amateur clubs. All members were professionals, because professional athletes belonged to them. Manos then announced he was forming a new club, the Athens Athletic Club, an amateur group, which would provide the only eligible Olympic athletes for the 1896 Games. He invited students of the university, the academies, and the high schools to join.[8] This search limited to student athletes recalls the strictures on the Athens 1875 Olympic Games.

Now the Panhellenic and National clubs were compelled to work in concert. Both Phokianos and Chrysafis quickly published strong replies to Manos's charges. Philemon and Constantine summoned the relevant committees to determine the question; they decided in Phokianos and Chrysafis's favor. But Manos would not accept defeat and convinced the crown prince and Philemon to refer the matter to the IOC; namely, to Vikelas and Coubertin. After consulting his closest Greek friend, A. Mercatis, the baron asked the French USFSA to make a ruling. Coubertin then wrote back to Athens, through Vikelas. Coubertin's decision, the IOC decision, went decisively against Manos: the amateur rules, Coubertin said, did not exclude members of such clubs as the Panhellenic and National Gymnastic Societies. They would be allowed to compete.

By this time, however, Manos had recruited athletes for his new Athens Athletic Club. They too would be eligible. They came from the aristocratic families of Athens. From England a coach, Charles Perry, arrived to train them in English athletic methods. Some observers at the training site complained about the heavy foreign influence and the un-Hellenic atmosphere. The athletes affected English manners and generally preferred to speak French, not Greek. French, not English, was the preferred language of the Greek aristocracy at the time. Under Manos's guidance, the subcommittee for the Greek national team, which included many aristocrats, openly began to favor the Athens Athletic Club over the others.

It also irked members of the longer established clubs that Constantine gave Manos important new offices on the main committee. Manos was appointed *alytarch*, a title from the ancient Olympics, which made him director of all the actual competitions. And Perry, Manos's import from Oxford, was named official timekeeper and put in charge of constructing the stadium track. Then Constantine made Manos one of the five official judges (*Hellanodikai*), again a title from the ancient Games. Except for the head judge, Prince George (born in Greece), Manos was the only Greek eventually appointed among the five.[9] The other three were an Englishman, R. Finnis, and two of Coubertin's friends on the IOC, Hungary's Franz Kemeny and Germany's Willibald Gebhardt, whom Coubertin had apparently appointed shortly before to help diffuse another great dispute.

Unlike the Manos affair, the German "ruckus" is well known to Olympic historians because Coubertin himself reported it, as "an extremely strange incident."[10] Despite his early nationalistic motivation resulting from the Franco-Prussian War, the baron hoped for German participation in the Olympic movement, so long as it did not alienate the French supporters he needed. His efforts to get German representation at the Paris congress met with French opposition and failed in Germany, but he did get one German, Baron von Rieffenstein, to attend the congress as an unofficial representative.

The Greeks, too, wanted German participation. In the fall of 1895, the Greek ambassador to Germany, Kleon Rangavis,[11] prompted the Germans to form an Olympic committee, with Dr. Willibald Gebhardt of Berlin as its secretary. Gebhardt began to organize a German team for Athens. But athletics (i.e., track and field) had scarcely begun there, where the special style of gymnastics known as *Turnen* was the national inheritance and focal point for all physical training—and the German *Turner* clubs resisted the Olympics.

The question of German participation had already been raised in several *Turner* publications. Many *Turner* disapproved of the coming international Olympics because a Frenchman had put them in motion. They also feared a kind of pollution from foreign sports would make the Games unsuitable to German character. Others, such as H. Raydt, proposed that instead of going to Athens, Germany should have its own national Olympic Games. The principal German physical education organization sent to Athens a formal refusal of the Greeks' invitation, blaming some words spoken by Coubertin in an interview six months earlier. In the interview published by the French newspaper, *Gil Blas*, in June 1895, Coubertin was purported to have said that Germany had not attended the 1894 Paris congress; they had been invited late, "perhaps on purpose." He was also quoted as saying the Greek royal family favored the French over the Germans.

This interview, naturally judged anti-German by the Germans, was later reported in Germany by German *Turner* publications. It caused an outrage against Coubertin in both Germany and Greece. By December 1895, German indignation climaxed and had reached Philemon and the Athenian press as well. Coubertin then sent a letter of protest and denial to the *National-Zeitung*, Gebhardt, and Rangavis in Germany and to Prince Constantine and some newspapers in Athens. The baron said he had simply been misquoted, that he had not said the things attributed to him in *Gil*

Blas. Von Rieffenstein and Rangavis quickly came to Coubertin's support in Germany, and the *National-Zeitung* printed his denial on January 3 (though it appended remarks suggesting it did not believe the denial).[12] The baron's letter then appeared in some Athens newspapers.[13]

In general, people accepted Coubertin's denial, but the episode clearly left some Germans and Greeks disheartened and less favorably disposed toward Coubertin. Philemon, on February 7, 1896, sent Coubertin a telegram saying, "Greek Committee never believed words attributed to you initiator revival Olympic Games." Coubertin thought the message had come too late and was insincere and that the Greeks continued to plot against him.[14] Gebhardt, who was somehow now a member of the IOC, tried to gain time and momentum for a German team. He asked Coubertin to postpone the Games until fall.[15] To judge from newspaper reports, either Coubertin then approached the Greeks about a postponement or Gebhardt invoked the baron's office in Paris when he himself requested a postponement from the Greeks. Gebhardt also published a lengthy essay on the question, "Should Germany participate in the Olympic Games." (His response was an emphatic yes).[16] In the end, he did muster the largest foreign team at Athens, but most were *Turner,* that is, gymnasts.

In January 1896,[17] the Athenian press kept a running account of the various committees' frenzied efforts to get ready and other Olympic news, including the German affair. I sum up some items gleaned from the *Nea Ephemeris.*[18] On January 4/16, the day after printing Coubertin's denial, the paper noted that Philemon had assured everyone the Games would take place, despite the German controversy. Some people, the newspaper said, wanted to postpone the Games, but there should be no postponement; the alleged grounds for postponement were not valid; the stadium would be ready; the city could accommodate the foreign tourists; their own athletes' unreadiness was not grounds to postpone (Jan. 12/24). The Games would take place. Despite reports resulting from a fear born in Paris concerning the postponement of the Olympic Games, the organizing committee here, when queried, rejected every notion of postponement; the Games would definitely start on March 24 (Jan. 14/26).

The interior of the stadium was being examined by the Germans; Gebhardt was active, and it was hoped that many Germans would come to participate (Jan. 16/28). The committee had received a letter from a British journalist and athlete wanting information on how to throw the discus; Greece must get her own athletes ready (Jan. 18/30). Bad news: Belgium would not come, nor would Switzerland and the Italian gymnasts; Holland refused, Greece being farther than Sweden. Sweden and Norway abstained as well, for lack of travel means (Jan. 19/31). Everyone was working hard to prepare, especially in the stadium. Every day new pledges to participate were arriving from abroad. It was hoped that in March Greece would see something truly beautiful, noble, and magnificent (Jan. 24/ Feb. 5).

There were not, in fact, many athletes preparing to come to Athens for the Olympic Games. Apart from Greece, the only truly national team was organizing in Hungary, where Franz Kemeny, strongly dedicated to the new Olympic movement, had succeeded in getting government support for the Olympic athletes. An official Hungarian team of eight prepared for the competitions. Besides Gebhardt's efforts in Germany, William Sloane, in America, was organizing a small contingent of Princeton athletes, and several members of the Boston Athletic Club had decided to go as a team. But nowhere else was an actual Olympic team forming. Athletes from a handful of other foreign countries eventually competed, but these men came as individuals, not as part of a team.[19]

Through these early months of 1896 one would expect a joyful Dr. W. P. Brookes to follow closely the intense preparations of the Greeks and to come to Coubertin's aid in assembling a British team. It was his life's dream—his own proposal—that the first modern international Olympics would take place in Athens. But Dr. Brookes had died in Wenlock on December 10, 1895, just before the outbreak of the German "ruckus."[20] He thus came close but did not fully succeed in his great wish for the plan that he, as newspapers then noted, had first promoted in the early 1880s:[21] "Brookes, this ardent philhellene, is now at work so that an International Olympic Festival may be held soon in Athens"; "[Brookes] hoped in a few years to see his efforts become successful." And that plan had not changed by 1892, when a newspaper said Brookes "hoped to go and witness an international festival at Athens, or upon the old spot where the Olympic Games were started."[22]

Brookes's wish to see the Olympics in Athens in person tempered, with his age, to a wish to rejoice in them vicariously, through Coubertin. As Brookes said of the coming Athens Olympics, in his last letter to the baron a year before his death, "I hope . . . that I shall live long enough to rejoice in the success of your patriotic and philanthropic undertaking."[23] In 1896, the doctor's dream was in the making, but he was not there to assist or enjoy it. Nor was there ever any mention of Brookes in connection with the 1896 Games—no mention by any Greek or by Coubertin. Coubertin claimed he himself was the forgotten man, the unsung mastermind behind the idea taking shape in Athens. Olympic historians believe him and extend him a kind of scholarly sympathy. The real forgotten man was Dr. W. P. Brookes. Yet, as Coubertin said of Brookes: "He did not care for immortality."[24] He cared only for Olympic Games.

TWELVE

The First International Olympic Games Begin, 1896

So long as a man lives
he has no greater glory
than what he wins
with the strength of his hands
and the speed of his feet
in the athletic games.

—*Homer,* Odyssey, *about 725 B.C.*

Sometime in March 1896, when work on the stadium was nearing its end, Coubertin finished an article, "Preface to the Olympic Games." It appeared that same week.[1] In it the baron repeatedly assigns the entire notion of an Olympic revival to himself alone. The first sentence begins, "From the moment that I wished to reestablish the Olympic Games. . . ." Apart from some brilliant comments on modern athleticism and on the Olympic Games' potential for peace,[2] the article is mainly a rather self-congratulatory account of how Coubertin conceived the Olympic idea, held the 1894 congress, and succeeded in getting the Greeks to implement his plan to revive the Games. In the end, he does give Constantine some credit for his efforts of the past year. But he clearly suggests throughout that no one before the baron himself had ever thought of reviving the Olympics. He had no way to know about Soutsos's 1830s proposals and his decades of work. But otherwise, he knew, in detail, all about the Zappas Olympics.[3]

Writing of the long gap between the ancient and the 1896 Athens Olympic Games and of the growth of the Olympic idea, Coubertin had opportunity—even cause—to mention not only the Zappas Athens Olympics but also the vision of W. P. Brookes as it now materialized. There was special reason to pay tribute to Brookes, since the doctor had died just a few months earlier. In fact, it seems most strange that Coubertin avoids all reference to Zappas and Brookes; for he knew their relevance full well. One can only conclude that already, just before the 1896 revival took place, the baron consciously ignored the contributions of his Olympic predecessors.

Even stranger is a companion piece in the same issue of the same journal, an article titled "The Revival of the Olympian Games," signed by John Gennadius. The bulk of the article reviews the ancient site at Olympia and the Olympic Games that were held there. But when Gennadius turns to the Games of the modern international revival, he writes:

> They are due to that sudden growth of the taste for athletic sports in France which was one of the healthiest signs of national recuperation after the war of 1870. That movement culminated in . . . an International Athletic Congress . . . in Paris . . . on June 16, 1894. . . . The Congress . . . decided to hold quadrennial meetings . . . to be known as the New Olympian Games. . . . The Congress finally decided to hold its first Olympiad in Athens in 1896. . . . In these circumstances, nothing less could be done than to elect the Greek delegate as chairman, in the hope that he would facilitate the necessary arrangements with the Greek government. This mission, however, was ultimately entrusted to Baron Pierre de Coubertin, the secretary and moving spirit of the Congress, whose intimate acquaintance with the questions involved is equal to the enthusiasm and energy with which he advocated the objects of the movement.[4]

This is the same man that Dr. Brookes had badgered with a barrage of letters—a dozen over the past decade or so—trying to interest Gennadius and the Greek government in his idea of reviving the Olympics on an international basis in Athens. Gennadius had last discouraged Brookes on international games and on the Olympic movement in 1893. It is surprising that Gennadius fails to name the "Greek delegate [elected] as Chairman," focusing instead on Coubertin as the "moving spirit"; Gennadius was the English language translator of Vikelas's best-known book. But I find it astonishing that Gennadius, after years of rebuffing Brookes and his own idea of establishing international Olympic Games in Athens, does not even refer to Brookes anonymously, yielding everything to France and to Coubertin.[5] Brookes's influence on Gennadius is clear in his title, where he uses Brookes's term, "Olympian Games," not Coubertin's "Olympic Games." I do not know details of Gennadius's association with Coubertin. But perhaps he knew that the baron wished credit for the very notion of a revival—and that even if Brookes "'did not care for immortality . . . '" Coubertin cared very much for immortality."[6]

Gennadius was not the only naysayer from the movement's past suddenly to reverse his field and jump on the Olympic revival bandwagon just as it appeared ready to succeed. We may recall the classical scholar, John

Mahaffy, the Irishman and would-be English gentleman, who had taken such delight in ridiculing any attempt to revive the Olympic Games and in generally belittling the modern Greeks and their neophyte modern nation. In 1875 he had begun his scornful account of the Athens Olympics held that year thus:

> The burden of great names and of a noble past seems to sit lightly on the modern Greeks. Were we to propose the resuscitation of the Olympic games in the Panathenaic stadium at Athens, we should be in anxious dread of comparisons with the victors of Pindar's day. . . . Nay we should fear an accusation of absurdity in transferring Olympia to Athens. . . . But the modern Greeks seem no ways daunted by these sentimental difficulties. An old gentleman called Zapa. . . .[7]

Now, in March 1896, we hear from Mahaffy again, in a newspaper report, which I here summarize: Deliyannis has received a letter from the famous professor, John Mahaffy, who says he will attend the Olympic Games so he can "marvel at the strength and dexterity of the Hellenic youth in the Panathenaic Stadium." [He had sneered at that same youth in that same stadium when he attended the 1875 Games.][8] In his letter Mahaffy identifies himself as "an old friend of the Greeks"—and asks that a seat in the stadium be reserved for him; Philemon sent him a warm response.[9] People have always been willing to do anything, it seems, for a stadium ticket.

Writing less than a month before opening day, W. Elliott, an American college professor, predicted that the Americans and the English would dominate the list of champions. "There should be but little question as to where the prizes will go. The Anglo-Saxon race is pre-eminently the athletic race of this age. The other nations of Europe are distinctly inferior." He also still expected contests in cricket, as well as tennis and "such other similar sports."[10]

On March 3, Vikelas arrived in Athens from Paris. The next day he went to the stadium. "I saw it and I marveled." Progress in stadium construction exceeded his expectations. It looked as if it would indeed be ready in time. But Vikelas was greatly concerned about something else. He was worried that few foreign athletes and tourists were preparing to come, partly because, as he knew, publicity and invitations had been poor, at best. Coubertin had not delivered well in this respect. Vikelas further feared that the chilly reception the Games had first received during Trikoupis's government would dissuade foreigners. He asked the committee to send out a series of telegrams to the foreign press, to distribute illustrated copies of the Olympic program, and to ask Greeks throughout the land to come to Athens as spectators.[11]

On March 21, an American Olympic team left Hoboken, New Jersey, bound for Athens, traveling first class on the German steamer *Fulda*.[12] This unofficial team numbered thirteen. But, as noted above, Vikelas's fears were well grounded. Coubertin himself perceived how ineffective he had been in fulfilling his assignment to recruit foreign athletes. By his own calculation he expected no more than a hundred foreign athletes and several thousand foreign spectators to come to Athens. He personally judged that a good start for international competition but knew the Greeks expected far more. "I did not dare tell my Greek friends [of these estimated numbers]," he reports.[13] Yet the Greeks had reason to expect more. For example, the organizing committee had somehow been informed that four foreign football (soccer) teams were to participate and proceeded to prepare the field and their own football teams. The football contests were not canceled until the time of the Games themselves, when no foreign football team actually showed up.[14]

The committee for the organization of the Greek national team held a three-day qualifying trials meet on March 21–23. These trials (track and field, weightlifting, wrestling, and gymnastics) were apparently held amid much acrimony and confusion.[15] But a Greek national Olympic team did emerge, generally two Greeks chosen to compete in each event, although each foreign team was allowed to enter as many as four per event.[16] The committee could afford to be generous with foreign teams; for they suspected that few teams would be there, and they needed all the competitors they could get.

As the month of March progressed and fears of poor numbers intensified, the baron felt compelled to defend himself in this matter by writing a letter to the Greek people. In this letter, addressed to the editor of the newspaper *Akropolis*, Coubertin says he knows that he has been accused of not trying hard enough to encourage foreigners to come, to make the Games succeed. He insists, however, that he did try, had tried, his best.[17] But toward the end of the month, people were indeed arriving in Athens for the Games. On March 24 a group of 210 spectators arrived from Egypt (presumably Greeks living in Egypt, as did Averoff). The newspapers said they expected the German team, many Romanian athletes, four Russians, seven Swedes, a Dane, and others to come as competitors within the week.[18]

The next day, March 25, Coubertin himself arrived in Athens—his second trip to Greece, more than a year after he had left it to its own Olympic devices in November 1894. A March 26 news item read, "Yesterday the General Secretary of the International Athletic Committee, Baron Coubertin, arrived, accompanied by Professor Pizos, formerly the Professor of the Museum in Constantinople." Madame de Coubertin accompanied her husband of one year to Athens.[19] It was not two weeks until opening day.

The organizing committee and all of Athens were abuzz with work to get the facilities and the city ready for the big event. All accounts agree that the city was in a festive mood, with shops and public buildings displaying flags and banners welcoming the foreign visitors to the Olympics. Each street seemed to be a light show with arcs of gas lighting spanning them. "Standing at the head of any of the principal thoroughfares, one seemed to look down a long tunnel of light. The parks were illuminated, and decorated with garlands and flags."[20] Athenians and other Greeks there gathered around the foreign athletes as they arrived and as they moved about town, asking them questions and talking Olympics and the coming contests. The Hungarians seem to have arrived first and were most prominent. Except for the Greek team, the Hungarian team was the only one sponsored by its government. Organized and led by Franz Kemeny, close friend of Coubertin and early Olympic activist, the team numbered only eight athletes, but they were to compete in the full spectrum of events. The Hungarians displayed their flags and their persons at every opportunity, attracting the attention they desired.

As if actors in a drama, the Americans apparently did not reach Athens until the night before the Games began.[21] The team went by a series of boats, stopping at Gibraltar, where they worked out. They docked at Naples and eventually crossed Italy by slow train to Brindisi; from there by slow boat to Patras, on the western Peloponnesus, then on to Athens by the slow train (there is no other). The Americans were met at the station by delegates from the Greek organizing committee; a brass band accompanied them on to their hotel. "From the moment of their arrival to that of their departure they were overwhelmed with kindly attentions from all classes, including the King and members of the royal family."[22] The thirteen-man American team, not an official state entry, had two contingents. There were four Princeton men, gathered by Sloane, who could not himself afford the time or money to attend. They were Robert Garrett Jr., Francis A. Lane, Herbert Jameson, and Albert Tyler, all track-and-field athletes. Garrett's banker father had paid their way. They were amateurs.

Sloane's Princeton athletes were joined by another group of track-and-field athletes from the Boston Athletic Club; namely, Thomas Burke, Ellery Clark, Arthur Blake, Thomas Curtis, and William Hoyt. Burke had graduated from Boston University, Curtis attended M.I.T.; the others were alumni or students of Harvard. James Connolly, of the Suffolk Athletic Club, a recent Harvard dropout, joined them, as did two brothers, Sumner and John Paine, who were pistol marksmen in the army, and a swimmer named Gardiner Williams. Williams paid his own way. A stockbroker, Arthur Burnham, and the governor of Massachusetts, Oliver Ames, paid the expenses for the rest of the Boston contingent.

Numbering nineteen, Gebhardt's German athletes made up the largest foreign team.[23] Though most of the Germans would compete and excel in the gymnastics contests, they also competed in track and field, wrestling, cycling, and tennis. Years earlier, in 1881, Brookes had hopes that many Englishmen "would gladly avail themselves of an opportunity of visiting the classic land. . . ; and of contending . . . with the Athletes of other nations, in the time-consecrated stadium at Athens"; Coubertin had once thought the same. But only five Englishmen made the trip to Athens from England, all independently of any club sponsorship. An Australian distance runner, Edwin Flack, went too, and—as a colonial—was considered part of the British team. He was, in fact, a member of the London Athletic Club. John Boland, whether tourist or not, entered the tennis competition for Great Britain and won.[24] Two employees of the British Embassy in Athens later entered the bicycle races. Some Englishmen in Athens tried to bar them on the grounds they were not amateurs but professionals, since they worked for a living. But the Greeks, like Coubertin and the IOC, shared Brookes's concept of amateur, not that of the English AAC and its strongly elitist tradition. The men competed, one of them, Mr. Keeping, finishing second in the twelve-hour cycling event.

Only a handful of French athletes made it to Athens, arriving earlier, on April 1; Coubertin had great trouble getting anyone in France to help defray athletes' expenses. Nearly all the French athletes were cyclists or fencers, and many were successful in those events. But one, Lermusiaux, distinguished himself on the track—without winning a medal—by entering various races—the 100-meter dash, the middle distance (he won a preliminary heat of the 800 meters), and the marathon (where he led for a while, before collapsing). By his quips and quaint manners, Lermusiaux also endeared himself to fellow athletes and later Olympic historians, thus leaving his mark for France on Olympiad 1. He was joined in the stadium by A. Tufféri, a French national who had grown up in Athens and trained with the Greek team. He was not part of Coubertin's USFSA. Another French athlete, Louis Adler, entered the discus and shot put.[25] Eventually, one or more athletes from other countries—Switzerland, Austria, Bulgaria, Sweden, and Denmark—came to compete as individuals, without official support.

On April 4 (March 23 by the Greek calendar), the day before the Greek Easter Sunday and the start of official festivities, the *Nea Ephemeris* announced: "The resurrection of Christ. The resurrection of the nation. The resurrection of the Olympic Games. What a fantastic combination!" That same day Vikelas spoke directly to the Greek people—but in Greek style, that is, by publishing a letter to the editor of a newspaper.[26] He began with a little scolding, telling them he knew that many found fault with the Olympic committee and their preparations, and indeed there were things worthy of blame. But he also pointed to all the good things, the many positive achievements of the committee, and assured them that the foreign visitors, unlike the native Greeks, would notice the good things more than the bad. "Let us keep recriminations to ourselves until the Games are over, and the foreigners are gone. We have no reason to be ashamed in front of them." And he rightly assured Greeks that good traditional Greek hospitality would send them away with nothing but a favorable impression. "Just do your best, and they will be grateful."

Last he inspired them with a patriotic appeal, reaching back, as he had at the final Congress meeting at the Sorbonne, into his genealogical bag of tricks.[27]

> Let's not forget that the idea which the Committee undertook to carry out was one of the highest national significance. It was a great honor for Greece to crown her as the first victor in the global Games. This is a new recognition of the eminent position which Greece, as from its name, holds in the civilized world. The people who come here from all places do not come as foreigners to a foreign land; they come as the spiritual children of ancient Greece, paying a tribute of gratitude to a common mother, the mother country of their civilization. Therefore the victory of every athlete, be it a Greek or not, bestows equal honor on Greece and should be equally applauded.[28]

Fortunately, the Greek people responded and cheered for all victors, starting a strong and remarkable Olympic tradition of good sportsmanship. It was salutary for the Olympics to start in Athens; for what we call good sportsmanship is something like a national code of honor and hospitality in Greece.[29]

The next day, April 5, was Easter Sunday (March 24 by the Greek calendar). In 1896 Greek Easter and Roman Easter fell on the same day, but it is perhaps in Greece more of a special day than in Western European settings. Easter is the most joyous, most powerful part of the Orthodox religious calendar; this Easter was also the day before Greek Independence Day, another day of national joy. But the weather was terrible that Sunday; rain began to pour, as it did during much of Olympiad 1. Somehow the Olympics conquered the weather. The people of Athens gathered at the entrance to the ancient stadium, now resplendent with its restored seats, row after row of carefully worked white marble. They came to witness the first Olympic ceremony, the dedication of the stadium and of the statue of the (second) man who had paid to rebuild it.

The new statue of Averoff had been placed by the entrance to the stadium, on the north. It stood erect, draped in a dripping Greek flag of canvas, the tarpaulin that covered it and awaited removal. A band of soldiers marched up in order, followed by members of the trade unions, who had their own bands and marched under their own banners. They had helped to create this day. Then came official guests, members of parliament, and the foreign dignitaries, including those members of the IOC who had come to Athens. Coubertin led them.[30] The organizing committee and the foreign athletes all assembled in the rain around Averoff's hidden statue. Prince Constantine headed the official party. Philemon gave a short speech; next Constantine briefly but highly praised Averoff and pulled the canvas flag off the statue. A Greek society and the Hungarian athletic team, led by Kemeny, placed wreathes at the feet of the statue. Then all marched away, drenched from the downpour.

The next day was Monday, opening day of the international Olympiad 1, March 25, Greek Independence Day—exactly as Soutsos had planned it in his first Olympic proposal half a century earlier. It was April 6 by our Western European calendar.[31] The weather was gloomy, but it did not rain on Monday. The city bustled, nearly vibrated, with activity. Bands from around Greece paraded in the vast central Syntagma (Constitution) Square. Carriages delivered spectators. Apparently, there had been little or no advance ticket sales. That same morning everyone was scrambling for tickets, which were being sold at a central location and by ticket vendors in the streets. The seats were assigned, marked by section and row. Prices seem reasonable, one drachma for an upper-section seat, two for the lower seats, nearer the track.[32] But many Greeks could not pay even that much and assembled on the hill above and outside the stadium, from which they could at least make out some of the bustle inside the stadium itself. The police watched carefully for scalpers.

Most of the crowd were Greeks, but there was truly international representation: "English, American, French, Italian, Hungarian, Russian, Swedish, &c., folk *en evidence* in every direction, the polyglottic confusion of tongues amounted almost to a Babel."[33] "Immediately after noon the endless trek to the stadium starts. From all sides of the city immense crowds of citizens set out, of all classes, all ages and both sexes." They convened as a mass of people entering the stadium to "the shrill cries of the refreshment vendors."[34] All witnesses agree that perfect order reigned everywhere as the people soon assembled in the stadium.

Estimates of attendance that opening day vary from forty thousand to seventy thousand; it may well have been the largest crowd ever gathered for a sporting event to that date. It was larger than any crowds at the IOC Olympiads II through VIII. Those seated on the hill above the stadium would swell the number to perhaps one hundred thousand.[35] Opening ceremonies were scheduled for 3:30 P.M. The crowd sat in the stadium, full of anticipation.

> The spectacle was brilliant in the extreme. The vast throng was attired in holiday dress, and certain sections of the amphitheatre were given over to officers of the army and navy. These were in full uniform, and their blue and red and white plumes made patches of bright color. A few minutes before three the royal party entered, marching down the ancient arena to the music of the national hymn and the "zetos" [shouts of "long live"] of many thousand throats. The royal party consisted of the King and Queen [and other family members]. They took their seats in the centre . . . where they were surrounded by the diplomatic corps, and the most prominent of the officials present.[36]

It was exactly as Soutsos had envisioned it in 1835—but even grander.

As head of the Athens organizing committee, the Olympic devotee Crown Prince Constantine approached his father and loudly, formally addressed him. He recognized the 1894 Paris congress and stressed that these new Games were indeed a revival of the ancient. Though his speech had a tinge of nationalism, it closed with recognition that the revived Olympics could be a force for international good will and physical and moral improvement.

> The fulfillment of the decision of the international congress of the Olympic Games which was convened in Paris that these be held for the first time in Athens, was one which imposed itself on the country in which these Games have their birth and prospered.
>
> In order to carry out that decision, whatever was possible was done in a short time. . . .
>
> May it be, Oh King, that the revival of Olympic Games binds closer the

links of mutual affection of the Greek and of other peoples, whose representatives for the Olympic Games we consider ourselves happy to welcome here. May it be that it brings new life into physical exercises and the moral outlook and that it contributes to the formation of a new Greek generation worthy of its ancestors.

With these hopes, I pray, Oh King, that you graciously agree to declare the opening of the first International Olympic Games.

Politicians are disposed to long speeches when given the chance, so perhaps Constantine's four paragraphs may be excused. But in reply, George set the standard of succinctness happily followed by most heads of state or other presiding officials who opened subsequent Olympiads. He added only several words of patriotism, which the fiercely proud Greek audience surely demanded: "I declare the opening of the first International Olympic Games in Athens. Long live the nation! Long live the Greek People."[37]

Many eagerly awaited the contests themselves with special expectations or hopes. Elliott, the American professor, and Robertson, the Oxford student, assumed the Anglo-Saxons would easily win most prizes. Phokianos had just assured the Greek people that the Greek athletes were ready; admitting his athletes "are not champions," he still had "great hopes for the predominance of the Greeks in the Games."[38] The Hungarians were a confident group, and Gebhardt's large contingent must have led the Germans there to be thinking, as Constantine and George made their speeches, that Germans would take their share of crowns. Coubertin sat with the distinguished foreign guests. Once hoping French athletes would be prominent at the Olympic revival, he could not have expected much from Lermusiaux. But much as Soutsos had taken personal pride in the 1859 Zappas Olympiad, Coubertin took his pleasure in watching his great plan unfold before his eyes. As the ceremony proceeded, Gebhardt reassured him, "All that is your work."[39]

By now the sun had come out and shone from a clear sky. The opening ceremony itself ended with the debut performance of our now well-known Olympic hymn, composed by Samaras, who had composed the comparable hymn sung at Constantine's 1893 Panhellenic Games.[40] The words this time, however, were written not by the Oxford student Constantinos Manos but by the noted poet Kostis Palamas. This same hymn has been performed at subsequent IOC Olympiads and will, I assume, be heard at Atlanta in 1996. This premier performance by the large orchestra, led by Samaras himself, was received with long applause, and Samaras obliged the crowd with an encore.

The silence which followed this impressive performance was one of intense expectancy; the Olympian Games were about to be resumed after the lapse of hundreds of years. Suddenly the clear, startling notes of a bugle were heard, and from the ancient tunnel under the Sphendone the contestants for the first event appeared. They were twenty-one in all, representatives of England, Germany, France, Hungary, Greece, and four Americans.[41]

Thus the Games were truly international, from that first event, three preliminary heats of the 100 meter dash. As planned, Prince George was the head judge; Manos was *alytarch* (director and "Chief Starter"); the track had been prepared under the supervision of his English friend, Charles Perry, now the official timekeeper. The Americans Lane, Curtis, and Burke each won his heat; Burke's time, 12 seconds flat, was the best. Second places went to a Greek, a Hungarian, and a German. The first two in each heat qualified for the final on Friday.

The next event was to be completed as a final, the triple jump. Tufféri, the Athenian of French nationality, was leading when Connolly, the Harvard dropout, came up in the rotation. Connolly, according to one source, walked out to Tufféri's mark and threw his hat down a meter beyond it; he then jumped on his hat and won.[42] His mark was 13.71 meters, a full meter beyond Tufféri, who held on to second. Connolly thus became the first winner in the first International Olympic Games. The victory ceremony soon followed, and the Olympic custom of raising the victor's national flag began. As the Stars and Stripes rose up the pole for the first of many times, the mainly Greek crowd cheered the first winner loudly and graciously. Members of Connolly's Boston contingent gave a "Rah, Rah" American college-style yell, surprising and amusing the European spectators.

Next came the 800-meter preliminary heats, the first won by the Australian Flack in 2 min. 11 sec. Lermusiaux won the other heat. There were no American entrants. Also qualifying for the finals were seconds Dani, of Hungary, and Golemis, of Greece. Only those four qualified.

The discus followed—an event that inspired intense Greek interest. Seven different countries were represented by the eleven entries. Each athlete would get three throws, and he who threw the farthest would be the final winner. The Greeks knew that the discus was not contested nor thrown outside of Greece, and they had two excellent, muscular, well-trained discus entries, Panagiotis Paraskevopoulos and Soterios Versis. Versis had been winning in major Greek athletic meetings ever since Phokianos's "Olympics" of 1889. The other veteran weightman, Miltiades Gouskos, was forgoing the discus to concentrate on the shot-put event. Both drew crowds of admirers at practice sessions and in the streets.[43]

Greeks were rather confident that the Greek flag would climb the victor's pole at the end of the discus event and probably in the shot put, as well.

The main foreign discus contender was Robert Garrett of Sloane's Princeton group. In America he had decided against entering the discus, since it was so unfamiliar to him. But in Athens he changed his mind and consulted Coubertin. Coubertin encouraged him to enter, so Garrett took his throws. He had never practiced the discus before, according to all reports. Yet the Greek throwers were hampered by their training in a compulsory style, which Greek coaches had determined by depending on an unreliable ancient author, who misinterpreted Myron's famous ancient statue, the Discobolus. Greeks felt constrained to keep their feet planted in a particular way—almost like a statue—without using the shifting weight of the body to add impetus and centrifugal force. They threw mostly with the arm. Paraskevopoulos was leading when Garrett made his last throw, modifying the style to take better advantage of the leverage of the legs and body. Greeks began to celebrate as the event concluded, not knowing that Garrett had barely beaten Paraskevopoulos, 29.150 meters to 28.995. As the American flag went up for the second time, the mainly Greek crowd at first murmured in disbelief. But when they saw it was true, they gave Garrett a generous and roaring cheer of congratulation. The American team gave him an American college cheer, as they had for Connolly.[44]

The last event of the first day saw preliminary heats in the 400 meters. Sixteen runners were divided into two heats; the first two in each would qualify for the finals. Again, both heats were won by Americans, Herbert Jameson of Princeton (56.8 sec.) and Burke of the Boston Athletic Club (58.4 sec.). The two other qualifiers were Hoffmann, of Germany, and Smelin, of England. It had grown cold long before the royal party left the stadium first, to music and loud cheers.

That evening was festive. The foreign athletes mingled with the citizens and exchanged good wishes. The people now made the victorious Americans their favorites, as they crowded around them more now than the Hungarians or their fellow Greeks. Everywhere there were lights, and bands played. The labor unions, which had played so strong a role in the affair since their first meeting with Vikelas, made a sparkling torchlight parade. It had been a good opening day.

THIRTEEN

IOC Olympiad I
One to Remember, 1896

There are persons who . . . behold the games of ancient Greece
as institutions never to be equalled, results never again to be attained.
I . . . am of the opposite opinion.
—*W. P. Brookes, Birmingham, June 27, 1867*

The house that Zappas built was the venue for the first event of day two, IOC Olympiad 1—fencing. The magnificent Zappeion, built with money Zappas had given to revive the ancient Olympic Games, had never seen any athletic contests before. As soon as the king arrived at 10 A.M., the fencing matches got under way. There were eight entries, five Greek and three French. After three preliminary rounds, Eugene-Henri Gravelotte, of France, beat his fellow countryman, Henri Callot, in the final, giving France its first Olympic victory. After the fencing, the Games were adjourned to resume in the stadium that afternoon.

The weather on day two was better than on the first day but too windy for comfort. The crowd was smaller. First were preliminary heats for the 110-meter high hurdles. Now a beautiful event, the highs were not pretty in those days. Athletes still stutter-stepped at each hurdle, then hopped over it, as a shepherd jumps a fence.[1] The times, too, were laughable by modern standards. Thomas Burke, an American, won his heat of four runners at 18 seconds flat. Grantley Goulding, of Great Britain, won the other heat at 18.2 seconds. Qualifying seconds went to Alajos Szokolyi, of Hungary, and William Hoyt, of the United States. Next on the program was the long jump. Ellery Clark, of the United States, fouled on his first two attempts. That left as leaders two other Americans, Robert Garrett, the previous day's discus champion, at 20 ft. 3.5 in., and James Connolly, who had won the triple jump, at 20 ft. 0.5 in. But on his last try Clark made a fair and winning jump, 20 ft. 10 in. (6.35 meters). The American flag went up again. After the long jump came the 400-meter finals. Thomas Burke and Herbert Jameson, the Americans who had won their preliminary heats the day before, finished in that order, time 54.2 seconds. Once more the

Stars and Stripes ascended the victory flagpole; the Americans wildly cheered, and again the crowd applauded the victor generously. Day two looked as if it might repeat the first day, Americans winning all. But the next event was the shot put, where the Greeks thought they would surely and finally win.

Greek hopes rested on their veteran strongman, Miltiades Gouskos, whom they called Hermes, comparing his magnificent body to that in Praxiteles' famous statue of the Greek god.[2] Of six who challenged him, only Robert Garrett, the American discus winner, seemed a contender. He had a good first throw. But Gouskos threw well, too, improving as the series progressed. His last throw seemed a sure winner, the crowd applauded excitedly, and the soldier assigned to post the winning athlete's number and raise the victor's national flag misunderstood the result. He put Gouskos's number on the pole.[3] A Greek newspaper reporter recounts the scene:

> Again the Americans win! There were some tears in Greek eyes. The victory of a Greek, the raising of the Greek flag on the pole where they post the victor's number, will send every Greek heart into a sea of enthusiasm. At one moment, deceived like everone else when the soldier put up the number of a Greek athlete, instead of an American, I placed my hat on the head of an American and shouted at him . . . "This time it's the Greeks' turn." He said, "That's fair enough." Suddenly the soldier changed the number, and the American flag was hoisted; then the American looked at me the cocky look of a victor, and cheered.[4]

Garrett's first throw had held up; Gouskos's best had fallen short by just a trifling two centimeters (¾ in.).[5] The meticulously honest men who did the measuring would not deceive themselves nor anyone else, despite the pressure for a Greek victory. Garrett won, fair and square. "Yet once more the American flag waves victorious and the enthusiasm of the Americans reaches its apogee. Their strange yells resound again and once more small American flags are waving. Most generously, however, the Americans congratulate the Greek Gouskos, who had had such bad luck, and give him a cheer."[6]

Yet Greek hopes for the day were not yet over. Their other strongman, Soterios Versis, third to Garrett in the discus, was entered in the next stadium event, weight lifting. But the best Versis could do was a tie for third place. There were two clearly better lifters, Viggo Jensen, of Denmark, and Lawrenceton Elliot, of Great Britain; they both lifted 111.5 kilos, but Jensen was given first place on the basis of a better technique.[7] In a follow-up event, a lift with one hand only, Elliot beat Jensen. The last event that day was the 1,500 meters. Eight runners lined up at the start, and Lermusiaux led for a while. But Edwin Flack, of Australia, overtook him as did Arthur Blake, of the United States, whom Flack outran to finish ahead at 4 min. 33.2 sec. When the Danish, British, and Australian flags ascended the pole, the American cheers were silenced. The Greek flag did not yet fly.

The third day, March 27 (April 8 by our calendar), was painfully cold. All events were held outside the stadium. There were preliminary rounds of rifle and pistol shooting at the barely completed shooting range in Kallithea; preliminary trials in the tennis grounds under a large tent not far from the Zappeion; and the first bicycle race at the new velodrome in Nea Phaleron, near the tomb of Soutsos's hero, Karaïskakis. But the cold chilled the bones of spectators there, and many left during the only race, the 100 kilometers, or three hundred times around the track. It took more than three hours. Frenchman Léon Flameng fell once but pluckily climbed back on his cycle and beat the one remaining competitor, G. Kolletis, Greece. Few were there to see the French flag go up the pole at the velodrome. The cold and winds kept the street crowds of the city small that night, as well.

The next morning, April 9, the bad weather continued, and it threatened to rain. But immediately Greece at last had its first Olympic victor, not in the stadium but in the rifle shooting at 200 meters: he was P. Karasevdas, a law student. Elimination matches continued in tennis. At the Zappeion, Greece got another victory when Ioannis Georgiadis won the fencing with sabers. The stadium lay in waiting for the afternoon's events.

The only track event was the 800-meter final—won in 2 min. 1 sec. by Edwin Flack, the 1,500-meter victor; Lermusiaux, who had won his qualifying heat, did not compete. Perhaps he was reserving himself for the next day and the featured race of the entire Olympiad, the first marathon run ever held. The hype for the marathon the next day had reached a crescendo by then, as various Greek businessmen were advertising that they would reward the marathon victor—if he were Greek—with free services, hotel rooms, tailored suits, and so on, in some cases as long as he should live.[8] After the 800, the stadium became dedicated to gymnastics, where the German and Greek teams were certain to beat the Americans, who had no gymnasts. There were three teams, the Panhellenic, the National Gymnastic Club, coached by the athlete and Olympic historian Chrysafis, and a German team led by Fritz Hoffmann. The German team won the first event, team parallel bars; Chrysafis's group finished third. Neither Greek team opposed the Germans in the team horizontal bar event; and Karl Schumann, of Germany, won the vaulting horse. Thus, three times in a row the German flag climbed the stadium pole. The Swiss flag went up next, as Jules Zutter won the side horse for Switzerland's only victory. Would the Greek flag ever be hoisted in that stadium? Yes! In the next event, the rings, Ioannis Mitropoulos, of Chrysafis's team, took the victory, and the Blue and White finally and proudly ascended the pole. "The enthusiasm bursts forth beyond control; tears damp the eyes, hats are hurled into the air and handkerchiefs waved frenziedly. The cheers and the endless applause of which the signal is given by the Royal Family constitute an indescribable sound."[9]

One competitor and spectator, George Robertson, an Oxford student, was not so pleased. In his subsequent eyewitness report he objected to the "absurd gyrations" of gymnasts being thought a sport worthy of the Olympic Games and to gymnasts being crowned the same as track-and-field Olympic victors.[10] English-speaking nations indeed seemed the leaders in track and field, but they had shown little interest or skill in gymnastics except in their own German communities. This day ended with the individual horizontal bar event, won by Hermann Weingärtner, of Germany. It was too cold and too late for any more.

"Fortunately," as the official Greek report says, the next day "dawned more serene." Indeed it did. Friday, March 29 / April 10, 1896—the day will live forever in the mind of every Greek. It was finally marathon day. Almost all the runners had traveled up to Marathon the previous day and were now making their mental and physical preparations. No one but the Greeks, in their team trials, had run a marathon race before. But all knew it would be an ordeal, not only novel but extroardinarily gruelling, an experience to remember, even to survive. Meanwhile in Athens, the streets were buzzing with vast numbers of people seeking tickets, and the stadium was beginning to fill to capacity, even in the morning; the crowd eventually reached more than seventy thousand. Everyone wanted a seat for the marathon finish later. Vast crowds assembled on the hill overlooking the stadium, as well.[11]

The marathon was not scheduled to begin until 2:30 P.M. In the morning event at the shooting range, John Paine, of the United States, won the military revolvers at 25 meters. At 10:00 A.M. the stadium program began, first finishing the gymnastic events postponed by the weather of the previous day. Alfred Flatow, of Germany, won the individual parallel bars, and Zutter, the Swiss victor in the side horse, took second; the German flag was raised. But in the rope climb, Nikolaos Andriakopoulos, of Greece, emerged the victor. The Blue and White went up for the second time in the stadium and excited a long ovation. But many in the Greek audience tended to agree with Robertson's verdict; they could not equate a gymnastic victory with a win in track and field.[12] They still awaited a victory on the track to feel fulfilled, vindicated, victorious, and happy. They waited, and all thoughts were on that road from Marathon to Athens. Both religious Greeks and doubters, Oikonomos says, were inwardly praying, "Dear God, make it be that the victor of the Marathon is a Greek."[13]

Americans won the remaining track-and-field events held in the stadium that day, the next four events. The first three were the now classic 100-meter finals, which Burke won at 12 seconds flat, while the German Hoffmann placed second; the high jump, where Ellery Clark, the long jump victor, doubled (1.81 meters, or 5 ft. 11¼ in.), beating his Boston teammate James Connolly, the triple-jump champion; and the 110-meter hurdles, where Thomas Curtis barely beat the highly regarded English hurdler, Grantley Goulding. It seemed the flagpole knew only one flag for track and field, the Stars and Stripes. Greece had entries in the pole vault, the next event. But only two Americans, William Hoyt and Albert Tyler, remained when something like bedlam broke out. Hoyt eventually won at 3.30 meters (10 ft. 10 in.); but by then no one cared.

"It's a Greek! It's a Greek!" came the deafening cry. There is so much history, legend, fiction, emotion, nationalism, and excitement hovering over this moment that it is hard to write about it. The Greek was Spyros Louis, entering the stadium first, to do the last lap of the world's first marathon run.

> When Louis arrived at the goal he was a pitiable object; his white costume was soaked with perspiration and covered with dust, his shoes were nearly worn from his feet, his face was purple and blotched with blood. As he stood reeling at the goal his father sprang into the arena, embraced him and kissed him upon both cheeks. At the same instant Crown Prince Constantine and Prince George rushed forward, put their arms around the victor's waist, and supported him into the dressing-room in the tunnel. Louis is now a great man in Greece.[14]

"A great man in Greece," is an understatement. It is an extended task to sift through the myriad conflicting stories about Louis's origins (Louis is described variously as a "well-to-do-farmer," a "herdsman," and a "donkey boy"); his preparations the previous night (he either prayed all night or ran off to see his girlfriend); his stops during his run from Marathon (apparently he really did stop at a taverna and drink a full glass of wine);[15] the race itself (the versatile and colorful, but luckless, Frenchman, Lermusiaux, prominently displaying the two interlocked rings of Coubertin's

USFSA, led for a while before falling down); the many rewards offered Louis (marriage, diamonds, haircuts, land); Louis's self-effacing modesty, his refusal of most of the prizes and the attention and his retirement into obscurity (until he was put on display at the Berlin Olympics, in 1936); and the heroic, proverbial status he achieved in Greece (*Eyine Louis*, "He became a Louis"; his father was compared to Diagoras of Rhodes, founder of the most famous and proverbial family of the ancient Olympics). All those things, so well and elaborately discussed by others, need no full retelling here.[16]

Coubertin, too, was most impressed with Louis's entry into the stadium first. He then and there astutely anticipated the now contemporary field of sport psychology: "It seemed that all of ancient Greece entered with him. The rising cheer was unprecedented. It is one of the most extraordinary sights that I can remember. Its imprint stays with me, and ever since I have been convinced that psychic forces play a far more powerful role in sport than we have allotted them."[17]

As Louis slowly headed for the finish line, someone let loose a number of white doves, who spread in the sky as if to tell the world, "It's a Greek."[18] Thus another venerable Olympic tradition began in 1896, although at subsequent Olympics the white doves are sent up at the opening ceremonies. Finally, at last, the blue and white Greek flag ascended that pole in a coveted track-and-field event. All else that day, that Olympiad, was obviously anticlimax. Seven minutes after Louis's finish, the second runner, Vasilakos, also of Greece, entered the stadium, with Kellner, of Hungary, not far behind him. The next five finishers were all Greek. When the pole vault finally ended and some of the jubilant spectators had left to celebrate, officials tried to hold the wrestling match. After a few bouts in darkness, by acclamation the rest were postponed. The crowd looked for Louis, hoping to give him gifts, just to see him; but he had gone back to his village with his friends. Tens of thousands took the train down to Piraeus, the port of Athens on the southern coast, for an official festival, which included the royal family, bands, and Venetian lanterns and was capped off by Olympic fireworks. "The festivities came to an end around midnight, and all left with tired bodies from the fatigue and deep emotions."[19]

The next day, Saturday, April 11, still seemed to be marathon day, Spyros Louis day. The morning newspapers spoke of little else, featuring Louis's picture, Louis stories, Louis tales. By then telegrams sent around the world, if not the doves, had told everyone about Louis, and congratulations were already returning to Athens. "Pictures of Louis, lithographs, photos, of every size and shape are sold from this day onwards in their thousands and are hung up in the houses and shops. Several shops take on the name of the Marathon victor."[20] For the completion of the interrupted wrestling contest, the committee opened the stadium gates, giving free access to the public. But few spectators came. For most, tomorrow had not come. In the wrestling final, Karl Schumann, of Germany, with some difficulty beat Georgios Tsitas, of Greece, and the German flag ascended the pole where the Greek flag had last flown. Schumann was accused of professionalism but withstood an inquiry and was vindicated as an amateur.[21] At the range, Ioannis Frangoudis, of Greece, and Sumner Paine, of the United States, won the rapid fire and free pistol events, respectively. Thus, both Paine brothers became Olympic victors.

The weather was good. The sun shone on the venue of the swimming events, the Marina Zea near the port of Piraeus. Besides enjoying great natural beauty, this small harbor is almost wholly encompassed by land, making nearly a full circle of extremely calm water, almost like an immense—unheated—circular swimming pool. King George and Prince Constantine were among the many spectators. Victory in the first swimming event, 100-meter freestyle, went to Alfred Hajos, of Hungary. As for the American, Gardiner Williams, reports conflict as to whether or not he finished the race.[22] Hajos's time will again seem to us almost ludicrously poor: 1 min. 22.2 sec. Hajos won the 1,200-meter freestyle, as well, while Paul Neumann, Austria, won the 500-meter swim.

At lunchtime the large crowd moved from the Marina Zea on to the velodrome, which was, in fact, near the Marina Zea. Paul Masson, of France, won all three races, the one-lap race, the two kilometers, and the ten. The French flag had now gone up four times in four cycling events. By that time, at the tennis grounds, back in the city center, John Boland, of England, had won the singles and had teamed with Fritz Traun, of Germany, to win the doubles. We find some good stories about Boland, too, and the 1896 tennis matches, in the work of an excellent, scholarly historian of Olympic tennis, to whom I defer.[23] With the good weather, the crowds, bands, and lights returned to the Athens streets and tavernas that night; many people attended an excellent performance of Sophocles' *Antigone*, performed in the original ancient Greek. It was another good day for the Olympics but a very bad day for their principal opponent. On this date, as all day long Greece basked in the joy of their marathon victory and the obvious success of the Games, Charilaos Trikoupis died in Cannes, France, presumably of unrelated causes.[24]

On Sunday, April 12, the sailing contests at Phaleron Bay were canceled, because only a Greek team showed up. At the shooting range, Orfanidis, of Greece, won the event in army guns at 300 meters, which had been left uncompleted two days before. But the event of the day was the marathon cycling race. It was still marathon day—or marathon day all over again for Greeks. The marathon cycling soon took on some of the importance, even some of the legendary quality, of its more famous namesake. But this marathon was eighty-seven kilometers, not just forty. The six cyclists left from downtown Athens; they were to cycle up northeast to Marathon, sign some papers, and then return to the velodrome itself, several miles south of Athens. Aristis Konstantinidis, of Greece, was the first to sign the papers at Marathon, one hour and fifteen minutes after leaving Athens. F. Battel, of Great Britain, was next. Soon after leaving Marathon, Konstantinidis's bicycle broke down, and he had to find another to borrow. By then Battel had passed him.

Konstantinidis, however, caught up to Battel, overtook him, and led into Athens. But in downtown Athens he skidded and fell badly. He got up to scramble for yet another bicycle. Battel passed him again, but Konstantinidis overtook him once again. Battel stayed in hot pursuit—until they got out of Athens, when he himself crashed. Battered and covered with mud, the plucky Konstantinidis pedaled victorious into the velodrome at Nea Phaleron, 3 hr. 2 min. 31 sec. The Greek flag was hoisted for another marathon first. "There follows, though on a smaller scale that which happened on Friday at the victory of Louis at the Stadium. There is an indescribable burst of enthusiasm." August Goedrich, of Germany, came in twenty minutes later. Somehow Battel, too, recovered well enough to finish third, though "badly bruised."[25]

Then came the torch parade, "[O]ne of the finest sights of the series of festivities." Thousands of participants zigzagged up and down central Athens (up Athinas to Omonoia Square; back down on Stadiou to Syntagma and the royal palace; then over to Aiolou Street and again up to Omonoia; then back southeast on Panepistimou before disbanding at the university). Many more thousands lined the streets to watch.

[T]he people had foregathered in thousands in the streets and squares, shining with lights. . . . By 8 P.M. the crowd in the central parts is suffocatingly dense. . . . [The marchers] continually foregather at Athinas Avenue. . . . [A] great number of men from the infantry . . . carry beacons and pine-wood torches . . . the high school pupils . . . two thousand students of the University . . . civilians, members of the trade unions. . . . When the torches were lit the whole of Athinas Avenue is lit from end to end. . . . the guards of the Stadium . . . carrying the flags of all the countries who have competitors in

the Olympic Games . . . philharmonic bands. . . . [T]his endless procession
. . . illuminated arches . . . river of torches . . . thousands of lanterns . . . magic
phantasmagory, while there is a strong reflection in the air, as if there is a
fire.[26]

That same evening, in his palace, King George gave a banquet for the
foreign athletes and dignitaries, all the victors, foreign and Greek, and the
foreign press, 260 people in all. Royal invitations read "Informal Dress,"
so the athletes came in coat and tie, not tuxedo—except for an anonymous
American, who came in his gym shorts. And Louis wore the traditional
Greek kilt-like *fustenella* that we all now expect from him. After dinner
George noted, "The revival of the Olympic Games in their classical cradle
has been crowned by full and unexpected success" and told his guests he
wanted to congratulate those responsible, Crown Prince Constantine, Averoff, the general secretary, Philemon, and other groups. He closed by
expressing the hope that the foreigners who honored Greece would "ap-
point our land as a peaceful meeting place of the nations, as a continuous
and permanent site of the Olympic Games." As Philemon obsequiously
replied ("The diamonds which dropped from Your mouth . . . Oh King!
shine with such brilliance. . . . I thank God that before I breathe my last
that He granted I should see such a day"),[27] Coubertin sat over his empty
plate, fuming silently.

Justifiably, I think, the baron was angry first of all because George's
speech did not thank Coubertin nor mention the IOC or the 1894 Paris
congress, all of which he and other Greeks had often mentioned before.
George perhaps purposely avoided those topics this time because of another item. A second source of Coubertin's anger was, I think, more important to him than justice or due credit. It was a crucial, substantive question about the very nature of future Olympiads. It more than nettled
Coubertin's personal pride; it cut his grand plan back to the quick: "our
land . . . a permanent site of the Olympic Games." The Paris congress
minutes and the letterheads Vikelas and Coubertin had been using read,
"Athens, 1896, Paris, 1900." Everything Coubertin had ever said, thought,
or written about the matter had suggested Paris in 1900. On the eve of
the Paris congress the baron wrote, "every four years . . . the youth of the
world assembling at the great capitals of the world." Upon hearing those
dread words, "permanent site," Coubertin saw that resistance at that point
was not feasible: "I decided to play the simpleton, the man who did not
understand. I pretended to ignore the King's speech on the pretext" that
the king's wording and language left his point incomprehensible to for-

eigners.[28] Like the baron, we pass over this moment for now—to return to it later.

As Monday, April 13, dawned, the good weather was over. It was cold again, and very windy. Although the organizers tried to set up the boat races and rowing matches down at Phaleron Bay and many spectators arrived, the winds and waves were so bad that they tossed the boats and barges back on the shore. As only Greek teams entered, the boat races and rowing were simply canceled. Only one event was held, the twelve-hour cycling race at the velodrome. Few spectators braved the cold wind and duststorms to watch a race that was tedious anyway. After "describing endless circles of the track" all day long, an exhausted Adolf Schmal, of Austria, beat the only other surviving contestant, F. Keeping, of England— the twelve-hour event, understandably, would never be held again. The weather was so bad that streets were empty that night, and the Acropolis could not even be illuminated. Tuesday was even worse. It was to be the grand day of closing ceremonies and the formal awarding of medals and prizes to the athletes. At 1 P.M. the stadium began to fill, despite the horrible weather, and members of the committees took up their special seats for the dignified ceremonies, as the cold rain began to pelt them in torrents. The weather was so bad that the whole affair had to be postponed till the next day.[29]

On the tenth day, Wednesday, April 15, the ancient Greek gods seemed to smile on the Olympic revival. At least Anninos was reminded of "the splendor of ancient days," when this day

> dawned radiant and the Spring sun was covered only from time to time by wisps of light cloud which tempered its heat. The stadium from the early hours started to have the appearance of the first days, the density of the crowds in the surroundings was incredibly great. By 10 A.M. the crowds in the stadium were about as many as on the day of the Marathon race.[30]

When the royal family had taken their seats, the officials opened up the gates free to the public, and the place overflowed with people and joy. Almost immediately George Robertson, the Oxford student, sixth in the discus—who would soon give us all a gift by writing up the Olympiad and his impressions in detail—approached the king and offered him a Pindaric ode praising the Games. He had composed it himself, in ancient Greek language and meter, and now recited it to the king and assembled multitude. George rewarded him with one of the olive branches that would be given to the athletes who had won. Coubertin was highly impressed with this ("Music had opened [the Games], and poetry was present at their close"), thinking it showed the union of poetry and feats of strength, of body and mind.[31] What I see underscored by Robertson's Pindaric ode is that antiquity and poetry—Soutsos's 1833 poems—had begun the Greek Olympic movement; ancient Greek poetry (albeit composed by an Oxonian) was there at its culmination in the stadium. And Pindar's own original poetry was recited in translation at the Los Angeles Olympics, in 1984.[32] We are reminded once again how authentic our own Games are because of genuine influences from ancient Greece.

After Robertson's poem, King George prepared to distribute the official prizes and a certificate for each athlete being honored. There were a few special prizes for specific events. For every victor there was a silver medal (not gold) and an olive branch, actually cut from the sacred grove of Zeus in Olympia, as in antiquity—another truly authentic link between the ancient Olympics and our own Olympiad 1. (Perhaps even now our modern victors, at least in events held at ancient Olympia, could get actual branches of Olympic olive taken from the olives that still grow there.) With their branch of olive and silver first-place medal, then, our first IOC Olympic victors received precisely the same prizes as were given at the 1859 and 1870 Zappas Olympiads, the olive of antiquity and a silver medal. The 1870 victors even received those prizes from the very same king. Some of Brookes's Olympians, too, had already received those same prizes.[33] To each second place winner, George gave a bronze medal and a branch of laurel, the prize awarded in the ancient Pythian Games—and at Brookes's very first Olympic Games, in 1850, before he fell under the heavy influence of the Zappas Olympics. It is not wholly coincidence that all these modern Olympics gave nearly the same prizes. All were seeking to restore the spirit of antiquity, to be true revivals in some ways, and were historically interconnected. The similar prizes stress once again the authenticity of their Games and, therefore, of our own.

At the call of a herald, who announced each victor's name, country, and event, the athlete came up to King George, who formally saluted each victor and, as he gave each his prizes, congratulated each athlete in his own native tongue. It was as Soutsos had hoped: "If in such a festival, you King!, the scepter of the Greek nation in your hands, should crown the [winners] . . . appear on your throne in the middle of the Greek amphitheater. . . . "—but with a different king, and a far more grand display than Soutsos's fondest dreams.

The large crowd cheered for each victor, especially those who had won their hearts, Greeks or foreigners. Naturally, Louis received the loudest cheers ("a rumble as of thunder burst from every side") and the most coveted prize, the silver cup that Bréal had, in Paris in 1894, promised the marathon victor. He also got a valuable, beautifully painted, authentic ancient Greek vase (which he later donated to the museum). "[P]airs of pigeons ... were released and flew above the arena." After second-place prizes were distributed, Dr. Gebhardt, of Germany and the IOC, presented Crown Prince Constantine, the principal organizer, with a laurel crown. Then followed the parade of champions (and runners-up) around the stadium, led by Manos, with Louis in the first row, not far behind. He received lusty cheers from the crowd, a Greek flag, and long-distance kisses, which he repeatedly returned. As the parade ended, King George loudly announced, "I declare the end of the First International Olympic Games."[34]

Though there had been fireworks at Friday's Piraeus event, there were no fireworks at the end, and the crowd left. But it was not yet satiated. The people and the organizing committee's Board of Twelve assembled outside the stadium, and with bands playing and stadium guards carrying the flags of the Olympic participant nations, the impromptu assemblage, led by Timoleon Philemon, marched to the royal palace, asking that the crown prince appear and receive it. Constantine responded graciously to the thanks expressed by two who addressed him, L. Deligeorgis, representing the Board of Twelve, and Orfanidis, representing the Olympic victors. Then the mass moved to the offices of the organizing committee, and Mr. Papamikhalopoulos addressed the group's thanks to Philemon, for his role as secretary-general, and to Demetrios Vikelas, in his capacity as president of the IOC. This is the same Papamikhalopoulos who had led the pro-Olympic Games lobby in Parliament, in December 1894, when other representatives came to his support, invoking Zappas's name and desires as good cause to support Coubertin, Vikelas, and the IOC.[35] Again, no one explicitly thanked Coubertin, who had organized the congress that had chosen Greece to be host. Coubertin later castigated Vikelas for not telling the crowd, "Go on over to the Grande Bretagne," to congratulate the baron who was staying at that hotel. So the group dispersed, and the Acropolis went ablaze with lights, in a way that probably would have inspired Soutsos to write a poem or burst from ecstasy. Ancient and modern were impressively juxtaposed—no, not juxtaposed—united harmoniously in an attractive whole. Revival.[36]

FOURTEEN

The Olympic Games Finally Revived

Pierre de Coubertin was overpowered by what he saw as he travelled. Young as he was, the power of O'Connell was in his being and he adopted the great reformer's motto: "agitate, agitate, and then agitate."

—*William Sloane*, Report of the American Olympic Committee, Seventh Olympic Games, Antwerp, Belgium, 1920

The Greeks knew they had produced a winner, and all foreign eyewitnesses agree. They are unanimous in asserting that the games were a total success. The American athlete, Ellery Clark—1896 Olympic champion in both the high jump and the long jump—gave one of the fullest judgments, perhaps the more valuable, because, writing from 1911, he had some perspective.

> Other Olympic games held later were to attract greater numbers of athletes, were to result in the making of more remarkable records, but for the *time* itself, nothing could equal this first revival. The flavor of the Athenian soil— the feeling of helping to bridge the gap between the old and the new—the indefinable poetic charm of knowing one's self thus linked with the past, a successor to the great heroic figures of olden times—the splendid sportsmanship of the whole affair—there is but one first time for everything, and that first time was gloriously, and in a manner ever to be remembered, the privilege of the American team in 1896.[1]

All others concur, and many find marathon day especially to be remembered, a once-in-a-lifetime experience. "The first celebration of the Olympic Games has thus been a stupendous success" (Waldstein). "Athletics moved on a high plane, and were carried on with a dignity that ought not soon to be forgotten.... As the participants and patrons of the games reflect on the events of the ten days their unanimous feeling is well expressed in the phraseology employed by one of their number. 'I am always an optimist,' said he, 'and I always expected a success; but I never expected such a success' " (Richardson). "[B]eyond question an unbounded success, without a hitch" (F.). "While the organization of the athletics was, with the above-mentioned exceptions, wonderful under the circumstances, the organization of the meeting generally seemed to us to be nearly perfect. ... Such was the scene [on marathon day], unsurpassed and unsurpassable. Who, who was present there, does not wish that he may once again be permitted to behold it" (Robertson). Of that "unsurpassable" marathon day, F. wrote, "Egad! the excitement and enthusiasm were simply indescribable." Coubertin said of the episode of Louis's victory and the Greek anticipation and response, "[O]ne of the most extraordinary sights that I can remember. Its imprint stays with me."

On at least one other major point all witnesses, including Coubertin, agree: the importance of the crown prince. "[The Olympic Games'] successful issue is largely owing to the active and energetic co-operation of the Greek crown prince Constantine" (Coubertin). "[The] untiring efforts of the three eldest Princes, whose absolute devotion—for we can call it nothing less—was of supreme importance to the general result" (Robertson). "[T]he Crown Prince of Greece, who proved himself the most capable and energetic organizer of all the work here" (Waldstein).[2]

On one crucial item, however, the baron strongly dissented from an otherwise generally unanimous judgment, the item on which he had "decided to play the simpleton, the man who did not understand"—the site of subsequent Olympic Games. Except for Coubertin, virtually all who attended, it seems, agreed that Greece should become the permanent site of the modern Olympic Games or at least regarded it as a reasonable proposition that should be carefully weighed. The entire American Olympic team—without whom Olympiad 1 would not have succeeded so well— drew up and signed a formal memorial, addressed to Constantine. After thanking him and all Greeks for their hospitality, praising it, the conduct of the games, and the physical structure of the stadium, and noting that Greece was the "original home of the Olympic Games," the American athletes unanimously agreed that "these games should never be moved from their native soil." Many Americans residing in Greece also signed this document.[3]

Although noting that the original impetus came from Paris and Coubertin, Horton writes, "The success of this first meeting in Athens has converted all those who had the good fortune to be here, into earnest partisans of this city as a permanent meeting place. There is much to be said in favor of this view." In the main and in the end, he clearly votes for Athens. So too does F.: "[The American athletes' proposal] has much to commend it, from the sentimental, if not the practical side of the question. At Athens, the games are international, but in a distinctively Hellenic setting. ...

Surely such a combination need not blush before the . . . greater cities and wealthier nations." The IOC members present in Athens met briefly there during the Games to decide the site for 1904, confirming Paris in 1900 without discussion. But after the Games, some IOC members favored making Athens the permanent site.[4]

Robertson and Richardson were less ready to vote than these others but still thought Athens had much merit as a permanent site. Writing of the sentiment to make Athens a permanent site, Robertson says no one would have opposed it at the end of the Games, "and even now, when the splendour has somewhat faded from the mind, it is difficult to criticize this impulsive proposal. Yet it has great practical difficulties to face. In the first place, it would have to meet French opposition of the most forcible kind. The French regard themselves as the nursing-fathers of the first Olympic Games." "The French," of course, totaled one man but a forcible power, nonetheless. Richardson names him, "Baron de Coubertin, the member of the International Committee for France, and perhaps more than any other one man the originator of the whole project of the revival of the Olympic Games."[5] Coubertin's opposition to the idea of Greece as a permanent site, which he suppressed at the king's banquet on Sunday, April 12, was no longer the potentiality that Robertson foresaw; it was, by then, reality. Coubertin had already expressed it in strong terms to Crown Prince Constantine, with whom he met on the last day of the Games. Also attending that meeting were Vikelas, Manos, and Charles Waldstein, of the American School, who had been the go-between for Coubertin and Constantine in April 1894, before the congress and before Athens had been chosen as the inaugural site.[6]

Though some Athenians wished it, the Greek officials did not insist that Athens be the only permanent site, as the Americans had proposed. They did not suggest Coubertin cancel the 1900 Olympics at Paris or that he move them to Athens. They wanted to repeat the International Olympic Games in Athens. They offered to intercalate their own Games with Coubertin's; that is, between each Olympiad in other cities of the world would come the Athens Olympics, so there would be Olympic Games every two years, not every four. Coubertin did not oppose Greece's holding additional Games, in between his. But he insisted they could not be called "Olympics," that he somehow had, now, a monopoly on the name. He told the Greeks to call their Games "Athenians," so they would not be confused with his own "Olympic Games." The controversy between the Greeks and the baron was simply over whether Greeks could use that Greek word out of their own great past and their most recent surprising glory. "What's in a name?" Shakespeare asked. The answer seems to be a great deal, if not everything.[7]

The meeting with Constantine ended in an impasse, neither side yielding on the question of the name; but that inconclusive issue must not have been clear to all. Some saw the truth, others said Coubertin prevailed. Still others reported a Greek victory: the international Olympics would always stay in Athens.[8] The *New York Times* reported that the IOC had met at Constantine's house and "arranged for holding the next Games in Athens."[9] The *Times* (London), on April 16, reported, "The wish is generally expressed that Athens should in the future become the permanent site of the Olympic Games." The reporter notes that Paris was already scheduled as the next Olympic site but interjects the hope "that the paramount claims of Athens will be recognized." The *Times* then explains the proposal for Games every two years, alternating between Athens and elsewhere. It approves that principle but stresses that, no matter what else, permanent Games, called Olympics, should be held in Athens. As soon as the *Times* reached Athens, where Coubertin still lingered, enraged, he fired off, on April 23, a bitter letter to its editor. He shot from the hip. The baron accused the *Times* of having as its correspondent some "philhellene enthusiast," since he had reported that "the Olympic Games were from now on scheduled for Greece." "Nothing of the kind," the baron snapped.

The next Games, Coubertin's letter insisted, would be held in Paris and after that in either New York, Berlin, or Stockholm. Coubertin carefully suggested that no Games were to be held in Athens. But he went farther than that and aspersed the motives of the Greeks: "It is wholly natural that the brilliant success which my undertaking has just obtained has inspired in the Greeks the desire to monopolize it to their profit. But I cannot agree to such a plan. For my part, since I wanted the Games at Athens back when the Athenians could not see it at all and rejected them. . . .[10] Coubertin then says he will not give up and signs as "President of the IOC, Athens, April 23."[11]

Coubertin surely knew this would anger the Greeks. Not only did he imply that Greece, then floating on Olympic euphoria, would never again hold Olympic Games, but he also impugned their motives in wanting them. He accused Greeks of personal greed while they cited the hallowed traditions of their ancestors. He accused Greece of being a latecomer to the idea of modern Olympics, while they, besides the ancient tradition, were recalling the Olympics of Zappas. He accused all Athenians of opposing the Games, when the charge applied only to Dragoumis, Trikoupis, and their clique. It did not apply to the royal family or to Vikelas and applied least of all to the Athenian public—who, with Vikelas and Constantine, had successfully fought those naysayers on their own behalf and Coubertin's to carry off the Games. So it did anger the Greeks, including those in that unique culture, the world of men and pundits in the Athens coffee shops. The newspapers report that those pundits viewed Coubertin's letter as "improper, audacious, rude, unseemly, insulting." Vikelas knew those reports would, in turn, anger the baron all the more and tried to mollify him ahead of time, writing two letters to Paris; they went astray, or Coubertin was slow to respond.[12]

On May 15, however, Coubertin got out his inkwell and told Vikelas what he thought:

> I don't care what the Greek newspapers say about me. When it comes to ingratitude, Greece easily wins first prize. One must be a very strong philhellene to keep on loving her after that kind of a test. You all got your "branch of olive"—so did even Mr. Robertson—in a full stadium from the hands of the King. I am the only one whose name, if ever mentioned, was spoken only in secret. That is all a shame. My wife is ill from the rudeness she endured in Athens. . . . Had I imagined how we would be treated, I would not have brought her with me. . . . As for the Games, I continue on my plotted course, as if nothing had ever happened.[13]

With no response from Paris, on May 19, before getting Coubertin's letter (they crossed in the mail), Vikelas wrote him a third letter, one not meant "for your eyes only" as was most of their correspondence. He had copies of this letter made by a calligrapher and sent to all members of the IOC. In it he told the baron that the Greek Games would indeed bear the name Olympics.

> As you know, the idea of reviving the ancient Games dates from far back. Evangelis Zappas . . . founded Games, to which he gave the name "Olympics." . . . and Olympic Games were then celebrated in the old stadium in 1859, 1870, and 1875.[14] These festivals, without an international character, had no reverberation. . . . The desire to organize their functioning again has been one of the results of the 1896 international Olympic Games' success. The government is preparing to draft a law . . . and contests would take place every four years in the restored stadium. These contests would have the name "Olympic Games."—We have seen that this name has been restored in Greece by the Zappas bequest.

Vikelas here assures Coubertin that the Greek Olympics would not compete against "the international Games instituted by the Paris Congress." They would be held at the intervals in between the moving Games and even bear their own series number and forgo the appellation "International," if need be—but they would be called Olympics. But, Vikelas adds, the Greek Olympics would indeed be international, and he prefers they be designated that way, with numbers united with the moving series: "The Games could thus be celebrated every two years, the one time at Athens, and the next time, alternately, in one of the major cities of Europe or America." Near the end of Vikelas's long letter, he expresses a desire to have a second international athletic congress, at which the IOC would consider his proposal about intercalary Athens Olympics. The letter closes explaining that Vikelas has had copies of the letter made to send to the other members of the IOC.[15]

On May 24, before Coubertin got this bombshell, Vikelas received Coubertin's bombshell of May 15, wherein Coubertin called the Greeks the most ungrateful people on earth, bitterly complaining that he got no olive branch when Robertson did and that Greece had maltreated his wife and made her ill. Vikelas quickly took up his pen and with some astonishment ("your letter caused me much pain, I won't hide it") tried to mollify the angry baron. But Coubertin was hard to mollify and wrote Vikelas another complaining letter:

> The last day of the Athens Games, when you replied to the crowd that was cheering you, you had the opportunity to say to that demonstration, "I thank you. . . . But now go on over to the Hotel Grande Bretagne, it's your duty." You didn't have the courage to say it then, and now—I know you well—you regret it. But don't be distressed about it. I don't hold anything against you. I remain with boundless respect for your character . . . and love for you as a person.[16]

Coubertin and Vikelas, these Olympic giants and close friends, continued to spar, for a few years, over the question and name of intercalary Athenian Olympics. Despite their real differences of opinion and aim and their irritability with one another, the profound respect and love they had for each other somehow survived. Full details are somewhat unpleasant and not needed here.[17] On December 16, 1899, Coubertin again wrote Vikelas, still complaining about his maltreatment in Athens in 1896, the "scandalous ingratitude of almost all your countrymen"; yet he ends with a splendid expression of his personal affection for the first president of the IOC: "I have already said to so many people when speaking of you, 'Vikelas, he is the most noble person there is on earth.' "[18] The body of the letter interests us most. Coubertin still tries to discourage Vikelas from pursuing the idea of intercalary Athenian Olympics.

The idea that Olympic Games be retained in Athens is irrational. Greece doesn't have anywhere near the means to carry it out successfully. You've known that full well from the start, but with time you've become the representative of the "Greek Committee," not of the "International Committee." I will defend the internationalization of the Games until the end of my existence. . . . With respect to the Games in Athens, may those who propose them see to it that they succeed. I'll give my blessing, but their success is impossible.[19]

Unfortunately, Coubertin was wrong about his own immediate abilities to hold international Olympic Games in the great cities of the world. Everyone agrees that the much awaited Paris Games in 1900 and the 1904 Games at St. Louis were fiascos. The Paris Games actually held in 1900 were organized by neither Coubertin nor the IOC; nor were they called Olympics at the time; the St. Louis Olympiad was hardly internationalized and was embarrassing in many ways. But fortunately, Coubertin was also quite wrong about Athens' total inability to hold further international Olympiads. After the Paris failure of IOC Olympiad II in 1900, Coubertin could not stem the tide of sentiment for Athens Games among the other members of the IOC. In 1901 the IOC officially approved Vikelas's intercalary International Olympic Games at Athens proposal. In the wake of the dismal Olympiad III, in St. Louis in 1904—when the Games and Olympic movement were on the verge of collapse—Athens implemented the IOC's intercalary decision and produced another winner Olympiad, the "unofficial" official IOC Olympiad of 1906. Henry states that the Olympics might well not have continued, that is, London would probably not have agreed to host the 1908 Olympiad, had the 1906 Athens Olympics not implanted a "feeling of sympathy for the Olympic movement" in England.[20] And all Olympic historians seem to concur that the Athens 1906 intercalary Olympics were so successful as to save the movement and our Games. They may well rank in historical significance above the 1908 London Olympics.[21] The 1906 Games were again organized by the crown prince, by then a veteran, not a frustrated, Olympian. Coubertin did not come, but most of the IOC did. Vikelas lived to see his own Olympic dream fulfilled, to sit in the stadium and watch international Olympic Games once more succeed in Athens.[22] He died two years later.

Thus the 1906 Athens Olympics, almost a repeat of 1896 but even better, confirmed and saved what was started there ten years before—when the weather was abominable and many of the winning marks abysmal. IOC Olympiad I was, against all odds, a glorious success, the grandest sporting event to that point in the history of earth. Ancient Greek Olympiads, despite no doubt vastly superior quality in the performances, had only Greek athletes, a tiny program limited to a few sports (nothing but track and field, with wrestling, boxing, a combination of the two, and equestrian contests); even in their heyday they never lasted more than five days. While the ancient Olympics attracted many spectators from all over the Greek world, the stadium, unlike those at Athens and Delphi, never had permanent seats for spectators (not even in Roman times); nor did it ever hold vast crowds comparable to those of Athens in 1896. England and America had already enjoyed great sport gatherings but nothing like this. Soutsos had foreseen the potential magnificence of a grand Olympiad in Athens but had not dreamed of so extensive or vast an international festival. Brookes had first conceived the idea of Olympic Games in Athens, which were realized in 1896, and he, like Soutsos, eventually thought in grand terms. But Coubertin succeeded where the other two appeared to have failed. We must ask why.

First and perhaps most importantly, the time was much riper for Coubertin. Soutsos and Brookes were far ahead of their times. When Soutsos began his Olympic campaign, there were no athletics in Greece and virtually none elsewhere in Europe. By Brookes's time, organization of and interest in athletic sports, apart from cricket, was little more than embryonic, even in England.[23] By the end of the nineteenth century, when Coubertin entered the scene, that interest in sports was spreading to the continent, and in America interest in athletics was already burgeoning; there is not yet any foreseeable downward turn. Just a decade or so before 1896, no foreign athletes would have shown up for international Olympic Games, anywhere.

Coubertin had the leisure time, a genuine talent for public relations, and certainly better help from others. What might Brookes have given for Constantine and Vikelas as his Greek contacts, instead of Gennadius? The constant rebuffs that met him in both England and Greece, even for a one-day Olympiad, surely would have made the grandeur and success of IOC Olympiad 1 hard for Brookes to believe. And, besides perhaps better luck generally, Coubertin had other advantages Brookes did not have: some superlative athletes, such as Spyros Louis and James Thorpe, who later teamed up with the Swedes in 1912 to seal, if not guarantee, the success of the modern Olympic revival movement signaled in 1896.[24]

In 1896 Coubertin and the Greeks had surpassed anything their predecessors could have dreamed. They had planned and then produced a magnificent nine-day Olympic festival (which took ten days). Much of the credit must go to Coubertin. He first formulated the principle, all sports, all nations, all people; he believed it in his heart and adhered to it in his acts. It proved to be the formula that succeeded then and succeeds today. Knowing that there was not much genuine interest in an Olympic revival—perhaps even realizing that Brookes's national revival and his Athens international Olympic proposal had failed for lack of support—he used the ruse of amateurism to assemble people at Paris, changed the goal of the conference, and then exploited the emotions of the moment. Those magic Olympic moments and emotions worked at Paris in 1894; they worked at Athens in 1896; and they still work today. As Brookes said, "what is right in itself . . . will ultimately prevail."[25] But it probably did take Coubertin's cunning and Athens' setting for "right" to succeed.

The idea and especially the tale, as we have it, of a single *renovateur,* Coubertin, is charming and romantic indeed, even wonderful.[26] But the full story, I think, is even better. The International Olympic Games are an authentic revival of the ancient Games and a truly international creation. The American Sloane, the Hungarian Kemeny, and the German Gebhardt played a part, especially by providing teams for the 1896 Games. But the principals are, first and foremost, a Frenchman, an Englishman, and a few Greeks. Several men—and some truly lucky acts of fate that intertwined them—are responsible for the revival of the Olympic Games; had any one of them not played his crucial role, I think it almost certain that we would not have the modern Olympic Games as we know them, and no Atlanta Golden Olympics in 1996. Certainly to be named in this select group are Zappas, Vikelas, and Prince Constantine.

Three others, dedicated visionaries, Soutsos, Brookes, and Coubertin, though each had other concerns and achievements, made the Olympic revival movement their principal life's work. Through his foresight, acute perceptions of history, past and future, and of reality around him, hard work, effrontery, and better help from others—we must not forget Louis and Thorpe—Coubertin succeeded best and well deserves the esteemed title, Olympic *renovateur.* But so also, I think, do the other two. Coubertin could—or rather would—not have done it without them. Soutsos's campaign led directly to the Zappas Olympic series, which, in turn, despite its spottiness, profoundly influenced King George, Constantine, many members of Greek parliament, and especially the Greek people. Greece was eagerly primed for modern Olympic Games. When Coubertin sought Greek help in producing IOC Olympiad 1, most of Greece was not so skeptical, recalcitrant, and incredulous as Trikoupis's clique and many others around the world. Brookes first told Coubertin of the Olympic idea; his own activity in England—his Olympic movements and the reactions to them—did much to spur the growth and exportation of British sports to the point where international Olympics were possible in 1896 and thereafter. Coubertin probably understood all this when he wrote, "[E]verything past affects the future, and no future can be built without taking the past into account."[27]

Coubertin's 1894 Paris congress and later Olympic efforts in many ways saved Soutsos's and Brookes's life's work, which might otherwise have been in vain. He picked up the torch. His 1894 choice of Athens as the first site was the critical factor that inspired Greece with patriotic zeal to hold outstanding Games. Arguing that Greece must not embarrass itself before the world's eyes, pro-Olympic Greeks cited the Paris congress's decision, more often than the Soutsos-Zappas tradition, as compelling cause to hold the 1896 Olympics.[28] Brookes, who first proposed international Olympics at Athens, was jubilant at Coubertin's march toward that goal; he relished the baron's expanded worldwide notion as a superb improvement over his own Olympic idea and trusted Coubertin as the torchbearer Gennadius had failed to become. Coubertin may now be compelled to share his title *renovateur*; but perhaps he merits an even loftier one. Despite the baron's shortcomings in sharing credit with others and his inactivity in 1895, his 1894 congress and his worldwide vision of Olympics aimed at "all sports for all people" might earn him yet another title, namely, *sauveur*, savior of the Olympic movement and its long-term success.[29]

These men's common achievement, culminating in Coubertin's, immense in magnitude, was the revival of the ancient Olympic Games—today transformed into something incomparably grand, an institution embracing the entire world, a source of peaceful national pride and the celebration of individual human achievement. That was the function of the ancient Olympics, too, which were revived in 1896 and now thrive with that expansive, renewed breath.[30]

Creatures of a day! What is a person? What is no person? Man is the dream of a shadow. But whenever the god-given gleam comes, a brilliant light plays upon men, and their life is sweet.

This poem, "Victory Ode for Aristomenes," was, according to the best available sources, the last poem Pindar wrote before he died. In his last public performance before his own death, Richard Basehart gave a reading of this same ode at the closing ceremonies of the 1984 Olympic Games at Los Angeles.[31]

Creatures of a day! Man is merely a shadow's dream. But when god-given glory comes upon him in victory, a bright light shines upon us, and our life is sweet.

Appendix
Note on Documents

This book makes frequent use of many unpublished documents now in archives in Greece, England, and Switzerland. I here explain what these documents are and how they are cited above.

Kivroglou Documents

This group consists of more than a score of original handwritten documents, dated 1856–65, pertaining to the establishment of modern Olympic Games in Greece, sponsored by Evangelis Zappas. Most are letters from S. Skoufos (Greek consul general to Romania) and from Zappas himself (in a secretary's hand) to Alexandros Rangavis (Greek minister of exterior) and the Greek government. These have been edited in Kivroglou, "Die Bemühungen." In an appendix to this thesis, Kivroglou includes, for each document, a photocopy of the original, his transcription into current printed Greek characters, and a German translation. Since the originals are in a tattered condition and written in a very difficult mid-nineteenth-century Greek script, Kivroglou is owed a great debt for his painstaking work.

Kivroglou locates these letters in the Historical Archives section, Greek Ministry of Exterior, with the exception of Kivroglou docs. 3, 6, 9, and 11–13 (all personal letters from Zappas to Rangavis), which are in the Research Center for the History of Modern Greece in the Academy of Athens (stored under Rangavis's name). These materials do not seem to have been catalogued by an archivist, nor have I myself examined them. I cite them according to their numbering in Kivroglou's appendix.

Dragoumis Documents

This group consists of sundry documents, mostly in Greek, both handwritten and printed, pertaining to the activity of the Greek Zappas Olympic committee from 1859 to after 1900. The committee had various official names over the period, and the files even include some printed documents of a former committee dating back to 1837. Some of the items, such as the official published reports of the Greek Olympic series of 1859–88, are, with difficulty, available in a few other places in Greece. But the unique, handwritten documents are of great importance (e.g., hand-drawn plans for Olympic buildings), especially the personal correspondence, including previously unknown letters from Pierre de Coubertin, W. P. Brookes, and Demetrios Vikelas (first president of the IOC).

Amounting to hundreds of items originally arranged in five large cartons, these documents were among the vast papers of Stephanos Dragoumis (1842–1923), prominent Greek politician and head of the Zappas Olympic committee for decades. He is the man notorious in Olympic histories for sending Coubertin a "get lost" letter in 1894 as Coubertin left for Greece to arrange for the first IOC Games at Athens in 1896.[1] Around 1985, Dragoumis's papers were willed to the American School of Classical Studies in Athens for preservation in the Gennadius Library, which it administers. They have recently been catalogued by Christina Varda, the excellent Gennadius archivist. Items especially relevant to Olympics are in *phakeloi* (envelopes) 231–35;[2] but the published catalogue does not list each individual item or give many details. I have myself spent months studying these documents and published a few of them (including parts of unknown letters from Brookes and Coubertin), before they were catalogued.[3] There is so far no other publication concerning these documents. I cite them here as "Dragoumis doc.," except in a few cases where, not knowing their present catalogue number, I cite them by their original carton number.[4]

"Congrès 1894"

This collection comprises more than a hundred documents (all, I think, dated 1894), almost all handwritten—personal letters, minutes of the meetings, and other items, and a few printed materials—pertaining to the June 1894 Paris Athletic Congress, organized by Pierre de Coubertin. That congress founded the IOC and made the decision to hold the first IOC International Olympic Games at Athens in 1896. These original documents (clearly assembled by Coubertin himself) are in the IOC archives, Lausanne; I have used a set of photocopies in a manila file folder marked "Congrès 1894," which is kept (or was in 1985 and 1987, when I examined them) in an upstairs room of (what was called then, at least) the IOC Library and Reading Room, in downtown Lausanne. I know of no archival catalogue for this file and cite items in it merely as "Congrès 1894."

I also use, in later chapters, "Correspondance, Pierre de Coubertin/Demetrius Vikelas, 1894–1905," a bound volume (photocopies) of original letters from Vikelas (first president of the IOC) to Coubertin shelved in the open stacks of the IOC Library in Lausanne.

Brookes Papers

This collection of documents, numbering in the thousands, was meticulously assembled by Dr. W. P. Brookes in Much Wenlock, Shropshire, from the 1840s to his death in 1895 (and continued for a time thereafter by others). Roughly half of this material is handwritten: original correspondence, minutes of meetings, financial reports, etc. The other half consists of newspaper clippings relating to various modern revivals of the Olympic Games, physical education, and Brookes's other interests, along with the printed programs for those Olympic Games with which Brookes was concerned. Contents of these papers are of uneven interest to the Olympic historian, since they contain everything from detailed reports about acquiring a railroad station at Wenlock to numerous, otherwise unknown, original letters from Coubertin and from John Gennadius (Greek ambassador to England), whom Brookes badgered throughout the 1880s in hopes of getting Greece to help Brookes realize his dream, the reestablishment of Olympic Games on an international basis. These letters (and even some newspaper clippings) have incalculable importance to Olympic history.

Brookes's copious archives are preserved in seven large albums of the type called scrapbooks in English. They are housed (at least as of 1991) in an old trunk in a second-story room of the Much Wenlock Corn Exchange Building. They are still kept under the auspices of the Much Wenlock Olympian Society. Their importance was recognized by Sam Mullins, former director of the Wenlock Museum, who has now published a brief but accurate popular account of Brookes and his Olympic activity: *William Penny Brookes and the Wenlock Games.* These same documents have been carefully studied and well interpreted by Neumüller, in "Die Geschichte." My own use of the Brookes documents comes mostly from my first-hand study of these archives in Wenlock, in the summer of 1991. But I have also used a microfilm copy of them, for which I am deeply indebted to Mullins, Rühl, and the British Olympic Association (especially Donald Anthony).

Brookes was clearly the first serious historian of the modern Olympic movement, keeping a continuous record from long before the first Greek Olympiad in 1859 through his friendship with Coubertin and the first issue of Coubertin's IOC *Bulletin* in 1894. But because he worked with so many diverse people for half a century on several projects and kept his scrapbooks on a daily basis, one cannot predict exactly what will be found where in them. I have found important letters in unexpected places, which Neumüller did not notice (e.g., Wyse's important February 10, 1859, letter to Brookes, about the pending Zappas Greek Olympics, and other matters of Brookes's correspondence with Coubertin and Gennadius).

In 1991 the Wenlock documents had not yet been catalogued, and I believe that is still the case. Neumüller developed a numbering system for the Wenlock scrapbooks (based, he says, on their chronological order), which I had hoped to follow here, for the sake of uniformity.[5] As an unpublished *Diplomarbeit*, Neumüller's is a superb achievement, far better than most published American doctoral dissertations; I have profited greatly from this work. But his "chronological order" is patently faulty, and there are serious problems with his citations. Occasionally and excusably, the citation is wrong; but more important, he states that some albums (volumes 3 and 7) are unpaginated, so he cannot cite them by page number. I find legible page numbers, even in the microfilm, and cite them by page. Furthermore, I find no mention of volume 1 in Neumüller, nor does the microfilm have any volume to equate with Neumüller no. 2 ("Minute Book of the Sanitary Board of the Much Wenlock Borough Council"). Neumüller never cites his no. 2, but my memory of the archives does not preclude such a volume. I cannot, however, believe that microfilm volume 1 could have such a description. Its contents (see description, below) have nothing to do with the sanitary board but concern very different things, sometimes important to Olympic history. Finally, Neumüller's description of the nature of some scrapbooks is misleading, and there are minor typos in the dates. I have reluctantly, therefore, recast the numbering system, basing it on the microfilm copy, which I suspect will be the form in which most future scholars will access these documents. But I stress the high quality of Neumüller's work and my own debt to it. Without it, I might have been lost.

The microfilm copy consists of two reels, the first containing four scrapbooks, divided as volumes 1–4; the second reel has three more books, called volumes 5–7. Since Brookes often pasted a multipage item on a single scrapbook page, in some cases several pages of a letter or published document may be cited by a single page. The microfilm photographer usually accounts for this more-than-a-page-on-one-page situation by opening the document page by page and taking repeated photos; but it appears that the photographer, after taking the front page of a multipage letter, sometimes forgot to open it up and photograph subsequent pages. In these cases, I rely on my own handwritten notes taken in Wenlock. I sometimes cite both the document itself and the page in Neumüller where it is mentioned, in case his thesis should reach the wider readership that it deserves. I here give a concordance of my citations with those given in Neumüller ("Die Geschichte," 296).

Microfilm	Neumüller doc. no. and description
vol. 1	(Neumüller omits volume 1)
vol. 2	7: "Sammelmappe der W.A.R.S."
vol. 3	6: "M(inute). B(ook). III"
vol. 4	3: "M.B. I"
vol. 5	4: "M.B. II"
vol. 6	5: "M.B. IV"
vol. 7	1: "Presscuttings of the W.A.R.S"

Volume 1 is not labeled; it opens with a poem by Brookes himself and contains a great variety of personal letters, some of Brookes's 1840 correspondence with medical boards and his Italian medical teachers, newspaper clippings spanning decades, Gennadius's last (1893) letter relative to the international Olympic movement, and the printed text of Brookes's speech at the 1866 London Olympics, from which Coubertin quoted in 1889.

Volume 2 is labeled, in Brookes's hand, "The Reading Society's Album" and headed with the seal of the Greek Delegation in London. It consists almost wholly of Brookes's personal correspondence over many years, a few important to the Olympics (including Wyse's handwritten results of the 1859 Zappas Athens Olympics). It closes with the printed bylaws of the Wenlock Olympian Society.

Volume 3 is labeled by a much later hand "1841–1860 Reports of the W.A.R.S." It contains the minutes of early meetings, a few newspaper clippings, a catalogue of trees that Brookes planted, and a variety of other items.

Volume 4 is labeled "Minute Book of the Wenlock Olympian Society." It opens with the Foundation Papers of the Wenlock Olympian Class in 1850 and contains many personal letters to and from Brookes, newspaper clippings, and many other WOC and WOS documents to 1876, minutes, athletic programs, etc., some handwritten, others printed.

Volume 5, the successor to volume 4, contains letters and other documents dated 1877–95 (including correspondence with Gennadius and Coubertin and early IOC documents).

Volume 6 is the successor to volume 5 and contains WOS documents dated 1891–1924, virtually all of them postdating Brookes's death and the first IOC Games in 1896 (I have no occasion to cite it here).

Volume 7 is labeled, not in Brookes's hand, "W.A.R.S.—Various Presscuttings, activities of 1841–1868," which is an adequate description of its contents; it contains newspaper clippings relating to physical education and Olympic Games, along with a few other unrelated topics.

Notes

ONE   The Birth of the Olympic Idea

1. Soutsos is regarded as the founder of romanticism in modern Greek poetry, but detailed biographical information on him is scarce, even in Greek. There is no article on him in the *Mega Hellenikon viographikon lexikon*, and the entry in the standard Greek encyclopedia is brief. There is a very brief English account of Soutsos in Politis, *History of Modern Greek Literature*, 139–40. I draw my information on Soutsos's biography and bibliography mainly from the rather meager front matter in several publications of his works, all in Greek.

2. These two poems, first published in serial form in *Helios* in 1833–34 (starting July 4, 1833), were soon republished as a book: Soutsos, *Nekrikos dialogos*.

3. Soutsos, *Nekrikos dialogos*, 15–16.

4. Ancient Greece was not a single political unit but a nonunified collection of discrete independent city-states sharing a language and a culture—but often at war with one another. The Panhellenic athletic festivals, such as the Olympics, were indeed almost the only institutions where there was a strong feeling of commonality and goodwill among the various Greeks of antiquity.

5. Soutsos, *Nekrikos dialogos*, 22–23.

6. With Soutsos, the ghosts were perhaps not wholly metaphoric. Since much of Coubertin's activity has been attributed to his "vision" at Rugby Chapel (see chapter 6, below), to compare Soutsos's experience with Coubertin's is relevant and reinforces the authenticity of our own Olympic revival: "I often sat, immersed in thought, on the beaches of Attica, where the shades of our great ancestors wander about." In Athens he would strain "to hear the voice of an ancient Greek"; expecting to come upon "Socrates philosophizing," he would "shudder"; see the first prologue to his *Messias*, 5.

7. Decker and Kivroglou state that Soutsos was a member of a "Committee" that proposed the revival of the Olympics in 1835 ("Die Begründung," 196, citing Kivroglou, "Die Bemühungen," 25). But it seems certain Soutsos acted on his own; there was no committee. Kivroglou must have misinterpreted these words in Soutsos's article in *Helios*, July 13, 1856: "In 1835 we wrote a memo concerning the establishment of the Olympic Games; the Minister of Interior, Iannis Kolletis, accepted it." Apparently the plural "we wrote" misled Kivroglou into presupposing a committee. But a close reading of the whole article makes it clear that Soutsos submitted the proposal as an individual. Nowhere in his article does Soutsos sug-

gest any committee; and—as editor of the paper—Soutsos regularly used the editorial "we," rather than "I," when referring to himself.

8. Soutsos knew Kolletis personally and had had a moving experience in Kolletis's home. There he met the great hero of the War of Independence, Georgios Karaïskakis ("a few days after the disaster of Mesolongion"). Karaïskakis told the young poet that he, Karaïskakis, was "the warrior" side of the renewed Greece; but that he, Soutsos, would be the intellectual, artistic side (Soutsos, *Tria lyrika dramata*, 90). Soutsos was but twenty years old at that time.

9. March 25 by the Greek Julian calendar, April 6 by ours. Greece did not adopt the modern Gregorian calendar until well into this century; to convert a nineteenth-century date from the Greek calendar to our own, add twelve days.

10. *Helios*, July 13, 1856.

11. Diamantes, "Protasis," 307–33. The original (French) text occupies 312–23. Because the document is signed by Kolletis, Dolianitis concludes that the ideas in the proposal are Kolletis's own ("Evangelos Zappas," 2–5). Again, a close reading of Soutsos's article in *Helios*, July 13, 1856, makes it clear that Kolletis is reproducing, while placing his own name and authority to it, the very proposal that Soutsos himself had drafted.

12. True to its early-nineteenth-century origins, the memo recommends the highest prize (ten thousand drachmas) for the philosophy prize, the lowest (two thousand drachmas) for the footrace. We shall often see the nineteenth century devaluing physical excellence compared to intellectual or spiritual achievement—an action not in keeping with the ancient Greek models and the very imbalance that Brookes and Coubertin devoted their lives to correct.

Similarly, the memo notes that young women ran in competition (in a separate festival) at ancient Olympia, but "[c]e coutume ne doit plus être imité" (Diamantes, "Protasis," 322).

13. While prosecuting the Jim Thorpe case, Coubertin wrote: "[A]ntiquity allowed participation in the Olympics only to those athletes who were irreproachable. Ought it not to be the same in the modern world?" (*Textes choisis*, 2:579). But the ancient Olympics enforced no such rule at all; see Young, *Olympic Myth*, 73 n. 70, especially the citation of Philostratus, *Gymnastika*, 152. Surprisingly, Soutsos does not propose an athletes' oath. For the history of actual Olympic oaths for athletes in English, Greek, and IOC Olympics, see comments on Brookes's 1867 Olympics in chapter 3 and on the 1870 Zappas Olympics in chapter 4, below.

14. See, for example, Mahaffy, "Olympic Games at Athens in 1875": "Were we to propose the resuscitation of the Olympic Games in the Panathenaic stadium at Athens . . . we should fear an accusation of absurdity in transferring Olympia to Athens" (324). Of course, with our IOC Olympiad 1 at Athens in 1896, we committed the very "absurdity" that Mahaffy ridicules.

15. The Greeks had many recurring athletic festivals in antiquity, some of them (Pythian, Isthmian, and Nemean Games) almost as prestigious as the Olympics. But the Olympics did, in fact, far eclipse all others; see Pindar *Olympian Odes* 1.1–7.

16. Soutsos, *Helios*, July 13, 1856, 2.

17. Royal Decree of Otto, King of Greece, dated January 25, 1837, reprinted in Epitrope ton Olympion, *Nomoi*, 1–8.

18. Some might suspect that the Oktoberfest of Otto's native Bavaria influenced him as much as Soutsos's proposal. But Otto did not at this time suggest October, and the law's details come far closer to Soutsos's proposal than to the Bavarian festival, even with its later use of the word "Olympics." For the Oktoberfest, see Lennartz, *Kenntnisse und Vorstellungen*, 172.

19. The official 1838 civil document, signed by the village secretary, is reproduced in Giannopoulos, "I epanadrysis ton Olympikon Agonon," 566–67. The document printed comes from the personal archives of Letrini committee member Giannopoulos, certified as to its minute accuracy by a descendant. The program mentioned in the document is very limited; it suggests the committee crown victors "in one or more events of the pentathlon."

20. Chrysafis, *Oi synchronoi diethneis Olympiakoi Agones*, 17, says his personal attempts in Letrini to uncover more on this matter produced nothing.

21. See the end of my discussion of the 1875 Zappas Games in chapter 4, below.

22. Soutsos, *Tria lyrika dramata*, 87–88.

23. Reported in *Helios*, July 13, 1856. Soutsos adds that this 1845 speech was then published, but I have not found it.

24. Soutsos, prologue to *Ta hapanta*, 33–37; reprinted in *Helios*, July 13, 1856.

25. My discussion of the 1835 Soutsos document (above) necessarily omits details such as "que chaque Commune de la première classe . . . soit tenue de présenter un char" (320).

26. A brief but accurate account of Brookes and his Olympic activity is found in Mullins, *Brookes and the Wenlock Games*. That by Cyril Bracegirdle, "Olympic Dreamer," 276–78, is so brief and inaccurate that it has no value. My own information on Brookes comes mostly from my first-hand study of the archives in Wenlock (see appendix). Much biographical information can be found there. There is as yet no biography of Brookes, but Helen Cromarty, researcher at Birmingham University, is writing one.

27. Minutes, WARS Meeting, Oct. 1, 1849 (Brookes papers, 3:85; Neumüller, "Die Geschichte," 45).

28. Minutes, WARS meeting, Feb. 25, 1850 (Brookes papers, 1:2), written in Brookes's own hand. Neumüller, "Die Geschichte," civ–cvi, gives a photocopy of these original minutes.

29. For the 104th Wenlock Olympian Games (1990), IOC member Princess Anne was the honored guest; there were some connections with the bid of Birmingham for the 1996 Games. The program for the 1991 Games (105th Wenlock Olympian Games, Much Wenlock) contains a brief history of Dr. Brookes and full lists of the competitors and events.

30. Strutt, *Sports and Pastimes of the People of England*, 63–64. English-Greek dictionaries and translations of ancient Greek texts often render the Greek *diskos* with "quoit." Brookes, in the *Shrewsbury Chronicle*, Oct. 9, 1858, uses "quoit" in his translation of the weight throw *(solos)* event in Homer *Iliad* 23; and "quoits" is the translation of the modern discus event *(diskos)* held at the 1859 Athens Olympics as given in the Wenlock archives (Brookes papers, 4:82).

31. Neumüller, "Die Geschichte," assembles the summary results of this (ii) and all subsequent Wenlock Olympian Games.

32. *Eddowes's Shrewsbury Journal*, Oct. 30, 1850 (Brookes papers, 4:6).

33. *Shrewsbury Chronicle*, Oct. 3, 1851 (Brookes papers, 4:11), whence comes the rest of this account.

34. A unique event was a footrace for older women. While other contestants received cash or a book of known value, the woman victor received a cup of tea. One might hope that this event—won by M. Speake—inaugurated women's competitions in Brookes's Games. But later female competitions seem limited to knitting, arithmetic, etc. This race "for old women" seems more like the men's "hopping on one leg" or later wheelbarrow races, perhaps aimed more at amusement than athleticism. The newspaper report calls this 1851 event "[t]he most amusing of all contests." In the Wenlock Museum, a recent painting depicts this 1851 "old women's race for a cup of tea."

35. So in ancient Athens, too, a few events were limited to Athenians, as ancient inscriptions prove: *IG* 2^2.2313 and 2314; see also Kyle, *Athletics in Ancient Athens*, 38. But all the events at Olympia were "open," and even in those Games at Athens all the events on the Olympic program were "open."

36. Several nineteenth-century photos of the tilting still exist in the Wenlock archives; and Brookes often described the event for others, most elaborately in "Tilting at the Ring": "The champion tilter of the preceding year accompanied by the herald . . . rides into the lists, when the herald, after a flourish of his trumpet, proclaims . . . '[name of defending champion], champion tilter of England, challenges all comers. If any one is willing to contend with him, let him enter the lists and take up his glove.' The champion tilter then throws down his gauntlet. A distant trumpet announces the approach of the intending competitors, who enter the lists."

The first challenger, dismounting, took up the glove and handed it down the line through the hands of all competitors. The entrants were then divided by lot into sets of three or four and, in succession, charged toward the ring. The first tilter to carry off the ring three times was declared victor.

> The victor, preceded by young girls casting flowers before him, and by a band playing "See the conquering hero comes," is escorted to the front of the stand when the herald proclaims him the champion tilter of England. Dismounting and kneeling on one knee, he is then crowned with an olive wreath by the lady paramount. . . . She also places over his shoulder and across his breast the champion's scarf, bearing the motto "Honour my guide." . . . The champion tilter's silver goblet, filled with champagne, is then handed to the queen of the tournament, who drinks to [his] health, a toast which is heartily joined in by his surrounding friends. The ceremony is concluded by the singing of one of the prize odes.

Cf. Coubertin, "Typical Englishman," 65, and photo on 64. Pubs in Wenlock now display rings from the nineteenth-century tilting.

37. "Sur certains points cependant, l'antiquité ne suffisait pas au Dr. Brookes; elle ignorait la galanterie. Il prit donc au moyen-âge quelques-unes de ses chevalresques coutumes, et voulut que le vainqueur de son tournoi ployât le genou pour recevoir des mains d'une dame le laurier symbolique" (Coubertin, "Les Jeux Olympiques à Much Wenlock," 708). On the next page, Coubertin describes Brookes's tilting event. These Wenlock impressions profoundly influenced Coub-

ertin's Olympic idea and made him equate medieval knights with ancient Greek athletes and jousting tournaments with the Olympic Games. So in his "La préface," 153, he writes: "Il y a eu en plein moyen-âge un retour de l'esprit athlétique: c'est la chevalerie. Cette veillée des armes qui précédait la fête toute de joie et d'activité physiques par laquelle le jeune chevalier inaugurait sa vie nouvelle, c'est peut-être ce qui, depuis quinze cents ans, a le plus ressemblé aux jeux olympiques."

38. Coubertin, "Typical Englishman," 64–65.

39. *Wolverhampton Chronicle*, Sept. 19, 1855 (Brookes papers, 4:26).

40. Too much meaningless nit-picking has been made of Olympic terminology in recent times. "Olympic Games" appears frequently in references to the Wenlock contests (e.g., *Wolverhampton Chronicle*, Sept. 19, 1855 [Brookes papers, 4:26]). Coubertin himself used "Olympic Games" in writing of Brookes's meetings ("Les Jeux Olympiques à Much Wenlock"), and his own friends used the term "Olympian Games" to denote the first IOC Games in Athens, in 1896 (Gennadius, "Revival of the Olympian Games"). Eyewitness accounts of those 1896 Games often call them "Olympian," not "Olympic" (see the titles of the articles by George Horton, Rufus Richardson, and Charles Waldstein). The ancient Greeks rarely used the term "Olympic Games" at all (a term not found in Pindar, the poet of the ancient Olympic Games). They tended to say simply "Olympiads" or "the contests at Olympia."

TWO   The First Zappas Olympiad

1. His name, "Evangelis," ends in *eta sigma* and accents the third syllable (despite current Greek practice, which ends such a name in *omicron sigma* and accents the second syllable). There is as yet no full biography of Zappas and nothing at all except in Greek. I mention two biographical pamphlets: Goudas, *Evangelis Zappas*, and Lykourgos, *Logos epitaphios eis to mnemosynon E. Zappa*. Very useful and more accessible is the entry for Zappas in the *Mega Hellenikon viographikon lexikon* (1:392–410). Part of the Zappas mystery arises because Zappas's business dealings are still not fully clear, nor is the manner in which Greece spent his money and Romania later took much of what was left. Further, Zappas was a man from the fiercely individual and unique culture of the mountains in northwestern Greece and southern Albania, whose customs differed from those of others. Lastly, the illness Zappas developed late in his life clearly included poor mental health. His biographers all deal gingerly with these topics.

2. Lambove is still in Albania. For the roles of Botsaris and his Souliots in the war and for Botsaris's fabled death, see Finlay, *Greek Revolution* (index, under "Botsaris"). Goudas compares the relationship of Zappas and Botsaris to that of Patroclus and Achilles in Homer's *Iliad* (*Evangelis Zappas*, 4–9).

3. Soutsos left Romania before Zappas arrived. Dimitra Pikramenou-Varfi says: "[Zappas] had already made up his mind in 1843 to finance the re-founding of the Olympic Games. However . . . [i]t was, in fact, in March 1865 that Evangelis Zappas . . . came forward with his offer of finance" ("Revival of the Olympic Idea," 71). But I cannot find her source, and surely Soutsos would have mentioned such earlier Zappas interest when he later gave a detailed history of his and Zappas's proposals.

4. Rangavis, *Apomnemoneumata*, 2:377; but I know of no article by Soutsos precisely fitting this description, and Rangavis himself says his own memory is vague on the matter.

5. Skoufos states (Kivroglou, "Die Bemühungen," doc. 1) that Zappas wanted the Olympic exhibition hall for works of "art and industry" (cf. Soutsos's proposal) to include a "museum of our antiquities": so also Soutsos, in *Helios*, July 13, 1856, says that his original proposal included "exhibitions of the inscriptions and antiquities that have been found."

6. Chrysafis, *Oi synchronoi diethneis Olympiakoi Agones*, 24, gives 1858, and I followed him (Young, "Origins," 274)—wrongly, in view of the original 1856 documents in Kivroglou. In fact, Zappas proposed that the first revived Olympic Games actually take place in 1857 (Kivroglou, "Die Bemühungen," doc. 1).

7. Kivroglou, "Die Bemühungen," 27, with relevant documents in the appendix.

8. Ibid., doc. 1.

9. This letter is not preserved, but Kivroglou, "Die Bemühungen," docs. 2–4 (Skoufos's and Zappas's July 15 letters, below) give July 10 as the date when Skoufos told Zappas of its contents.

10. Rangavis published at least three different paraphrases of his own July 1856 letter. I follow the earliest version from "Ypomnematikoi Semeiosis" [Berlin], July 9/21, 1886; reprinted in *Mega Hellenikon viographikon lexikon*, 1:396); for there Rangavis admits that Zappas forced him to compromise by adding athletics to the proposed Olympic program. In *Apomnemoneumata* (which Kivroglou, "Die Bemühungen," 29–30, follows), Rangavis suggests that he offered the compromise himself but told Zappas: "[Nations become distinguished] not by physical strength and ability but through intellectual activity and development" (2:378). A third and yet different version is in *Hestia*, Jan. 10/22, 1888, 17.

11. Kivroglou, "Die Bemühungen," docs. 3, 4.

12. "July" is legible, but not the day, on Skoufos's letter (Kivroglou, "Die Bemühungen," doc. 2). This letter is long, with clear references to Rangavis's earlier letter and to Zappas's July 15 letter and gift of money.

13. *Helios*, July 13, 1856.

14. E.g., in a December 1856 letter from Skoufos to Rangavis (Kivroglou, "Die Bemühungen," doc. 7).

15. Rangavis clearly did not share Soutsos's antiquarian views. According to Linos Politis, *History of Modern Greek Literature*, 141, Rangavis was a cousin of Panagiotis Soutsos and his brother, Alexandros Soutsos. In view of the clash on athletic Olympics (and Alexandros's political imprisonment in December 1858), one wonders whether that family relationship helped or hindered other relations between these men; it is not likely to have been irrelevant.

16. Rangavis, *Apomnemoneumata*, 2:380–81.

17. In Paris, Minoides, in a postscript dated "13 August 1858" (*Philostrate sur la Gymnastique*, 132–43), knows of the forthcoming Olympic decree through newspapers, though the decree was not yet published.

18. *Helios*, Aug. 29, 1858, where Soutsos prints parts of Zappas's letter.

19. Epitrope ton Olympion, *Nomoi*, law dated August 19, 1858; the Committee

for the Encouragement of National Industry had been established by Otto's 1837 decree; whether it had ever been active in the meantime is unclear.

20. *Agonothete*, the ancient Greek term for a sponsor of the athletic Games.

21. I have not determined the exact location of this first Olympic building in Athens. Photograph 49, with the caption "The Building of the Olympics," in *To pnevma kai to soma*, 82, must have some error; for the text with that caption places the illustrated building on Vasilissis Olgas Avenue; the 1859 exhibition building, newspaper accounts make very clear, was near the Piraeus Road. Inquiries in Athens have not resolved the problem.

22. *Helios*, Aug. 29, 1858.

23. Minoides, *Philostrate sur la gymnastique*, 132–43.

24. Brookes papers, 7:100.

25. There is no good alternative to this local-newspaper-item-caught-his-eye explanation of how Brookes began to correspond with Athens. Their letters clearly show that Brookes wrote Wyse first. A much later account (*Wellington Journal*, Sept. 10, 1892 [Brookes papers, 5:206]) quotes Brookes as then saying that in 1858 "he was in correspondence with Sir Thomas Wyse . . . , the result being that he received a letter from Sir Thomas asking him for advice as to restoring the games, which he readily gave." The tone of Wyse's extant letters strongly suggests that the Greeks had not asked Wyse for help.

26. These conclusions come from Wyse's Feb. 10, 1859, letter (Brookes papers, 3:74) and from Brookes's gift of a prize for the Greek victor in tilting at the ring, which he clearly expected to be held at his suggestion (that event, unique to Wenlock, had just been introduced there in 1858). Wyse's letter refers to Brookes's "23 Dec." 1858 letter by exact date (see also previous note for the account in *Wellington Journal*, Sept. 10, 1892). Neumüller, "Die Geschichte," 95, does not seem to know of this Feb. 10, 1859, letter nor of any of the 1859 Brookes-Wyse correspondence. Yet he dates Brookes's first contact with Greece to 1858, by misreading the origin of the *Eddowes's Shrewsbury Journal*, Oct. 6, 1858, item (above).

27. Wyse's letter of July 14, 1859 (Brookes papers, 3:75), acknowledges receipt of the February 24 letter and the prize money, which, he says, the Greek committee now has. Yet another letter from Wyse, dated September 15, 1859 (ibid.), acknowledges two more letters from Brookes, whose pattern of persistent letters recurs later in his correspondence with Gennadius and Coubertin.

28. Neumüller, "Die Geschichte," 96, suggests that the soaped pole climb in the 1859 Greek program was included at Brookes's suggestion, since Brookes had introduced such an event in the 1857 Wenlock Games. But the 1858 Wenlock program seems not to include the pole climb event, and Brookes's influence, if any, on the Greek program remains a question.

29. The September 30 announcement is reprinted in Chrysafis, *Oi synchronoi diethneis Olympiakoi Agones*, 30–34.

30. The Greeks obviously mistook a handwritten *ch* for a *d*. A special edition of the newspaper *Hestia* (Oct. 1859, 10) garbled the committee's announcement even more, claiming that the "Boxing Club of Mikitenlok in England" had offered a prize of ten pounds for the victor in boxing, which would go—in the absence of that event—to the Olympic distance victor (Rühl, "L'idéal de l'amateurism," 9,

with n. 44; Kivroglou, "Die Bemühungen," 57 n. 2). The *Hestia* reporter must have confused Brookes's term, tilting at the ring, with a boxing ring. In the handwritten Greek version of the October 24 Wenlock prize announcement Wyse sent to Wenlock (Brookes papers, 3:75), the name is correct.

31. The original laws and official announcements are reprinted in the committee's official report, *Olympia tou 1859;* the October 24, 1859, addendum announcing Brookes's prize is on 47.

32. *Athena*, Oct. 21, 1859, *Helios*, Oct. 24, 1859 (Soutsos).

33. *Helios*, Oct. 24, 1859.

34. "Poetic" here—though literally true—is also chosen defensively for the word *impractical*, used by critics such as Rangavis (above); Coubertin often uses the word *utopian* in precisely the same way, as a defense against critics who describe his ideas as impractical.

35. Obviously the first time such a division was ever made; but it is a special case for an event where professional drivers already existed in the world of travel and business; it had nothing to do with athletes who made money. I know no evidence that either the word or the concept "amateur" athlete in this sense had been invented yet.

36. On the pistols' value, see Chrysafis, *Oi synchronoi diethneis Olympiakoi Agones*, 44; on the ancient race, see Pindar *Pythian Odes* 5.49–53. For details of the race, see *Athena*, Nov. 4, 1859, and *Auge*, Nov. 4, 1859. For the winner in the professional category, *Athena* gives the name as Elias Voulgaris ("Bulgarian"); *Auge* has Elias Georgiou Makedon ("Macedonian"); the version Wyse sent to Brookes (Brookes papers, 4:82) has "Christos Vassiliou, Bulgaria."

37. He thought that the private owner asked far too much money; he decided there were better places to spend Zappas's gift. He apparently used Zappas funds to excavate the famous Theater of Dionysus at the base of the Acropolis: Rangavis, *Apomnemoneumata*, 2:383–84. Kivroglou, "Die Bemühungen," doc. 27, states that Zappas had given Rangavis three thousand florins (which Kivroglou, "Die Bemühungen," 37, equates with thirty-nine thousand 1858 drachmas—an immense sum at the time) for purchase of the Olympic land alone.

38. I myself (*Olympic Myth*, 30 n. 34) and almost all Greek sources have been confused about the exact location of the 1859 athletic Olympics, because the name Plateia Loudovikou (named for Otto's father) was later transferred to a wholly different square (Kotzia). In 1859 the site was neither Kotzia Square nor Omonoia. Early maps and von Strantz, "Plan von Athen, 1862" (map 3) place the Plateia Loudovikou at that square now officially named Plateia Eleftherias (Freedom Square) but known locally only as Koumoundourou. That location, contiguous with Piraeus Street, suits exactly the 1859 newspaper reports and is surely the actual site of the 1859 Olympic Games. The only scholar known to me to locate the site correctly is Evangelos Pavilinis, *Istoria tis gymnastikis*, 396.

39. My account is based on contemporary 1859 Greek newspapers. Unfortunately, even the best historians, when it comes to Greece (and Greek), have perforce relied on second-hand, even fifth-hand, twentieth-century non-Greek sources, which are already flawed by confusion and prejudice and badly misrepresent what actually took place. To correct all the errors would take a separate article. I have twice elsewhere (*Olympic Myth*, 39–40; "Origins," 273, 290–91 nn. 7–8)

detailed many errors in the accounts of the Zappas Games in Mandell, *First Modern Olympics*, 34–36, MacAloon, *This Great Symbol*, 151–52, and several others (Mezö, *Modern Olympic Games*, Grombach, *Official 1980 Olympic Guide*, Banciulesco, "Forerunner," Santas, *Olympia*). But here, for those who have read other accounts, I correct major, widely published misconceptions: there was no milkcow given as a prize at the 1859 Olympics, no standing broad jump, high jump, rope climb, tug-of-war, or wrestling events (Mandell); no blind beggar won an event (Santas), nor, it seems, did any blind man or beggar sing a song for the king or for the crowd (Mandell, Grombach [quoted by MacAloon], Banciulesco, and others); only one mounted policeman drove back a few spectators who had flowed over into the infield—not a large group of cavalry soldiers (Mandell) or mounted police charges (Banciulesco; cf. Grombach and MacAloon), who charged the crowd (Banciulesco) and "with sheathed swords hit at the surging spectators, including many women and small children" (Mandell). Nor can I find any contemporary source whatsoever for the repeated report that police arrested some athletes, mistaking them for spectators (Grombach, Banciulesco, Mandell, and MacAloon). A few of these many errors result from gross exaggeration of actual events. Some may come from a misreading of Bourdon's French. But most result from pure fancy and the endless perpetuation—even embellishment—of a mistake once it sees print. Even Redmond's brief account ("Pseudo-Olympics," 78), otherwise rather free of such errors, has the 1859 program of events seriously wrong. Grombach's brief paragraph seems the source of most English language accounts of the Zappas Greek Games, and I speculate on the origins of his own faulty version (he cites no source) in my "Origins," 290 n. 8.

Virtually all non-Greek—and even some Greek—accounts of the Zappas Olympics go back to Bourdon (Coubertin's associate), who himself announces his prejudiced motive for writing his article: "to discredit the Olympic Games" of Greece (see remarks on his erroneous damning judgments of the 1870 Athens Olympics in chapter 4, below).

40. One, Benoukas, winner of one of the jumps, was from Zappas's own district and was perhaps some descendant of the famous Souliots with whom Zappas campaigned in the war.

41. *Aion*, Nov. 16, 1859.

42. *Athena*, Nov. 18, 1859.

43. The actual distances were precise equivalents of the ancient Olympic distances for the sprint *(stadion)*, middle-distance *(diaulos)*, and distance *(dolichos)*—600, 1,200, and 4,200 feet, respectively (although scholars still dispute the length of the distance race). Thus what I give as the "1,500 meters" was really only 1,280.16 meters. The information on results given here comes from several contemporary newspaper reports (*Auge*, Nov. 16, 1859; *Helios*, Nov. 28, 1859; *Aion*, Nov. 16, 1859; and *Athena*, Nov. 18, 1859), the summary results that Wyse sent to Brookes (in Brookes papers, 4:92), and Chrysafis, *Oi synchronoi diethneis Olympiakoi Agones*, 36. Although each of these has some detail that the others do not have, they show a surprising consensus. I do not note minor differences in the spelling of names unless it seems significant.

44. A misreading of an ancient text misled the organizers into thinking there was an ancient discus competition "in height": Chrysafis, *Oi synchronoi diethneis*

Olympiakoi Agones, 36 n. 1. But the published rules for the event (34–35) prove that it was not so impossible to judge as it may sound: the criterion was accuracy, not height: "In the discus throw in height, the first one hitting the center of the circle wins, or the one coming closest." Two sources give "Kosta(s)/Konstantinos" as this athlete's first name, two others give it as his last.

45. The phrase, "beyond the ditch" *(hyper ta eskammena)*—we would say "beyond the jumping pit"—is an ancient Greek term for any act that far exceeds all probability and expectation (first in Plato *Cratylus* 413a). It should not be taken literally, any more than when we say "Babe Ruth hit the ball a mile." Used of a fifth-century B.C. jumper, Phayllos of Croton, centuries after his death, it was wrongly taken literally by some benighted A.D. writers (e.g., Zenobius 6.23), who then flippantly guessed the length of Phayllos's jump at 55 feet. (For good arguments against Phayllos's supposed 55-foot jump, see Gardiner, "Phayllos and his Record Jump" and "Ancient Long Jump.") Equally benighted modern scholars, attempting to account for Phayllos's reported 55-foot record jump, decided the only explanation of so incredible a feat must be that the ancient jump was a triple jump. The modern Greek organizers of the 1859 Olympics seem to have accepted that scholarly error and called the triple jump the "jump beyond the pit." The rules for the triple jump in the 1870 Athens Olympics read "they will jump beyond the pit . . . in three leaps" (Chrysafis, *Oi synchronoi diethneis Olympiakoi Agones*, 55–56). The *askoliasmos* jump, also on the 1859 program, was a wholly different event, in which the contestants leaped onto an inflated wine skin and sought to maintain their balance (Kivroglou, "Die Bemühungen," 54 n. 1).

46. *Athena*, Nov. 18, 1859.

47. *Auge*, Nov. 16, 1859.

48. And I, at least, find it difficult to believe that anyone actually blind could run a seven-lap distance race, almost a mile, on a tricky, untried course under these far from ideal conditions.

49. "Brookes qui possédait le programme complet d'Athènes, parla à partir de cette époque-là moins de la 'rencontre annuelle' de Wenlock que des 'Jeux Olympiques' de Wenlock" (Rühl, "L'idéal de l'amateurisme," 9).

THREE The Olympic Movement in England

1. Neumüller, "Die Geschichte," 89, notes the addition of a javelin event to the program but then states that it was not contested in the actual Games; and in his summary results for 1859 (xxi), the javelin event has the notation "not competed for." This seems an error, for the *Shrewsbury Chronicle*, July 29, 1859 (Brookes papers, 4:55), gives the javelin victor here as "Wm. Owen, Ironbridge."

2. *Shrewsbury Chronicle*, July 29, 1859 (Brookes papers, 4:55; Neumüller, "Die Geschichte," 92).

3. Brundage, "Why the Olympic Games?" 22. One could fill pages with quotations from both Coubertin and Brundage restating the same theme. The international element, stressed by the two IOC presidents, was absent in Soutsos's conception and still missing in this Wenlock 1859 speech of Brookes. But Brookes himself was the first to add it (in 1880: see chapter 5, below). For a similar Olympic

ideal expressed by a Greek newspaper, see the discussion of the 1875 Athens Olympiad in chapter 4, below.

4. Brookes papers, 2:75–77, 4:82–88 (a photocopy of printed Wyse letter in Neumüller, "Die Geschichte," cviii); Coubertin, "Les Jeux Olympiques à Much Wenlock," 712.

5. Newspaper clipping (Brookes papers, 4:64), without name or date; its phrasing suggests that the meeting took place in late February or March 1860. If so, I cannot account for the delay in notifying Velissariou.

6. *Eddowes's Shrewsbury Journal*, Mar. 31, 1860, according to Neumüller, "Die Geschichte," 97 (I have been unable to confirm his citation).

7. *London Review*, Sept. 15, 1860 (Brookes papers, 4:74): "An account has been forwarded to us of the manner in which the classical games of antiquity were revived near Athens, under the auspices of the government, and the full approbation of the Attic community." After listing the various events on the program, the report says, "The largest prize was contributed by a committee of gentlemen in England, and in their honour was designated 'The Wenlock Prize' "; it adds the winner's name, Velissariou.

8. Handwritten minutes in Brookes papers, 4:60–61 (Neumüller, "Die Geschichte," 98).

9. Mullins, *Brookes and the Wenlock Games*, 16, dates the medal to 1860; but Neumüller, "Die Geschichte," 141, seems to date it to 1868. Since this medal as illustrated in Mullins, 17, is inscribed as given to Brookes on "June 11th, 1867," the 1868 date cannot be correct. I cannot confirm the 1860 date. Brookes himself describes the medal in detail on the printed program for the 1868 Wenlock Olympics (Brookes papers, 4:234).

On the actual medal, the text of Pindar's Greek (not legible in either Mullins, 17, or Neumüller, 141, but legible in Neumüller, cxxvi, and in Mullins, "Museum Information Sheet") has one letter in error. Pindar's actual Greek says *eukleon ergon apoina* (in return for glorious deeds) (*Isthmian Odes* 3.7), which is what the Wenlock organizers always thought their medal said. But the medals and all transcriptions of them (e.g., Neumüller, "Die Geschichte," 283 n. 313) have *eukleon erion apoina*, which means "in return for glorious wool." In the Greek alphabet, *gamma* and *iota* differ only in the length of one tiny horizontal stroke, and the die-maker could have easily mistaken or made the one for the other. (When I inspected the die in the Wenlock Museum, the letter looked more like an *iota* than a *gamma*.) Only a classicist can appreciate the change of Pindar's powerful phrase to "in return for glorious wool."

10. Edwards's "Address to the Olympian Class" (Brookes papers, 4:70, 140). He then, "in the light of modern warfare," belittles the Games as military training, saying that modern armies have no need of physical fitness, only good marksmanship. He thus makes the very criticism that Philip Ioannou would later make in Greece (see chapter 4, below), the criticism that drew frequent, strong, and public dissent from both Brookes and Coubertin (see chapter 6, below).

11. Program for the July 5, 1861, London performance, in Brookes papers, 7:155.

12. Coubertin, "Typical Englishman," 65; MacAloon, *This Great Symbol*, 150–

51. The matter is important because MacAloon, compounding Coubertin's errors, misdates Brookes's very first contact with Greece and thus finds further proof of Coubertin's dishonesty and "obfuscation" about the Zappas Games. After mentioning the London performance of this ode, Coubertin wrote: "A curious circumstance is connected with this celebration. An account of it found its way into London papers, and there met the eye of the Greek minister. . . . He communicated with the managers of the festival, inquiring whether any memento of an occasion so interesting to a descendant of the ancient Greeks could be transmitted to his sovereign. The committee forwarded in response a silver decoration awarded to victors in the Wenlock games, also a silver waist belt clasp . . . to Queen Amalia." But this is all wrong; Brookes sent the gifts on his own initiative, not at the ambassador's request.

Assuming the baron's account to be true and that Trikoupis's supposed solicitation of a memento from Wenlock was Brookes's very first contact with the Greeks, MacAloon is drawn even further astray. He adduces a passage from Coubertin's *Campagne*, 53, where the baron writes that "at the time of King Otto and Queen Amalia" Brookes had sent a "cup" as a prize for "the winners of the footraces decorated with the name 'Olympics' " and concludes, "This passage is a frank misrepresentation, for Coubertin was only too aware of the history of the pre-1896 Greek Olympics." Since the 1859 Games were the only Olympics held during Otto's reign, MacAloon continues: "[I]f Brookes's first contact with the Greeks was in 1860, . . . [it] gives us reason to believe that Brookes posted his cup to King George and not to King Otto, . . . and the switch of sovereigns' names may be more defensive obfuscation." But many actual 1859 documents disprove MacAloon's premise that "Brookes's first contact with the Greeks was in 1860." The first contact was 1858, and many others were made in 1859. The baron indeed misrepresented his knowledge of the Zappas Games elsewhere, precisely as MacAloon claims, but not here. MacAloon's misdating of Brookes's first contact with Greece must not be left to confuse Olympic history.

13. Before he sent them, Brookes made a copy of each letter, dated merely "October 1890," without the day of the month (Brookes papers, 4:90–92).

14. This one-page document, the list of "Honorary Members of the Wenlock Olympian Society," is in Brookes papers, volume 5, just inside the front cover.

15. A copy of the letter is in Brookes papers, 4:89.

16. Trikoupis to Brookes, Nov. 21, 1861 (Brookes papers, 4:90); for Coubertin and C. Trikoupis, see Coubertin, *Mémoires*, 15, and *Campagne*, 112.

17. So reads the page listing honorary members mentioned above. In 1859 Greeks referred to Brookes's group as the Wenlock Olympic "committee" *(epitrope)* or "society" *(hetairia)* but never "class" *(taxis)*. But this linguistic matter is too complex to examine here.

18. At a public meeting of the WARS, the Rev. W. H. Wayne argued for removing the Olympian Class from the society, objecting to "the mixing of the physical with the mental. The two should be separated." This notion that a simultaneous union of physical and mental training is bad harks back to Aristotle *Politics* 1339a–b; but it directly contradicts all modern Olympic philosophy and was the very feature of nineteenth-century education that Brookes and Coubertin spent their lives combating. Wayne further charged that the Olympic Games encouraged bet-

ting and drunkenness (for the minutes of that meeting, Nov. 16, 1860, see Brookes papers, 3:210–11, and *Shrewsbury Chronicle*, Nov. 23, 1860 [Brookes papers, 7:146]; Neumüller, "Die Geschichte," 102–3, gives more information). Those charges were unfounded, as Brookes readily proved; but several days later a special session of the Olympian Class met to decide "whether the general interests of the class would not be best promoted by a separation from the W.A.R.S." The separation, desirable to both sides, carried. This frequent antiathletic stance of the Christian clergy goes back to St. Paul; see my "On the Source of the Olympic Credo," 18, with notes. It was often identified and denounced by Coubertin (e.g., "La préface," 154).

19. Brookes papers, 4:93–94.

20. This important letter (Brookes papers, 4:95) is not among the documents that Neumüller lists or mentions.

21. *Shrewsbury Chronicle*, May 24, 1861 (Brookes papers, 4:98–100); Neumüller, "Die Geschichte," 104.

22. For the total absence of amateurism, even the concept, from the ancient Olympics, see my book, *Olympic Myth*. *Mens sana* was the motto of the Muscular Christianity movement, to which John Hulley and the Liverpool group belonged; it became a catchword in all parts of the British Olympic movement. The first such use I know of is in Hulley's December 4, 1861, Liverpool speech, reprinted in Shropshire Olympian Society, ed., *Opinions of Eminent Men on the Importance of Physical Education* (1863), 5 (see Brookes papers, 4:139). By 1864 one could write: "The motto which the Olympian Societies of Great Britain have universally adopted, points to the highest conception of humanity. To have *mens sana in corpore sano*" (*Shrewsbury Chronicle*, Sept. 9, 1864, [Brookes papers, 7:180]). Brookes himself repeated the motto in his speech during Coubertin's 1890 visit, and the baron quotes him and it in 1890 ("Les Jeux Olympiques à Much Wenlock," 706), attributing it first to Charles Kingsley. But Coubertin had already himself espoused this same catchphrase before his Wenlock visit (*Textes choisis*, 1:151); there he attributes it to "the ancients." He quoted it approvingly for some time but soon began to demur (*Textes choisis*, 3:335 [1902]). He eventually rejected *Mens sana* altogether as far too bland and replaced it in his own philosophy with *Mens fervida in corpore lacertoso* (first in *Revue Olympique*, July 1911; see *Textes choisis*, 1:603). In 1917 he rendered that as "un esprit ardent en un corps entraîné" (*Textes choisis*, 2:446); Dixon translates "an ardent mind in a trained body" (Coubertin, *Olympic Idea*, 61). Coubertin often defended his *Mens fervida* motto, saying it was carefully designed and researched (*Textes choisis*, 2:455). Robert Barney tells me that *Mens sana* was also the motto of the nineteenth-century German *Turner* clubs in America.

Despite the repeated use of *Mens sana* in connection with athletics, I have never seen anyone cite the ancient source. The original Latin version comes from the first-century A.D. writer Juvenal (*Satire* 10.356; cf. Plato *Gorgias* 479b). A glance at Juvenal's context quickly shows an unexpected result: the phrase has not, and in antiquity never had, anything whatsoever to do with Olympics or athletics. Juvenal is merely telling the ordinary person what content he should put in his prayers. The answer? *Mens sana*—good health, a sound mind in a sound body; pray not to get sick and not to go crazy. That is all the passage is about, nothing more (Coubertin's very reason for rejecting it). Nor is it remotely similar to any Greek phrase or concept associated with the ancient Olympics. *Mens sana* is a nice old adage, but it is ill suited for the purpose we use it. There is now a universal belief that the ancient Olympics and athletes pursued an ideal of a balanced, harmonious development of mind and body. I intend to write a separate article showing that that belief is pure fiction. The hard ancient evidence shows that it has no historical basis whatsoever; what evidence there is suggests the opposite conclusion.

23. Keuser, "Die Geschichte," 21–23.

24. Ibid., 21–23, 25–32. Redmond, "Pseudo-Olympics," 79–80, has three good paragraphs on the Liverpool Olympic Games; his principal source is R. Rees, "Olympic Festivals." For the traditional Christian opposition to athletics, see the above account of the WOC's separation from the WARS.

25. Keuser, "Die Geschichte," 31–32, citing the program printed in the *Liverpool Courier,* May 31, 1892; Keuser says it is not wholly clear whether the event was a true discus throw or the game of quoits well known in England (citing inconsistent reports in the *Liverpool Mercury,* June 16, 1862, and *Bell's Life in London,* June 15, 1862). Keuser (45) notes that there was no discus event in subsequent Liverpool Games: "Diese Disziplin schien dem Publikum des 19. Jahrhunderts wahrscheinlich zu fremd." Mahaffy indeed listed the discus as a most ludicrous anachronistic event in his criticism of the 1875 Athens Olympics (dicussed in chapter 4, below).

26. *Liverpool Mercury,* June 16, 1862 (Keuser, "Die Geschichte," 33–34); Keuser presents the summary results on 65.

27. *Eddowes's Shrewsbury Journal,* Oct. 1, 1862 (Brookes papers, 4:126; Neumüller, "Die Geschichte," 106–7); cf. Brookes papers, 4:139.

28. Keuser, "Die Geschichte," 37–38, citing the *Liverpool Daily Post,* June 12, 15, 20, 1863 (international call, pageantry, and "truly Olympic"); *Liverpool Mercury,* June, 15, 20, 1863 (swimming and summary results); *Liverpool Porcupine,* June 20, 1863, 92 (objection to trainers). Amateurism's objection to trainers, founded here, receives especial attention in the film, "Chariots of Fire."

29. Keuser, "Die Geschichte," 39–40; Redmond, "Pseudo-Olympics," 80.

30. *Liverpool Mercury,* July 2, 11, 1864 (Keuser, "Die Geschichte," 49–50). For Coubertin's adoption of "chivalry" as an Olympic idea, see the section on Brookes's tilting in chapter 1, above. But on one point he would have differed sharply with the *Mercury*'s reporter, who also wrote, "the festival has no religious significance." Coubertin insisted that his modern Olympic movement should be a religion.

31. "[M]y friend Mr. Hulley, of Liverpool, whom you have elected an honorary member of this society, and whom you have awarded your silver medal" (Brookes, in an address to the WOS, quoted in the *Shrewsbury Chronicle,* Oct. 14, 1864 [Brookes papers, 4:149]). Yet Hulley's name does not appear on the special (select?) roll-page of honorary members, where Velissariou's and Coubertin's names are listed first and fifth among only five.

32. Besides Shropshire and Liverpool, in his 1864 address to the WOS, Brookes listed the following as already having Olympic organizations: "Lancashire, Cheshire, Somersetshire, and other counties."

33. The IOC charter is printed in many places, e.g., Miller, *Behind the Olympic Rings.* The only conspicuous difference from the above NOA document is its in-

clusion of the word "moral" in the IOC's first stated aim: "physical and moral qualities." But the omission of the word "moral" in the NOA charter probably comes more from an assumption so strong that it did not need to be stated than from inattention to that category. The Olympic aim of "moral" improvement was implicit in every one of Brookes's Olympic acts and, apart from this 1865 NOA document, always explicit from the beginning. So in the original 1850 foundation papers of the first Olympian Class, the aims read—in Brookes's hand—"for the moral, intellectual, and physical improvement of the Inhabitants of the Town and Neighbourhood of Wenlock and especially of the Working Classes" (Brookes papers, 4:2 [photocopy in Neumüller, "Die Geschichte," civ]).

34. Foundation Charter of the NOA, Nov. 6, 1865 (Brookes papers, 4:161–62; Neumüller prints a photocopy in "Die Geschichte," cvxi).

35. The first actual international Olympic competition seems to have been at the Liverpool Olympics of 1867, when competitors came from, among many other places, "Paris, Marseilles, and London," *Liverpool Mercury*, June 29, 1867 (Keuser, "Die Geschichte," 42).

36. I find no evidence of a dispute between Brookes and Hulley on this point; perhaps the class-exclusive "Gentleman Amateur" element of the Liverpool Games was due more to Melly than to Hulley. On this same point Brookes later convinced Coubertin and thus strongly influenced the IOC rules (Rühl, "L'idéal de l'amateurisme," 7–8).

37. Lovesey, *Official Centenary History*, 18–19 (cf. Neumüller, "Die Geschichte," 121, and Keuser, "Die Geschichte," 55).

38. The Mincing Lane Athletic Club, later renamed the London Athletic Club (Pash, *Fifty Years of Progress*, 73).

39. Quercetani, *World History*, xv–xvi; Quercetani's frontispiece is a photo of the original program for that meeting.

40. See Young, *Olympic Myth*, 18–26, with notes; there I also show how the American, Caspar Whitney, sought to enforce class-exclusive amateurism in this country. For the formal AAC rule excluding "mechanics, artisans, and labourers," see below, on the 1867 NOA Olympic Games. That class-elitist rule (normally called "the mechanics clause") continued to be operative in English amateur sport long after it was formally abandoned. "In 1892 . . . if Lord Burghley had been seen competing with the 'mechanic, artisan, or labourer' admitted . . . to athletic competitions as an amateur, it would have been considered a surprising thing," Pash, *Fifty Years of Progress*, 74.

41. Neumüller, "Die Geschichte," 121; at Oxford in 1978 I saw a man nearly refused service at a downtown pub because he was from Newcastle.

42. *Sporting Gazette*, Dec. 23, 1865, in Lovesey, *Official Centenary History*, 19 (Neumüller, "Die Geschichte," 123, Keuser, "Die Geschichte," 56).

43. Lovesey, *Official Centenary History*, 21.

44. Ibid., 22.

45. *Sporting Life*, Aug. 4, 1866 (Brookes papers, 4:178). The only three "prominent London athletes" were Guy Pym (AAC), who won the high jump, C. G. Emery (AAC), victor in the 100- and 175-yard dashes, and A. King (Thames R. C.), third in the half mile. From the AAC, besides Pym and Emery, were W. Collett (2d, 175 yards) and T. Collins (3d, hurdles).

46. Neumüller, "Die Geschichte," 127–28, makes a comparative compilation of the available marks and judgments.

47. They are not mentioned at all in either Mandell, *First Modern Olympics*, or MacAloon, *This Great Symbol* (who follows Coubertin, "Typical Englishman," 65, in mere mention of " 'Olympian festivals' . . . in Birmingham, Shrewsbury, and Wellington," with nothing of dates or London [150; cf. Boulongne, *Pierre de Coubertin*, 146]). In 1890 Coubertin could still briefly refer to the London Olympics: "Un essai fut bien tenté vers 1866 pour étendre et généraliser les jeux olympiques. Un festival eût lieu cette année-là au Palais de Cristal." But after the baron himself decided to propose the Olympic revival in 1892, he seems to have had amnesia about the London 1866 Games; Olympic historians apparently caught the same malady. Even the rather comprehensive Redmond, "Pseudo-Olympics," says nothing of major 1866 Olympic Games in this major city of the world. As is often the case, Mullin's booklet, *Brookes*, briefly includes this important information lacking in better-known histories (20–22).

48. *Eddowes's Shrewsbury Journal*, Aug. 8, 1866 (Brookes papers, 4:175); *Bell's Life in London*, Aug. 4, 1866 (Brookes papers, 7:210). The following account of the 1866 London Olympic Games is a composite based on these two reports and that in *Sporting Life*, Aug. 4, 1866, above. Subsequent references in this chapter to the three publications refer to the accounts in these issues.

49. Erected first at Hyde Park for the great Exhibition of 1851, the Crystal Palace was then taken down and reerected (1852–54) at Sydenham Hill in upper Norwood, where the 1866 Olympics took place. It measured 563 meters long, 124 meters wide, and 33 meters high, and it remained a site for exhibitions and athletic contests until it burned in 1936.

50. Brooke (no relation to Brookes) would later twice win the special all-around competition at Wenlock. In 1869 he won the Wenlock "first class silver medal" valued at more than fourteen pounds, and in 1870 he again won a "first class silver medal and olive crown" (Neumüller, "Die Geschichte," xlix, lii).

51. "[T]o run one mile at the double, in 10 minutes, and 440 yards at full speed, wearing uniform and carrying arms and thirty-six rounds" *(Sporting Life)*. In the *hoplites* event of the ancient Olympics, athletes ran a 400-meter race wearing helmet and greaves while carrying their shields.

52. "A rattling race to the finish was carried off by Emery, who won by a yard from Pelly, . . . Wear close up" *(Bell's Life in London)*.

53. According to *Sporting Life*; the "1 min. 32 sec." given in *Eddowes's* seems an error.

54. This event was otherwise unknown to British track and field except in Wenlock, whence it surely came through Brookes to London. Brookes obviously got it from the 1859 Greek Olympics.

55. "(Draw) . . . (Tie)": newspaper accounts are not wholly consistent, but it seems that the officials, because of the lateness of the hour, stopped or canceled the final eliminations in the catch-as-catch-can wrestling and lightweight boxing events and gave the remaining contestants equal prizes. The heavyweight boxing final was not canceled but postponed to the next day.

56. "[L]adies class for athletics—what will they not do when honour is to be attained!" *(Sporting Life)*.

57. In the presence of an Englishman I once tried to explain to an American Grace's position in British sport by saying he was "the Babe Ruth of England"; the Englishman objected strongly, saying, "No! Babe Ruth is the W. G. Grace of America!"

58. *Bell's Life in London*. Grace's age at the race is given by Lovesey, *Official Centenary History*, 22.

59. For the 1866 description: see *Sporting Life;* on the history of the steeple-chase event, see Quercetani, *World History*, 176–83, who tells an anecdote [without source] about a recreational steeplechase run by Oxford men in 1850 but otherwise begins his account with the 1900 Paris Olympics, not mentioning the 1866 London Games. Wallechinsky, *Complete Book of the Olympics*, 64, says, "The steeple-chase event appears to have been introduced in Edinburgh in 1828" but does not elaborate.

60. *Bell's Life in London.*

61. *Sporting Life; Oxford Journal*, Aug. 25, 1866 (Brookes papers, 4:178). The Oxford paper continues, "Through the efforts of [Brookes], the athletic societies of the country have now become connected in one grand body."

62. In chapter 6, below, I show that in 1889 Coubertin read this speech and quoted directly from it; one copy of Brookes's printed 1866 text is in Brookes papers, 1:104–11, others elsewhere.

63. Keuser, "Die Geschichte," 46–48, who notes Hulley's and Melly's attention to the NOA, their gym, and neighboring festivals in the mid-1860's. Hulley was "the conductor of the sports" at a Grand Olympic Festival in Lancaster in 1865 (newspaper clipping reproduced in Keuser, 84–85); perhaps that Lancaster Olym-piad passed for the 1865 Liverpool Games.

64. *Shrewsbury Chronicle*, June 14, 1867 (Brookes papers, 4:185). There is a photo of this very medal in Mullins, *Brookes and the Wenlock Games*, 17.

65. On the NOA regulations, see the printed Program Prospectus for the Sec-ond Annual Festival, National Olympian Society (copy in Brookes papers, 4:186–87; photocopy in Neumüller, "Die Geschichte," cxvii–cix). On the AAC regula-tions, see Wilkinson, *Athletic Almanack*, 1868 (quoted at greater length in Bailey, *Leisure and Class in Victorian England*, 131; confirmed in Pash, *Fifty Years of Progress*, 19). The mechanics clause was destined to play its own role in the history of En-glish athletics, a frequent topic of discussion (see, e.g., Pash, 19, 32, 73). Even owners of small businesses and employers were not welcome as athletes, since, "engaged in selling goods," they were considered " 'tradesm[e]n,' a word at which many Victorians shuddered" (although the athletic clubs happily cashed these tradesmens' checks: Pash, 32). The mechanics clause is sometimes called the Hen-ley Rule, after the regulations for entry in the Henley Regatta, the most class-exclusive sporting event in all England. But the Henley rules actually went a further step; besides barring mechanics, artisans, and laborers, they explicitly ex-cluded from competition anyone who had ever "engaged in any menial duty" (quoted—with high approval—by the American Caspar Whitney, *Sporting Pilgrim-age*, 163).

66. There is a full write-up of these Olympic Games in the *Birmingham Daily Post*, June 26–28, 1867 (Brookes papers, 7:212–13); Neumüller, "Die Geschichte," 133–37, has a good summary, based mainly on *Aris's Birmingham Gazette*, June 29,

1867 (Brookes papers, 4:190). He has also compiled the figures that compare the NOA track-and-field marks with those of the 1867 AAC meeting.

67. According to the *Birmingham Daily Post* (Brookes papers, 7:213); but Neumüller ("Die Geschichte," 136) gives 10.50; whichever is correct, the NOG 100-yard race was faster than the 1867 AAC mark of 10.75 seconds.

68. Its somewhat obscure foundation date may even antedate the founding of the AAC; further details in Neumüller, "Die Geschichte," 137–38, with n. 305. There is a need for a full, separate study of Brookes's decades-long struggle with the question of amateurism; his various attempts to settle the question and still be fair; his battles with class-exclusive amateurism; and the influence of Brookes's amateur principles on Coubertin and, therefore, on the whole history of amateurism in the modern Olympics. Rühl, "L'idéal de l'amateurisme," is an excellent start, but the precise chronology needs to be followed closely in its relation to all the other simultaneous developments in English amateurism.

69. Program of the Autumn Festival of the Amateur Class, Nov. 1, 1867 (Brookes papers, 4:194).

70. Coubertin, (*Textes choisis*, 2:466–68; *Olympic Idea*, 15–16); "l'établissement du serment . . . cette solution que nous avons toujours préconisée" (*Textes choisis*, 2:579); on the first performance of the oath, at Antwerp in 1920, see *Textes choisis*, 2:273. Coubertin insisted that he himself carefully phrased the wording of our present Olympic oath (*Textes choisis*, 2:306–7); he was proud it had no explicit reference to "amateurism" (ibid.); but it was, indeed, intended to enforce amateurism (*Textes choisis*, 2:476). "Avery Brundage had tried to change the Olympic Amateur Oath by adding a controversial clause involving a commitment by every Olympic athlete that he or she would never become a professional, as well as swearing that he or she had never been a professional" (Grombach, *Official 1980 Olympic Guide*, 25). The modern Olympic oath mainly just says that the athlete will obey the rules, much like the ancient Olympic oath, which the baron imitated (Pausanias 5.24.9; my *Olympic Myth*, 74 n. 70). For the 1870 Zappas Olympic oath, see chapter 4, below; for post-1920 IOC oaths, see Wendl, "Olympic Oath."

71. Program prospectus, copy in Brookes papers, 4:221.

72. *Wellington Journal and Shrewsbury News*, Aug. 29, 1868, has a full write-up of the 1868 Wellington NOG, even down to the dinner menu (Brookes papers, 7:218–19, 4:224); a brief account is in Neumüller, "Die Geschichte," 143.

73. Neumüller, "Die Geschichte," 144.

FOUR   The Olympic Movement in Greece

1. According to Ketseas, "Restatement," 56. I do not find those very words in the long, elaborate will, but they well reflect what Zappas expressed in his 1856 letter (Kivroglou, "Die Bemühungen," doc. 1) and Soutsos's revival proposal, which Zappas sought to implement.

2. The will, dated November 30, 1860, is published in many places (e.g., *Mega Hellenikon viographikon lexikon*, 1:405–8); it became subject to great international legal controversy when Zappas's cousin (often wrongly identified as his brother) and executor, Konstantinos Zappas, died in 1892. The will speaks pointedly but briefly of the stadium, since Zappas had long before specified how he wanted it

rebuilt, including marble seats for spectators. In 1859 he had given two hundred thousand drachmas to that end. Rangavis, "Peri tou Zappeiou idrymatos."

3. Kousoulas, *Modern Greece*, 36–53. Kousoulas (40, without source), tells a good anecdote about a conversation between Otto and Rangavis concerning Otto's inability to rule.

4. Chrysafis, *Oi synchronoi diethneis Olympiakoi Agones*, 51.

5. The official report (Chrestides, *Olympia tou 1870*) appends a balance sheet of income and expenses for the entire second Olympiad. The expenses included 66,099 drachmas for the "temporary building" for these exhibits, 17,665 for display cases, tables, etc., for them, and 1,396 drachmas for "Olympic speeches" (Ioannou's antiathletic speech), but noticeably less, only 1,108 drachmas, for salaries of the head athletic coach and his assistants. A few other athletic expenses (e.g., five discuses at 3 drachmas each; 1,500 drachmas for the athletes' cash prizes), even with the 8,521 drachmas spent on excavating the stadium, make the total athletic budget still less than 6 percent of the total expenditures, 192,779 drachmas (not even half of the listed assets).

6. The German archaeologist E. Ziller excavated the stadium in 1869 (when one of the famous herms was found), continuing his work there for several years after the 1870 Olympic Games. Ziller's excavation report, along with plans and sketches, is found in his *Ausgrabungen am Panathenaïschen Stadium*.

7. Chrestides, *Olympia tou 1870*, 55 ff., articles 14–16, 8, Program of the Athletic Games. The 1870 oath seems modeled after the simple oath of antiquity (we have only Pausanias's [5.24.9] paraphrase, "they swear that no fraud will enter the games on their account") and not unlike our present oath. The 1870 version reads, "I promise that I will compete honorably within the rules and regulations, and not cheat my fellow competitor."

8. Ibid., articles 3, 4, 12, and 13.

9. The sizes of early Olympic crowds are given piecemeal (without source) in Schaap, *Illustrated History of the Olympics*. Before the Paris Games of 1924, the only IOC crowds that might compare with Athens in 1870 were seen during brief periods in 1908 (at soccer football games, not track-and-field events) and 1912. Attendance figures at the 1900 Paris Games (there were no crowds in the normal sense), the St. Louis Games in 1904 ("Attendance averaged about ten thousand and went as high as twenty thousand only on the last [day]," Schaap, 73), and the 1920 Olympics ("[A]ttendance rose above ten thousand only late in the games," Schaap, 139) were all far below the thirty thousand at the 1870 Olympics (so also most of the time in 1908 and 1912). Of course, the 1896 and 1906 Athens Olympics topped all IOC attendance records, even Paris in 1924, until the 1932 Los Angeles Games.

10. On Ening as head coach, see Chrestides, *Olympia tou 1870*, 170, and Chrysafis, *Oi synchronoi diethneis Olympiakoi Agones*, 72; on Ening as Vikelas's childhood teacher, see Vikelas, *I zoi mou*, 116–17.

11. My account of the 1870 Olympic Games is a compressed composite of the newspaper accounts mentioned below, which show remarkable unanimity and no significant discrepancy.

12. Chrysafis, *Oi synchronoi diethneis Olympiakoi Agones*, 78–79. The summary results are available (only in Greek) in several other places and agree (with only minor spelling differences) in the names for all three places in the ten events.

13. Chrysafis quotes accurately and at length (ibid., 79–83) two wholly favorable newspaper reports (*Aletheia* and the usually critical *Aion*, both Nov. 16, 1870). I quote briefly from another (*To Mellon*, Nov. 17, 1870) to complement and corroborate Chrysafis: "[I]n the ancient stadium . . . the second version of the Olympics resurrected by Evangelis Zappas. . . . [There were] 40 athletes . . . 30,000 spectators. . . . The rite began with the . . . Olympic Hymn. . . . The first event was the 400 meters. . . . Complete order reigned. Everyone enjoyed the height of satisfaction, and there was universal gratitude to the organizing committee." Despite the contrary statements of modern Olympic historians who have not read the original Greek sources, I find no negative comment about the 1870 Games from any contemporary source (apart from Ioannou's complaint about some winners' social class).

14. Otto insisted on being called founder of the Olympics *(idrytes ton Olympion)* for the 1859 Games, and on the medals he termed Zappas the producer of the Games *(agonothete)*. But the founder title was given to Zappas himself in 1870 accounts: "Let the Founder of the Olympics E. Zappas take comfort, if those in the other world have any perception, as he sees that his hopes were not deceived. . . . [The 1870 Olympic Games] enjoyed, as is well known, unbelievable success" (Chrestides, *Olympia tou 1870*, 218–19).

15. This speech was published separately in 1870 (there is a copy in the Gennadius Library in Athens); a portion is reprinted in Chrysafis, *Oi synchronoi diethneis Olympiakoi Agones*, 76; for the notion that "high-tech" nineteenth-century warfare rendered physical fitness of little or no military value, see the discussions of Edwards's speech in chapter 3, above (he agreed with Ioannou) and the strongly dissenting views of Brookes and Coubertin in chapter 6, below.

16. "Official Judge's Report," in Chrestides, *Olympia tou 1870*, 171–72 (much of the report is reprinted in Chrysafis, *Oi synchronoi diethneis Olympiakoi Agones*, 84).

17. See my *Olympic Myth*, 21 n. 24.

18. See the account of Bourdon, below; this comment, wholly directed at questions of social class, was expressed only in Ioannou's judge's report, not by the Greek public.

19. Chrysafis, *Oi synchronoi diethneis Olympiakoi Agones*, 86–87.

20. Amateurism had recently reached American shores, as well, but here our strong egalitarian tradition so confused the issue that almost no one, not even those who professed it, could determine what amateurism was. See my *Olympic Myth*, 22–27; Smith, *Sports and Freedom* (index, under "amateurism"); Redmond, *Caledonian Games*, 50–53, etc.

21. "Dr. W. G. Grace . . . was a doctor, a cricketer, and an amateur [and, we now know, an Olympic victor: see above, on the 1866 London Games]. Since he . . . did not need money from the game in order to survive, Grace was able to receive money openly and still retain his amateur status. [In public he accepted two checks, for fifteen hundred and nine thousand pounds]. Yet Grace was an amateur; his background and career made him so" (Cohen, "More than Fun and Games," 91–92).

22. Chrysafis, *Oi synchronoi diethneis Olympiakoi Agones*, 89.

23. *Ephemeris*, May 15, 1875 (a large portion is also in Chrysafis, *Oi synchronoi diethneis Olympiakoi Agones*, 99).

24. My account is a compressed composite of contemporary newspaper reports, mainly *Aion*, May 19, 1875, and *Ephemeris*, May 20, 1875; both are reprinted in full in Chrysafis, *Oi synchronoi diethneis Olympiakoi Agones*, 100–107. The newspapers show remarkable unanimity and must, I assume, be generally accurate. I also cautiously use Mahaffy's report, "Olympic Games at Athens," obviously even more exaggerated yet not conflicting substantively with the Greek newspapers (except where he misread them).

25. As well, Phokianos's brother had died from a fall from the parallel bars (Chrysafis, *Oi synchronoi diethneis Olympiakoi Agones*, 118 n. 1).

26. MacAloon, *This Great Symbol*, 152, trustingly quotes Mahaffy's report, "Olympic Games at Athens," 326, that Athenian newspapers were "in high delight and admiration" of the 1875 Games. Obviously false, Mahaffy's account then draws MacAloon into even further error ("outpouring of civic joyfulness unabated," etc.: see my discussion of the 1888 Zappas Olympiad in chapter 5, below). Mahaffy, professor of ancient Greek in Dublin, had trouble reading modern Greek. Here he mistakes a newspaper comment ("almost ridiculous" *[schedon geloion]*, *Ephemeris*, May 20, 1875, below) about the 1859 Olympiad (which he misdates to 1867) for a comment on the 1870 Olympiad. Then, ignoring that same reporter's highly favorable comparison of the 1870 to the 1875 Games, he states what is the opposite of the truth, namely, that all Greece judged the 1870 Olympiad as even worse than that of 1875.

27. Coubertin, *Campagne*, 117, 121, 125; Coubertin, *Mémoires*, 19–25.

28. Rangavis founded this antiathletic, anti-Olympic tradition (see chapter 2, above); I discuss its obstruction to Brookes's and Coubertin's Olympic efforts in Greece in chapters 5 and 9, below.

29. Their comments on classes appear in chapter 3, above.

30. Since this book focuses on modern origins, I say little here about Mahaffy's false notion that ancient Greeks were amateurs; but see my comment on his 1879 article, below.

31. Mahaffy, "Olympic Games at Athens in 1875," 324–27.

32. Mahaffy gives the only mark recorded for the Zappas Olympics, stating that some athletes threw the discus "about thirty yards"—not astonishingly shorter than the 95 ft. 7¾ in. throw by R. Garrett, of the United States, that won the first IOC Olympiad in the same stadium in 1896.

33. I omit a full critique of Mahaffy's version of the 1875 Olympiad. It is clearly an inaccurate journalistic hatchet job; I elaborate its errors in *Olympic Myth*, 34–40.

34. Stanford and McDowell, *Mahaffy*, 89, borrowing from Hesketh Pearson, *Life of Oscar Wilde*. See also Young, *Olympic Myth*, 35.

35. Mahaffy, "Old Greek Athletics," 61–69. Anachronism, his equation of ancient Greece with Victorian England, was one of Mahaffy's known habits. I have shown the major errors of this second article and its amazingly harmful influence on scholarship, and even on modern athletes and athletics, in my *Olympic Myth*, 44–56, etc. Giving amateurism, especially elitist amateurism, just the hallowed precedent it wanted—ancient Greece—Mahaffy's article retains some influence to this day.

36. Mandell, *First Modern Olympics*, 34–36, MacAloon, *This Great Symbol*, 51–

52; for Mahaffy's reputation in his own day as a poor and inaccurate scholar, see Stanford and McDowell, *Mahaffy*, 145–48 (a part is quoted in my *Olympic Myth*, 47 n. 44).

37. Bourdon, "Athènes essaye de faire revivre Olympie," 20. A member of its organizing committee, Bourdon was a featured speaker at Coubertin's 1892 USFSA jubilee, where the baron first uttered his own suggestion to revive the Olympics. On that occasion Bourdon spoke on ancient Greek athletics (MacAloon, *This Great Symbol*, 163, Mandell, *First Modern Olympics*, 80, Coubertin, *Textes choisis*, 2:115–16, 325, 331); see also *Textes choisis*, 1:177. Boulongne, *Pierre de Coubertin*, 139, says that Bourdon "hated" *(haïsset)* Coubertin; if so, he hid his hatred well here.

38. Bourdon, "Athènes essaye de faire revivre Olympie," 21. Bourdon's account seems nothing but a badly garbled version (to 1870 only) of an early stage of Chrysafis's own research, which, Bourdon says (19), Chrysafis himself "graciously communicated to me" while Chrysafis was still in the midst of his study. Yet Bourdon explicitly rejects Chrysafis's information (and the 1870 statement of Chrestides) that the 1870 Greek Olympiad was a great success (grasping at Ioannou's 1870 judges' report, instead, 21).

39. Especially Grombach, *Official 1980 Olympic Guide*, Mandell, *First Modern Olympics*, and MacAloon, *This Great Symbol*; I detail these authors' errors, badly prejudicial to evaluating the Greek Olympic contribution, in *Olympic Myth*, 42, and "Origins," 290–91, with nn. 7–8. They all ultimately derive from Mahaffy and Bourdon.

40. Epitrope ton Olympion, *Olympia tou 1875*, 192. The formation of the 1838 Letrini committee is recounted in chapter 1, above.

FIVE   National Failures, International Dreams

1. Neumüller, "Die Geschichte," 141, with n. 133; at Wenlock the half-mile hurdles replaced the London half-mile run. Neither pentathlon program was much like that won by Jim Thorpe at the Stockholm Olympics (200- and 1,500-meter races, javelin, discus, long jump), which was closer to the ancient pentathlon (200 meters, javelin, discus, long jump, and wrestling); the current "modern" (military) pentathlon is unrelated.

2. See Brookes's remarks on France's defeat and military deficiency quoted in chapter 6, below.

3. To the successful 1871 edition of the Wenlock Olympics came good athletes from the Birmingham Athletic Club and Ravenstein's German group from London. A modern track-and-field program had thirteen adult contests; eleven are Olympic events today. Besides the high jump, long jump, 200-yard dash, quarter-mile and mile runs, 150-yard hurdles, mile hurdles, and pentathlon, it included a steeplechase, "putting the shot," and "throwing the hammer." Some winning marks seem respectable for the day (men's 200 yards: 21 seconds); others may make us shudder (high jump: 5 ft. 5½ in.; the weight of the hammer, won by Mr. Clement at 63 ft. 2 in., is not specified). A newspaper said these twenty-second annual Wenlock Olympian Games in 1871 were "carried out with unparalleled success"

and "the most brilliant of any yet held" (*Eddowes's Shrewsbury Journal*, June 7, 1871, [Brookes papers, 4:276; Neumüller, "Die Geschichte," 154, with 1871 program on lii–liv]). These Games also included, for the last time, an event (the quarter mile) specifically for "non-amateurs," with a cash prize of two pounds. Subsequent programs seem to have no more of such open events, they do designate cash prizes (and value prizes continued on).

4. Neumüller, "Die Geschichte," lvii–lviii; conspicuous is the absence of such children's contests as knitting, sewing, and history.

5. Prospectus of the Fourth Festival of the National Olympian Association (Brookes papers, 4:311).

6. See, e.g., Mandell, *First Modern Olympics*, 67.

7. Neumüller, "Die Geschichte," 167, who seems to cite Disraeli as quoted in Baugh, *Victoria History*, 3:133.

8. Hughes, himself a Rugby graduate, wrote his novel about a Rugby student named Tom Brown. Like Hulley and Melly, Hughes was active in the movement called Muscular Christianity. Coubertin saw him and his novel as the quintessential source for an almost perfect English school system. See the discussion of Hughes's heavy influence on Coubertin in chapter 6, below. It is typical of our story that it connects Hughes to Brookes before Coubertin.

9. There is a long write-up of these NOA Games in the *Wellington Journal*, May 25, 1874 (Brookes papers, 4:316), and a shorter report in *Field*, June 6, 1874 (Brookes papers, 4:332). On the comparison with AAC marks, see Neumüller, "Die Geschichte," 165–67.

10. Prospectus of the Twenty-fifth WOG, May 18, 1875 (Brookes papers, 4:339); *Wellington Journal and Shrewsbury News*, May 22, 1875 (Brookes papers, 4:340).

11. *Shrewsbury Chronicle*, June 9, 1876 (Brookes papers, 4:351); Neumüller, "Die Geschichte," 173–76 (with photo of the winning bicycle and cyclist, T. Sabin).

12. Their roles are explained in chapters 8–10, below.

13. I know no biography of Gennadius, but there is a pamphlet in English, available at the Gennadius Library: Nicol, *Ioannes Gennadius*.

14. Gennadius to Brookes, dated August 8, 1877 (Brookes papers, 5:12); a picture of the cup, with transcription and translation of its Greek inscription, is in Neumüller, "Die Geschichte," cxxv.

15. Coubertin has errors in his piecemeal reports of the history of Olympic gift exchanges between Brookes and the Greeks, and MacAloon's account adds more (chapter 3, above); MacAloon, *This Great Symbol*, 150, dates George's 1877 gift to 1867 (Coubertin has it right, "17 years" after Brookes's 1860 gift to Queen Amalia, i.e., 1877, "Typical Englishman," 65). But MacAloon's error that George's cup was given to the "Wenlock [A]ssociation" comes from Coubertin's original. The cup's inscription clearly states its occasion and the site. The "Association" mentioned by both Gennadius and Coubertin is the NOA, not the WOS (a "Society"). By 1897 Coubertin might well have forgotten the cup's exact occasion and recipient; but also by 1897 the words "Modern Olympics of the British, 1877," sponsored by the "National Olympian Association," might have made him cringe.

16. Quoted in *Shrewsbury Chronicle*, Oct. 19, 1877 (Brookes papers, 5:14).

17. *Athletic World*, May 24, 1878 (Brookes papers, 5:25).

18. Quoted in *Shrewsbury Chronicle*, Sept. 28, 1878 (Brookes papers, 5:17).

19. Neumüller, "Die Geschichte," 145, 186–94.

20. Program of the Thirtieth Wenlock Olympian Games (Brookes papers, 5:46); *Shrewsbury Chronicle*, May 21, 1880 (Brookes papers, 5:50); *Wenlock and Ludlow Express*, Oct. 16, 1880 (Brookes papers, 5:56–57); for the downward trend, see Neumüller, "Die Geschichte," 195–99.

21. Some of the correspondence Gennadius received is kept among his papers in the Gennadius Library in Athens. But Christina Varda, archivist, found no letter from Brookes in that collection.

22. I summarize a longer section here; the photo is indeed in Wenlock (Brookes papers, 1:115), along with that of Coubertin (Brookes papers, 5:176), who, like Gennadius, apologized for its quality. Brookes was fascinated with photographs and sought to exchange them with his new friends.

23. The full letter seems extant only in the original (Brookes papers, 5:59) in the trunk in Wenlock; it is not mentioned in Neumüller, "Die Geschichte." The microfilm omits all but the first page.

24. Address of the Committee for 1880, Jan. 21, 1881 (Brookes papers, 5:52).

25. Coubertin himself, as late as 1897, still recognized Brookes's primacy here, although he was careful to emphasize how Brookes's plan was impossible until his own "Paris Congress" met ("Typical Englishman," 65). But after 1897, Coubertin forgot all about Brookes's primacy in proposing the international Olympic revival—therefore, Olympic history forgot it, too.

26. I elaborate below on this difference when commenting on Gennadius's October 16, 1883, letter to Brookes; and I attempt to account for it in the discussion, in chapter 7, below, of Brookes's May 22, 1894, letter to Coubertin. The difference proved crucial.

27. WOS balance sheet, 1880, Jan. 21, 1881 (Brookes papers, 5:55); Neumüller, "Die Geschichte," 288 n. 409.

28. I found the full original newspaper in the Old Vouli library in Athens. On his newspaper clipping (Brookes papers, 5:65), Brookes has written "by Socrates A. Parasyrakis"; someone has made an English translation on Brookes papers, 5:66. Because the masthead of this newspaper (not in Wenlock) lists "S. Papandonopoulos" as its London correspondent, one would expect him to be the author. Yet since Brookes must have known Parasyrakis, he was not likely to err here.

29. *Shrewsbury Chronicle*, Sept. 29, 1882 (Brookes papers, 5:74–75). The account also gives a brief history of the NOA, including the successful 1866 London Olympics.

30. *Shrewsbury Chronicle*, June 6, 1883 (Brookes papers, 5:86; Neumüller, "Die Geschichte," 209).

31. See Young, *Olympic Myth*, 21, and sources there. At the reorganization meeting at the Randolph Hotel in Oxford on March 24, 1880, the class-exclusive amateurism did not give up easily (some names and details are found in Neumüller, "Die Geschichte," 282 n. 295 [based mainly on Pash, *Fifty Years of Progress*, 19–20, 43]). " 'In those days there was a burning question. People did not want to see anybody competing who was not a gentleman!' (Laughter)" (Pash, 26). "When the A.A.A. decided to throw the sport open to all who had neither competed nor

taught for money, many heads were shaken and doleful doubts expressed as to the future, and it was many years before the debates on the wisdom of abandoning the 'Henley definition' died away" (Pash, 73).

32. Reported in Pash, *Fifty Years of Progress*, 38 (Neumüller, "Die Geschichte," 210).

33. Quoted in *Shrewsbury Chronicle*, June 6, 1883 (Brookes papers, 5:86; Neumüller, "Die Geschichte," 209). Brookes's tribute to O'Connell anticipates William Sloane's 1920 description of Coubertin: "[T]he power of O'Connell was in his being and he adopted the great reformer's motto: 'agitate, agitate, and then agitate' " (see also the epigraph at the beginning of chapter 14; *Report of the American Olympic Committee*, 75). Daniel O'Connell (1775–1847) was an Irish political activist famous, not long ago, for his dedication to a cause and persistence in pursuing it. That same dedication and persistence in the face of repeated opposition indeed linked Brookes and Coubertin, making their careers comparable. Their connection through O'Connell's model is apt.

34. Gennadius to Brookes, Oct. 16, 1883 (Brookes papers, 5:89).

35. Gennadius to Brookes, June 4, 1886; June 23, 1886 (modern Greek "Olympian Games"); see also May 23, 1887 ("I'd love to come to Wenlock to watch the Olympic Games, but I can't"); and June 18, 1887 ("I'm very sensible to your warm attachment to Greece"; he thanks Brookes for the letter and photo and for the invitation but regrets that he can not come to Wenlock to watch the Olympic Games (I paraphrase a lengthy section; see Brookes papers, 5:107, 138, and 124, respectively).

36. Coubertin, *Campagne*, 109, 112, and *Mémoires*, 14–15.

37. Quellenec and Zinopoulos, *Rapport*; the construction took place under three phases and three contractors: 1872–79, 1879–84, 1884–88 (and may have involved some malfeasance). The Dragoumis documents (see appendix) contain a very old, original, hand-drawn suggested design for the Zappeion (when and by whom is not given); but it is not close to the actual design of this building. In *Hestia*, Jan. 10/22, 1888, 17, Rangavis states that Zappas wanted the building in the shape of an ancient Greek open theater.

38. The official announcement, dated March 9, 1888 (Dragoumis envelope 234, doc. 3), stated that "on the last Sunday of October, starting at 1 P.M., there will be held in the Panathenaic Stadium the following events, forming a part of the Olympic Festival": the list of events includes 200- and 1,500-meter footraces (*stadion* and *dolichos*), hurdles, triple jump, and horizontal and parallel bars. And on October 2, 1888, *Deltion tes Hestias*, 1–2, after listing the prizes to be awarded in agriculture, music, etc., says, "and for the athletic contests to be held in the Panathenaic stadium, 45 prizes." Amazingly, just several days before the athletic games were to take place, the committee still pretended that it would hold them—when anyone in Athens could surely see the truth. Perhaps the committee feared legal action if it canceled the athletic games officially.

39. A poster (loose original in Dragoumis envelope 234) dated October 18, 1888, announced that "[t]he interment of the remains of the venerable Evangelis Zappas will take place at the right entry post of the circular stoa in the Zappeion at 10 A.M. 20 October, 1888." So it did, with much ceremony and in the presence of Zappas's aged cousin and executor Konstantinos Zappas, who came from Ro-

mania (see *Le Messager d'Athènes*, Dec. 9, 1888, for further details). Dragoumis envelope 234 contains many crumbling original letters, in (to me) undecipherable scripts with official seals, all dated mid-1888; they seem to come from sundry dignitaries, who are accepting or sending regrets in response to an invitation to attend. The official report of the 1888 Olympiad gives much detail on the agro-industrial exhibits and winners but omits all mention of athletics.

40. "Either because it lacked the material means that even an impromptu preparation of the stadium for such a festival would require, or because it feared a repetition of the 1875 scene, the Olympic Committee from the outset failed to concern itself with the question [of athletic games in the stadium] and slowly abandoned it altogether," Chrysafis, *Oi synchronoi diethneis Olympiakoi Agones*, 117. A third possibility is ideological.

41. Mandell, *First Modern Olympics*, 35; MacAloon, *This Great Symbol*, 151: "and Olympic Games were held . . . in 1889 (there is confusion as to the last year of the festival)." MacAloon's note continues, "Otto Szymiczek . . . gives it as 1887. The display at the Museum . . . in Olympia makes it 1888. Grombach is firm in dating it to May 18, 1889" (319 n. 136). Several other Olympic histories waver between 1888 and 1889. Why Szymiczek, who knew Greek Olympic history well, should say 1887, or why Norbert Müller says 1877 (in his preface to vol. 2, Coubertin, *Textes choisis*, 2:8), I do not know; they are perhaps typos.

42. *Akropolis*, quoted in Chrysafis, *Oi synchronoi diethneis Olympiakoi Agones*, 121 (without precise date).

43. For more detailed accounts of the 1889 "Olympics," see Young, *Olympic Myth*, 40–42, and Chrysafis, *Oi synchronoi diethneis Olympiakoi Agones*, 118–27 (whence most of my account comes), with full summary results. Chrysafis himself attended and writes an eyewitness version, admitting that he and the other pupils of Phokianos had misbehaved and were to blame. There he also reprints several 1889 newspaper accounts. MacAloon's desideratum ("Unfortunately, I have failed to turn up eyewitness accounts of the 1889? festival" [*This Great Symbol*, 152]) is thus fulfilled; but the rest of his sentence ("but improvements were likely made and the outpouring of civic joyfulness unabated") was a wrong guess and misleads.

44. Dolianitis, "Evangelos Zappas," 23, with doc. 44. Dolianitis also has in his private collection a poster that announces, in large print, these Athens Olympic Games for 1892.

45. Ibid., 23, with doc. 45; *Ephemeris tis kyberniseos*, June 28, 1891.

46. Chrysafis, *Oi synchronoi diethneis Olympiakoi Agones*, 134–39.

47. Ibid., 148–49, where Manos's words (not much like Palamis's in our present Olympic hymn) are given. The second day began with "[b]oth free and pedagogic exercises on the parallel bars by students of the Dioskorides High School: I. E. Chrysafis, coach." Chrysafis himself was named "co-winner in the parallel bars," (*tetheis ektos synagonismou*, which seems to mean "ranked beyond competition"). His covictor was Soterios Versis (see next note). Chrysafis, a careful historian, was intimately involved with the Greek Games of this period and is an excellent witness.

48. For the importance of Soterios Versis and Miltiades Gouskos (1893 Panhellenic victors) in IOC Olympiad 1, see MacAloon, *This Great Symbol*, 209, 217–18, 219; see also the detailed account of the 1896 Olympics in chapters 12 and 13,

below. Versis had won the rope climb in Phokianos's 1889 "Olympics" and in the 1891 Panhellenic Games (where he won a cash prize of one hundred drachmas). He won the parallel bars in the 1893 Panhellenic Games. Gouskos won the 1893 Panhellenic weight-lifting event and had many other victories in Greek athletics before the IOC Games of 1896. These men were not neophytes in 1896.

49. Chrysafis, *Oi synchronoi diethneis Olympiakoi Agones*, 151–56.

50. Brookes papers, 1:114; I find no more; Neumüller, "Die Geschichte," omits this one.

51. Coubertin's 1892 proposal is explained in the discussion of his jubilee of that year (chapter 7, below). True, when Coubertin calls Brookes "my oldest friend" ("Typical Englishman," 62), he puns on Brookes's chronological age; but Coubertin knew English perfectly, and the pun proves he knew what he was saying.

52. Brookes to Coubertin, May 22, 1894 (in "Congrès 1894"; quoted and studied further in chapter 7, below). I see only two possible reasons—neither at all likely—why Coubertin might wish to keep Brookes in the dark about his own proposal: (1) he wrongly feared that Brookes would not approve his idea of worldwide sites—anticipating the 1896 controversy over Athens as a permanent Olympic site (see chapter 14, below); or (2) he correctly perceived that Brookes was not in favor with the amateur athletic clubs of London, whose support for his proposal he strongly wished to obtain.

53. Gennadius, "Revival of the Olympian Games," 71; see the full discussion of this article in chapter 12, below.

SIX   Enter Pierre de Coubertin

1. Coubertin's own version, found piecemeal through his sundry works, is most complete in *Campagne*, 1–7; he wrote extensively about Arnold in *L'éducation en Angleterre* (1888, extracted at *Textes choisis*, 1:48–56).

2. Guttmann, *Olympics*, 6–10; cf. Mandell, *First Modern Olympics*, 54–62, MacAloon, *This Great Symbol*, 52–82, Boulongne, *Pierre de Coubertin*, 103–24; in the following paragraphs, names in parentheses refer to these pages of the three American authors.

3. MacAloon, *This Great Symbol*, 39, 54.

4. "Public school" in England means, of course, a private school open to the public, as opposed to state schools funded by the government. These public schools were expensive and attended only by the upper and upper-middle classes in England, as Brookes's 1869 Manchester speech (below) recognizes.

5. Coubertin, *Campagne*, 2–3. Thomas Hughes, *Tom Brown's School Days*; the book was so popular that it had reached six editions by 1868 and has enjoyed scores of reprintings since then. Coubertin first read an 1875 French translation. Hughes himself had attended Rugby (Neumüller, "Die Geschichte," 164), and in the book "Hughes romanticized his memories" (Guttmann, *Olympics*, 9).

6. See the discussion of Hughes's presence on the council for Brookes's 1874 Wenlock National Olympian Games in chapter 5, above.

7. Since I argue that Coubertin got his Olympic idea, even many of his ideas about physical education, more from Brookes than from Hughes and Arnold, I do not enter the knotty controversy over exactly how much Hughes misrepresented

Arnold's activity or how much Coubertin misrepresented Hughes and misunderstood Arnold; nor do I assess Arnold's place in the history of physical education (see Mandell, *First Modern Olympics*, 58–60; MacAloon, *This Great Symbol*, 60–68).

8. We can not be certain of the source, unable to enter a dead man's mind. But Coubertin certainly could not have got the idea from Hughes's *Tom Brown* or Rugby's Thomas Arnold. Mandell, *First Modern Olympics*, 62, implies that Didon (whose *Les Allemands* [1884] contained the notion of French physical weakness versus German strength) contributed to the baron's interest in that theme (and that is, indeed, likely). MacAloon implies that Le Play and Taine contributed to the baron's thinking on German relative to French physical and military strength (*This Great Symbol*, 45–56, 86), but no one cites a Coubertin reference to either French author for that specific theme. Yet by 1889 Coubertin was apparently reading Brookes's statements on this same theme; he quoted him in June of that year (quoting a passage immediately following Brookes's comparison of the French and German soldier) and, in January 1890, cited him by name (see below).

9. "[Brookes's] attention was first attracted to physical exercises in 1830, by taking up a book . . . on his way to Paris, . . . with the subject of weavers who died in the third generation, and this, the author argued, was caused by long confinement and want of out-door recreation and exercise. This book made a great impression on his mind," *Shrewsbury Chronicle*, Feb. 17, 1882 (Brookes papers, 5:74). Brookes, in his 1862 Wenlock speech at the Shropshire Olympics, had said that degeneracy would make poor soldiers and called for a "race . . . of . . . youths . . . whose bodily power . . . would inspire far more terror on the battlefield . . . than the arms they bore" (Brookes papers, 4:126, quoted more fully in chapter 3, above; cf. Brookes papers, 4:67).

10. So the printed text reads; the man's name was Johann Christoph Friedrich Guts Muths (sometimes hyphenated); see Lennartz, *Kenntnisse und vorstellungen*, 54.

11. The printed speech, as Coubertin read it, is in Brookes papers, 1:104–9, and elsewhere in Wenlock scrapbooks (see appendix).

12. See Edwards's words quoted in chapter 3, above; Brookes here attributes the offending remarks to an anonymous Englishman "the year before last." Ioannou expressed an identical criticism of Olympics a few years later in Greece (see chapter 4, above).

13. For example, in an 1872 speech quoted in the *Wellington Journal*, May 25, 1872 (Brookes papers, 4:288; Neumüller, "Die Geschichte," 159), where Brookes described "the French as undersized, thin, slightly-developed . . . with . . . little external evidence of stamina, whilst the Germans, on the contrary, were thick powerful fellows . . . hard and muscular."

14. Brookes to Archdeacon Allen, Oct. 1, 1869 (a copy in Brookes papers, 4:245; Neumüller, "Die Geschichte," 149).

15. For the Hadley speech, see *Shrewsbury Chronicle*, Feb. 17, 1882 (Brookes papers, 5:74; Neumüller, "Die Geschichte," 204–5); for the Wenlock speech, see *Shrewsbury Chronicle*, June 7, 1884 (Brookes papers, 5:95; Neumüller, "Die Geschichte," 211).

16. Brookes papers, 5:135 (Neumüller, "Die Geschichte," 221, with notes). Brookes never stopped: "Consider . . . what a wonderful improvement in the

health, strength, and physique of the British race could be effected in two genera-
tions were bodily training introduced into our elementary school" (*Wellington
Journal*, June 15, 1889 [Brookes papers, 5:152], the very day Coubertin quoted
Brookes's 1866 speech in Paris).

17. Coubertin, *Textes choisis*, 1:111, (from *L'éducation anglaise en France*, 1889,
but signed "27 Oct. 1888"). Grousset's proposal (MacAloon, *This Great Symbol*,
111) was not actually for a revival of the Olympic Games; he merely proposed a
modern athletic institution that would reflect the nature of contemporary French
culture as the Olympics reflected that of ancient Greece. In his final chapter, "La
république vraiment athénienne," Grousset (quite wrongly) suggests that the ancient playwright Euripides was an "athletic victor in the Olympic Games." Then
his exact words are: "Jeux Olympiques: le mot est dit. Il faudrait avoir les nôtres"
[Olympic Games: the word has been said. We ought to have our own]. The rest of
the page outlines the school system and festival that he proposes, but neither "revival" nor "Olympic Games" occurs in the proposal itself (*Renaissance physique*,
256). Grousset's manuscript was signed the same month as Coubertin's, "Oct.
1888."

18. See Boulongne, *Pierre de Coubertin*, throughout (Le Play, at 94–101), Mac-
Aloon, *This Great Symbol*, 45–57 (Taine), 83–93 (Le Play), 97–112, 128–38 (French
athletic organizations). MacAloon suggests that Taine's 1872 *Notes sur Angleterre*
led the young baron to read *Tom Brown*, which was pivotal even to some of Taine's
own work.

19. MacAloon believes that this "vision" was one of the most formative episodes
in Coubertin's whole life. He devotes several pages to it (*This Great Symbol*, 59–60,
294–95), often refers to it elsewhere (e.g., 51, 96), and even titles his third chapter
"The Vision at Rugby Chapel" (cf. Guttmann, "indisputable vision," review of
This Great Symbol, 98). But perhaps MacAloon makes too much of too little (cf.
Guttmann, ibid.). The only source MacAloon cites for this "vision" is a single
sentence in Coubertin's *Campagne*, 5: "Combien souvent, au crépuscule, seul dans
la grande chapelle gothique de Rugby, tenant les yeux fixés sur la dalle funéraire
où s'inscrit sans épitaphe ce grand nom de Thomas Arnold, j'ai songé que j'avais
devant moi la pierre angulaire de l'empire britannique." Coubertin describes what
was clearly a very moving experience. But he does not call it a vision; he says "I
dreamed that" (*j'ai songé que*). Arnold himself does not even appear to him; instead,
the baron "dreams" that he has before him "the cornerstone of the British Empire." If Coubertin is calling Arnold a cornerstone, he writes metaphorically; and
the French verb *songer*, "to dream," hardly need imply an actual vision. It is often
used metaphorically, meaning little more than "to think" or "to imagine" (according to the dictionaries; cf. Boulongne, *Pierre de Coubertin*, 54). I do not doubt
that Coubertin's experiences in the chapel were fateful for him, but I suspect they
have only minor relevance to our Olympic Games. Coubertin's encounters at
Rugby Chapel are amazingly like Soutsos's experiences when he sat on Attic
beaches and on the Pnyx, shuddering as he sought to hear the voices of the ancient
Greeks there (see the notes to my account in chapter 1 of how Soutsos formed his
ideas).

20. He departed for America on July 17, 1889 (MacAloon, *This Great Symbol*,
113); but a month before, on June 15, he had quoted verbatim Brookes's 1866

Olympic speech about French physical degeneracy and the need for physical education in the schools (see next note).

21. There is one inconspicuous exception. Mullins, in his little-known 1986 booklet, *Brookes and the Wenlock Games*, 23, notes that in 1889 Coubertin quoted from Brookes's 1866 NOA speech. Guttmann, *Olympics*, 9, is probably alone among prominent Olympic historians in even acknowledging that Brookes had "influence" on Coubertin's thinking at all; but some small influence from Brookes seems implied in MacAloon, *This Great Symbol*, 147–49, and Boulongne, *Pierre de Coubertin*, 145–46.

22. Coubertin, "Typical Englishman," 62; *Revue Athlétique* 1 (Jan. 25, 1890), discussed below, n. 28.

23. Coubertin, *Campagne*, 35–41; Mandell, *First Modern Olympics*, 75–77; Mac-Aloon, *This Great Symbol*, 135–39. None of these sources gives any details on Coubertin's congress presentation, in which he quoted Brookes. In fact, MacAloon (316 n. 76) says of this presentation, "Unfortunately, the text has not survived." We have at least part of it now, in Brookes's archives; see below.

24. Brookes papers, 5:144; Coubertin's speech containing these words may be in the Coubertin bibliography, *Textes choisis*, 3:717, top entry (which I have not found; the item at Brookes papers, 5:144, could be nothing but a snippet of the full text); Coubertin, *Campagne*, 39, refers to its oral delivery. The baron here quotes verbatim (in French) a passage where Brookes warns that if England allows her youth to degenerate, to "abandon the exercises of the gymnasium," then her "long cherished freedom and with it the power . . . of this great empire" will "pass away." (Coubertin could not have missed the immediately preceding passage, in which Brookes assesses the relative fitness of the French and German soldier.) Coubertin explicitly cites Brookes's words of warning in order to praise nascent French athleticism, which now, he says, leads the French youth to manly exercises; "Voilà pourqoi les libertés, la puissance et le bonheur de la France ne périront pas."

Brookes's ideas on physical education deserve a separate study and perhaps an edition of his copious articles and speeches on the subject, something like Norbert Müller's edition of Coubertin, *Textes choisis;* together, Coubertin and Brookes state a similar and powerful nineteenth-century case from both sides of the Channel.

25. "[C]'est de citoyens plus que de soldats qu'elle a besoin" and "Ce n'est pas le miltarisme qu'il faut à notre éducation, c'est la liberté" (Coubertin, *Textes choisis*, 1:78, 79); on the degradation of military "muscle" in education, see *Textes choisis*, 1:85. In fact, he says there (85) that "military training" and "school training" have nothing at all to do with each other.

26. Coubertin fails to mention Brookes's name as well ("a perspicacious speaker"); but in an oral address, such details are often omitted. He praised Brookes by name a few months later. But the omission of the name "Olympics" is another matter, if Coubertin were already obsessed with the notion of their revival. It is too far-fetched to think he was already covering up the tracks of his Olympic predecessors; that would require a foresight, a cunning, and a meanness that Coubertin simply did not have. It is far easier—and kinder to Coubertin's memory—to conclude that at this point the baron simply had no interest in Olympic Games,

especially since even shortly after his Wenlock visit, he still had no interest in Olympics.

27. *Shrewsbury Chronicle*, Nov. 1, 1889 (Brookes papers, 5:163; Neumüller, "Die Geschichte," 227).

28. "Quelques documents intérressant nous sont parvenus par les soins de M. W.-P. Brookes, qui suit avec une vive sympathie, de sa résidence de Much Wenlock (Angleterre) . . . le mouvement de renaissance physique en France," *Revue Athlétique* 1 (Jan. 25, 1890): a copy in Brookes papers, 5:144; Neumüller, "Die Geschichte," 229.

29. MacAloon, *This Great Symbol*, 157–62, Mandell, *First Modern Olympics*, 78–80, Boulongne, *Pierre de Coubertin*, 48–59; these are founded mainly on Coubertin's account in *Campagne*, 43–51.

30. Coubertin to Brookes, Aug. 9, 1890 (Brookes papers, 5:172–73 [the microfilm has only the first of four pages]). Coubertin's "when we meet in October" suggests that the two had already discussed this visit and had settled on a date.

31. Brookes papers, 5:176, reproduced in Mullins, *Brookes and the Wenlock Games*, 29; Neumüller, "Die Geschichte," 234.

32. Neumüller, "Die Geschichte," 229, draws the same conclusion from the total lack of reference to Olympics in Coubertin's several mentions of Brookes's work antedating his visit.

33. Mandell, *First Modern Olympics*, 77, misdates Coubertin's visit in Wenlock by a year, to the fall of 1889, before the baron returned to France from America.

34. Coubertin, "Les Jeux Olympiques à Much Wenlock," 708.

35. My account uses all three: Coubertin, "Les Jeux Olympiques à Much Wenlock" and "Typical Englishman" and *Wellington Journal*, Oct. 25, 1890 (Brookes papers, 5:169).

36. *Wellington Journal*, Oct. 25, 1890 (Brookes papers, 5:169). Precedents for the special autumn edition are explained in chapters 3 and 5, above.

37. Brookes tended his trees meticulously; Brookes papers, vol. 3, has a section on specific, individual trees: notes in Brookes's hand locate and date the planting of each tree, its Latin botanical name, the special honoree or occasion for that particular tree, and the history of its growth. Now and then he states—almost an obituary—that the tree died (a cedar of Lebanon, "killed by severe weather, 1890–91"; Brookes papers, 3:222).

38. Coubertin, "Les Jeux Olympiques à Much Wenlock," 709.

39. "This practice, and the idea of victory ceremonies themselves, were planted in Coubertin's imagination at Wenlock," MacAloon, *This Great Symbol*, 149, who quotes extensively Coubertin's account of Wenlock pageantry and well appreciates its hold on the baron. The Raven Inn, still open today, much as it was then, now exhibits a few mementoes and reminiscences of Coubertin's visit.

40. *Wellington Journal*, Oct. 25, 1890 (Brookes papers, 5:169).

41. That Brookes consciously viewed the baron as his Olympic successor (the more successful hammerer)—or hoped that he would carry on his own Olympic work after he was gone—is proved by the way he pasted items into his current minute book. For example, Brookes papers, 5:206, has two items juxtaposed: one, Coubertin's letter dated July 20, 1892; the other, a newspaper clipping (*Wellington*

Journal and Shrewsbury News, Sept. 10, 1892, quoted in chapter 7, below), which reports the entire history of Brookes's Olympic movement, from his first contact with Wyse in 1858 about Zappas Olympics to his proposal to found international Olympic Games in Athens. Brookes was, in fact, the first historian of the modern Olympics, and a superb one, making the task much easier for the rest of us.

42. Coubertin, "Les Jeux Olympiques à Much Wenlock," 712; "Typical Englishman," 65.

43. Coubertin, "Les Jeux Olympiques à Much Wenlock," 712. I discuss this passage more fully and quote the original French in chapter 7, below, where I assess the evidence of those who date Coubertin's Olympic revival idea to 1888 (e.g., Boulongne, *Pierre de Coubertin,* 54).

SEVEN   The Baron at Work

1. Coubertin, "Les Jeux Olympiques," 705.

2. Ibid., 708; "La préface," 153. Cf. Coubertin, "Typical Englishman," 65: "The scene was indeed strange, because of its derivation from three very different forms of civilization," etc.

3. "Ce mouvement ne fut pas inutile. . . . Mais . . . on n'eût plus besoin d'invoquer les souvenirs de la Grèce et de chercher des encouragements dans le passé. On aimait le sport pour lui-même" ("Les Jeux Olympiques à Much Wenlock," 712). His attack on Grousset (*Textes choisis,* 1:111) is quoted in chapter 6, above. Coubertin's rivalry with Grousset perhaps explains his initial coolness to Brookes's Olympic ideas, since he otherwise approved of Brookes's activity. To approve Brookes's Olympic idea here might have seemed to approve Grousset's.

4. Boulongne, *Pierre de Coubertin,* 54–55: "Dès 1888—il s'en est entretenu en Amérique avec son ami Sloane—il a songé à faire renaître les Jeux Olympiques"; Boulongne cites no source, making only vague reference to Coubertin's *Universités transatlantiques.* Müller, too (preface to vol. 2, *Textes choisis,* 7–8, with n. 14), writes as if Coubertin's "project of modern Olympic Games" already existed before the American trip of 1889. And "[i]t is possible" that his meeting with Sloane in 1889 encouraged *(renforcer)* Coubertin in his Olympic project. Müller also cites *Universités transatlantiques* (for the American visit, not claiming that the book records Olympic talk in 1889). But my perusal of *Universités transatlantiques* yields no indication that Sloane and Coubertin discussed Olympic Games in 1889. Boulongne may have concluded that Sloane and Coubertin talked Olympics from a forgivable misreading of *Textes choisis,* 2:354 (dated 1928); there, Coubertin does say that Sloane appreciated his Olympic idea "immediately." But he does not, I think, refer to the 1889 meeting; rather, he means in 1893. I have yet to see convincing evidence that Coubertin had any notion of reviving the Olympics himself before he visited Brookes in 1890.

5. Coubertin, ("Les Jeux Olympiques à Much Wenlock," 712). The subject ("he") of Coubertin's verb, *favorisa,* is not expressed, but context shows it is Brookes, not "the Greek King." The "contest at Wenlock" was the NOA Olympiad at Shrewsbury (see chapter 5, above).

6. I come upon no 1870 or 1875 Athens Olympics results nor any clear reference to them in Brookes's papers. The Greeks knew of Brookes's interest, and it is

hard to believe that the ardent Brookes knew nothing of the 1870 or 1875 Athens Games, although it appears possible.

7. Coubertin, "Typical Englishman," 65.

8. Coubertin, *Campagne*, 108. See my "Demetrios Vikelas," 97, with n. 49; "Origins," 287 (and chapter 14, below).

9. Coubertin to Brookes, Apr. 21, 1891 (Brookes papers, 5:187).

10. Coubertin to Brookes, July 20, 1892 (Brookes papers, 5:206).

11. I doubt that Coubertin at this point already planned to take all credit for the proposal for himself and therefore cunningly kept Brookes in the dark about his own plans.

12. *Wellington Journal and Shrewsbury News*, Sept. 10, 1892 (Brookes papers, 5:206).

13. Coubertin, *Mémoires*, 5; *Campagne*, 90; Lucas, *Modern Olympic Games*, 31; Henry, *Approved History*, 21, and others; cf. Mandell, *First Modern Olympics*, 81, MacAloon, *This Great Symbol*, 162–64 (who, however, notes the audience could not have been so dumbfounded as the baron said, for "many had heard the proposal before").

14. Coubertin himself explains that "[t]he baby was switched." See his *Mémoires*, 5; MacAloon, *This Great Symbol*, 162; Guttmann, *Olympics*, 11–12.

15. Coubertin, *Mémoires*, 6; *Campagne*, 90. Jusserand had taken Coubertin's gift of a medal to England for Brookes; Bourdon, friend or enemy, later wholly discredited the Zappas Olympics as an earlier Olympic revival (see the discussion of Bourdon in chapter 4).

16. French *songeur*. Should we then speak of Coubertin's boyhood "vision" of Olympia (see my comments on his "vision" at Rugby Chapel in chapter 6, above)?

17. Coubertin, *Campagne*, 89–90.

18. MacAloon, *This Great Symbol*, 81–82, 139, counts only two minor references to Olympia in Coubertin's voluminous pre-1892 writing. One of these ("la poussière olympique," *Textes choisis*, 1:153) certainly comes not from any study of ancient Olympia but from his reading the Latin poet, Horace (*Odes* 1.1.3); the other seems to come from his reading Taine (MacAloon, 304 n. 258). For Coubertin's errors concerning ancient Greece, see my *Olympic Myth*, 10, 73. His major reference to Olympic Games before meeting Brookes may well be, I fear, his negative comment on Grousset's proposal.

19. Coubertin, *Campagne*, 90; "opera-house," I think, refers to the 1893 San Francisco Revival of the Ancient Greco-Roman Games (see below).

20. In *Mémoires*, 6, to clarify how far his 1892 audience was from understanding his intent, Coubertin compares the naïveté of an American woman at the 1896 Athens Games, who told him, "I have already attended Olympic Games," referring to a theatrical production in San Francisco (for which see my *Olympic Myth*, 181, and my discussion of Coubertin's 1893 visit to San Francisco, below). The lady, Coubertin means, could not conceive of true Olympic Games.

21. I discussed Gennadius's important reply (Gennadius to Brookes, Jan. 12, 1893, Brookes papers, 1:114) and its implications in chapter 5, above.

22. Here Brookes reveals not only his mortality but also his humanity and humor: he tells Coubertin that he had to miss the Forty-third Annual Wenlock Olympian Games because "[I] fractured my left leg and seriously injured my ankle

joint, thereby reducing my position to that of a limping instead of an Olympian member of the Society."

23. Brookes to Coubertin, May 30, 1893 (photocopy given to me in Wenlock, May 1991, by a member of the WOS).

24. The words "only contests" recall Leonidas's words in Soutsos's poem quoted in chapter 1, above: "And let the only contests that you have be those national games, the Olympics."

25. See my *Olympic Myth*, 182–83; and, e.g., Glader, *Amateurism and Athletics;* Paddock, "Amateurism," and the works cited there.

26. Coubertin, *Campagne*, 90–91.

27. Coubertin, *Mémoires*, 10; MacAloon, *This Great Symbol*, 164–65.

28. Coubertin, *Mémoires*, 10.

29. Ibid., 6 (see notes 19–20, above); Young, *Olympic Myth*, 181. A full program of the Olympic Club Fair and Revival of the Ancient Greco-Roman Games, Apr. 17–23, 1893, is extant in the UCLA Library; the *San Francisco Chronicle* for those days reported them in great detail. I hope to write a separate account of these San Francisco "Olympics." Here I merely note that Coubertin was right; they were much more a theatrical production than a serious athletic contest and were not relevant to the history of our own Olympic Games.

30. Sloane's contribution included his help at Paris in 1894 and his recruitment of an American team of athletes for Athens in 1896; but his participation increased after 1900 (which lies beyond the scope of this study). The letters in the IOC collection (Sloane, "Correspondance") reveal an extremely close and touching personal relationship between Sloane and Coubertin, who seemed always willing to bare his innermost feelings to his American friend. John Lucas offers an excellent study of Sloane's Olympic work: "Professor William Mulligan Sloane: Father of the United States Olympic Committee."

31. Of Herbert, Coubertin said, "[L]a partie technique du programme l'intéressait quelque peu; il ne voyait rien de viable ni d'utile dans le mouvement olympique" (*Campagne*, 92–93); Coubertin, *Mémoires*, 10; a good summary of all these events is in MacAloon, *This Great Symbol*, 164–68.

32. The original eight-point January circular is reprinted in Coubertin, *Mémoires*, 9, and my *Olympic Myth*, 180, with notes (from an English version in the journal of the Olympic Club in San Francisco, *Olympic* 1, no. 6 (May 17, 1894). Most books (e.g., Mandell, *First Modern Olympics*, 85, MacAloon, *This Great Symbol*, 167, Coubertin, *Olympic Idea*, 2) wrongly state that Coubertin sent the ten-point version (which differs greatly with respect to Coubertin's Olympic plans) in January; even Coubertin later became somewhat confused and has it wrong himself in *Mémoires*, 9 (see my *Origins*, 295 n. 46; cf. *Olympic Myth*, 61–63, 179–81). Müller has now corrected this error by reproducing (from IOC archives), with a January date, the eight-point agenda (*Textes choisis*, 2:106) and the ten-point version, dated to May (*Textes choisis*, 2:110). The journal *Herkules* (Budapest, Apr., 1, 1894: 38–39) printed, in Hungarian translation, the flyer Hungary received; it is the eight-point version (the translation by Franz Kemeny, as his letter in "Congrès 1894" shows). I thank Dr. T. Ajan of the Hungarian Olympic Committee, J. Bartoszek, and A. Lukacsfalvi for getting me a photocopy of the *Herkules* article.

33. "[I]l est permis de croire que ces luttes pacifiques et courtoises constituent le meilleur des internationalismes," *Textes choisis*, 2:104–5.

34. See "Pax Olimpica," *Revue Olympique* 12 (July 1912); the article is unsigned but written by Coubertin's friend, Rev. Laffan (according to Coubertin, *Mémoires*, 79); the *Revue Olympique* printed only opinions that conformed closely to the philosophy of its editor. For Coubertin, the Olympics, and peace, see also my "Riddle of the Rings," 271–76. Many, John Lucas foremost (*Future of the Olympic Games*, 20–21; and often), have observed that Coubertin's Olympic movement was a "peace movement." But that feature deserves more study than it has received, more than I can give it here. A small step in the right direction has now been made, in the publication of Quanz, "IOC Founding."

35. Hungarians clearly got the earlier version at some point (see the note on the eight-point flyer, above). Of the eighty or so responses to Coubertin's invitation in the "Congrès 1894" file, most, my notes record, date from May and June. None dated before late April seems to have clear reference to the ten-point version. Some earlier respondents got the eight-point program: e.g., W. House, of Australia, on April 16 refers to the "preliminary program" of "the international congress of amateurs" and responds, point for point, to the eight points (all exactly as printed in the journal *Olympic* [see the note on the eight-point flyer, above]). Herbert, in a January 10 letter (on AAA letterhead), tells the baron to send multiple invitations to potential distributors in the "Colonial Clubs": "Send some dozen invitations enclosed to Leonard A. Cuff ... New Zealand," etc. Cuff received them, with a letter from Coubertin dated January 16, replied extensively, and became one of Coubertin's more helpful supporters and a charter member of the IOC.

36. The honorary members were still accepting in early April (R. Feldhaus on April 9, H. Pratt on April 14; "Congrès 1894" file).

37. de Courcel to J. J. Jusserand, Mar. 29, 1894 ("Congrès 1894"), proves that, as of that date, Coubertin and de Courcel had never met one another and de Courcel had not yet accepted presidency of the congress (in fact, he seems unsure what Coubertin wants of him). A meeting was arranged for early April. Coubertin himself prints some of this letter in *Campagne*, 95, but omits its date.

38. The list is published in *Textes choisis*, 2:113, and the *Bulletin*, no. 1 (July 1894): 2.

39. Coubertin, *Campagne*, 94. Coubertin met Waldstein (an American, but German educated) in Cambridge during the baron's 1886 travels in England (*Textes choisis*, 1:47).

40. Coubertin, *Campagne*, 94, Chrysafis, *Oi synchronoi diethneis Olympiakoi Agones*, 203. Chrysafis's account is somewhat fuller than Coubertin's and says Coubertin asked Waldstein to get the royal family "to have a hand in" (*na balei cheri*) Coubertin's project. I do not know if Chrysafis heard that from Waldstein (whom he knew) or somewhat overinterpreted Coubertin's own account. Waldstein says in his 1894 excavation report (*Argive Heraeum*, 77) that the royal family, in this April visit, "remained with us over four hours." At the end of chapter 8, below, I propose that Waldstein and Constantine may have discussed Athens as the site of IOC Olympiad 1.

41. For the eight-point program, see *Textes choisis*, 2:106; the May ten-point program (*Textes choisis*, 2:110) retains that paragraph.

42. Brookes's letter (see below) seems to treat the points of the circular as if he had just received it and as if his personal opinion had not been solicited.

43. Brookes to Coubertin, May 22, 1894, in "Congrès 1894."

44. Compare Coubertin's "successivement près des grandes capitales du monde" in "Le rétablissement," 184.

45. Coubertin, *Campagne*, 53.

46. Coubertin, "La préface," 153.

47. For the difficulties of international Olympiads after 1896, see the discussion of that topic in chapter 14, below. Since Coubertin indisputably knew of Brookes's rotating British Olympics, perhaps he even derived that feature of his proposal from Brookes, too.

48. Circular (dated "6-94") reproduced at *Textes choisis*, 2:112–14. Some Parisians did not get their first invitation until June; they responded to an invitation to the Congress for the Re-establishment of the Olympic Games (e.g., the Paris YMCA, June 13, and the Office of Primary Education in Paris, June 9 ["Congrès 1894"]).

49. Coubertin, *Mémoires*, 11 (cf. MacAloon, *This Great Symbol*, 170).

50. Coubertin, *Mémoires*, 65; cf. *Mémoires*, 8: "Amateurism, an admirable mummy that one could transport to the museum of Boulak as a specimen of modern embalming! A half a century has passed and it does not appear to have suffered from the constant manipulations of which it has been the object. It seems intact. Not one of us counted on such endurance.... [The amateurism congress] provided me with a valuable screen" (again, the French word for "screen" is *paravent*). Yet he was early a master at feigning true belief, writing even of ancient Greek amateurism with "zeal": "Il y a toujours eu distinction et souvent querelle entre 'amateurs' et 'professionals.' Les conditions d'amateurisme imposées aux concurrents des jeux olympiques dépassent en exigence ce que pourrait inventer, de nos jours, le comité le plus pointilleux," *Textes choisis*, 2:101 (1893). ·

51. Introduction to Lambros and Politis, *Olympic Games*, 110 (1988; in the 1896 edition, 6–7).

52. Brookes to Coubertin, June 13, 1894, "Congrès 1894"; I explain more about Brookes's recommendations on amateurism in chapter 8, below.

53. See the account of those gifts in chapter 3, above.

54. Brookes to "S. Trikoupis, Prime Minister," now Dragoumis envelope 235, subfolder 1, doc. 92. I published some of this letter in my "Origins," 280, 296, before Dragoumis's papers were catalogued.

EIGHT   The 1894 Paris Congress and D. Vikelas

1. In 1895 Coubertin apparently tried to resign from the IOC (Vikelas, "Correspondance," 2). If Vikelas had not forged ahead, in effect refusing to accept the baron's resignation, the 1896 Athens Olympics would have taken place—if at all— as a wholly Greek affair; and Athens would no doubt have become the permanent site of subsequent Olympiads. See the discussion of Vikelas, "Correspondance," Jan. 17, 1894, and the word "resignation" at the end of chapter 10, below.

2. For a more detailed account of Vikelas and his work, including his relations with Coubertin, see my 1988 "Demetrios Vikelas." Before that article, little of Vikelas was known outside of Greece and almost nothing published on him except in the Greek language (all sources remain in Greek). I drew most of my 1988 material on Vikelas from the extensive "Vikelas" entry in the *Mega Hellenikon viographikon lexikon.* I add much more in this book, taken from Oikonomos, *Dimitrios M. Vikelas,* a long, detailed biography in Greek, and the previously unknown letters reproduced in Linardos, *Panellinios G. S.* I use Oikonomos especially for particulars of Vikelas's relations with Trikoupis and Coubertin. Vikelas's autobiography, *I zoi mou,* contains nothing noteworthy about the Olympic Games.

3. Vikelas, "Oi diethneis Olympiakoi Agones." "June" is an error; he replied by telegram on May 26 (see below).

4. Rangavis was by then a member and advisor of the Panhellenic (see chapter 2, above); apart from his choice of Vikelas to represent the society in Paris, I know of no other connection of Rangavis to Vikelas, the 1894 congress, or the 1896 Games. The original of Vikelas's affirmative telegram response to Rangavis, dated May 26, 1894, is reproduced in Linardos, *Panellinios G. S.,* 52; the original of his May 28 letter to Rangavis (noting that Rangavis had suggested his name) is in Linardos, 50. On the princes, see Coubertin, *Bulletin,* no. 1 (July 1894): 1. On Waldstein's role in Coubertin's invitation to the Panhellenic, see Coubertin to Phokianos (as president of the Panhellenic), Apr. 26, 1894 (original reproduced in Linardos, 37).

5. Coubertin, *Campagne,* 96.

6. Coubertin, *Bulletin,* no. 1 (July 1894): 3. I argue in "Riddle of the Rings," 266–67, that the five interlocked rings of the IOC were probably suggested by the two interlocked rings of Coubertin's "Union," the USFSA (illustrated at *Encyclopédie des sports,* 145, 165; Coubertin, *Mémoires,* 21). Mandell, *First Modern Olympics,* 33, with n. 22, says fireworks and Olympics were proposed together by William H. Drayton in the 1779 U.S. Congress (citing the *South Carolina Historical Magazine* 61 [1960], 146–47). There were fireworks at the Liverpool Olympics and at a ceremony attached to the 1896 Athens IOC Games.

7. Letter (in Greek), Vikelas to Rangavis, dated May 28, 1894: "Yesterday I tried to call on Baron de Coubertin, in order to find out something of what I should do; but unfortunately I did not find him at home. I'll try again." The original of this remarkable letter is reproduced in Linardos, *Panellinios G. S.,* 50 (printed transcription on 68). Since the congress was not to begin for more than two weeks, perhaps Vikelas succeeded in meeting Coubertin on a later attempt.

8. "Procès-Verbal," handwritten minutes of the 1894 Paris International Athletic Congress, in "Congrès 1894." For Coubertin's statement ("il fallait Athènes"), see *Campagne,* 98.

9. I do not know if Mr. Herbert ever arrived. No mention of his presence is made, and I suspect he did not attend.

10. The London motion left its undetected shadow in the *Deutsche Turn-zeitung* 28, 1894 [12.7]: 548, where a report on the Paris congress headed "Neue Olympische Spiele" states, "Since Paris has chosen the date 1900 for its next World's Fair, it was arranged that the second holding of the Games would be in the French capital and the first in London in 1896" (reprinted in Koebsel, *Dokumente,* 5). "[I]n

London in 1896" makes no sense within received Olympic history but is easily explained by the suppressed London motion. Perhaps the *Turn-zèitung* reporter attended the June 19 meeting but left the congress before June 23, expecting the delegates to continue voting for London.

11. *Hestia*, May 7/19, 1895, 147. See my "Origins," 282–83, where I quote Vikelas's version at length; to quote that long text again here would exaggerate its importance, since much of it seems fiction.

The question whether Vikelas or Coubertin first proposed Athens is further confused by two more letters of Vikelas. First, the day before Coubertin's own Athens proposal, Vikelas wrote Phokianos that he intended to add Athens to the list of future Olympic host cities (Vikelas to Phokianos, June 18, 1894 [in Linardos, *Panellinios G. S.*, 68–69]). But Vikelas does not here say he would propose Athens as the initial site. Second, Linardos, 74, prints the text of a second letter, Vikelas to Phokianos, dated "2 June, 1894," in which Vikelas writes of a plan to hold IOC Olympiad I in Athens. But other items in the letter ("Coubertin is coming to Athens in Autumn"; Vikelas is already president of the IOC) prove that "2 June" is an error (by Vikelas or Linardos), July 2 probably being the correct date.

12. I do not think Vikelas misrepresents out of malice or egoism; he wrote what he and Coubertin decided should be the only version made public then. Coubertin became more candid later.

13. For their (very excusable) errors (Mandell, *First Modern Olympics*, 91, 183 n. 27; MacAloon, *This Great Symbol*, 173) and Coubertin's own inconsistency, see my "Origins," 272, 283–85, with notes (esp. 54, 60). I do not repeat those discussions here, but I do note that the mistakes and confusions are even more complex and manifold than I perceived when I wrote "Origins."

14. Coubertin, *Bulletin*, no. 1 (July 1894); similar in his introduction to *Olympic Games*, 110.

15. Coubertin, *Campagne*, 98. Coubertin's version in *Mémoires*, 12, is also candid and generally accurate, but rather obscure.

16. Vikelas, "Correspondance," 20–21.

17. "Très sensible à la demande si courtoise du baron de Coubertin, je le prie ainsi que les membres du Congrès, de recevoir, avec mes remerciements sincères, mes meilleurs voeux pour le rétablissement des Jeux Olympiques. George" (Coubertin, *Bulletin*, no. 1 [July 1894]: 4). "[B]efore a vote had even been taken on the matter, a telegram was received from the king of Greece thanking Coubertin and the members for having declared the revival," MacAloon, *This Great Symbol*, 170. MacAloon (n. 58) then quotes a *Times* (London) version (June 23, 1894), which inexplicably translates the French *demande* ("question," "request," "petition") as "act."

18. Coubertin, *Bulletin*, no. 1 (July 1984): 4, says that Criésis transmitted George's telegram to him.

19. Mandell, *First Modern Olympics*, 183 n. 27. Cf. MacAloon, *This Great Symbol*, 170 ("But the Congress was not, for all this, a sham"), 173, with n. 72; and Chrysafis, *Oi synchronoi diethneis Olympiakoi Agones*, 203–4.

20. Vikelas, *Hestia*, May 7/19, 1895, 147: "Was I not compelled to propose Athens as the site of the first Olympic Games?—I had no such charge or permission" (*den eikha toiauten entolen e adeian*; cf. Vikelas's similar denial in Linardos,

Panellinios G. S., 71). I translate more from this same article in my "Origins," 282, and in chapter 9, below.

21. Vikelas to Phokianos, June 22, 1894 (in Linardos, *Panellinios G. S.*, 69–70).

22. Coubertin, *Campagne*, 98, citing his own "Le rétablissement" in the *Revue de Paris* for the proposed 1900 starting date. Coubertin there indeed says (184), a month before the congress opened, that "the 20th century" would, if Olympic Games were revived, see contests of youths every four years "near the great capitals of the world." But I find nothing about a precise initial site and date there. And one does not know when this article, published May 15, 1894, was written; it could easily have been before April 15. Nor, if posted from rather remote Argos, would Waldstein's April letter have arrived speedily.

23. See the discussion of Coubertin's preparations for the congress in chapter 7, above.

24. There were many obstacles—from the king's point of view, Trikoupis high on that list; and from Coubertin's view, the Duvals among his delegates, who judged Greece backward and out of the way.

NINE The IOC: First Faltering Steps

1. That his speech directly followed dinner ("ensuite") and the order of speakers Coubertin himself clearly states in a full account of the evening in *Bulletin* 1 (July 1894): 3. MacAloon, *This Great Symbol*, 173, makes him the very last speaker of the evening, after Vikelas and others; cf. Mandell, *First Modern Olympics*, 90–91. Both MacAloon and Mandell (183, n. 7) place the nomination and approval of Athens for 1896 at this final banquet in the Jardin d'Acclimatation. But *Bulletin* 1 (July 1894): 2–4 carefully separates the *fêtes* (dinners, excursions—and the final banquet) from the business meetings, *travaux*, held in rooms of the Sorbonne—including the Athens proposal. Vikelas's proposal of Athens was surely made at a daytime business meeting; his evening speech, like others after Coubertin, was just a brief formality, and invitation to, not a proposal for, Athens.

2. The French text is in *Bulletin*, no. 1 (July 1894): 3; the English text in *Olympic Idea*, 6–7 (followed here); selections are in Mandell, *First Modern Olympics*, 90–91, and MacAloon, *This Great Symbol*, 173.

3. See n. 1, above. Vikelas, "Oi diethneis Olympiakoi Agones, " 147, puts the Athens proposal just after a debate and vote on each question of amateurism, unlikely at a formal evening banquet.

4. Vikelas, "Correspondance," 20–21.

5. Vikelas, "Oi diethneis Olympiakoi Agones," 147 (also in my "Origins," 282–83). Mandell, *First Modern Olympics*, 90, suggests that Vikelas's speech did not survive; we have now at least a paraphrase. This surely true paraphrase comes after a fictitious account of how Vikelas first conceived the "Athens in 1896" idea the night of June 22. I cannot judge if his tale of encouragement from a "wealthy Greek" who visited that same night is fictitious or not. If it is true, one wonders who the wealthy visitor was—or if "he" was a telegram from Constantine.

6. Coubertin, *Bulletin*, no. 1 (July 1894): 1.

7. Bréal's successful marathon innovation is well known (there was no precedent

for this race in antiquity: see MacAloon, *This Great Symbol*, 173, 225; Mandell, *First Modern Olympics*, 89); but Bréal did not propose it until "some time after" the congress (Coubertin, *Campagne*, 96). Absent from the list of events approved by the delegates (*Bulletin* 1 [July 1894], 4), the marathon is first mentioned in *Bulletin* 2 (Oct. 1894), 4. That same official list, however, recommends that the modern Olympics include a pentathlon, which had been proposed by both Vikelas and Brookes (Vikelas *ibid.*; Brookes to Coubertin, 13 June, 1894 [above, chapt. 7]. Conversely, in Coubertin's revised program issued months later, the marathon replaced the pentathlon (*Bulletin* 3 [Jan. 1895], 1).

8. Coubertin, *Bulletin*, no. 1 (July 1894): 1; no. 2 (Oct. 1894): 1, 4. For Coubertin's preference for titled nobility, see my *Olympic Myth*, 73.

9. Coubertin, *Campagne*, 108.

10. Brookes papers, 5:219.

11. Coubertin, *Campagne*, 108.

12. Vikelas, "Correspondance," 5–8.

13. Coubertin, *Bulletin*, no. 2 (Oct. 1894): 3.

14. Vikelas, "Correspondance," 9–17; Coubertin, *Campagne*, 108–9, *Mémoires*, 14.

15. In 1865, soon after leaving London, Trikoupis asked Vikelas to send him razor blades from England, better than what he found in Greece. Vikelas sent the blades but took the opportunity to criticize some of Trikoupis's politics, especially his coolness toward King George and the monarchy itself. Trikoupis took the matter ill and shot back a defensive letter. The next year Trikoupis's letters to Vikelas address him with the formal plural pronoun "you," not the familiar singular used among friends. When Vikelas publically criticized Trikoupis's economic policies in 1893, Trikoupis's sister (who had borrowed money from Vikelas's uncle) announced she would never speak to Vikelas again (Oikonomos, *Dimitrios M. Vikelas*, 136–39).

Although Trikoupis and King George were both often practical enough politicians to work together, their relationship, lasting two decades, was probably always strained (Kousoulas, *Modern Greece*, 58–60, 73–81).

16. Oikonomos, *Dimitrios M. Vikelas*, 463.

17. Dragoumis doc. 93, dated Oct. 3/15. Vikelas sought to quell Dragoumis's doubts about the Games, saying that failure to hold them would cause "the worst impression abroad." He also said, "The presence of Baron de Coubertin in Athens will help to dissolve the doubts." My thanks to Christina Varda for help in reading several Greek letters in these archives. All citations of the Dragoumis documents in this chapter are to envelope (*phakelos*) 235.

18. Cf. Coubertin, *Campagne*, 109, 111.

19. The October 20 letter of introduction (in French) and the October 22 letter (in Greek) are in Dragoumis docs. 97, 98, respectively.

20. Coubertin, *Campagne*, 109–11. MacAloon, *This Great Symbol*, 183–84, gives a summary (cf. Mandell, *First Modern Olympics*, 96). In the Dragoumis documents, envelope 235 preserves Dragoumis's own copy of the original. When Coubertin published the letter in 1908, he observed that Dragoumis's assertion that Greece had no notion of "Athletic Sports" was false, pointing to the gymnastic and other sporting societies in 1894 Athens.

21. Mandell, *First Modern Olympics*, 96, gives that exact date (without source), which seems about right; I find no confirmation. The rest of Mandell's account is wrong; Vikelas, of course, was not even in Athens.

22. Coubertin, *Campagne*, 111–12. Coubertin states that he immediately replied to Dragoumis's letter, but I do not find that reply among Coubertin's letters in the Dragoumis archives. Coubertin stayed at the Hotel Grande Bretagne, then, as now, the most prestigious hotel in the city. It is located near the royal palace and the Zappeion.

23. Ibid., 112–13; Coubertin, *Mémoires*, 16–17, where he says he had "two long conversations" with the crown prince.

24. *Textes choisis*, 2:372; Coubertin, *Campagne*, 113. The full (French) speech was published shortly thereafter (in *Le Messager d'Athènes*: see *Textes choisis*, 2:364–75). The version in *Bulletin*, no. 3 (Jan. 1895): 4 (also at *Olympic Idea*, 7–10), gives only selections from the original speech and has little value for the historian. Lambros and Politis stayed with the project to the end, as editors of the official report (Lambros and Politis, *Olympic Games*), where Politis's article on the stadium is the second after Coubertin's own article. In his narrative in *Mémoires*, 16, Coubertin wrongly says this Parnassus speech was given several days after the organizational meeting in the Zappeion, but in fact it preceded it (see n. 32, below).

25. I have written a separate article, "On the Source of the Olympic Credo," on this saying, which is variously called the Olympic creed, code, device, or motto. There, I argue that Coubertin did not get the saying from Bishop Talbot, as he himself suggested in 1908 (*Textes choisis*, 2:449; *Olympic Idea*, 20) and some recent scholarship would affirm; for Talbot's words are not close. I argue that Coubertin later subconsciously recalled the phrase from his own Parnassus speech, and its use there was a subconscious recollection of his reading, as a boy at school, this phrase from the ancient Latin poet Ovid: "Nec tam turpe fuit vinci quam contendisse decorum est" (*Metamorphoses* 9.5–6). For more on this saying, its possible sources, bibliography, etc., see my article.

26. Coubertin, *Mémoires*, 16; *Campagne*, 115. I date the meeting to November 17 or 18 on the basis of the baron's November 19 letter to Dragoumis (see below).

27. Coubertin, *Campagne*, 115.

28. Dragoumis docs. 101, 95, 94, all three dated Nov. 19.

29. Both meetings "yesterday" in Dragoumis doc. 99 (see next note).

30. Dragoumis doc. 99. The letter is dated merely "Thursday," but that was November 22. Besides the hand-written "Confidential," the top of the letter bears the printed letterhead of the Committee for the Olympic Games, boldly followed by the words, "Athens, 1896" and "Paris, 1900."

31. *Nea Ephemeris*, Nov. 11/23, 1894.

32. In *Mémoires*, 16, Coubertin wrongly gives November 12 as the meeting date; in *Campagne*, 115, he dated it correctly to November 24. The discrepancy arises from the difference between the Greek calendar and that used by the rest of Europe, for the twelfth was the Greek date for our twenty-fourth. The baron himself had made it all clear in the *Bulletin*, no. 3 (Jan. 1895): 2, "12/24 November." But by 1931 he had forgotten.

33. Dragoumis, in *Ephemeris ton syzitiseon tis Voulis*, 178.

34. Coubertin, *Campagne*, 115; the report in *Nea Ephemeris*, Nov. 14/26, em-

phatically states: "The President is Crown Prince Constantine." So also Skouloudis, in *Ephemeris ton syzitiseon tis Voulis,* 179, who says that Coubertin "announced that the Crown Prince had agreed to accept as President of the committee to be selected." In view of the unanimity of these contemporaneous sources, Philemon's version (Lambros and Politis, *Olympic Games,* 111–12) seems in error. Philemon says that Constantine was merely "Honorary President" of the initial committee and only later assumed the "actual presidency." Perhaps it was Constantine who suggested that Coubertin invite Melas and Mercatis, who "had been Constantine's boyhood friend" (MacAloon, *This Great Symbol,* 187).

35. Coubertin, *Campagne,* 115–16. Other vice presidents were Colonel Manos, Commandant Soutsos (perhaps somehow related to Soutsos, who first proposed the Olympic revival in the 1830s), and Mr. Retzinas, mayor of Piraeus. Mercatis and Melas were Coubertin's closest new friends in Athens; the former was later named to the IOC. The prince apparently did not attend the meeting in person. Virtually all details of Coubertin's version of these events are confirmed by Dragoumis and by Skouloudis himself—who adds, however, that he himself left in the middle of the meeting only to find out later that, after he had left, he was named a vice president (*Ephemeris ton syzitiseon tis Voulis,* 178–79). The number attending, thirty-two, is from Skouloudis's account.

36. Coubertin, *Bulletin,* no. 3 (Jan. 1895): 2; *Nea Ephemeris,* Nov. 16/28.

37. Coubertin, *Campagne,* 89; see Coubertin's explanation of his idea's genesis in a fascination with Olympia, quoted in chapter 7, above.

38. Coubertin, *Mémoires,* 17; *Textes choisis,* 2:415.

39. MacAloon, *This Great Symbol,* 6–7. The IOC archives in Lausanne contain several documents and newspaper clippings about the entombment of Coubertin's heart at Olympia. The Museum of the Modern Olympics in Olympia village displays the box in which the heart arrived, along with photographs and reports of the ceremony. The marble pillar containing the heart long stood at the entrance to the ancient archaeological site; it is now on the grounds of the International Olympic Academy, not far from the ancient stadium. Wreathes are regularly placed at its base by the IOA.

40. Coubertin, *Mémoires,* 17; *Bulletin,* no. 3 (Jan. 1895): 2.

TEN   Politics, Trade Unions, and Wedding Bells

1. Coubertin, *Campagne,* 116: "[Skouloudis] was a close friend and confidant of Trikoupis." So Zygomalas, in *Ephemeris ton syzitiseon tis Voulis,* 179.

2. Skouloudis said he had left the November 24 organizing meeting in its middle and only later found out that, in his absence, he had been appointed a vice president. He at once began to submit his resignation to Coubertin, but others urged him not to do so. He decided, instead, to view the committee as a study committee, not a commitee of action. The members studied the question and, finding that there was not enough time, and especially not enough money, to hold the Games, decided to resign (*Ephemeris ton syzitiseon tis Voulis,* 179). Coubertin's version differs only slightly and, whatever his source, seems accurate. Coubertin further says that Skouloudis slyly assembled the other three vice presidents first—not inviting the two secretaries, the baron's own friends Mercatis and Melas—to

convince them to reject Coubertin's budget and resign (Coubertin, *Campagne*, 116–17).

3. Coubertin, *Campagne*, 116–17; *Mémoires*, 19; Greek sources agree, e.g., Philemon, in Lambros and Politis, *Olympic Games*, 112. Skouloudis (see below) suggests an unimportant difference in the timing of these events.

4. By the Greek calendar the date was November 24. The exact words of each of the speakers, the parrying against opponents, and the frequent appeals to Greek patriotism are all preserved in the published *Ephemeris ton syzitiseon tis Voulis*.

5. *Ephemeris ton syzitiseon tis Voulis*, 177–79. I omit the speeches of several other delegates who intervened in the course of Zygomalas's remarks and the bulk of what he himself said.

6. Sloane, *Report of the American Olympic Committee*, 79. See also my *Olympic Myth*, 70–71, and Ketseas, "A Restatement," 56. Sloane's statement, confirmed by no other source that I know, raises many questions. But if true, it might resolve some financial difficulties, such as how the sale of commemorative stamps could bring in the high amount reported (400,000 drachmas: Philemon, in Lambros and Politis, *Olympic Games*, 118; cf. Coubertin, *Campagne*, 118).

7. The account of the debate given (without source) in Coubertin, *Campagne*, 116, is generally accurate; his minor mistakes (Trikoupis indeed spoke) do not misrepresent the event as a whole.

8. *Nea Ephemeris*, Nov. 27/Dec. 9, Nov. 28/Dec. 10, Dec. 10/22, respectively.

9. Oikonomos, *Dimitrios M. Vikelas*, 473–74.

10. *Nea Ephemeris*, Dec. 15/27 (for reports of gifts) and Dec. 21/Jan. 2 (on athletic clubs). The paper then reports over the next several months numerous private donations, large and small.

11. *Nea Ephemeris*, Dec. 28/Jan. 9.

12. Vikelas, "Correspondance," 25–27.

13. Ibid., 35–36.

14. Coubertin, *Mémoires*, 21.

15. Vikelas, "Correspondance," 1–3.

16. Oikonomos, *Dimitrios M. Vikelas*, 476, who quotes the speech on 475–76. See also Vikelas, "Correspondance," 2; *Asty*, Jan. 5/17; cf. *Nea Ephemeris*, Jan. 5/17. All speeches for the Games emphasized Greek patriotism; all opposed to them stressed finances. This alliance between the royalist Vikelas and the working-class Athenians may be surprising; yet classicists may recall ancient Greek politics, wherein monarchists and plebeians often united against the aristocracy.

17. Oikonomos, *Dimitrios M. Vikelas*, 476; Delivorrias, *Athens, 1839–1900*, caption to photograph 359, "The Funeral of Charilaos Trikoupis."

18. Oikonomos, *Dimitrios M. Vikelas*, 476; *Nea Ephemeris*, Jan. 11/23, 1895 (Kousoulos, *Modern Greece*, 80, gives the date as Jan. 23). Coubertin, *Campagne*, 117, suggests that Constantine's failure to approve Skouloudis's committee's decision to abandon the Olympics so angered Trikoupis that it triggered his animosity against the crown prince and the events that led to his resignation "in circumstances unrelated to my main topic." In *Mémoires*, 19, Coubertin states that Trikoupis "seized the pretext of an incident arising from a labor strike" to compel King George "to choose between his son and his Prime Minister." MacAloon, *This Great Symbol*, 196, agrees that the Olympic dispute contributed to the tension between

the two men but thinks Coubertin wrong about the labor strike; the real reason was a "dispute over military discipline" (cf. Mandell, *First Modern Olympics,* 184 n. 10). Both these other causes are probably half right: "military discipline" may refer to the prince's January 20 act in Ares Park, and "labor strike" to Vikelas's recruitment of the trade unions against Trikoupis, surely a partial cause of the Ares Park rally. Neither event is mentioned by Coubertin, MacAloon, or Mandell. Thus the Olympic dispute probably has more bearing on Trikoupis's departure than scholars have previously recognized.

19. Philemon quotes Constantine's speech in Lambros and Politis, *Olympic Games,* 112–14.

20. Coubertin, *Mémoires,* 21.

21. Brookes to Coubertin, Dec. 11, 1894; photocopy given to me in Wenlock, 1991, by a member of the WOS. Brookes's own hand clearly dates it "December 11th, 1895," an obvious mistake for "1894"; for Brookes died the day before that 1895 date. This letter is seven pages long, and interesting throughout. I discuss only its highlights here.

22. This is apparently Brookes's last letter to Coubertin; he died almost exactly one year later, December 10, 1895, at the age of eighty-six. The wish to "live long enough" thus went unfulfilled.

23. "Finally! I have received your letter, and what a good letter! I . . . express to you my best wishes, my sincerest blessings [and to] Mademoiselle Rothan, please tell her how much I would like to present her my congratulations and respects in person. I sent your letter on to Col. Sapountzakis [Constantine's aide-de-camp] . . . the good news . . . will be published in tomorrow morning's *Asty,*" Vikelas, "Correspondance," 1.

24. Vikelas, "Correspondance," 1–3; in the IOC Library in Lausanne, in the stack collection of photocopies, this letter is bound out of chronological sequence, because Vikelas carelessly dated it January 5/17, 1894, whereas the correct year was 1895 [1894 is clearly impossible]. People often make that mistake in January.

25. Vikelas, "Correspondance," 37–39, Jan. 18; 40–42, Jan. 23; 43–45, Jan. 24 ("As for the velodrome, people are still waiting for your instructions. Write ASAP also with regard to the invitations that the Athenian Committee should make"); 46–47, Jan. 27 ("I'm promising everywhere that next winter you will be here. I consider you to be committed to that. Put it in your marriage contract"). These pleading letters prove quite false the charges Olympic historians make against the Greeks; namely, that they ignored Coubertin in making preparations (e.g., Mandell, *First Modern Olympics,* 102–3, cf. 112; and MacAloon, *This Great Symbol,* 199, says, "Even his design for the velodrome . . . was rejected by the Hellenic committee"). Vikelas's letters begging for the velodrome plan prove that Coubertin's velodrome plan was not rejected; it came too late. More in my "Origins," 286, 299–300.

26. Coubertin, *Campagne,* 119–21.

27. Vikelas, "Correspondance," 57–58. Jebb was a highly prominent classical scholar. Since he worked on, among other things, ancient authors who wrote on the Olympics, he may well have been associated with contemporary athletics, as well. Vikelas's correspondent at Oxford might have been Constantinos Manos, whose role in the 1896 Olympics unfolds in chapters 11 and 12, below.

28. Robertson, "Olympic Games," 944–45. See, further, MacAloon, *This Great Symbol*, 198–201, Mandell, *First Modern Olympics*, 109–10, 113.

29. Vikelas, "Correspondance," 59 (Feb. 9, 1895).

30. MacAloon, *This Great Symbol*, 203–6.

31. MacAloon, *This Great Symbol*, 204–5, citing only Eyquem, *Pierre de Coubertin*, 132, but cautiously noting that Eyquem cites no sources at all. Elsewhere (e.g., MacAloon, 284 n. 83), MacAloon shows that Eyquem often invents her own material, even putting quotation marks around sentences, attributing them to Coubertin or those associated with him—when both the words and the sentiments are wholly of Eyquem's own invention (cf. MacAloon, 327, nn. 57–58). Unhappily, I find Eyquem's book without historical merit—a work of outright historical fiction. I think we should say so. An index of Eyquem's reliability comes from her reports of the conversations between Coubertin and Vikelas in Athens in November 1894—verbatim accounts of conversations between the two. Eyquem, *Pierre de Coubertin*, 143–44, relates how, upon the baron's arrival in Athens, Vikelas gave him a copy of Dragoumis's "get lost" letter. " 'What are you going to do?' Vikelas asked. 'Visit the ruins of the stadium,' " Coubertin supposedly replied. So also, as the two of them went around Athens, Eyquem's Vikelas asks, " 'What are you thinking, my friend?' 'Of America,' " Eyquem's Coubertin replies. But the whole episode is patently false, for Vikelas was in Paris the whole time (see above, chapter 9; Mandell, *First Modern Olympics*, 96–97, unfortunately took Eyquem's bait and embellished this wholly false historical-fiction scenario [see my "Origins," 291]).

32. MacAloon, *This Great Symbol*, 204. Several critics judge Coubertin's history book (*L'évolution française sous la Troisième République*) excellent, the best that Coubertin ever wrote. Some reviews were good, others not; one reviewer explicitly judged it inferior to his father-in-law's work (see MacAloon, *This Great Symbol*, 206–7).

33. "Je comprends que les présidents donnent leur démission. Mais je ne comprends pas celle de vôtre. Cela m' a surpris, et je suis plein d'inquiétude. Que va-t-il se passer en France?" Vikelas, "Correspondance," 2 (Jan. 17, 1895; see fuller translation above, in text).

34. MacAloon, *This Great Symbol*, 205–6.

35. In 1915 Coubertin indeed resigned, for a brief period, as president of the IOC, since he wished to enlist as a soldier for World War 1. The French army did not accept him, and he soon came back to the IOC. This letter of resignation is published in Mayer, *A travers les anneaux Olympique*, facing 33.

ELEVEN   The Greeks at Work

1. Philemon himself gives a useful outline of the Greek committees and organization in Lambros and Politis, *Olympic Games*, 111–20. Coubertin says little, perhaps because he had little to do with it (*Mémoires*, 21–23, *Campagne*, 118–25). Since he was rather silent on the matter, the accounts in MacAloon, *This Great Symbol*, and Mandell, *First Modern Olympics*, are sparse. Chrysafis, *Oi synchronoi diethneis Olympiakoi Agones*, 210–310, has great detail on the Greek athletes' preparations and the controversies concerning them and some material on the individual committees' work. Since Chrysafis was a participant and an eyewitness, he seems a

most important source. But some of his information also seems to come from Coubertin and Politis. I also use material from contemporary Athens newspapers.

2. Oikonomos, *Dimitrios M. Vikelas*, 476–77.

3. *Nea Ephemeris*, Dec. 15/27; in the Dec. 22/Jan. 3 issue, that paper said the directorship of the Academy for Industry and Business was collecting individual Olympic donations (one thousand drachmas recommended).

4. Philemon, in Lambros and Politis, *Olympic Games*, 117; biography of Averoff in *Mega Hellenikon viographikon lexikon*. I find no precise date for Philemon's visit to Egypt or Averoff's gift in Greek sources. In *Hestia*, May 7/19, 1895, 148, Vikelas says Averoff's gift was not known on April 5, 1895. But Coubertin knew of Averoff's gift before his June 12, 1895, interview with the newspaper *Gil Blas* (reprinted in Koebsel, *Dokumente*, 21; discussed below). In "Olympic Games of 1896," 40, Coubertin suggests there had been "eighteen months" work on the stadium when the Games opened in April 1896. That cannot be correct; he must here count from his own first view of the stadium, November 1894.

5. One may still wonder if the four hundred thousand from the sale of stamps might somehow relate to Sloane's statement (*Report of the American Olympic Committee*, 79) that Coubertin's friend Mercatis got Zappas money for the 1896 Games (see the end of the section on the parliamentary debate in chapter 10, above).

6. Vikelas, "Oi diethneis Olympiakoi Agones." So far as I can determine, the speech was published only in Athens, in Greek.

7. Chrysafis, *Oi synchronoi diethneis Olympiakoi Agones*, 245–61.

8. I here summarize Chrysafis, *Oi synchronoi diethneis Olympiakoi Agones*, 259–84, which is highly detailed and acrimonious; for he and his club were among Manos's targets. I take his prejudice into account here but cannot be sure I fully succeed. Apart from the *Asty* article, I know no version from Manos's side.

9. Chrysafis, *Oi synchronoi diethneis Olympiakoi Agones*, 313; Anninos, "Description of the Games," 133 (where "Chief Starter" is an inadequate translation of *alytarch*).

10. Coubertin, *Campagne*, 123–25; *Mémoires*, 22–23; Chrysafis, *Oi synchronoi diethneis Olympiakoi Agones*, 290–92; Mandell, *First Modern Olympics*, 92–94 (who calls it a "brouhaha" and a "ruckus"); MacAloon, *This Great Symbol*, 201–3. See also Koebsel, *Dokumente*, where a number of pertinent documents are reprinted.

11. Chrysafis, *Oi synchronoi diethneis Olympiakoi Agones*, 292. Kleon was the son of Alexandros Rangavis (see chapter 2, above). MacAloon's index to *This Great Symbol*, 357, prints this man's first initial as "M."

12. *Gil Blas*, June 12, 1895, reprinted (in W. Gebhardt's German translation) in Koebsel, *Dokumente*, 20–22; almost all the other documents are reprinted in *Dokumente*, 22–41.

13. *Nea Ephemeris*, Jan. 3/15, 1896 (the letter was addressed to the *Ethniki Ephemeris*).

14. Coubertin, *Mémoires*, 23.

15. On Gebhardt's appointment to the IOC, see MacAloon, *This Great Symbol*, 326 n. 41; on the proposal to postpone, see MacAloon, *This Great Symbol*, 202, with n. 44, and Mandell, *First Modern Olympics*, 111. Gebhardt's January 20 letter to Coubertin appears in Koebsel, *Dokumente*, 57.

16. *Soll Deutschland*, which published many original documents and news items; some of the essay is reprinted in Koebsel, *Dokumente*.

17. A typographical error in Coubertin, *Mémoires*, 23, misleads; for "16 janvier 1895," read "16 janvier 1896."

18. All items in this and the next paragraph come from the *Nea Ephemeris;* the date given is first the Greek date, then our own.

19. MacAloon, *This Great Symbol*, 199.

20. Mullins, *Brookes and the Wenlock Games*, 30; the date is carefully inscribed on Brookes's tombstone in Wenlock.

21. Coubertin, *Campagne*, 53, says, "Dr. Brookes, already very aged in 1890, lived long enough to see the Olympics reborn, and his joy was immense." Brookes lived to know the Games were scheduled to take place, so Coubertin's statement is not really wrong. Yet Brookes always focused on the athletes and the Games themselves; he had hoped to take joy in the actual event. He was, as Coubertin said, "a practical philanthropist" ("Typical Englishman," 65).

22. *Kleio* (Trieste), June 25, 1881; *Shrewsbury Chronicle*, Sept. 29, 1882 (Brookes papers, 5:74–75); *Wellington Journal and Shrewsbury News*, Sept. 10, 1892 (Brookes papers, 5:206).

23. Brookes to Coubertin, Dec. 11, 1894 (see above, chapter 10).

24. Coubertin, "Typical Englishman," 65.

TWELVE   The First International Olympic Games Begin

1. The article is in French: "La préface des Jeux Olympiques"; the date "March 1895" clearly appears at the end, but the last sentence says the Games will start "in a week." Thus "1895" is an error for "1896." Other statements (e.g., "eighteen months"; that the stadium is now lined with marble [158]) prove the date of writing is 1896.

2. I note examples of Coubertin's penetrating remarks. In "La préface," he perceptively identifies opposition to athleticism as a holdover from medieval Christianity's "hatred of the flesh" (154). He cannily predicts that "[t]he 'athletic renaissance' will be considered, later, as one of the characteristics of the nineteenth century. Yet today the word makes people smile" (153). The article also contains the first instance that I know of the neologism "Olympism" (150). For the theme of Olympics as an agent of peace, see, especially, 156.

3. Besides actually viewing the summary results of Zappas Olympiad 1 (see the discussion of his visit to Wenlock in chapter 6, above), in 1894 Coubertin had edited and published Vikelas's brief, sketchy account of the entire Zappas Olympic series (a part is quoted in chapter 9, above).

4. Gennadius, "Revival," 71; the article is in English. Unlike Coubertin's, Gennadius's article bears no date; but it, too, seems written in March 1896 with a view toward publishing by early April. It says the Games will start in "the present month."

5. Gennadius writes one paragraph on Zappas and his Games (70). But his brief account is indifferent, if not plainly negative, and Gennadius has many facts quite wrong. He says, "[Zappas's] purpose was to combine periodical industrial exhibi-

tions with athletic meetings." Then, after mentioning the 1859 Olympiad, he writes, "[A]fter an interruption due to political circumstances, the exhibitions, with an increasing element of athleticism, have since been held more regularly, in the Zappeion." The Zappeion had not yet been built in 1870 and 1875, and though it hosted agro-industrial Olympics in 1888, it had not yet seen any athletic contests.

6. I borrow this happy turn of phrase from MacAloon, *This Great Symbol*, 149.

7. There is a detailed discussion of Mahaffy in chapter 4, above.

8. "[I]f any one desires to see beauty at Athens, he must wander through the bazaars and markets, and the lowest parts of the town, where he will find among the children remarkable beauty, especially in the form of the head. . . . But among the richer classes (they can hardly be called upper, as all Greeks profess to be equal) there is no beauty at all" (Mahaffy, "Olympic Games at Athens in 1875," 324).

9. *Nea Ephemeris*, Feb. 28/Mar. 12, 1896.

10. Elliott, "New Olympic Games," 49.

11. Oikonomos, *Dimitrios M. Vikelas*, 489. Robertson, "Olympic Games," 945, 955, blames poor foreign representation in athletes and spectators on the "French" and the lack of information given by the "so-called agents of the committee."

12. Clark, *Reminiscences*, 127; Mandell, *First Modern Olympics*, 116–17.

13. Coubertin, *Campagne*, 123.

14. See *Nea Ephemeris*, Jan. 24/Feb. 5, 1896, where football matches still appear as part of the official program; Chrysafis, *Oi synchronoi diethneis Olympiakoi Agones*, 294–95, 331.

15. Over the strong objections of Phokianos and Chrysafis (representing the Panhellenic and National clubs), the crown prince appointed as director of these trials his Greek friend, the Oxford student Constantinos Manos, already named head official for the international Olympic events themselves. These two directors of the older athletic clubs thought Manos prejudiced against their own athletes while favoring athletes from his own new Athletic Club of Athens. They filed protests over some of the official judging and ranking of athletes. Apparently the Athenian press, too, felt Manos had bungled things. All the unpleasantness—with summary results even of the disputes, both athletic and journalistic—is reported with anger and detail by Chrysafis (*Oi synchronoi diethneis Olympiakoi Agones*, 297–308). A quick check of the results suggests that no performance in these trials surpassed the winning marks of the IOC Games themselves.

16. For a few events only, more than two Greeks were chosen; namely, 1,500 meters and discus (three entries each) and marathon (five Greek entries). Three entries were eventually named in the pole vault, to settle a dispute over the judging of the places in the national trials (Chrysafis, *Oi synchronoi diethneis Olympiakoi Agones*, 298, 303–4). Phokianos said the team was selected from some five hundred young Greeks who wished to enter (*Nea Ephemeris*, Mar. 24/Apr. 5). Chrysafis complained that Manos had created chaos by announcing the trial games "open to all comers"—so long as they swore an oath that they were amateurs (297).

17. Reprinted in *Nea Ephemeris*, Mar. 12/24, 1896.

18. *Nea Ephemeris*, Mar. 13/25, 1896.

19. *Nea Ephemeris*, Mar. 14/26, 1896, which does not further identify Pizos nor mention Marie de Coubertin at all. In fact, I know no printed mention of Marie

de Coubertin's presence in Athens in 1896, either in the Greek press or in any of Coubertin's own published writings. But—though Eyquem may well have invented Madame Coubertin's presence in the stadium (Eyquem, *Pierre de Coubertin*, 151) and her conversation with the baron on their return through Corfu (155–56), she did not invent Marie Coubertin's presence in Athens. For in a private letter to Vikelas, dated May 15, 1896, Coubertin bitterly complained to Vikelas about the lack of attention his wife received in Athens (Oikonomos, *Dimitrios M. Vikelas*, 496–97; I print a portion of this letter in chapter 14, below). Otherwise we might not even have known she was there.

20. Horton, "Recent Olympian Games," 216.

21. That unlikely, dramatic, last-minute arrival on April 5, the night before the contests began, seems true: see Curtis, "Glory," 21–22, Clark, *Reminiscences*, 129–30; Robertson, "Olympic Games," 950, says the American marathon runner arrived "five days before the race." The athletes had difficulty declining the retsina wine the Greeks urged on them as they arrived.

22. Horton, "Recent Olympian Games," 216. Curtis, "Glory," and Clark, *Reminiscences*, agree.

23. *Nea Ephemeris*, Mar. 23/Apr. 4, 1896.

24. See the account of the tennis matches in chapter 13, below.

25. "[Yesterday] five French athletes arrived," *Nea Ephemeris*, Mar. 21/Apr. 2, 1896. MacAloon, *This Great Symbol*, 198, says the French team consisted of only a "handful—a long-distance runner, two cyclists, and four or five fencers"; Mandell, *First Modern Olympics*, 110, reports "two cyclists, some fencers, a runner, and a couple of French tourists with amateur credentials who happened to be in Athens." The runner is obviously Lermusiaux; for Tufféri, see Chrysafis, *Oi synchronoi diethneis Olympiakoi Agones*, 314, and Anninos, "Description of the Games," 134. Anninos, 134, says an unnamed French athlete entered the discus; and Wallechinsky, *Complete Book of the Olympics*, 99, 103, lists Louis Adler of France as placing fourth in both weight-throwing events. The otherwise unnoticed Adler may have been one of Mandell's tourists. Lermusiaux is front and center (prominent because of the two interlocked circles of the USFSA on his shirt) in an often reproduced photo of the marathon runners just before the race began (Coubertin, *Mémoires*, 21; cf. MacAloon, *This Great Symbol*, plate 14).

26. Reading newspapers is now, at least, a kind of national pastime in Greece. Many Greeks read several newspapers a day.

27. I refer to the sentence citing Victor Hugo and continuing, "[T]he whole world has a common grandmother in ancient Greece, but we [Greeks] have her as our mother," which I quote from Vikelas's June 23, 1894, speech in chapter 9, above.

28. *Hestia*, Mar. 23/Apr. 4; reprinted in full in Oikonomos, *Dimitrios M. Vikelas*, 489–90.

29. "It was a happy thought of the committee to bring the first contest to Greece, the mother of athletics. The visiting contestants were forced into contact with history. . . . The visitors are unanimous in their praise of the adequate and warm hospitality afforded them by the Athenian people," Richardson, "New Olympian Games," 270. All foreign reports agree the Greek people and athletes showed outstanding good sportsmanship. See Robertson's comment ("Olympic

Games," 954) on the Greek "gentlemanly feeling" (which I myself have often encountered). It set the tone for everyone else there, and thereafter: "[My account of the marathon] cannot illustrate the generous joy and enthusiasm which moved the Greeks and all the visitors at each victory, to whatever nation it might have fallen," Waldstein, "Olympic Games at Athens."

30. MacAloon, *This Great Symbol*, 210, citing Coubertin's own silence on the matter, says, "Whether the baron was present for the stadium dedication is unclear." But Chrysafis, who was surely there, says Coubertin was "at the head of the delegation of Distinguished Foreigners" (*Oi synchronoi diethneis Olympiakoi Agones*, 309). He had attended mass at the Catholic cathedral, where his Parisian friend, Father Didon, preached the sermon. Didon, an ardent supporter, had come to Athens for the Games (here MacAloon is correct; that Didon was "residing in Athens" at the time is an error of the English translator in Lambros and Politis, *Olympic Games*, 132).

31. "Saturday, April 5," in Mandell, *First Modern Olympics*, 123, is an error.

32. These prices are given in Richardson, "New Olympian Games," 274, who equates a drachma with a franc or U.S.$0.12 at that time.

33. F., "Olympic Games," 440. "The audience, like the athletes, was cosmopolitan. All the tongues of Europe were heard. But all the foreigners together amounted to only a few thousand. At least nineteen-twentieths of the mass were Greeks," Richardson, "New Olympian Games," 275.

34. Anninos, "Description of the Games," 131.

35. See MacAloon, *This Great Symbol*, 212; Clark, *Reminiscences*, 137, gives "150,000" on marathon day.

36. Horton, "Recent Olympian Games," 218.

37. Quoted in Anninos, "Description of the Games," 132.

38. *Nea Ephemeris*, Mar. 24/Apr. 5, 1896.

39. Quoted in Coubertin, *Mémoires*, 24.

40. On the sunshine, see Anninos, "Description of the Games," 132; on Samaras, see the discussion of the Panhellenic Games in chapter 5.

41. Horton, "Recent Olympian Games," 218. The *sphendone* is the circular end portion of an ancient stadium, at Athens, the south end. On the east side, as the *sphendone* joins the *diazomata*, or straight rows of seats, there was in antiquity a tunnel that led below the seats and was used for the entrance of the athletes. Excavators preserved it, and modern athletes entered at the same spot as the ancient ones.

42. Horton, "Recent Olympian Games," 219–20; others do not mention this bold act, but Horton, "the United States Consul at Athens" ("Revival of Olympian Games"), seems unlikely to have invented it.

43. For their previous careers, see the discussion of the 1893 Panhellenic Games in chapter 5 (with notes), above; on their crowds of admirers, see Mandell, *First Modern Olympics*, 119 (citing no source, but what he says in this section seems believable and authoritative).

44. My account of the discus event here is a composite of Anninos, "Description of the Games," 134, Horton, "Recent Olympian Games," 222, Coubertin, "Olympic Games of 1896," 45, Robertson, "Olympic Games," 949–50, MacAloon, *This Great Symbol*, 217–18, Mandell, *First Modern Olympics*, 126–28, and Chrysafis,

Oi synchronoi diethneis Olympiakoi Agones, 231 (who explains the origins of the Greek-style throw; Phokianos had issued a pamphlet, "How to Throw the Discus," based on Myron's statue and the benighted ancient writer, Philostratus). I cannot confirm MacAloon's statement that Versis retired "after two [throws], leading the contest."

THIRTEEN   IOC Olympiad 1: One to Remember

1. Clearing the hurdles with the lead leg extended and taking just three steps between hurdles was introduced the next time, in Paris in 1900, by Alvin Kraenzlein, a German American who later taught track and field in Germany. By that innovation Kraenzlein improved Burke's 1896 Olympic record by an almost incredible 2.2 seconds, with a time of 15.4 in 1900 against Burke's 17.6.

2. Richardson, "New Olympian Games," 277, with Robertson, "Olympic Games," 949. Mandell, *First Modern Olympics,* 130, says Gouskos was only about 5 ft. 8 in. tall but weighed over two hundred pounds (apparently citing Connolly's later novel about the Games, which is not wholly historical).

3. MacAloon, *This Great Symbol,* 218, and Mandell, *First Modern Olympics,* 130, say the Greek flag was actually raised at this point, but the error seems not to have gone that far. *Nea Ephemeris,* Mar. 28/Apr. 9, 1896, Robertson, "Olympic Games," 954, and Richardson, "New Olympian Games," 280, all note the error in raising the victor's number but not the hoisting of the Greek flag.

4. *Nea Ephemeris,* Mar. 28/Apr. 9, 1896.

5. Again Garrett's winning mark, 11.22 meters (36 ft. 9¼ in.), seems ridiculously low even compared to the 1900 new Olympic record set by Richard Sheldon, of the United States, at 14.10 meters (46 ft. 3¼ in.). Despite failing as an Olympiad, the 1900 Olympics saw much better marks.

6. Anninos, "Description of the Games," 136 (I have slightly retranslated from 35).

7. F., "Olympic Games," 441: "on some technicality of style." Wallechinsky, *Complete Book of the Olympics,* 536, says Elliot (whose first name is variously spelled) "moved one foot while lifting." Elliot was exceptionally tall, muscular, and fair, attracting wide admiration from the Greeks (Mandell, *First Modern Olympics,* 130–31). Chrysafis, *Oi synchronoi diethneis Olympiakoi Agones,* 322, calls Elliot a "giant," naming him "the best-looking *(ho kallistos)* of all the athletes there, without exception" (316). The ancient athletic Games in Athens gave a prize for "the best-looking" athlete (Kyle, *Athletics in Ancient Athens,* 36); this was no doubt more of a body-building competition than a beauty contest.

8. Anninos, "Description of the Games," 140. Others simply offered cash. But the statement in Hopkins's history, *Marathon*—that the "most spectacularly generous offer" was from Averoff himself, who offered a million drachmas and his daughter's hand in marriage—is surely false, one of the myriad fictitious, apocryphal tales of Louis and his marathon victory. No contemporary source I know mentions Averoff's offer. The story is probably an embellishment of Maurras's unconfirmed tale of the Greek lass, "Mlle. Y.," who offered herself in marriage to the marathon victor but reneged when she discovered Louis's station in life (MacAloon, *This Great Symbol,* 227, 235).

9. Anninos, "Description of the Games," 140.

10. Robertson, "Olympic Games," 946, whose paragraph ends, "An Olympic wreath is far too precious a thing to be squandered on good form in hopping over a horse or swarming up a rope." His article is signed by "G. S. Robertson . . . a competitor," and Wallechinsky, *Complete Book of the Olympics*, 103, lists a George Robertson, of Great Britain, as sixth in the 1896 discus. I conclude they are one and the same but notice no reference to his participation in the discus in his article.

11. Anninos, "Description of the Games,"140. Richardson, "New Olympian Games," 273 (followed by MacAloon, *This Great Symbol*, 226), says "the Stadion was filled to its utmost capacity, i.e., with 50,000 people." But Horton, "Recent Olympian Games," 226, says, "On Marathon day 71,800 tickets were sold." That figure sounds as if Horton had more precise knowledge than Robinson's ball-park estimate, and it accords well with other eyewitness reports: "The noon time church bells had hardly sounded. . . . The movement in town was indescribable. In all the streets, in all the corners of the city the populace moved. . . . All means of transport were called into service. . . . At 1:30 P.M. the City of Athens was deserted and the stadium was full. After half an hour there was not an empty seat in this vast place" (Anninos, "Description of the Games," 141; see his 140 for morning ticket sales and commotion).

12. Richardson, "New Olympian Games," 279, reporting about the previous day, suggests the importance Greeks placed on a gymnastic victory compared to one on the track: "But the gymnastic exercises did not fill the Stadion as the running matches had done, and the individual contest in vaulting the wooden horse . . . and the horizontal bar contest . . . nearly emptied it."

13. Oikonomos, *Dimitrios M. Vikelas*, 491.

14. Horton, "Recent Olympian Games," 223–24; Coubertin's "He reached the goal fresh and in fine form" ("Olympic Games of 1896," 46) seems an exaggeration, the only source to clash with Horton's vivid description of a wholly fatigued runner; but others were indeed worse off.

15. According to Anninos, "Description of the Games," 143.

16. See especially MacAloon, *This Great Symbol*, 225–41, where there is an excellent, full, and generally accurate account of these matters; cf. Mandell, *First Modern Olympics*, 135–40, 156 (and many others). I merely add some information on Louis's physical appearance and reiterate some comments on his social standing. Waldstein, "Olympian Games at Athens": "I saw the victor . . . slightly over medium height, slim and strong, with fine features, clear bright gray eyes, and dark hair. He is quite simple and unspoilt. . . . He remains the true Greek peasant—a hardy, clear-headed, honest and kind tiller of the soil—than which no better type of man exists in the world." Coubertin, "Olympic Games of 1896," 46, also says Louis was a "peasant" (as does Hugues le Roux, in Anninos, "Description of the Games," 151; Clark, *Reminiscences*, 138). For "a well-to-do farmer," see Richardson, "New Olympian Games," 281; for "herdsman," see Maurras, in MacAloon, *This Great Symbol*, 235; for "donkey boy," see Curtis, "Glory," 56. Anninos, likely to know, says that Louis had been in the army and belonged to a "large, industrious and honorable family" (original Greek on 45, *filergos kai entimos oikoyeneia;* the French translation on 94 is inaccurate, the English on 145, unclear). Some con-

temporary Greek sources give Louis's first name as Spyros, others the variant, Spyridon. I also elaborate on the comparison with Diagoras of Rhodes, who, after a long boxing career, finally won the Olympic boxing crown in 464 B.C. His three sons, Damagetos, Akousilaos, and Dorieus, all athletes in combative events, later won a total of six Olympic victories from 452 to 432 B.C.; then his grandsons, Eukles and Peisirhodos, one by each daughter, took Olympic crowns in 404 (Moretti, *Olympionikai*, victories 287, 299, 300, 322, 326, 330, 354, and 356). A Greek proverb, "Die, Diagoras; for you cannot reach heaven," which first appeared in antiquity (a famous Latin translation by Cicero, *Tuscul. Disput.* 1.46.111), is still used in Greece today to suggest that someone has reached the pinnacle of human achievement. A man who himself wins in the Olympics, then sees his son win, too, has known the best a human can know (Pindar, *Pythian Odes* 10.22–29); there is nothing more for him to achieve; he may die happy now. Louis's father was no Olympic victor, but because of Diagoras's proverbial value as the happiest of Olympic victors' fathers, Anninos, "Description of the Games," 150, draws the comparison (cf. Richardson, "New Olympian Games," 281).

17. Coubertin, *Mémoires*, 26; quoted in MacAloon, *This Great Symbol*, 232.

18. Coubertin, "Olympic Games of 1896," 46, Clark, *Reminiscences*, 138, and Curtis, "Glory," 56 ("thousands of white pigeons") all mention the white doves or pigeons flying at the finish of the marathon. Anninos, "Description of the Games," 154, says that doves were released at the closing award ceremony on Wednesday, April 15, too. Coubertin, *Mémoires*, 24, says there was a "release of pigeons" at the opening ceremony. But no 1896 account, not even Coubertin's own, mentions doves at the opening ceremony. By 1931 Coubertin perhaps misremembered exactly when they were released.

19. Anninos, "Description of the Games," 145. Louis's village was the nearby Maroussi (also Amarousi), only eight miles northeast of the stadium. It is now just a suburb of sprawling modern Athens. By coincidence, Horton had paid special attention to Maroussi in his scouting of the Attic countryside months before the Games: "At Amarousi, famous for its cold, clear water, we clambered down from the train to start in search of donkeys. . . . In about ten minutes . . . we were off: through narrow tumble-down streets with projecting balconies, through shady olive orchards . . . through stretches of fragrant purple heather" ("Revival of Olympian Games," 270). For fireworks at the Olympics, see the report (in chapter 8, above) on the *fête de nuit* at Coubertin's Paris congress on June 21.

20. Anninos, "Description of the Games," 145.

21. Richardson, "New Olympian Games," 282. Robertson, "Olympic Games," 946, says that Schumann was "a little, elderly man" (Chrysàfis, *Oi synchronoi diethneis Olympiakoi Agones*, 323, makes a similar observation) who won the wrestling by "sheer pluck and presence of mind" and that Schumann "seemed to compete in every event"—so that some even "termed [him] 'the best all-around athlete at the games.' " But Robertson had little true admiration: "[H]e would have served his reputation better, had he refrained from exhibiting himself in many of the events."

22. Anninos, "Description of the Games," 146–47, twice prints the Hungarian's last name as "Hajos (Guttman)" but in the victory summary, 154, as "Hajos Guttman" (without parentheses). The original Greek and French versions omit the

name Guttman (except in the summary). Both Mandell, *First Modern Olympics*, 143, and MacAloon, *This Great Symbol*, 236, tell the wonderful tale wherein Williams, who had come all the way from America at his own expense for his chance at this big moment, leaped forward into the water at the gun with the rest of the swimmers—only to jump out immediately and back onto the starting platform, swearing and complaining of the "freezing" cold temperature of the water. Both cite only Curtis's "Glory," 56, and I find no other source. Curtis wrote this tale in 1932. But the official eyewitness account, Anninos, "Description of the Games," 146, reads: "Of the fourteen registered only thirteen participate, of whom two Hungarian, one American, one Dane, one Swede, and the remainder Greeks. With the shooting of the pistol they all set forth swimming rapidly, and the first to . . . finish . . . is the Hungarian Hajos." This will not accommodate Williams's in-and-out-of-the-water story, which I admit is good fun. Either Curtis misremembered in 1932 or embellished far beyond the truth (the great story is no good if Williams actually swam the race) or one of Anninos's 1896 statements reprinted above is simply false.

23. Heiner Gillmeister, *Geschichte der Olympischen Tennisturniere*, has an excellent chapter on the 1896 tennis competitions. Robertson, "Olympic Games," 948, says Boland just "happened to be in Athens as a visitor, purchased the requisite equipment on the spot, and was victorious" (cf. Mandell, *First Modern Olympics*, 146, where he is described as "a tourist"). Thus began a quaint story that Boland decided to enter on a whim, searched Athens to buy a tennis racket, and so on. But Gillmeister has determined that Boland had already helped his Greek friend, fellow Oxford student, and director of the 1896 Olympics, Constantinos Manos, recruit English athletes for Athens. That he was there racketless, as a mere tourist, is highly unlikely. For he and Traun both turn out to have been very good, experienced tennis players, not neophytes (see Gillmeister, "Olympic Tennis," 23, where he reports that neither the U.S. Tennis Association nor a major American publisher of sport research finds an English translation of his Olympic tennis history book financially worthwhile; let us hope someone eventually does).

24. Kousoulas, *Modern Greece*, 80, says, "after a short illness." Trikoupis's political enemy, Prince Constantine, participated in the march at Trikoupis's funeral (see photo 359, in Delivorrias, *Athens, 1839–1900*, with caption).

25. Anninos, "Description of the Games," 148–49.

26. Anninos, "Description of the Games," 149; I recast about four words in the translation.

27. Anninos, "Description of the Games," 150–51.

28. Coubertin, *Mémoires*, 25; for "great capitals," see Coubertin, "La préface," 154.

29. Anninos, "Description of the Games," 152.

30. Anninos, "Description of the Games," 153.

31. Coubertin, "Olympic Games of 1896," 50. Coubertin was quick to see "body and mind" *(le muscle et l'esprit, Campagne*, 200) united whenever poetry and art were related to the Olympics. In his article, "Olympic Games," Robertson mentions the ode but not that he himself composed and recited it (only in England do students compose ancient Greek poetry in meter). I know no preservation of

the text of Robertson's Pindaric ode, so I cannot pass judgment on its merit. Mac-Aloon, *This Great Symbol*, 252, plausibly suggests that "prize-winner" in his title refers to the olive branch (MacAloon says "laurel") that the poem won him. My term "olive branch" comes from Coubertin's private letter to Vikelas, May 15, 1896 (Oikonomos, *Dimitrios M. Vikelas*, 496–97, quoted in chapter 14, below). Anninos, "Description of the Games," 153 (where Robertson is wrongly called a "professor") and Coubertin (above) both recount this episode.

32. See the end of chapter 14, below.

33. At the 1870 Wenlock Olympics, H. W. Brooke, winner of the general competition, won a "first class silver medal and olive crown" (Neumüller, "Die Geschichte," xlix, lii).

34. Anninos, "Description of the Games," 153–55; that Louis gave the ancient vase to "the museum": Richardson, "New Olympian Games," 282 (according to Anninos, "Description of the Games," 153, John Lambros had donated the vase from his private collection "so the ancient world may appear to be celebrating with the modern"; Crown Prince Constantine had donated a silver cup for the discus victor, which Garrett received); that King George saluted each athlete and spoke their language to them: Oikonomos, *Dimitrios M. Vikelas*, 493. George is likely to have known all the needed languages (even Jensen's Danish, since he himself was a Dane); only on Hajos's Hungarian might he have needed coaching.

35. See the account of the Parliament debate in chapter 10, above.

36. Horton, "Recent Olympian Games," 226, gives a vivid description of the night lighting of the Acropolis: "The inhabitants strove to entertain their guests by night as well as by day. Of all their efforts in this direction none will be so long remembered as the illumination of the Acropolis.... The effect was grandly wierd. On a dark night the ruins are indistinguishable, but when the lights were suddenly ignited the columns of the ancient temples were revealed with startling distinctness.... When the red lights were turned on the ruins were wreathed with a lurid glow, and looked like a castle on fire." This was probably the very origin of the periodic *son et lumière* ("sound and light") shows on the Acropolis that are now among the most spectacular and popular tourist attractions in Greece. After all, the Greeks have something unique to work with. F., "Olympic Games," ends, "To my mind, the immortal ruins of the Parthenon, and the glorious Attic sky, cannot be matched anywhere" (441).

Coubertin's complaint that Vikelas did not direct the crowd to congratulate him is quoted in chapter 14, below (personal letter, Coubertin to Vikelas, May 31, 1896). IOC Olympiad 1 was now officially over; the next day saw only an unofficial banquet in honor of the foreign athletes, hosted by the mayor of Athens and attended by Constantine and other dignitaries. Franz Kemeny, of Hungary and the IOC, made the final toast. The participants then went their own way, the foreigners going home. But Coubertin stayed on a while. The American team stayed "about ten days," according to Curtis, "Glory," 56. Constantine surely consulted the Americans on sports (Horton, "Recent Olympian Games," 216) and perhaps asked for a demonstration of baseball at a later picnic. But that a cane served as the bat and an orange as the ball—which splattered all over the catcher, the crown prince, on the first pitch (Curtis)—may be apocryphal.

FOURTEEN   The Olympic Games Finally Revived

1. Clark, *Reminiscences*, 140.
2. Waldstein, "Olympian Games at Athens," Richardson, "New Olympian Games," 282, F., "Olympic Games," 440–41, Robertson, "Olympic Games," 953–54, 956 (cf. 954, "the whole scene can never be effaced from one's memory"—remarkable in light of Robertson's general imperturbability and peevishness), Coubertin, *Mémoires*, 26.
3. Full text in Richardson, "New Olympian Games," 284.
4. Horton, "Recent Olympian Games," 228; F., "Olympic Games," 441. "New York, Berlin, or Stockholm" were named as candidates for 1904, but no decision was made; Kemeny was assured that Budapest would host Olympics "later on": Minutes of the IOC Meeting, Athens, Apr. 12, 1896 (see Coubertin, *Textes choisis*, 2:596–97, where the March 12 date is an error). MacAloon, *This Great Symbol*, 210–11 (with notes citing Mayer, *A travers les anneaux*, 43–44, who lists six meetings, Apr. 4–14), dates the decisions recorded in these minutes to IOC meetings held on April 6 and 11; Müller's date in *Textes choisis* is founded on a reprinting of these minutes in *Le Messager d'Athènes*, Apr. 16. Perhaps, after the Games, Coubertin conflated several discussions of IOC members into the minutes of one "meeting" and predated it when he gave the text to *Le Messager*; the published text indeed suggests a later date and that Coubertin already sought to repel the question of Athens as the permanent site when he wrote it. Horton, "Recent Olympian Games," 228–29, knows the post-Games preference of "several IOC members" for Athens as permanent site from Vikelas (but Coubertin himself, *Campagne*, 127, admits as much).
5. Robertson, "Olympic Games," 957 (who disagrees with F. about the internationalism of future Athenian Games); Richardson, "New Olympian Games," 286.
6. Waldstein, "Last Word on the Olympic Games," lists "M. Manos," Constantine, Coubertin, and himself; I add Vikelas (whose presence might be expected) because of Vikelas's July 1 letter to Coubertin (Vikelas, "Correspondance," 81–83), which speaks of "our interview with the Crown Prince" (I read *notre* rather than *votre*, though initial *n* and initial *v* are often hard to distinguish in Vikelas's French hand). Cf. Coubertin, *Campagne*, 128, Richardson, "New Olympian Games," 286, MacAloon, *This Great Symbol*, 250, Lucas, *Olympic Games*, 48 (where "Thr[asyboulos] Manos," Constantinos's father, may be correct). MacAloon, I think rightly, dates the meeting to "Tuesday night or Wednesday morning" on the basis of April 16 accounts in the *New York Times* and the *Times* of London. Waldstein's role remains somewhat unclear; but since he was a mutual friend of Constantine, Coubertin, and Vikelas, it merits pursuing.
7. Ironically, it was the 1900 Paris Games that did not bear the official name Olympics: Coubertin, *Campagne*, 136–52 (esp. 138, 150); cf. Mandell, *First Modern Olympics*, 165–66. When Coubertin saw that A. Picard, president of the Paris 1900 Exposition, adamantly refused to allow Olympic Games to be any part of the program and forbade the "physical exercises" (not called Olympics) to be held near the main exposition in central Paris, the baron tried to organize an Olympiad himself, wholly apart from the exposition. He appointed his own Paris Olympic

organizing committee, chaired (and partly financed) by the wealthy aristocrat, Ch. de La Rochefoucauld. But the committee made no progress, de La Rochefoucauld resigned, and the committee and Coubertin's plans for an independent Olympiad II dissolved (*Campagne*, 138–45). He was then constrained to declare the nameless Games that the government held at the Bois de Boulogne the "IOC Olympiad II" or to lose, besides all else, a sequence-number.

8. Richardson, "New Olympian Games," 286, saw the impasse; but Waldstein, "Last Word on the Olympic Games," thought Coubertin won: "[T]he games to be held at Athens will have another name, the term 'Olympic' being reserved for the rotary cycle . . . and the name of the celebrations at Athens will thus be *International Panathenaic Games*." Horton, "Recent Olympian Games," 229, says, "Unfortunately, the International Committee . . . definitely decided upon Paris for 1900. Therefore the next games must take place there."

9. *New York Times*, Apr. 16, 1896, dating those next Games "in 1898."

10. *Times* (London), Apr. 30, 1896, 12 (the letter is in French). Coubertin, *Campagne*, 128, mentions this "letter of rectification." MacAloon, *This Great Symbol*, 250, clearly implies that this letter was sent to the *New York Times*, and Müller, in Coubertin, *Textes choisis*, 2:163, prints the very same text I find in the *Times* of London, Apr. 30, 1896, 12, giving its source as "*New York Times*, 30 avril 1896, 12" (signed, with no date, "Paris, 31, Rue de Lubeck," not "Athènes"). Perhaps Coubertin sent that letter to both newspapers; he sent one to a French newspaper (see Oikonomos, *Dimitrios M. Vikelas*, 496) and a similar, less inflammatory letter to *Le Messager d'Athènes* (Coubertin, *Textes choisis*, 2:164–65). Despite MacAloon and Müller, I can find no letter from Coubertin, nor any item related to Olympic Games, in the *New York Times*, Apr. 30, 1896, 12 (only real estate transfers and legal notices).

11. Vikelas had formally turned over the IOC presidency to Coubertin, apparently the moment the Games ended (Coubertin, *Campagne*, 127–28).

12. Oikonomos, *Dimitrios M. Vikelas*, 496 (in Greek, *akosmos, thraseia, kapiliki, aprepis, ibristiki*); in his May 24 letter (Vikelas, "Correspondance," 72), Vikelas speaks of "your silent response to my previous two letters." These two letters are not in the collection in Vikelas, "Correspondance."

13. Coubertin to Vikelas, May 15, 1896. This letter, along with those of Coubertin to Vikelas dated May 31, 1896, and Dec. 16, 1899 (see below), is so far preserved only in Oikonomos's Greek translations of excerpts (*Dimitrios M. Vikelas*, 496–98). I print above my own translation of Oikonomos's Greek version of the original French (though Oikonomos preserves Coubertin's original French at the end of the 1899 letter). I admonish readers that the text above is a translation of a translation, in which much can happen; but Oikonomos was devoted to Coubertin, and I have tried to be accurate. I do not think there is any gross misrepresentation. Oikonomos implies that these otherwise unknown letters of Coubertin were in Vikelas's papers when he saw them. A few years ago, when I sought access to Vikelas's papers, I was told they were "held up" in a grand legal battle after the recent death of one of his heirs. Now Wolfgang Decker's student at Cologne, Andreas Morbach, is on their trail. For the sake of Olympic history, let us hope he succeeds; Coubertin's unknown letters are only a small part of the important Olympic documents that are likely to be among them.

14. Vikelas's site of the 1859 Zappas Olympiad is simply wrong.

15. Vikelas, "Correspondance," 62–65 (the original in Vikelas's own hand), 66–71 (Coubertin's copy of the version by a calligrapher, sent to all members of the IOC). Coubertin, *Campagne*, 130–31, gives his own account of and reaction to Vikelas's letter, proposition, and action.

16. Coubertin to Vikelas, May 31, 1896, in Oikonomos, *Dimitrios M. Vikelas*, 497; see the explanation of these letters' source, above.

17. In my "Origins," 287–88, and "Demetrios Vikelas," 94–97, I publish parts of Vikelas's letters to Coubertin and note the end of Vikelas's IOC career. I have translated here some, but not all, excerpts from Coubertin's letters to Vikelas that Oikonomos, *Dimitrios M. Vikelas*, 496–98, prints in Greek translation.

18. Here Oikonomos preserves Coubertin's original French: "J'ai dit déjà à tant de gens en parlant de vous: 'Bikélas, c'est ce qu'il y a le plus noble sur la terre!' " Oikonomos says he retains the French "as a proof of the style of this sentimental Frenchman, equal to that of his knightly ancestors of the thirteenth century" (*Dimitrios M. Vikelas*, 498). Coubertin, with his love of medieval chivalry, would have liked Oikonomos's tribute perhaps even more than Vikelas liked Coubertin's.

19. Coubertin to Vikelas, Dec. 16, 1899, in Oikonomos, *Dimitrios M. Vikelas*, 497–98. In this letter, Coubertin also assures Vikelas, "I love your country very much."

20. "Great Britain participated enthusiastically in the Athenian Olympic games of 1906, and as a result there was built up in England a feeling of sympathy for the Olympic movement that was responsible for a cordial welcoming of the offer to hold the games of Olympiad IV in London when it became evident that they could not be held in Rome," Henry, *Approved History*, 69. Henry's comment is surprising, since his book—literally—received Coubertin's imprimatur.

21. "Baron de Coubertin could not know that these unofficial games of 1906 would give a boost to the whole Olympic movement and keep the modern Olympic Games from early extinction," Lucas, *Modern Olympic Games*, 56. Mandell, *First Modern Olympics*, 167, notes that at the 1906 Athens Olympics "the standard of festivity, the breadth of international participation and the performance levels were, as a whole, superior to the Olympic Games of 1896, 1900, 1904, and 1908"; cf. Henry, *Approved History*, 67–68, MacAloon, *This Great Symbol*, 270. Even Coubertin, *Mémoires*, 53, himself grudgingly admits that the 1906 Athens Olympics were "plus brillants et mieux organisés que les premiers"—that is to say, the best to that date. "Unofficial" is the later designation of Coubertin (*Mémoires*, 50) and Olympic historians; in 1906 they were indeed official. For the failure of Paris, 1900, and St. Louis, 1904 (Olympiads II and III), see MacAloon, *This Great Symbol*, 271–74 ("disasters"), Mandell, *First Modern Olympics*, 165–67, and Coubertin, *Campagne*, 136–61. Though Coubertin helped pro-Olympic Greeks fight anti-Olympic Greeks in their government, no one came to help Coubertin persuade the Dragoumises of Paris; Coubertin lost in his own native city. Even his friend St. Claire called what took place an "incommensurable fiasco" (*Campagne*, 150). Coubertin later called it IOC Olympiad II. Only Gebhardt and Kemeny, of all the IOC members, went to St. Louis for IOC Olympiad III; Coubertin later heard reports about it, including the now infamous Anthropology Days (where untrained native Americans contended with pygmies and other men with exotic backgrounds

from a local sideshow); that elicited from Coubertin the comment, "Among Americans, anything is possible" (*Campagne*, 161–62).

22. Coubertin stayed in Paris, where he had scheduled a counter-Olympic event, the Fourth Olympic Congress, with the theme of Olympics and art: Coubertin, *Mémoires*, 50. The IOC met without him in Athens and voted to restructure the IOC and make Constantine the "Honorary President"; as IOC president, the baron later simply vetoed the actions that his colleagues took in Athens (*Mémoires*, 53). One must wonder exactly what those actions were (see further my "Demetrios Vikelas," 96, with notes). For Vikelas (no longer an IOC member, see my "Demetrios Vikelas," 95) and the 1906 Olympics, see Oikonomos, *Dimitrios M. Vikelas*, 597–98.

23. I must pass over the Scottish Highland Games, referring readers to Gerald Redmond's excellent works, *Caledonian Games* and *The Sporting Scots.* The history of German and Scandinavian gymnastics is another subject, with its own extensive literature.

24. Coubertin's own vast Olympic writings have little to say about specific individual athletes, without whom there would be no Games. Books such as Mandell, *First Modern Olympics*, and other recent works, however, well note the athletes' importance and give good accounts of them; Bill Mallon's journal, *Citius, Altius, Fortius*, is helping to rectify the imbalance further. One could well argue that it was the Herculean efforts of athletes such as James Thorpe and Spyros Louis, not the acts of the various organizers studied above, that saved the Olympic Games.

25. *Shrewsbury Chronicle*, June 6, 1883 (Brookes papers, 5:86; Neumüller, "Die Geschichte," 209).

26. Coubertin himself, it must be said, did much to promote this image; his writings teem with phrases like his title, "Why I Revived the Olympic Games." Though he eventually claimed he wanted no credit and regretted the necessary "I's" and "me's" of his accounts (*Mémoires*, 136, 138), he could have done much more to credit others. I suspect he even consciously sought to minimize or obscure others' contributions. From Vikelas he knew in detail all about the Zappas Olympiads ("Correspondence," 62 [1896]; see pg. 164). Yet he later even went so far as consciously to misrepresent what he knew and to mislead history about the purpose of Zappas's bequest, even denying in print that any Zappas Olympiads had ever taken place (*Campagne*, 108, reprinted with comments in my "Demetrios Vikelas," 97, with n. 49). I do not think that Coubertin ever said a bad or false word about Brookes, Constantine, or Vikelas, only favorable praise. He wrote a touching obituary for Vikelas, in the *Revue Olympique*. And "A Typical Englishman" is a kind of extended, narrative, laudatory obituary of Brookes. But as the years passed, he distanced himself from Brookes's memory and influence. In *Campagne* (1908), 53, Coubertin merely calls him an "English doctor, from another age, who had made his little village into a metropolis of popular sports." And in recounting what he himself saw in Wenlock, he focuses on "pig-sticking" (of which event I have no memory from any Wenlock program), saying nothing of Brookes's involvement in the track and field of the day, nor of Brookes's National Olympian Games, nor of Brookes's international Olympic proposals. I do not find Brookes's name in *Mémoires* (1931). But, as Coubertin said of Brookes, "He did not care for immortality" ("Typical Englishman," 65). Were he somehow given the choice either to be pro-

claimed worldwide as the "renovateur" in the Olympic stadium at Atlanta in 1996 or to sit in it anonymously for just five minutes to watch his first International Olympic Games, I am certain Brookes would choose the five minutes.

27. Coubertin, quoted at Durántez, *Pierre de Coubertin*, 62 (Durántez cites Coubertin, "Mémoire concernant l'instruction supérieure des travailleurs manuels et l'organisation des universités ouvrières. Special brochure, p. 1," at 69). A slightly different translation, by Müller, is quoted and cited in Rioux, *Pierre de Coubertin*, 4–5).

28. Vikelas to Dragoumis, Oct. 3/15, 1894, Dragoumis envelope 235, doc. 93; Papamikhalopoulos, in *Ephemeris ton syzitiseon tis Voulis*, 176 (and other delegates that day, though they more often mentioned Coubertin by name); Constantine's January 25, 1895, speech to the reformed committee (Lambros and Politis, *Olympic Games*, 112); *Nea Ephemeris*, Jan. 13/25, 1895; Vikelas, letter to the editor, *Hestia*, Mar. 23/Apr. 5, 1896 (reprinted in Oikonomos, *Dimitrios M. Vikelas*, 490); for Constantine's opening ceremony speech, see Anninos, "Description of the Games," 132; these and others explicitly cite Coubertin's 1894 congress's decision as justification for hosting the Games. An appeal to the Paris congress's choice of Athens is implicit in the countless Greek warnings that the "whole world is watching us; we must do well."

29. Further research might suggest that Constantine should have some share in that title; besides his excellent organization of both the 1896 Games and the 1906 Games, which saved a floundering Olympic movement, his role in Athens's 1894 choice may not yet be fully known. Coubertin's phrase "all sports for all people" *(tous les sports pour tous)* is recurrent in his works, e.g., in his January 1919 letter to IOC members, Coubertin, *Textes choisis*, 2:344 (also in *Olympic Idea*, 71, where Dixon translates "every sport for everyone").

30. Cf., e.g., Guttmann, *Olympics*, xi. As many Olympic historians from Coubertin to Lucas have often observed, our Olympics, despite all their real problems—which must be addressed—have yet unknown positive potential. There is no truly excellent, accurate, and full account of ancient athletics and the Olympic Games. The best is Finley and Pleket, *Olympic Games*. That book, if supplemented by my own articles, "Athletics" and "Pindar," will adequately serve those who wish to understand the meaning of the ancient Greek institution.

31. Pindar, *Pythian Odes* 8.95–97; the translation (that given above is mine) is difficult, especially the two brief questions in the first line, and open to some variation: see my "Pindar," 168. The best translation of all Pindar's *Odes* is by Nisetich, *Pindar's Victory Songs*. Nisetich's book includes, for the nonclassicist, a long, excellent introduction to Pindar's poetry and the Games (for which see also my own "Athletics"); it ends with a good glossary and indexes.

Pindar wrote this poem to celebrate the wrestling victory of Aristomenes of Aegina in the final at the 446 B.C. Pythian Games, after three grueling preliminary elimination bouts (81–87). His maternal uncle, Theognetos, had won an Olympic wrestling crown in 476 B.C. (Moretti, *Olympionikai*, victory 217). "Creatures of a day" means that human beings, unlike gods, are short-lived (though that phrase, too, is disputed by some Pindar scholars); the "dream of a shadow" is a metaphor for something insubstantial and transient.

The translation read at Los Angeles in 1984 was adapted from Nisetich's version.

Appendix

1. Coubertin, *Mémoires,* 14–15.
2. Varda, *Archeia oikogeneias Dragoumi,* 254–57.
3. Young, "Origins of the Modern Olympics."
4. Ibid., 289.
5. Neumüller, "Die Geschichte," 296.

Bibliography

Anninos, C. "Description of the Games." In Lambros and Politis, *Olympic Games*, 129–55.

Bailey, Peter. *Leisure and Class in Victorian England.* London, 1978.

Banciulesco, Victor. "A Forerunner of the Revival of the Olympic Games." *Bulletin du Comité International Olympique* 83 (1963): 55–56.

Baugh, G. C., ed. *Victoria History of the Counties of England.* Vol. 3. London, 1979.

Boulongne, Yves-Pierre. "The Decline of the Olympic Games." Paper presented at meeting of the International Olympic Academy, Ancient Olympia, 1990.

———. *La vie et l'oeuvre pédogogique de Pierre de Coubertin.* Ottawa, 1975.

Bourdon, G[eorges]. "Athènes essaye de faire revivre Olympie." In *Les Jeux de viiie Olympiade: Paris, 1924,* 19–21. Paris, 1926.

Bracegirdle, Cyril. "Olympic Dreamer." *Olympic Review* 284 (June 1991): 276–78.

Brookes, William P. Papers. 7 vols. Collection of the Much Wenlock Olympian Society. Much Wenlock Corn Exchange Building. Much Wenlock, Shropshire, England.

———. "Tilting at the Ring." *Organ of the National Physical Recreation Society* 1, no. 3 (1888).

Brundage, Avery. "Why the Olympic Games?" In *Report of the United States Olympic Committee: Games of the xivth Olympiad, London, England, 1948,* 21–26. [New York, 1949?].

Chrestides, D., ed. *Olympia tou 1870.* Athens, 1872.

Chrysafis, I. E. *Oi synchronoi diethneis Olympiakoi Agones.* Athens, 1930.

Clark, Ellery. *Reminiscences of an Athlete.* Boston, 1911 (chapter 6, 124–41, is "Olympic Games of 1896").

Cohen, Steven. "More than Fun and Games." Ph.D. diss., Brandeis University, 1980.

"Congrès 1894." Collection (photocopies from IOC Archives) of documents relating to the Paris International Athletic Congress of June 1894. IOC Library, Lausanne.

Coubertin, Pierre de. *Batailles de l'éducation physique: Une campagne de vingt-et-un ans, 1887–1908.* Paris, 1908.

———. *Bulletin du Comité International des Jeux Olympiques,* no. 1 (July 1894); no. 2 (Oct. 1894); no. 3 (Jan. 1895).

———. Introduction to Lambros and Politis, *Olympic Games*, 108–10.

———. "Les Jeux Olympiques à Much Wenlock." *La Revue Athlétique* 1 (Dec. 1890): 705–13.

———. *Mémoires olympiques* (1932). Rev. ed. Lausanne, 1977.

———. "Olympic Games of 1896; by their Founder, Baron Pierre de Coubertin." *Century Magazine* 53 (1896): 39–53.

———. *The Olympic Idea.* Edited by Carl-Diem Institut. Translated by John G. Dixon. Stuttgart, 1967. A collection of various writings.

———. "La préface des Jeux Olympiques." *Cosmopolis* 2 (1896): 146–59.

———. "Le rétablissement des Jeux Olympiques." *Revue de Paris* 1 (May 15, 1894): 170–84.

———. *Textes choisis.* Edited by Norbert Müller. 3 vols. Zurich, 1986. A large collection of Coubertin's writings, some reprinted in full, some extracted, and miscellaneous related documents, with commentary (and bibliography, at the end of vol. 3).

———. "A Typical Englishman: Dr. W. P. Brookes of Wenlock in Shropshire." *Review of Reviews* 15 (1897): 62–65.

———. *Universités transatlantiques.* Paris, 1890.

Curtis, Thomas. "The Glory That Was Greece." *Sportsman* 12 (July 1932): 21–22, 56. A somewhat briefer version is found in *Review of Reviews* 86 (1932): 50.

Daryl, Phillipe [Paschal Grousset]. *Renaissance physique.* Paris, 1888.

Decker, Wolfgang, and Kivroglou, Anastase. "Die Begründung der Nationalen Olympischen Spiele in Griechenland durch Evangelos Zappas im Lichte neuer Quellen." In Luh and Beckers, *Umbruch und Koninuität im Sport,* 192–200.

Delivorrias, A., ed. *Athens, 1839–1900: A Photographic Record.* Athens, 1985.

Diamantes, K. A. "Protasis kathieroseos ethnikon epeteion kai demosion agonon kata to protypon ton eorton tes archaiotetos kata to etos 1835." *Athena* 73–74 (1972–73): 307–23.

Dolianitis, George. "Evangelos Zappas: 'Olympia' 1859, 1870, 1875, 1888." Paper presented at meeting of the International Olympic Academy, Ancient Olympia, 1992.

Dragoumis, Stephanos. Papers. American School of Classical Studies. Gennadius Library, Athens.

Durántez, Conrado. *Pierre de Coubertin: The Olympic Humanist.* Lausanne, 1994.

Elliott, W. M. "The New Olympic Games." *Chatauquan* 23 (1896): 47–51.

Encyclopédie des sports. Vol. 1. Paris, 1924. Contains articles by Bourdon on the USFSA and nineteenth-century French sport.

Ephemeris ton syzitiseon tis Voulis. Proceedings of the Greek Parliament. Synedriasis 17, Nov. 24, 1894, 176–84. Contains the full text, speaker by speaker, word by word, of the day's debates in the Greek Parliament relating to the 1896 Olympic Games.

Epitrope ton Olympion. *Nomoi.* [Athens, 1890?]. A collection that reprints laws pertaining to the Olympic revival by the committee (and its predecessors), starting with Otto's 1837 decree.

———. *Olympia tou 1859.* Athens, 1860.

———. *Olympia tou 1875.* Athens, 1876.

———. *Olympia tou 1888.* Athens, 1889.

Eyquem, Marie-Thérèse. *Pierre de Coubertin: L'épopée olympique.* Paris, 1966.

F. (no other signature). "The Olympic Games." *Bailey's Magazine of Sport* 65 (1896): 439–41.

Finlay, George. *A History of the Greek Revolution*. London, 1971. Revised reprint of vols. 6 and 7 of original edition (1877).

Finley, M. I., and H. W. Pleket. *The Olympic Games: The First Thousand Years*. New York, 1976.

Gardiner, E. N. "The Ancient Long Jump." *Journal of Hellenic Studies* 24 (1904): 179–94.

———. "Phayllos and His Record Jump." *Journal of Hellenic Studies* 24 (1904): 70–80.

Gebhardt, Willibald. *Soll Deutschland sich an den olympischen Spielen teilnehmen*. Berlin, 1896.

Gennadius, John. "The Revival of the Olympian Games." *Cosmopolis* 2 (1896): 59–74.

Giannopoulos, G. P. "I epanadrysis ton Olympikon Agonon; I proti idea." *Deltion tes historikes kai ethnologikes hetaireias tes Hellados* 9 (1926): 576–77.

Gillmeister, Heiner. *Geschichte der olympischen Tennisturniere (1896–1992)*. Saint Augustine, Germany, 1993.

———. "Tennis bei Olympischen Spielen (1896–1924)." *Stadion* 11 (1985): 193–262.

———. "Olympic Tennis: Some Afterthoughts." *Citius, Altius, Fortius* 3, no. 1 (1995): 23–24. *Citius, Altius, Fortius* is the journal of the International Society of Olympic Historians, published in Durham, N. C.

Glader, Eugene. *Amateurism and Athletics*. West Point, N. Y., 1978.

Goudas, Anastasios. *Evangelis Zappas*. Athens, 1870.

Grombach, John. *The Official 1980 Olympic Guide*. New York, 1980. Other editions have slightly different names and pagination.

Grousset, Paschal. See Phillipe Daryl.

Guttmann, Allen. *The Olympics: A History of the Modern Games*. Urbana, 1992.

———. Review of *This Great Symbol: Pierre de Coubertin and the Origins of the Modern Olympic Games*, by John J. MacAloon. *Journal of Sport History* 8 (1981): 97–99.

Henry, Bill. *An Approved History of the Olympic Games*. 4th ed. Los Angeles, 1984.

Hopkins, John. *The Marathon*. London, 1966.

Horton, George. "The Recent Olympian Games." *Bostonian* 4 (1896): 215–29.

———. "Revival of Olympian Games." *North American Review* 162 (1896): 266–73.

Hughes, Thomas. *Tom Brown's School Days*. London, 1857.

Ketseas, John. "A Restatement." *Bulletin du Comité International Olympique* 83 (1963): 56.

Keuser, Anette. "Die Geschichte der 'Liverpool Olympics' (1862–1867) und ihre Bedeutung für die Wiederbelebung der Olympischen Spiele." *Hausarbeit (für Lehrämter)*, Deutsche Sporthochschule, Cologne, 1991.

Kivroglou, Anastase. "Die Bemühungen von Ewangelos Sappas um die Wiedereinführung der Olympischen Spiele in Griechenland unter besonderer Berücksichtigung der Spiele von 1859." *Diplomarbeit*, Deutsche Sporthochschule, Cologne, 1981. The documents cited in this work appear in Kivroglou's *Anhang* (appendix).

Koebsel, V., ed. *Dokumente zur Frühgeschichte der Olympischen Spiele.* Cologne, 1970.

Kousoulas, D. George. *Modern Greece.* New York, 1974.

Kyle, Donald. *Athletics in Ancient Athens. Supplements to Mnemosyne* (Leiden) 95 (1987).

Lambros, S., and N. G. Politis, eds. *The Olympic Games: 776 b.c.–1896 a.d.* 2 vols. Athens, 1896 (German-English version). Vol. 2 reissued (Greek, French, English), with new English translation (anonymous, Athens, 1966), by the Committee to Prepare for the Olympic Games, Athens, 1988. I cite the 1988 edition, for its English translation is superior (sometimes I cite both).

Lennartz, Karl. *Kenntnisse und Vorstellungen von Olympia und den Olympischen Spielen in der Zeit von 393–1896.* Schorndorf, 1974.

Linardos, Petros. *Panellinios G. S.: 1891–1991.* [Athens, n.d.]. A history of the Panhellenic Gymnastic Society.

Lovesey, P. *The Official Centenary History of the Amateur Athletic Association.* Enfield, Great Britain, 1979.

Lucas, John. *The Future of the Olympic Games.* Champaign, Ill., 1992.

———. *The Modern Olympic Games.* South Brunswick, N.J., 1980.

———. "Professor William Mulligan Sloane: Father of the United States Olympic Committee." In Luh and Beckers, *Umbruch und Koninuität im Sport,* 230–42.

Luh, Andreas, and Edgar Beckers, eds. *Umbruch und Koninuität im Sport—Reflexionen im Umfeld der Sportgeschichte (Festschrift für Horst Ueberhorst).* Bochum, Germany, 1991.

Lykourgos, Alexandros. *Logos epitaphios eis to mnemosynon E. Zappa.* Athens, 1865.

MacAloon, John J. *This Great Symbol: Pierre de Coubertin and the Origins of the Modern Olympic Games.* Chicago, 1981.

Mahaffy, John. "Old Greek Athletics." *Macmillan's Magazine* 36 (1879): 61–69.

———. "The Olympic Games at Athens in 1875." *Macmillan's Magazine* 32 (1875): 324–27.

Mandell, Richard. *The First Modern Olympics.* Berkeley, 1976.

Mayer, Otto. *A travers les anneaux Olympiques.* Geneva, 1960.

Mega Hellenikon viographikon lexikon. Edited by K. Vovolinis. 4 vols. Athens, 1958–61.

Mezö, Ferenc. *The Modern Olympic Games.* Budapest, 1956.

Miller, Geoffrey. *Behind the Olympic Rings.* Lynn, Mass., 1979.

Minoides, Mynas, ed. *Philostrate sur la gymnastique.* Paris, 1858.

Moretti, Luigi. *Olympionikai, i vincitori negli antichi Agoni Olimpici: Atti della accademia nazionale dei Lincei.* Rome, 1957.

Müller, Norbert. Préface to vol. 2 of *Textes choisis,* by Pierre de Coubertin, 1–22.

Mullins, Sam. *William Penny Brookes and the Wenlock Games.* Leicester, 1986. English text with facing French translation.

———. "Museum Information Sheet No. 9." Shropshire County Museum Service. A brief summary of *William Penny Brookes.* This paper has been distributed at the Wenlock Museum and at several recent sports history conferences.

Neumüller, Benno. "Die Geschichte der Much Wenlock Games." *Diplomarbeit,* Deutsche Sporthochschule, Cologne, 1985.

Nicol, D. M. *Ioannes Gennadius: A Biographical Sketch.* Athens, 1990.

Nisetich, Frank J. *Pindar's Victory Songs*. Baltimore, 1980.

Oikonomos, Alexandros A. *Dimitrios M. Vikelas*. Vol. 2 of *Treis anthropoi*. Athens, 1953.

Paddock, Robert. J. "Amateurism: An Idea of the Past or a Necessity for the Future?" *Olympika* 3 (1994): 1–15.

Pash, H. F., ed. *Fifty Years of Progress, 1880–1930: The Jubilee Souvenir of the Amateur Athletic Association*. London, 1930.

Pavilinis, Evangelos. *Istoria tis gymnastikis*. Thessaloniki, 1977.

"Pax Olimpica." *Revue Olympique* 12 (July 1912).

Pikramenou-Varfi, Dimitra. "The Revival of the Olympic Idea and the 'Olympia.'" In *Hellada athletismos politismos: Greek Sports and Culture*, 70–73. Athens, 1988.

To pnevma kai to soma. Athens, 1989.

Politis, Linos. *History of Modern Greek Literature*. Oxford, 1973.

Quanz, Dietrich. "The IOC Founding: Birth of a New Peace Movement." *Citius, Altius, Fortius* 3, no. 1 (1995): 6–16.

Quellenec, I., and A. Zinopoulos. *Rapport sur la vérification de la construction du Zappeion*. Athens, 1888.

Quercetani, Roberto L. *A World History of Track and Field, 1864–1964*. London, 1964.

Rangavis, Alexandros. *Apomnemoneumata*. 2 vols. Athens, 1895.

———. "Peri tou Zappeiou idrymatos." *Hestia* 25 (1888): 18–20.

Redmond, Gerald. *The Caledonian Games in Nineteenth-Century America*. Cranbury, N.J., 1971.

———. *The Sporting Scots of Nineteenth-Century Canada*. Toronto, 1982.

———. "Toward Modern Revival of the Olympic Games: The Various 'Pseudo-Olympics' of the Nineteenth Century." In *The Olympic Games in Transition*, edited by Jeffrey O. Segrave and Donald Chu, 71–87. Champaign, Ill., 1988.

Richardson, Rufus. "The New Olympian Games." *Scribner's Magazine* 20 (1896): 267–86.

Rioux, Georges. *Pierre de Coubertin and History*. Lausanne, n.d.

Robertson, G. S. "The Olympic Games." *Fortnightly Review* 65 (1896): 944–57.

Rühl, Joachim K. "L'idéal de l'amateurisme et l'influence de la Grèce sur les 'Jeux Olympiques' à Much Wenlock." Paper presented at meeting of the International Society for the History of Sport and Physical Education (HISPA), Ancient Olympia, 1989.

Santas, Alexander. *Olympia; Olympiakoi Agones; Olympionikai*. Athens, 1966.

Schaap, Dick. *An Illustrated History of the Olympics*. New York, 1975.

Sloane, William. "Correspondance Pierre de Coubertin/William Sloane, 1897–1924." Bound volume (photocopies) of Sloane's letters to Coubertin. IOC Library, Lausanne.

———. "The Greek Olympiads." In Sloane, *Report of the American Olympic Committee*, 59–83.

———. *Report of the American Olympic Committee: Seventh Olympic Games, Antwerp, Belgium, 1920*. Greenwich, Conn., n.d.

Smith, Ronald A. *Sports and Freedom: The Rise of Big-Time College Athletics*. New York, 1988.

Soutsos, P. *Messias*. Athens, 1839.

———. *Nekrikos dialogos kai ta ereipia tes palaias Spartes*. Athens, 1835.

———. *Ta hapanta*. Athens, 1851.

———. *Tria lyrika dramata*. Athens, 1842.

Stanford, W. B., and R. B. McDowell. *Mahaffy: A Biography of an Anglo-Irishman*. London, 1971.

von Strantz, C. "Plan von Athen, 1862." In *Sieben Karten von Athen*, edited by Ernst Curtius. Gotha, Germany, 1868.

Strutt, J. *Sports and Pastimes of the People of England*. London, 1903.

Varda, Christina. *Archeia oikogeneias Dragoumi: Evretiria* (Archives of the Dragoumis Family: Catalogue). Athens: 1989.

Vikelas, Demetrios. "Correspondance, Pierre de Coubertin/Demetrius Vikelas, 1894–1905." Bound volume (photocopies) of Vikelas's letters to Coubertin. IOC Library, Lausanne.

———. "Oi diethneis Olympiakoi Agones." *Hestia Eikonographimeni* (May 7, 1895): 145–50.

———. *I zoi mou*. Athens, 1908.

Waldstein, Charles. *Argive Heraeum*. Vol. 1. Boston, 1902.

———. "A Last Word on the Olympian Games." *Harper's Weekly*, May 23, 1896.

———. "The Olympian Games at Athens." *Harper's Weekly*, May 16, 1896.

———. "The Olympic Games at Athens." *Harper's Weekly*, Apr. 18, 1896.

Wallechinsky, David. *The Complete Book of the Olympics*. 2d ed. New York, 1988.

Wendl, Karel. "Olympic Oath: A Brief History." *Citius, Altius, Fortius* 3, no. 1 (1995): 4–5.

Whitney, Caspar. *Sporting Pilgrimage*. New York, 1895.

Wilkinson, H. F. *Athletic Almanack*. 1868.

Young, David C. "Athletics." In *Civilization of the Ancient Mediterranean*, edited by Michael Grant, 2:1131–42. New York, 1988.

———. "Demetrios Vikelas: First President of the IOC." *Stadion: Internationale Zeitschrift für Geschichte des Sports* 14 (1988): 85–102.

———. *The Olympic Myth of Greek Amateur Athletics*. Chicago, 1984.

———. "On the Source of the Olympic Credo." *Olympika* 3 (1994): 17–25.

———. "The Origins of the Modern Olympics: A New Version." *International Journal of the History of Sport* 4 (1987): 271–300.

———. "Pindar." In *Ancient Writers: Greece and Rome*, edited by T. J. Luce, 1:157–77. New York, 1982.

———. "The Riddle of the Rings." In *Coroebus Triumphs*, edited by Susan J. Bandy, 257–76. San Diego, 1989.

Ziller, E. *Ausgrabungen am Panathenaïschen Stadium*. Berlin, 1870.

Index

Library of Congress Cataloging-in-Publication Data

Young, David C.
    The modern Olympics : a struggle for revival / David C. Young.
      p. cm.
    Includes bibliographical references (p.   ) and index.
    ISBN 0-8018-5374-5 (alk. paper)
    1. Olympics—History. I. Title.
GV721.5.Y68   1996
796.48—dc20

96-16496
CIP

Printed in the United States
836500003B